SWT: THE STANDARD WIDGET TOOLKIT, VOLUME 1

the eclipse series

SERIES EDITORS   Erich Gamma ▪ Lee Nackman ▪ John Wiegand

Eclipse is a universal tool platform, an open extensible integrated development environment (IDE) for anything and nothing in particular. Eclipse represents one of the most exciting initiatives hatched from the world of application development in a long time, and it has the considerable support of the leading companies and organizations in the technology sector. Eclipse is gaining widespread acceptance in both the commercial and academic arenas.

The Eclipse Series from Addison-Wesley is the definitive series of books dedicated to the Eclipse platform. Books in the series promise to bring you the key technical information you need to analyze Eclipse, high-quality insight into this powerful technology, and the practical advice you need to build tools to support this evolutionary Open Source platform. Leading experts Erich Gamma, Lee Nackman, and John Wiegand are the series editors.

Titles in the Eclipse Series

John Arthorne and Chris Laffra, *Official Eclipse 3.0 FAQs*, 0-321-26838-5

Kent Beck and Erich Gamma, *Contributing to Eclipse: Principles, Patterns, and Plug-Ins*, 0-321-20575-8

Frank Budinsky, David Steinberg, Ed Merks, Ray Ellersick, and Timothy J. Grose, *Eclipse Modeling Framework*, 0-131-42542-0

Eric Clayberg and Dan Rubel, *Eclipse: Building Commercial-Quality Plug-Ins*, 0-321-22847-2

Steve Northover and Mike Wilson, *SWT: The Standard Widget Toolkit, Volume 1*, 0-321-25663-8

SWT: THE STANDARD WIDGET TOOLKIT, VOLUME 1

Steve Northover
Mike Wilson

♦▾Addison-Wesley

Boston • San Francisco • New York
London • Munich • Paris • Madrid
Capetown • Sydney • Tokyo • Singapore • Mexico City

Many of the designations used by manufacturers and sellers to distinguish their products are claimed as trademarks. Where those designations appear in this book, and Addison-Wesley was aware of a trademark claim, the designations have been printed with initial capital letters or in all capitals.

The authors and publisher have taken care in the preparation of this book, but make no expressed or implied warranty of any kind and assume no responsibility for errors or omissions. No liability is assumed for incidental or consequential damages in connection with or arising out of the use of the information or programs contained herein.

The publisher offers discounts on this book when ordered in quantity for bulk purchases and special sales. For more information, please contact:

U.S. Corporate and Government Sales
(800) 382-3419
corpsales@pearsontechgroup.com

For sales outside of the U.S., please contact:

International Sales
(317) 581-3793
international@pearsontechgroup.com

Visit Addison-Wesley on the Web: www.awprofessional.com

Library of Congress Cataloging-in-Publication Data
Northover, Steve.
  SWT : the standard widget toolkit / Steve Northover, Mike Wilson.
    p. cm. -- (The Eclipse series)
  Includes bibliographical references and index.
  ISBN 0-321-25663-8
  1. Graphical user interfaces (Computer systems) I. Wilson, Mike, 1960-
II. Title. III. Series.
QA76.9.U83N67 2004
  005.4'38--dc22

                                              2004011503

For information on obtaining permission for use of material from this work, please submit a written request to:

Pearson Education, Inc.
Rights and Contracts Department
75 Arlington Street, Suite 300
Boston, MA 02116
Fax: (617) 848-7047

ISBN 0-321-25663-8
Text reprinted on recycled paper
1 2 3 4 5 6 7 8 9 10—CRS—0807060504
First printing, June 2004

To Deb and Dennis,
forever.
—McQ

To Anita, thank you for our life together.
—Steve

Contents

Foreword by Erich Gamma   xiii

Preface   xv

Introduction   xix

Part 1 ○ **Widgets**   **1**

           If You Don't Read Anything Else...   3

Chapter 1   *Widget Fundamentals*   **7**
       1.1   What Is a Widget?   7
       1.2   Widget Hierarchy   14
       1.3   Events and Listeners   17
       1.4   Application Data   25
       1.5   Querying the Display   26
       1.6   Summary   26

Chapter 2   *The Keyboard*   **27**
       2.1   When a Key Is Typed, Where Does It Go?   28
       2.2   Keyboard Events and the Focus Control   28
       2.3   Traversal   39
       2.4   Accelerators   48
       2.5   Window System Keys   50
       2.6   Summary   51

Chapter 3   *The Mouse*   **53**
       3.1   Mouse Events   54
       3.2   Selection   61
       3.3   Summary   63

Chapter 4   *Control Fundamentals*   65
      4.1   Bounds   65
      4.2   Client Area   66
      4.3   Moving and Resizing   68
      4.4   Visibility   72
      4.5   Z-Order   74
      4.6   Enabling and Disabling   74
      4.7   Preferred Size   76
      4.8   Painting   77
      4.9   Repainting and Resizing   82
      4.10   Filling the Background   86
      4.11   Summary   88

Chapter 5   *Display*   89
      5.1   Naming Your Application   90
      5.2   Display Life Cycle   90
      5.3   Events and Listeners   91
      5.4   Event Filters   93
      5.5   Runnable "Execs"   95
      5.6   The Event Loop   96
      5.7   Multithreaded Programming   100
      5.8   Timers   108
      5.9   Putting It All Together: Multithreading, Timers,
             Events, and the Event Loop   111
      5.10   Monitors, Bounds, and Client Area   112
      5.11   The Active Shell, All Shells, and Focus Control   115
      5.12   Cursor Control and Location   116
      5.13   Display Depth and DPI   118
      5.14   Updating the Display   121
      5.15   Application Data   122
      5.16   Coordinate Mapping and Mirroring   124
      5.17   Miscellaneous   127
      5.18   Summary   128

Chapter 6   *Native Widgets*   129
      6.1   Native Widgets Summary   130

Chapter 7   *Basic Controls*   135
      7.1   Class Label   135
      7.2   Class Button   140
      7.3   Class Text   147

7.4	Class List	164
7.5	Class Combo	173
7.6	Summary	179
Chapter 8	**Tool Bars and Menus**	**181**
8.1	Classes ToolBar and ToolItem	181
8.2	Classes Menu and MenuItem	194
8.3	Summary	206
Chapter 9	**Advanced Controls**	**209**
9.1	Classes Tree and TreeItem	210
9.2	Classes Table, TableItem, and TableColumn	226
9.3	Classes TabFolder and TabItem	251
9.4	Summary	257
Chapter 10	**Range-Based Controls**	**259**
10.1	Class ProgressBar	259
10.2	Class Scale	262
10.3	Classes ScrollBar and Slider	265
10.4	Summary	272
Chapter 11	**Controls, Composites, Groups, and Shells**	**273**
11.1	Class Control	273
11.2	Class Composite	277
11.3	Class Group	279
11.4	Class Shell	280
11.5	Summary	294
Chapter 12	**Canvas and Caret**	**295**
12.1	Class Canvas	295
12.2	Class Caret	298
12.3	Summary	302
Chapter 13	**Draggable Controls**	**303**
13.1	Classes CoolBar and CoolItem	303
13.2	Class Sash	313
13.3	Class Tracker	315
13.4	Summary	321
Chapter 14	**Dialogs**	**323**
14.1	Creation	323
14.2	Opening a Dialog	324

14.3	Setting the Title	324
14.4	MessageBox	325
14.5	FileDialog	328
14.6	DirectoryDialog	334
14.7	ColorDialog	337
14.8	FontDialog	338
14.9	Summary	341

Chapter 15   Layout   **343**

15.1	When Are Layouts Invoked?	344
15.2	Class Layout	345
15.3	Layout Data	346
15.4	Class FillLayout	347
15.5	Classes RowLayout and RowData	350
15.6	Class GridLayout	360
15.7	Defining the Grid	363
15.8	Class FormLayout	377
15.9	Assigning Width and Height Hints	390
15.10	Which Layout Should I Use?	392
15.11	Forcing a Layout	392
15.12	Forcing Controls to Wrap	394
15.13	Summary	399

Part II ○ Graphics   **401**

Chapter 16   Graphics Fundamentals   **405**

16.1	Points and Rectangles	405
16.2	Class Point	406
16.3	Class Rectangle	407
16.4	The Graphics Context	409
16.5	Graphics and Threads	410
16.6	Line and Figure Drawing	412
16.7	Clipping and Regions	421

Chapter 17   Colors   **427**

17.1	Class RGB	427
17.2	Class Color	430
17.3	System Colors	433

Chapter 18	Fonts	437
18.1	Class FontData	437
18.2	Class Font	442
18.3	Drawing Text	448
18.4	Class FontMetrics	451

Chapter 19	Images	461
19.1	Class ImageData	461
19.2	Class Image	473
19.3	Animation	481
19.4	Loading Images	486

Chapter 20	Cursors	497
20.1	System Cursors	498
20.2	Custom Cursors	501

Part III ○ Applications   **511**

Chapter 21	Minesweeper	513
21.1	How to Play	513
21.2	Implementation Notes	515

Chapter 22	FileExplorer	519
22.1	Features	519
22.2	Implementation Notes	521

Part IV ○ Next Time   **527**

Index		529

Foreword

I enjoy programming user interfaces in Java, but users don't need to know that—they shouldn't be able to spot that I was using Java from the surface of my application. SWT solves this problem by providing an efficient portable native widget kit. The widget kit is rich enough to build full-fledged applications that look and feel like a native application developed for a particular target platform.

I first used the Standard Widget Toolkit (SWT) several years ago. I was part of the team with the mission to build a Java based integrated development environment for embedded applications that was shipped as the IBM VisualAge/MicroEdition. We used Swing/AWT as the underlying UI technology. We enjoyed being on the bleeding edge of the brand new Swing toolkit. After several months we could finally start to "eat our own dog food" and develop with the IDE we were building. We felt pretty good about what we had achieved! However, our early adopters didn't feel as good as we did... they complained about the performance and most importantly about the fact that the IDE didn't look, feel and respond like a native Windows application. Some of the performance problems were our fault and some of them could be attributed to Swing. The performance problems didn't bother us that much; they could be engineered away over time. What worried us more was the non-native criticism. While we could implement a cool application in Swing that runs on Windows, we couldn't build a true Windows application. Fixing this problem required more drastic measures. Fortunately, there was another team with a lot of experience in portable UI libraries leveraging native widgets for Smalltalk. The next chapter of the story was obvious: transfer these native widget skills and technology to Java and SWT was born. A downside of this decision was that we had to move back several steps and reimplement the user interface of our development environment once more with SWT. This was an intense time with sometimes heated but valuable discussions with the SWT team. Our reward was that the IDE not only became faster but it also started to look and feel like a native application. In particular, users didn't notice anymore that the application was implemented in Java. The final chapter is public history; based on the lessons learned from the IBM VisualAge/MicroEdition effort, we have moved on to Eclipse and built it on top of SWT.

Since our initial steps with SWT in VisualAge/MicroEdition, SWT has evolved a lot. It now covers more native features with its API and even more importantly, it supports almost all platforms that are popular today. The missing piece was an in-depth book about SWT. I'm glad to see that this gap is now filled. This book comes right from the source—Steve and Mike are the original SWT designers and implementers. They bring amazing depth and broad experience with native widgets to the table. When I hear them telling a horror story about an exotic feature of some native widget, I'm grateful to be on the other side of the API.

This book will give you insights into how the various platform realities shaped particular SWT solutions. You'll find explanations and snippets that illustrate how to program SWT that will support both developers building an eclipse contribution and developers using SWT as a standalone application. Steve and Mike have opened a window into SWT that will profit both beginners and experienced developers!

—Erich Gamma
May 2004

Preface

When we began this book, our Grand Vision was to create a complete reference for every aspect of SWT. It was not until we began identifying the range of topics that we would need to cover that we realized that SWT is *big*—not big in size but big in terms of features, uses, and the energy that is behind it. The community that has built up around SWT has pushed it in many directions, everything from PDAs, to stand-alone desktop applications on several platforms, to Eclipse[1] and the many commercial IDEs that have been built from it. We had to narrow the focus.

We decided to cover only those aspects of SWT that every developer would need to know.

- How to get and install SWT and how to invoke it from your programs.
- The fundamental systems that make up SWT: mouse and keyboard handling, graphical user interface components, drawing routines, etc.
- The native operating system-based user interface controls.

These topics, covered in depth and with many examples, are exactly what you will find on the following pages.

To give you some idea of the scope of the original problem, here are some of the topics that we are *not* going to cover in detail.

- Frameworks built from SWT (e.g., JFace and GEF)
- Coding patterns specific to using SWT in Eclipse
- The custom widgets package created for Eclipse
- Drag-and-drop and clipboard support

---

1. See the Introduction for more on Eclipse.

○ Platform-specific features, such as OLE support on Windows

○ Building your own new widgets, dialogs, and layouts

○ Bidirectional language (BIDI) support

○ Implementation strategies used by SWT

○ The HTML browser widget

○ Printing

○ OpenGL support

We touch on these topics when they come up in context and attempt to provide pointers to more information, but as one of our reviewers said, "It cries out for a Volume 2." We are aware of this. Once we get this one out the door and have enough time to remember who our families are again, we will start thinking about it.

Another very interesting element of this book is the inclusion of some of the history behind SWT and the design decisions that led to it having the shape that it does. We felt that, as two of the original designers, we could provide a better insight into this than you are likely to find elsewhere. Although this content represents only a small portion of the total, we hope that you find it interesting.

Contributing to SWT

As you learn more about SWT, it is worth keeping in mind that SWT is not a closed system. If you are new to the open source community, you may be used to thinking in terms of code libraries coming from "somewhere else," in which you have little say in the design, direction, or development. SWT, and indeed the entire Eclipse project, follows a different path.

SWT is supported by a community of developers. Anyone who wants to contribute time and energy can become part of that community. The first step is to keep in mind that whenever you find what you think is a bug in SWT, you should enter a Bugzilla report that describes the problem at https://bugs .eclipse.org/bugs/. SWT developers like bug reports and use them to communicate and organize their work.

If the bug that you have found (or any other bug, for that matter) is causing you grief, ask a question on the SWT newsgroup[2] and start a discussion about it. Given that the entire source for SWT is available, *you* can also try to fix the problem by doing the following.

---

2. See news://news.eclipse.org/eclipse.platform.swt.

1. Figuring out what is wrong.

2. Changing your copy of the SWT code to make it stop happening.

3. Attaching a patch that shows the changes to the Bugzilla report.

If you get stuck, ask the other developers whether they have suggestions. The best place to have this discussion is on the developer's mailing list, which you can find by following the links from http://eclipse.org/mail/index.html.

The SWT developers look at every patch that is submitted. Because they have a wide understanding of the implications of a given change, you may be asked to submit a new patch that takes into account aspects of the problem that you missed. Keep trying. When you get to the point where the other developers trust that code you submit can be added and it is clear that you are going to continue to contribute, a vote will be taken to give you the right to change the SWT source that everyone uses. This is called *earning your commit rights*. If any of this appeals to you, go for it. We would love to have your help!

Conventions

The following formatting conventions are used throughout the book:

Bold Boldface is used to indicate method names at the start of their descriptions and for points of emphasis in the text.

Italics New terms are italicized where they are defined. Italics are also used for emphasis and to indicate package names, fields, and equivalent code patterns in the text.

`Courier` Courier is used exclusively for embedded code examples.

`Courier Bold` In code examples, boldface is used to identify important lines that are described in the text.

Acknowledgments

We wish to thank everyone who took the time to read and comment on fragments of the book, especially Silenio Quarti and the other SWT committees (in particular Veronika Irvine, Carolyn MacLeod, Christophe Cornu, Felipe Heidrich, and Grant Gayed) who fixed a number of bugs so we wouldn't have to talk about them.

We would also like to thank the following individuals who reviewed our manuscript and offered many significant and helpful suggestions: Simon Archer, Ronald van Rijn, Sherry Shavor, and Joe Winchester.

Special thanks are due to Carolyn MacLeod for her Herculean effort to make us sound literate. (Uh oh, Car, more commas!)

Without Dave Thomas, there would have been no SWT. Thank you, Dave, for being an inspiration, encouraging hard work, and reminding us that it should always be fun.

We are grateful to John Neidhart and Raquel Kaplan for helping us with the wonderful, arcane process of book publishing, and to all the staff at Addison-Wesley Professional for their painstaking efforts in the production of this book.

Steve says: "Buy this book and I'll get this guitar."

Mike says: "Thanks, Steve, for SWT and for the energy to get this book done."

Above all, we owe more thanks than we can ever give to our families for their willingness to handle all the details of real life over long periods of writing.

Introduction

The Standard Widget Toolkit, typically called SWT, is a *graphical user interface* (GUI) toolkit for the Java programming language. It was created by the developers of the Eclipse Project to provide access to the native user interface facilities of the operating systems that host the *Eclipse universal tools platform*. Further information about the Eclipse Project is available at the Web site http://www.eclipse.org. The SWT component home page is http://www.eclipse.org/swt.

Although this book is intended to cover all versions of SWT, it was written during the development of R3.0 of Eclipse. Some of the features that are described here are not available on earlier versions of SWT. For particularly significant additions, this is called out in the text, but for minor differences such as bug fixes, it is not.

In addition to being the standard user interface library for Eclipse development, SWT has proven to be useful for a wide range of stand-alone Java applications on both desktop and handheld systems. This book is aimed at experienced Java programmers who want to use SWT to build modern, GUI-based applications. It is broken into five main parts.

Introduction The introduction, which you are currently reading, contains an overview of SWT and the details of how to get SWT, install it, and make it available to your applications.

Widgets Widgets are the building blocks of a GUI. In SWT, the code that implements the appearance and behavior of the widgets is provided by the underlying operating system; we call this "using *native widgets*." This part of the book is the largest, because it describes all of the various kinds of native widgets provided by SWT in detail. It also covers the general aspects of widgets, such as their life cycle, how they interact with the user, how they are arranged into a GUI, and how to access non-widget support resources, such as system dialogs.

Graphics The SWT graphics routines provide access to fonts, colors, images, and primitive graphics operations, such as line and circle drawing. Using these routines, it is possible to configure the appearance of native widgets, to draw application-specific graphics, or to create entirely new *custom widgets* whose presentation is drawn by your application.

Applications This section provides a pair of example applications that are intended to show best practice uses of SWT in real-world situations. They represent both good starting points for new application development and valuable sources of information on how it all fits together. The intent is to take the book beyond being just a reference for the SWT *application programming interface* (API) by showing you what a *good* SWT program should look like.

We believe that the programmer's equivalent of the old adage, "A picture is worth a thousand words" is "A program is worth a thousand words," so throughout the book, whenever there is an important topic or a new feature to be described, you will always see a snippet of code that shows exactly how to use that feature alongside the description. To the greatest extent possible, this code represents either a complete program that you can run and test out or a fragment of such a program. The source code for all examples is available for download at http://www.awprofessional.com/title/0321256638.

The rest of the introduction consists of an overview of the rationale and history behind SWT, followed by a description of how to get it and use it in your applications.

SWT Overview

The SWT component home page on eclipse.org states the following.

> The SWT component is designed to provide efficient, portable access to the user interface facilities of the operating systems on which it is implemented.

This is as strong an embodiment of the design philosophy of SWT as can be found anywhere.

Certainly, part of the reason why SWT is efficient is because it is predominantly a compatibility layer on top of the user interface facilities of the underlying operating system. Most of the "real" work is done by the highly optimized, platform-specific code that the operating system vendors have implemented. There is more to it than that, however. To the greatest extent possible, anything that would put extra overhead between the running program and the operating system has been avoided. For example, SWT does not have a separate internal implementation hierarchy, as is found in the *AWT peer* layer. This removes a layer of indirection from every public entry point and significantly reduces the size of the library. The trade-off with this strategy is that SWT implementations (called *ports*) have the same implementation hierarchy *shape* on every platform,[1] and there is very little sharing within the internals of the ports. This made the initial design of SWT somewhat challenging but in practice has not turned out to be a significant issue since then.

Implementations of SWT are available for all of the major desktop operating systems and some handheld devices.[2] Over time, areas of missing platform functionality that would have prevented particular operating systems from being targets for full SWT implementations (and thus, candidate Eclipse platforms) have been covered by emulated versions of that functionality. Using the emulated versions simplifies the task of getting an initial port of SWT running, making it possible to fill in the details incrementally.

Porting SWT

Because much of the implementation of SWT must be re-created for each port, SWT was carefully designed to make this as simple as possible. The first step in creating a new port is to construct a *platform interface* layer that mimics in Java the native (typically) C-based API of the platform's user interface library. To the greatest extent possible, this layer has the same entry points with the same names and arguments as the native routines. Typically, only a subset of the platform's user interface library (those that are needed by the SWT port) is required. It even keeps the operating system's standard naming conventions for data structures and variables. Programmers who are familiar with the API for a particular platform can develop the SWT port using their full knowledge of that API. A side effect of this is that it is also possible for knowledgeable programmers

---

1. In this book, the word *platform*, without qualifiers, is frequently used as a synonym for the GUI library provided by the operating system. In some cases, when the phrase *operating system* is used, it is also intended to have this meaning, although this is technically less correct because some operating systems (Linux, for example) provide more than one graphical user interface library, which they call *window system*s.

2. You can determine which platforms are supported and their port status at www.eclipse.org/swt.

to use the SWT platform interface to code platform-specific functionality in their applications, although a discussion of that is beyond the scope of this book.

Once the platform interface has been created, all of the interesting aspects of the port can be written in Java. This allows the full power of the Eclipse Java development tools to be used to implement and debug the new library, including *hot code replace* (modifying the code of a program while it is running) and *remote debugging* (debugging a program on one system while it is running on a different one).

Before starting out on a port, interested programmers should contact the SWT developers on the *platform-swt* mailing list at eclipse.org.

Another way that SWT maintains efficiency is by avoiding the trap of attempting to "fix" fundamental limitations in the underlying operating system. There are three significant ways that this is visible in SWT.

1. The SWT API has been designed to take the limitations that are common to all (or almost all) of the modern operating systems into account. An example of this would be the notion of a distinguished "user interface thread" to model the canonical operating system limitation that cross-threaded access to widgets is either limited or not allowed.

2. The SWT API allows for the existence of platform-specific limitations, as long as they are in areas that most applications will not encounter. For example, most operating systems have a limit on the amount of text that can be passed to a single text drawing call. For some operating systems, this is based on the number of characters; for others, it is based on the number of pixels covered by the rendered result. Because this limit is typically quite large—32768 pixels, for example—most applications are not affected; thus, SWT neither constrains the amount of text that can be passed nor attempts to work around the limitation.

3. Some of the capabilities SWT provides are not available on all platforms. Although this runs counter to the notion of a *portable* API, the SWT designers felt that it was important for SWT to provide more than the lowest common denominator of functionality. Because of this, the API allows programmers to provide *hints* that platform-specific capabilities should be used. In these cases, when it is possible for the SWT implementation to *fall back* to more generic capabilities, it will do so; otherwise, the requests are ignored. For example, some operating systems allow buttons to be rendered with either a default three-dimensional appearance or a "flat" appearance. SWT provides access to these two styles if

they are available. If a particular operating system does not provide the capability, SWT simply renders all buttons using the default style.

Despite these potential sources of platform-specific behavior, writing SWT applications that run well on multiple operating systems is not difficult. Certainly, the star example of this is the Eclipse universal tools platform. SWT has also been used for many other applications ranging from simple text editors to development environments and large vertical market applications. By allowing access to platform-specific functionality but not requiring that you use it, SWT allows you to choose whether to optimize for a platform that is particularly important to you or to provide the same capabilities everywhere.

Look and Feel

Applications built with SWT native widgets *inherently* take on the appearance and behavior (the *look and feel*) of the platforms they run on because the widget implementations are provided by platform-specific code that the operating system vendors have written. Although the SWT API makes it simple to create applications that run on any supported platform, it is important to test your applications on each platform on which you intend to ship. You should expect the look and feel of the application to change to match the norm for the platform in any or all of the following ways.

○ The canonical sizes of widgets may vary. Every platform specifies, either through programming guidelines or by providing API, the appropriate size for each widget. SWT uses this information when computing the preferred sizes of widgets.

○ In some cases, platform-specific size constraints are applied. For example, Microsoft Windows does not allow applications to change the height of combo boxes, so SWT Combo widgets also exhibit this behavior on Windows.

○ The location of some of the standard user interface elements may change. The prime example of this is the menu bar that appears at the top of the screen on the Macintosh but within each application window on all other platforms.

○ Even the behavior of the widgets may change, as it does, for example, in the case of the Microsoft Windows "feature" that causes radio buttons to become selected in the user interface whenever they are given focus. Here, SWT generates a matching selection event on Windows so that the application will behave as though the user explicitly selected the button, and no special-case handling is required in your code.

In general, platform-specific differences in *behavior* are handled by the SWT implementation, either by modeling the platform-specific aspects in terms of the portable API (as was done in the Windows radio button selection case described above) or by introducing new abstractions to describe the differences. For example, the SWT.MenuDetect event was introduced to indicate that the user had performed the appropriate action to request a pop-up menu. The sequence of button and/or key presses and releases that are required to do this varies from platform to platform, but portable SWT application code can be written by simply watching for the SWT.MenuDetect event.

To handle platform-specific differences in *appearance*—the size differences, size constraints, and location differences described above—SWT provides a powerful framework for dynamically positioning and sizing widgets based on *layouts*. By associating a layout with a collection of widgets, it is possible to arrange them in terms of various kinds of abstract constraints. Within these constraints, the layouts and widgets will collaborate to ensure that the expected platform appearance is maintained without requiring platform-specific code to be written. Layouts are described in detail in the Layout chapter.

Custom Widgets

During the creation of Eclipse, two issues were uncovered that have affected the nature of SWT.

1. Some of the features that people expect in the user interfaces of modern development tools cannot be provided by any of the native widgets that are available on any platform.

2. To make Eclipse more recognizable and give it a style all its own,[3] some of its user interface elements need to maintain the same appearance (specified by the Eclipse user interface design team) on every platform.

Neither of these issues could be addressed by the native widget-based capabilities of SWT, so a set of support classes, called the *custom widgets package,* was designed for the specific needs of Eclipse. These classes are implemented entirely in terms of existing SWT API, requiring no new native routines. They can be found in the package *org.eclipse.swt.custom.*

It is important to note that the custom widgets package is not the basis of the Eclipse user interface. Most of what you see in Eclipse—shells, trees, tables, lists, text fields, labels, menu bars and menus, tool bars, dialogs, scroll bars, progress bars, etc.—is created from native widgets. Thus, Eclipse gener-

---

3. Using the standard vernacular: "to give Eclipse a distinct *brand.*"

ally takes on the look and feel of the platform. The custom widgets package provides the "icing" on the user interface that makes it distinctly Eclipse.

Despite the fact that the custom widgets classes were created for Eclipse, they have been designed to be generically useful. If you are looking for a feature that the native widgets do not provide and can live with the fact that the appearance of the result may not necessarily match the platform look and feel, it is worth checking out the classes in the custom widget package. Some of the things you will find there include the following.

❍ A powerful text editor framework (StyledText)

❍ Support for adding editable fields to tables and trees (ControlEditor)

❍ Labels (CLabel), combo boxes (CCombo), and tabbed views (CTab-Folder) that avoid some of the limitations of their platform widget-based counterparts

❍ Tools to simplify common coding patterns, such as resizing (SashForm) and scrolling subviews (ScrolledComposite), showing activity (BusyIndicator), and creating "stacks" of widgets that occupy the same area of the user interface (StackLayout).

As stated above, the custom widgets package is implemented entirely in terms of the existing SWT API. The widget and event handling support they use is described in the Widgets part of the book. The graphics routines that were used to draw them are covered in the Graphics part.

History

SWT was created by the group within the Rational Division of IBM—then Object Technology International, Inc. (OTI)—that had been responsible for implementing the user interface for IBM's VisualAge/Smalltalk product. Much of the design philosophy of SWT has its roots in the VisualAge/Smalltalk work, so a brief discussion of this history is in order.

At the time of VisualAge/Smalltalk's creation, most Smalltalk implementations used user interfaces that were drawn entirely by simple graphics primitives (BitBlt). By doing this, the Smalltalk environments had complete control over the presentation of the user interface and provided what were at the time state-of-the-art capabilities. However, the other side of the coin was that Smalltalk programs did not look or interact like native platform applications. Attempts were made to extend the standard Smalltalk user interface to be "pluggable," so that Smalltalk code could be written to emulate the appearance of native widgets on each platform. These were successful to some extent but never to the point where users were unable to tell the difference. Applications that were built using this user interface failed in at least three ways.

1. Common interactions, such as scrolling and typing, typically felt different in Smalltalk applications than in native applications. Users found this more disconcerting when the application *looked* like a native application than they did when the application looked markedly different.[4]

2. Native operating system features that relied on interoperability, such as drag-and-drop support, document embedding, and systemwide national language support, were either not available or incompletely implemented.

3. As new releases of the native operating systems came out, their appearance changed, leaving the Smalltalk applications looking "dated" because they continued to run code that emulated the old look and feel.

There was a growing sense among Smalltalk developers that these user interface issues significantly limited the acceptance of Smalltalk within the larger software developer community, despite the many advanced capabilities that the environment provided: pure object-oriented programming, garbage collection, pointer safety, cross-platform portability, and integrated development and debugging (with hot code replace support), to name just a few. Solving the problem would require the construction of a Smalltalk user interface that used the native widget code rather than emulating it.

The first incarnation of this was done at OTI to implement a simple, native widget-based user interface for the Digitalk Smalltalk/V Mac product. Although the implementation strategy used was closely tied to the Macintosh operating system, and the set of native widgets and their API was limited to the requirements of the existing Smalltalk/V GUI, it clearly showed that building Smalltalk user interfaces from native widgets was practical. Digitalk produced similar native widget-based user interfaces for OS/2 and Windows.

The VisualAge/Smalltalk user interface, called *CommonWidgets*, was implemented using a strategy that was similar to the one used by Smalltalk/V, but it differed from it in at least two interesting ways.

1. The CommonWidgets API was modeled on the premier GUI library of the day, X/Motif, rather than on historical Smalltalk user interfaces. This meant both that the API was more familiar to a wider range of developers and that there was a simpler mapping between the Smalltalk user interface classes and the underlying native widgets.

---

4. This is a variant on the "near human" problem in computer animation, which states that the more humanlike an animated figure appears to be, the easier it is to recognize the flaws in the animation.

2. CommonWidgets had consistent, clearly defined rules for how the interface to the operating system API should be implemented. These included ensuring that the operating system API functions and structures, and the Smalltalk code that modeled them had the same names and arguments (modulo Smalltalk's unusual function call syntax).

VisualAge/Smalltalk provided excellent portability across all of the supported platforms: Microsoft Windows 3.11, 95, NT3.51 and NT4.0, OS/2 Warp 3.0 and 4.0, and X/Motif. Implementations for MacOS and OpenLook were also started but not completed. At the time, OTI did not have a business case that made it worth the effort to "productize" them.

To simplify the task of creating the various non-X/Motif implementations, *another* layer, called the *OSWidget* layer, was constructed that more closely matched the programming model of Windows and OS/2. The CommonWidgets API was implemented in terms of this layer, and it in turn was implemented on each of the platforms.

By the time Java began its massive rise to fame, VisualAge/Smalltalk was a robust, mature product. However, design decisions that had seemed to be perfectly reasonable at the inception were now definitely showing their age. Most notably, selecting X/Motif as the basis for the API now seemed positively arcane, given that Microsoft Windows had become the overwhelmingly dominant desktop platform.

In any case, it was clear that the world was moving to Java. OTI continued to use Smalltalk for its internal development long enough to create the award-winning VisualAge/Java development environment (with a GUI built from CommonWidgets), but beyond that, any new development would almost certainly be done with Java.

When work began on the next programming environment from OTI—a tool for developing embedded systems in Java that became IBM VisualAge/MicroEdition—Java was, as expected, chosen as the implementation language. The developers initially built a prototype of the user interface using AWT/Swing but in the process of doing so, they discovered a number of appearance and performance problems. They attempted to work around the problems but eventually came to the conclusion that *at that time*, AWT/Swing was not ready to be used as the basis for commercial application development. In addition, it seemed that Swing's use of emulated widgets was going to be prone to all of the negatives that the "emulated look and feel" Smalltalk user interfaces had been shown to exhibit.

At this point, a question needed to be answered: Would AWT and Swing mature sufficiently quickly that applications built using them would be commercially acceptable by the time VisualAge/MicroEdition went to market?

And even if that happened, would an emulated approach effectively enable the implementation of tools that would appeal to demanding developers? After considerable internal discussion, it was decided that a different approach was required.

Given the amount of effort that had already gone into CommonWidgets, an obvious choice of action would have been to translate the existing Small-talk code into Java and take that as the basis for a new toolkit. However, using X/Motif as the model for an API no longer seemed reasonable. The OSWidget layer that had been used to provide portability between the various non-X/Motif implementations was equally powerful and had a simpler API. This, then, filtered through the constraints of the new programming language and with the opportunity taken to clean up a few of the suboptimal design decisions but keeping the original philosophy and overall structure, became the basis for SWT.

Since then, SWT has continued to advance, with the conversion to open source; its use by Eclipse and the addition of the custom widgets package; new ports available for Windows CE, GTK 2, and Macintosh OS X; and many other new features. Despite the new capabilities, the philosophy remains the same: Make the platform capabilities available, keep the layers as thin as possible, and give people the tools they need to make real platform applications in a portable way.

Using SWT

So far, we have been looking at the rationale and history behind SWT. Before we begin taking a closer look at its structure and how to use it, we pause for a moment to show you some code.

Your First SWT Program

SWT applications almost always have the same shape. They begin by creating a connection to the platform window system, then they create a window using that connection, then they react to the events that are generated by the platform window system until some action by the user causes the application to exit. Here is an example of what that looks like in the form of a simple SWT "Hello World"[5] program.

---

5. See the "ACM Hello World Project" (http://www2.latech.edu/~acm/HelloWorld.shtml).

```
import org.eclipse.swt.widgets.*;

public class HelloWorld {
    public static void main(String[] args) {
        Display display = new Display();
        Shell shell = new Shell(display);
        shell.setText("Hello, World.");
        shell.open();
        while (!shell.isDisposed()) {
            if (!display.readAndDispatch())
                display.sleep();
        }
        display.dispose();
    }
}
```

If you want a complete breakdown of what the code in the HelloWorld program does, you can check the introduction to Part 1 (see HelloWorld in SWT). You can also see the subsection Running SWT Applications for detailed information about compiling and running SWT applications. Ignoring those details for the moment, if you invoke the HelloWorld program, it will cause a window to open that looks something like Figure I.1

Figure I.1 Result of running the HelloWorld program.

A Few Words about Screen Shots

SWT runs on many platforms. On each one, applications that are built with SWT take on the look and feel of the underlying window system. For example, the screen shot in Figure I.1 was made on Macintosh OS X. Figure I.2 shows what the window produced by running the HelloWorld program would look like on Microsoft Windows XP.

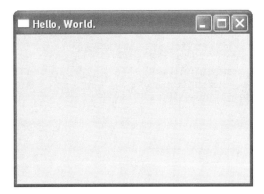

Figure I.2   The HelloWorld program on Windows XP.

To remind you that SWT applications take on the native look and feel of the platform, some of the screen shots in this book are taken from each one—at least each one that we could convince to do screen captures. The choice of platform for a particular screen shot is arbitrary unless the point under discussion is specific to that platform.

SWT Packages

The SWT library is divided into a number of Java packages, based on logical groupings of functionality. In Eclipse terms, most of these packages are defined to be *API packages*, meaning that all publicly visible elements contributed by the package (i.e., the definitions of the public and protected classes, methods, and fields) are available for your use and will remain constant over time, except in certain very restricted circumstances.[6] In practice, releases of SWT are binary-compatible, meaning that a program compiled against the API packages of a previous version of SWT will run on later versions without recompilation.

The SWT library also includes packages that are *not* API. These packages are identified by the word *internal* embedded in their package names. You should treat these packages purely as part of the implementation of SWT, even when they contain public elements. Typically, they have been marked as public only so that they can be shared by several parts of the implementation. There are **absolutely no guarantees** that the classes and methods visible in internal packages will continue to be available from release to release.

---

6. For a description of how and when the API could change, see the Eclipse.org article "Evolving Java-based APIs" (http://www.eclipse.org/eclipse/development/java-api-evolution.html).

Another way that the SWT packages are characterized is based on the platforms on which they are available: Packages that exist on only one platform contain the unique name for the platform (called the *platform code*) embedded in their package name. Because SWT is intended to be portable, platform-specific packages are almost always also internal. As of the writing of this book, the only platform-specific API package is the one that provides access to OLE (also called Active X) in Microsoft Windows.

A list of the SWT API packages and the functionality they provide can be found in Table I.1. Note that this list reflects the situation at the time this book was written.

Table I.1   SWT API Packages

Package Name	*Purpose*
org.eclipse.swt	Contains the class SWT, a global constant pool, and classes to model exceptions and errors
org.eclipse.swt.widgets	Native widgets and related classes, including menus, platform dialogs, low-level (untyped) event support, abstract superclass Layout, etc.
org.eclipse.swt.events	High-level (typed) events, listeners, and adapters
org.eclipse.swt.layout	Standard layout classes FillLayout, RowLayout, GridLayout, FormLayout, and support classes
org.eclipse.swt.graphics	Fonts, colors, images, and primitive graphics operations, such as line and circle drawing
org.eclipse.swt.custom	Custom widgets and other classes implemented specifically for Eclipse; platform-neutral (i.e., same implementation used in all SWT ports)
org.eclipse.swt.dnd	Classes that provide portable access to platform drag-and-drop support
org.eclipse.swt.accessibility	Extensions to support platform tools that assist people with disabilities
org.eclipse.swt.printing	Printers and print dialogs

Table I.I   SWT API Packages (continued)

Package Name	Purpose
org.eclipse.swt.program	Contains class Program, which provides simple program launching, operating system document type mapping, and icon lookup; also created for Eclipse but is platform-specific (i.e., a separate version of this package for each SWT port)
org.eclipse.swt.browser	Provides a Web browsing widget and related support classes; uses native Web browser for the implementation
org.eclipse.swt.awt	Support for building user interfaces from a mix of SWT and AWT widgets
org.eclipse.swt.win32.ole	Available only on Microsoft Windows; provides access to Object Linking and Embedding facilities

In this book, we will be looking predominantly at the first five packages.

- ❍ org.eclipse.swt
- ❍ org.eclipse.swt.widgets
- ❍ org.eclipse.swt.events
- ❍ org.eclipse.swt.layout
- ❍ org.eclipse.swt.graphics

These packages represent the "meat" of SWT; almost all applications will make use of them, and understanding them is fundamental to using SWT. The remaining packages will be touched on in context but will not be covered in detail.

SWT Packages and Memory Constraints

This section will predominantly be helpful to you if you are planning to use SWT in a context where there is limited memory. However, it also provides some useful insight into the relationship between various SWT packages.

The SWT API packages have been arranged into a dependency hierarchy, so that classes defined in packages that are lower in the hierarchy never reference objects that are in higher packages. Aside from being simply good programming practice, making it simpler to separate and debug different areas of functionality, this has two other significant benefits.

1. Only a subset of the packages needs to be ported to a new platform before testing can begin.

2. The SWT library can be pruned in a natural way to deal with situations where memory is constrained, such as in embedded systems or handheld devices.

The simplest way to reduce the size of the library is by removing entire packages that contain functionality not required by your application. Table I.2 shows the dependencies between the SWT packages.

Table I.2   Package Dependencies

Package Name	*Required by*
org.eclipse.swt	all
org.eclipse.swt.graphics	org.eclipse.swt.widgets
org.eclipse.swt.events	org.eclipse.swt.widgets (required by API but not by implementation)
org.eclipse.swt.accessibility	org.eclipse.swt.widgets, but can be replaced by a stub implementation, as is done on platforms that do not have accessibility support
org.eclipse.swt.widgets	org.eclipse.swt.custom
org.eclipse.swt.dnd	org.eclipse.swt.custom
org.eclipse.swt.printing	org.eclipse.swt.custom
org.eclipse.swt.layout	none
org.eclipse.swt.custom	none
org.eclipse.swt.program	none
org.eclipse.swt.browser	none
org.eclipse.swt.awt	none
org.eclipse.swt.win32.ole	org.eclipse.swt.accessibility and org.eclipse. swt.browser (on win32 only)

From the table, you can see that the packages that provide program, printing, layout, drag-and-drop support, the Web browser, SWT/AWT interoperability, and the custom widgets package can be deleted if their functionality is not needed. The custom widgets package, by virtue of the high-level function-ality it provides, ends up tying together most of the other packages.

The *org.eclipse.swt.events* package is interesting because although the *typed* event mechanism it implements is used throughout the native widget *API*, the native widgets themselves use a simpler, *untyped* event mechanism internally. Because of this, it would be possible to remove the events package, as well, if the matching API methods in the native widgets package were also removed. Obviously, this type of pruning would be attempted only if space constraints were critical. Event handling in SWT, both high-level and low-level, is described further in the section Events and Listeners.

After all this, if SWT was still too large to fit your required memory foot-print, the native widgets package *(org.eclipse.swt.widgets)* can also be removed! At this point, all you are left with is the ability to use the graphics routines to draw directly on the screen and platform-specific API methods in the native interface layer to handle input. Although this is beyond the require-ments of almost all reasonable situations, it is still possible, should extreme circumstances arise.

The SWT implementers are serious about making SWT useful across the widest possible range of targets. In addition to making it possible to remove unused packages as described above, care has been taken to minimize the set of features that SWT uses from the standard Java base class libraries. This means that SWT does not need the most current Java Runtime Environment to run. In fact, SWT will run on Java2 Micro Edition (J2ME), because any Standard Edition features that are used by the native widgets and graphics packages have been factored out, and J2ME-compatible versions have been created. For example, both J2SE and J2ME versions of SWT for Microsoft Window CE on ARM processors have been prebuilt and are available at Eclipse.org. These versions have had the custom widgets removed and have only a 500K footprint.

Running SWT Applications

To run an SWT application, you need two sets of components.

> **SWT Jars**   These jars contains the Java classes that make up the SWT library on a particular platform. It is important to note that there is a *different* set of JAR files for each platform, and you will need to get the ones that match your environment. Note that when you *compile* an application that references SWT classes, you also need to make sure that the JAR files are available to the compiler. Because the SWT API is common across all platforms (with the exception of the *org.*

eclipse.swt.win32.ole package), you can compile your application on one platform and run in it on all of the others.

SWT shared libraries   These are shared libraries in whatever form they take for the particular platform (i.e., ".so" files on Linux, ".DLL" files on Windows, etc.). They contain the implementations of the native methods that make up the SWT platform interface layer. Because SWT is designed to do all the interesting work in the Java code, these methods are nothing more than one-to-one Java Native Interface (JNI) wrappers for functions in the platform GUI API. In other words, for each C code function in the platform API (that was needed to implement SWT), there will be a native method definition in one of the shared libraries with the same name and matching arguments. The name of the SWT shared libraries will contain both the platform code indicating where they will run and the version number of the SWT build with which they are compatible. For example, the name of the Windows version of the main SWT shared library from build 3015 of SWT is *swt-win32-3015.dll*. Typically, you can ignore the details of the library names, because the SWT JARs and matching shared libraries are always shipped together.

Getting SWT

SWT is available from www.eclipse.org. The link to the main download page is http://www.eclipse.org/downloads/index.php. Eclipse is a very dynamic, active project, and this page can provide you with a bewildering number of choices for drops (i.e., versions) of Eclipse to choose from. You need to pick one of these to get to a page that contains both full Eclipse drops and *separate SWT drops* for each platform. There are really only two interesting choices here.

1. You should pick the *latest release* if you want the version of SWT that was shipped with the last full release of Eclipse. This version of SWT was thoroughly tested at the time of the release. However, it can be as much as a year behind the most up-to-date version.

2. You should pick the most recent *stable build* if you want the version of SWT that was shipped with the last milestone build of Eclipse. Eclipse milestones are intended to be points of stability during the development cycle, which occur every six weeks. For a milestone, all the Eclipse teams ensure that they have solidly working, stable versions of their code released. Testing is done but not as much as would be done for a release. The intent is that all Eclipse developers can move to each stable build.

For most uses, the stable build is the best choice. You would only pick the latest release if the extra product testing is worth sacrificing the new features and bug fixes that were made since then. Of course, if you are shipping a product based on SWT, you might consider this extra testing to be important.

There are also weekly *integration builds* that are even more current than stable builds. You would move to an integration build only if it provided a missing feature or a particular bug fix that **you needed in your application** that was not available in the last stable build.[7] Integration builds are typically stable, but this is not always the case. Very little testing is done beyond running the automated regression test suites. In most cases, waiting for the next stable build is a better choice.

Once you have picked which drop you want, you need to select the version of SWT that is appropriate for your platform. The drops Web page enumerates the available choices. If you scroll to the bottom of the page, you will find stand-alone SWT drops for the platforms shown in Table I.3.

Table I.3   Available Drops and Supported Platforms

Drop Name*	Platforms
swt-...-win32.zip	Microsoft Windows 98, Me, 2000, and XP
swt-...-linux-motif.zip	Current Linux x86 distributions (tested on RedHat and SuSE) for the X/Motif GUI (based on included OpenMotif)
swt-...-linux-gtk.zip	Current Linux x86 distributions (tested on RedHat and SuSE) for the GTK2 GUI
swt-...-solaris-motif.zip	Sun Microsystems Solaris-based version for the X/Motif GUI
swt-...-qnx-photon.zip	QSSL QNX-based version for the Photon GUI
swt-...-aix-motif.zip	IBM AIX-based version for the X/Motif GUI
swt-...-hpux-motif.zip	Hewlett-Packard HP-UX-based version for the X/Motif GUI
swt-...-macosx-carbon.zip	Apple Macintosh OS X (10.2+) based version for the Carbon GUI

---

7. This can happen. The SWT implementers work hard to address problems that are found by the community. If you have reported a problem, the developer who makes the fix will notify you (by updating the bug report) of the integration build in which it is fixed.

Table I.3   Available Drops and Supported Platforms (continued)

Drop Name*	Platforms
swt-...-win32-ce-arm-ppc.zip	Windows CE for PocketPCs using the ARM processor; subset version for small memory spaces
swt-...-win32-ce-arm-ppc-j2me.zip	Windows CE for PocketPCs using the ARM processor and a J2ME install; subset version for small memory spaces

*Where the ellipses (...) would be replaced by the drop's version identifier.

The list of supported platforms changes over time. There are always efforts within the open source community to produce versions for new platforms. As these mature, they will be added to the list. The dual of this is that if the support for a particular platform disappears, it will be removed from the list. The mainstream platforms, at least, will continue to be supported for the foreseeable future. The Eclipse Project Draft Plan, available at www.eclipse .org, contains a full list of supported platforms, including operating system version numbers.

Regardless of the SWT drop you choose, the ZIP file will contain at least the following files.

❍ An *about.html* file that indicates that the drop is being made available under the Common Public License (CPL) and provides a pointer to the text of that license at eclipse.org.

❍ The SWT JAR files containing the SWT Java classes

❍ The *shared libraries* containing the native method implementations that match the provided JAR files

❍ An *swtsrc.zip* file that contains all the Java and C source code that was used to create the drop, along with makefiles, Ant scripts, and any other support files that are needed to re-create it.

Depending on the platform you are running, there may be several shared libraries provided with the drop. For example, the drops for Linux and the various Unix variants contain, in addition to the main shared library, one or more shared libraries that provide SWT with access to the active desktop manager (Gnome, CDE, etc.). In addition, the Linux X/Motif-based version includes the OpenMotif shared libraries that it requires.

It is also possible to have more than one JAR file included in the drop. For example, the GTK port of SWT has *three* JAR files, swt.jar, swt-pi.jar, and swt-mozilla.jar. The swt.jar file contains the SWT implementation classes. The swt-pi.jar file contains the Java code for the GTK platform interface routines. Similarly, the swt-mozilla.jar contains the classes that interface to the Mozilla browser code. In this case, for each JAR there is a matching shared library.

All JARs and shared libraries that are included with a given SWT drop must be accessible when your application runs. The next section describes how to do this.

Installing as an Extension

Once you have an SWT drop, you need to make the classes that it contains available to your programs. There are various ways to do this, but the simplest by far is to install SWT as a *Java extension*. This makes SWT available to all Java programs in exactly the same way as the Java base classes.

The steps to create an extension vary, depending on the platform and the VM you are running, so you may need to check the documentation that came with your Java install. If you are using the **Sun Java VM on Windows**, you would do the following.

1. Copy the SWT JARs to the JRE *lib\ext* directory

2. Copy all swt*-win32-NNNN.dll files to the JRE *bin* directory,

where *NNNN* is just the four-digit SWT build number that shows up in the DLL included with the drop.

Similarly, to install SWT as an extension on *Solaris*, you would do the following.

1. Copy the SWT JARs to the JRE *lib/ext* directory

2. Copy all libswt*-motif-NNNN.so files to the JRE *lib/sparc* directory,

where, as above, *NNNN* is the four-digit build number that shows up in the names of the .so files included with the drop.

When SWT is installed as an extension, you can compile the HelloWorld example by simply typing

```
javac HelloWorld
```

then run it by typing

```
java HelloWorld
```

This makes developing using SWT as simple as developing using AWT or any other part of the Java base libraries.

Using Command Line Arguments

If you want to make SWT available to a single program, you can reference the SWT library using command line arguments. The swt.jar file and any other JAR files that are included need to be added to the classpath using the *–classpath* or *–cp* options when compiling and running the application, and the directory containing the shared library files must be added to the *java.library.path* system property using the *–D* command line argument when the application is run.

As an example of what this looks like in practice, if you had installed the *GTK* version of SWT in your /home/me/swt directory, you could run the HelloWorld example on *Linux* like this.[8]

```
java \
  —cp .:/home/me/swt/swt.jar:/home/me/swt/swt-pi.jar \
  —Djava.library.path=/home/me/swt \
  HelloWorld
```

In order to run the *Linux X/Motif* version, you need to make sure that the OpenMotif libraries that are included with the SWT distribution are visible. This can be achieved by setting the *LD_LIBRARY_PATH* to include the directory where they are found. Thus, if you had installed the X/Motif version of SWT in your /home/me/swt directory, you could run the HelloWorld example as follows.

```
export LD_LIBRARY_PATH=/home/me/swt
java \
  —cp .:/home/me/swt/swt.jar \
  —Djava.library.path=/home/me/swt \
  HelloWorld
```

If you are using command line arguments to specify the SWT information, you will typically build a batch file or shell script to invoke your application.

Stand-Alone SWT and Mac OS X

As of the writing of this book, the Java VM on Macintosh OS X has some oddities that make running stand-alone SWT programs problematic. The issues have been reported to Apple, and the hope is that they will eventually be resolved, but to work around them in the meantime, a custom Java

---

8. Note that the swt-mozilla.jar file would also need to be included on the classpath if the example used the classes in the *org.eclipse.swt.browser* package.

launcher was created. This launcher is embedded within the Eclipse application but is also included in the Macintosh SWT drops.

Given java_swt, you can run a stand-alone SWT application by passing in the locations of the swt.jar file and shared library directory exactly as you would on other platforms. For example, if java_swt were in the current directory and SWT were installed in the swt subdirectory, you could run the HelloWorld program by typing the following command into a Terminal window.

```
./java_swt \
  —cp .:./swt/swt.jar \
  —Djava.library.path=./swt \
  HelloWorld
```

Unfortunately, there are several problems with this approach, not the least of which is that most Macintosh users would rather not type commands in Terminal windows. In addition, the menu bar of the resulting application has "java_swt" as the name of the application. What is really needed here is a "distiller," such as the *MRJAppBuilder* that is included with the OS X developer tools, that creates double-clickable SWT applications.

The SWT implementers are actively working on improving the integration between SWT and Macintosh OS X. We hope that in the near future, the Macintosh version of Eclipse will include extensions for creating double-clickable applications directly from within the environment. Whatever form this takes, it will almost certainly support creating SWT applications, because using it to create the Eclipse application itself would be an important requirement.

Using Eclipse to Get SWT

When you download an SWT drop, you get only the subset of the codebase that is applicable to a particular platform. That is **almost always the right answer** for a stand-alone application developer.

This section describes how to get the full source for SWT. It is a relatively complex process, and you can safely skip this section if you are not one of the following.

❍ An Eclipse plug-in developer who, for some reason, needs to work with SWT from source

❍ Someone who wants to know how the SWT team works with the code

Even if you are using Eclipse to develop your application, you can still download SWT and configure your environment as described in the previous section.

For those who want to see the full picture of SWT across all platforms, the first step is to connect to the Eclipse CVS repository. The repository can be found at dev.eclipse.org, and it accepts anonymous pserver connections. The main SWT project module is called *org.eclipse.swt*. This contains the SWT Java code for all supported platforms.

Included in the org.eclipse.swt project are a number of XML files with names of the form

```
.classpath_<platform>
```

or

```
.classpath_<platform>_j2me
```

where <platform> is the platform code that identifies a particular implementation of the SWT library. The *_j2me* variant is intended for use on Java2 Micro Edition virtual machines; the other version is for use with J2SE and J2EE. Table I.4 shows the possible values of <platform>.

Table I.4 SWT Platform Codes

<platform>	**SWT Version**
carbon	Macintosh OS X
gtk	Linux GTK 2
gtk1x	**No longer supported!** Was an incomplete version of SWT for GTK 1.x
motif	All X/Motif platforms (Linux, AIX, HP-UX, and Solaris)
photon	QNX Photon
win32	All Microsoft Windows versions (including Windows CE)

The .classpath files describe which subdirectories in the SWT source need to be included in order to create a working SWT implementation for that platform. They are human-readable and could presumably be used manually to select the subdirectories to compile and use, but the best way to deal with them is the same way that the SWT implementers do: Use Eclipse.

Assuming you are familiar with Eclipse,[9] you can *check out* either the HEAD stream or a version of the org.eclipse.swt project from the repository, using the CVS Repository Exploring perspective. The versions are named with tags that contain the same build numbers found in the SWT shared library files.

---

9. There are several good books, including *Contributing to Eclipse Principles, Patterns and Plug-ins* by Erich Gamma and Kent Beck, that explain how Eclipse works. There are also many good articles about using Eclipse at www.eclipse.org and elsewhere on the Web. We recommend Eclipse as the best tool for developing SWT applications.

Once you have checked out the project, you will need to select which platform you are going to develop for. To do this, take the following steps.

1. Switch to the Resource perspective.

2. Find the .classpath_<platform> file that matches the platform you want to use.

3. Select it, then use the context menu to *Copy* then *Paste* it back into the same location.

4. When prompted to provide a new name for the copy, type in the name *.classpath*, which is the name of the file that Eclipse uses to hold the Java build path for the project.

When the .classpath file is modified, Eclipse will automatically recompile the project if the *Perform build automatically on resource modification* preference is enabled (as it is by default).

By requiring the extra step of setting the classpath when loading the project, the code for all SWT implementations can be kept in one project. This makes simultaneously managing all the platforms much simpler.

At this point, you have the SWT Java code configured for use on a particular platform. To allow it to be referenced from another project in the workspace, you need to select the org.eclipse.swt project in the *Java Build Path* (pop up the context menu on the project and select *Properties*) of the project you want to compile.

To run an application from within Eclipse that uses the SWT you have loaded, you will also need the shared libraries that match it. For each platform, there is a project in the dev.eclipse.org repository named *org.eclipse.swt.<platform>* where <platform> is one of the platform codes described above. These projects contain all of the required shared libraries for that platform. You should load the version of the appropriate org.eclipse.swt.<platform> project with the version tag that matches the version of org.eclipse.swt you are using.

Locate the shared libraries within that project; the path is different for each platform to allow the libraries for more than one platform to be installed in a single location (for example, to allow Linux GTK and X/Motif versions to coexist). To run your application, create a *Run...* launch configuration as you normally would, then add a *–Djava.library.path=...* line to the *VM Arguments* that points at the directory containing the libraries.

Now you are ready to go. You should be able to run and debug both applications that use SWT and the SWT code itself from within Eclipse.

Developing Eclipse Plug-ins

This section has shown you how to get the full source for SWT and how to configure it for development with Eclipse on a particular platform. If you are building an Eclipse plug-in that uses SWT, you do not need to perform these steps, because the Plugin Development Environment (PDE) will manage the configuration of SWT for you.

Onward

This part of the book has provided you with the rationale and history behind SWT and the details of how to compile and run SWT-based applications. The remainder of the book covers the SWT widgets and graphics API in detail, then provides some real-world examples of applications built with SWT.

PART I

Widgets

Traditionally, a widget is thought of as an abstract device that is useful for a particular purpose. The term is popular in economics. If you have ever studied economics in university, the professor probably asked, "How does an increase in supply affect the price of widgets?" when discussing the laws of supply and demand. We software developers have co-opted this word to represent those self-contained packages of code that are used to build most modern graphical user interfaces.[1] SWT is called the *Standard **Widget** Toolkit* because widgets really are the basis of any application built in SWT.

---

1. You could argue that many user interfaces are now built from HTML or other XML-based descriptions. For example, although widgets are typically used to *implement* the input areas and scrolled frames that are found in Web pages, this is not relevant to the page designer. Despite this, all currently popular operating systems use widgets as the basis for their visual interfaces and devote a considerable portion of their code to implementing them.

1

Because widgets are so fundamental to developing applications, they are covered in detail in this part of the book. Each chapter covers a different aspect of the topic.

Widget Fundamentals: an overview of widgets and user interaction

The Keyboard: interacting with widgets via the keyboard

The Mouse: interacting with widgets via the mouse

Control Fundamentals: behaviors that widgets called *controls* share

Display: the connection between widgets and the underlying platform

Native Widgets: an overview of the native widgets

Basic Controls: the simplest controls in SWT

Tool Bars and Menus: controls that perform actions

Advanced Controls: tree, table, and tab folder controls

Range-Based Controls: controls that describe numeric ranges

Controls, Composites, Groups, and Shells: the container controls

Canvas and Caret: drawing area controls

Draggable Controls: controls that can manipulate the user interface

Dialogs: self-contained information windows and prompters

Layout: widget positioning and resizing support

The first four chapters describe what widgets are, their life cycle, and how users interact with them.

The Display chapter covers the class that represents the root of all widgets. Both its relationship to the rest of SWT and the specific API it provides are covered.

The Native Widgets chapter lists and briefly describes each of the native widgets. Following this chapter, there are a number of chapters that together provide complete descriptions of all of the native widgets provided by SWT: Basic Controls; Tool Bars and Menus; Advanced Controls; Range-Based Controls; Controls, Composites, Groups, and Shells; Canvas and Caret; and Draggable Controls.

The remaining two chapters provide both general descriptions of dialogs and layouts; they also have specific sections on each of the dialogs and layouts that are included with SWT.

If You Don't Read Anything Else…

If you are one of those people who learn by reading code and running it, this section is for you. In it, you will find "HelloWorld," a minimal SWT program with a short description of each line of code and a list of the widget packages. If you want to run this code, you should read the section Running SWT Applications, but that's it. Enjoy!

HelloWorld in SWT

Here once again is a complete SWT program that creates and displays a new window on the desktop with "Hello, World." in the title bar. This is a slight variation of the one described in the Using SWT chapter. Figure P1.1 shows the result of running this program on Windows XP.

```
01  import org.eclipse.swt.widgets.*;

02  public class HelloWorld {

03  public static void main(String[] args) {
04      Display display = new Display();
05      Shell shell = new Shell(display);
06      shell.setText("Hello, World.");
07      shell.setSize(200, 100);
08      shell.open();
09      while (!shell.isDisposed()) {
10          if (!display.readAndDispatch())
11              display.sleep();
12      }
13      display.dispose();
14  }
}
```

This is what the code does.

Line 1 Most widgets are found in the package *org.eclipse.swt .widgets* (native widgets). The other packages that you will need to investigate are *org.eclipse.swt* (constants), *org.eclipse.swt.events* (typed events), *org.eclipse.swt.layout* (layout algorithms), and *org .eclipse.swt.custom* (nonnative widgets).

Line 4 Every SWT program must create a display to establish the connection between SWT and the underlying window system. For readers who are familiar with the X Windows system, a display is equivalent to an X Windows display. You need to create a display before you can do anything interesting with SWT.

Lines 5–7   These lines create a shell, then set its title and size. Top-level windows are instances of the class Shell and are created on a display. It is not necessary to set the title, position, or size of a shell when it is created. If they are not set, the title will be empty, and the initial position and size will be chosen by the operating system.

Line 8   Shells are invisible when created. This line makes the shell visible, brings it to the front on the desktop, and sets user input so that when keys are typed, they go to the shell.

Lines 9–11   SWT supports an event-driven user interface that requires an explicit event loop. These lines repeatedly read and dispatch the next user interface event from the operating system. When there are no more events, the program goes to sleep waiting for the next event, yielding the CPU. The loop terminates when the programmer decides that the program has ended, typically when the application's main window is closed.

Line 13   This line disposes of the display. Strictly speaking, it is not necessary to dispose of the display because this will happen when the program exits to the operating system. However, it is bad form not to do this because explicitly disposing of the display allows the full life cycle to complete.

As long as the shell remains open, the event loop keeps Java alive, and the SWT program keeps running. When the shell is closed, the program terminates.

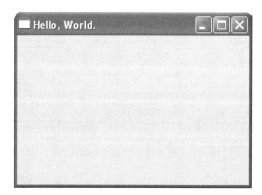

Figure P1.1   The result of running the HelloWorld program on Windows XP.

Obviously, there is *much* more to using SWT than this, but almost all SWT programs have this same basic shape. The many complete examples included in the source code that is provided with this book are also good starting points for exploration. Run them, change them, and watch the results.

You should also feel free to read the rest of the book. It provides many tips and tricks that are subtle enough that it is worth taking the easy road to discover them.

CHAPTER 1

Widget Fundamentals

This chapter provides an overview of the classes contained in the packages *org.eclipse.swt.widgets* and *org.eclipse.swt.events*. We begin by defining what a widget is, then cover the fundamental relationships between widgets, and finally cover how widgets interrelate with each other and the user.

1.1　What Is a Widget?

A widget is a graphical user interface element responsible for interacting with the user. Widgets maintain and draw their state using some combination of graphical drawing operations. Using the mouse or the keyboard, the user can change the state of a widget. When a state change occurs, whether initiated by the user or the application code, widgets redraw to show the new state. This is an important distinguishing feature that all widgets share. It means that when you set a property on a widget, you are not responsible for telling the widget to redraw to reflect the change.

1.1.1　Life Cycle

Widgets have a life cycle. They are created by the programmer and disposed of when no longer needed. Because the widget life cycle is so fundamental to the understanding of the Standard Widget Toolkit (SWT), we are going to cover it in detail here.

1.1.2 Creating a Widget

Widgets are created using their constructor, just like any other Java object. Some widget toolkits employ the *factory* pattern to instantiate their widgets. For simplicity, SWT does not.

When a widget is instantiated, operating system resources are acquired by the widget. This simplifies the implementation of SWT, allowing most of the widget state to reside in the operating system, thus improving performance and reducing memory footprint.[1] There is another important benefit of acquiring operating system resources in the constructor. It gives a clear indication when resources have been allocated. We will see that this is critical in the discussion of widget destruction (see Disposing of a Widget).

Finally, constructors take arguments that generally cannot be changed after the widget has been created. Note that these arguments are create-only **from the point of view of the operating system** and must be present when the widget is created.

Standard Constructors

Widget is an abstract class, so you will never create a Widget instance. In the discussion that follows, note that references to the class Widget actually apply to the subclasses of Widget. This is because subclasses of Widget share the same constructor signatures, giving widget creation a strong measure of consistency, despite the different kinds of widgets and their implementation.

There are four general forms of widget constructor implemented by the subclasses of the class Widget.

1. Widget ()

2. Widget (Widget parent)

3. Widget (Widget parent, int style)

4. Widget (Widget parent, int style, int index)

---

1. If this were not the case, fields would be needed to keep track of values not yet stored in the operating system. When the operating system widget was created, state would need to be copied back and forth between SWT and the operating system, slowing things down and introducing potential inconsistencies. The same application code operating on a widget that has been created in the operating system must *not* behave differently when that widget has yet to be created. Although different behavior can be characterized as a bug, the potential for these kinds of problems is large, especially when multiplied by the number of platforms.

The concept of *hierarchy* (see Widget Hierarchy) is very important in SWT, so much so that the parent widget is the first parameter in most widget constructors.[2] The following sections describe each of the parameters in detail.

A Word About Parameters, Exceptions, and Error Checking

In SWT, methods that take parameters that are Objects check for null and throw IllegalArgumentException ("Argument cannot be null") when the argument can't be null. Besides being more informative, checking for null helps to ensure consistent behavior between different SWT implementations. Barring unforeseen circumstances, such as catastrophic virtual machine failure, an SWT method will throw only three possible exceptions and errors: IllegalArgument-Exception, SWTException, and SWTError. Anything else is considered to be a bug in the SWT implementation.

The Parent Parameter

Widgets cannot exist without a parent, and the parent cannot be changed after a widget is created.[3] This is why the parent is present in almost every constructor. The type of parent depends on the particular widget. For example, the parent of a menu item must be a menu and cannot be a text editor. Strong typing in the constructor enforces this rule. Code that attempts to create a menu item with a text editor parent does not compile, making this kind of programming error impossible.

It is also possible to query the parent of a widget using getParent() but this method is not found in the class Widget.

Why Is getParent() Not Implemented in Widget?

We could have implemented getParent() in class Widget but the method would need to return a Widget. This would require the programmer to cast the result

---

2. Note that the no-parameter version of the constructor is very rare and occurs only as a convenience constructor in the class Shell, so it will not be discussed here.
3. For an exception to this rule, see Control.setParent(), which allows you to change the parent on *some* platforms.

to the appropriate type, despite the fact that the correct type was provided in the constructor. By implementing getParent() in each subclass, the type information that was specified when the widget was created is preserved. One of the design goals of SWT is to preserve as much type information as possible in the API, reducing the need for application programs to cast.

The Style Parameter

Styles are integer bit values used to configure the behavior and appearance of widgets. They specify create-only attributes, such as choosing between multiple- and single-line editing capability in a text widget. Because these attributes cannot be changed after creation, the style of a widget cannot be changed after it has been created. Style bits provide a compact and efficient method to describe these attributes.

All styles are defined as constants in the class org.eclipse.swt.SWT.

Class SWT

SWT uses a single class named (appropriately) *SWT* to share the constants that define the common names and concepts found in the toolkit. This minimizes the number of classes, names, and constants that application programmers need to remember. The constants are all found in one place.

As expected, you can combine styles by using a bitwise OR operation. For example, the following code fragment creates a multiline text widget that has a border and horizontal and vertical scroll bars.

```
Text text = new Text (parent,
    SWT.MULTI | SWT.V_SCROLL | SWT.H_SCROLL | SWT.BORDER);
```

The list of the style constants that are applicable to each widget is described in the Javadoc for the widget. Styles that are defined in a given superclass are valid for the subclasses unless otherwise noted. The constant SWT.NONE is used when there are no applicable style bits.

The widget style can be queried after it has been created using getStyle().

getStyle() Returns the actual style of the widget represented using a bitwise OR of the constants from class SWT. Note that this can be different from the value that was passed to the constructor because it can include defaults provided by the widget implementation. In addition, if a style requested in the constructor cannot be honored, the value returned by getStyle() will not contain the bits. This can happen when a platform does not support a particular style.

The following code fragment uses a bitwise AND to test to see whether a text widget displays and can edit only a single line of text.

```
if ((text.getStyle () & SWT.SINGLE) != 0) {
    System.out.println ("Single Line Text");
}
```

The Position Parameter

The position parameter allows you to create a widget at a specific index in the list of children or by the parent.[4] The other children in the list are shifted to make room for the new widget. For example, the position parameter could be used to create a menu item and make it the third item in a menu. By default, if the position parameter is not provided, the child is placed at the end of the list.

Why is there no widget "add()" method to add a child to the children list of its parent? For an add() method to do something reasonable, it would require that you be able to remove a widget from the children list without destroying it. Given that a widget cannot exist without a parent, this would leave the child in a state where it knows about its parent but the parent does not know about the child.

Convenience Constructors—Just Say No

Some programmers demand convenience constructors using arguments such as, *"Every time a button is created, I always set the text so there should be a button constructor that takes a string."* Although it is tempting to add convenience constructors, there is just no end to them. Buttons can have images. They can be checked, disabled, and hidden. It is tempting to provide convenience constructors for these properties, as well. When a new API is defined, even more convenience constructors are needed. To minimize the size of the widget library and provide consistency, SWT does not normally provide convenience constructors.

---

4. The position parameter is the natural expression of the rule that widgets cannot exist without a parent. Because the parent-child relationship is specified in the constructor, the child will be placed in the list of children when it is created.

1.1.3   Disposing of a Widget

When a widget is no longer needed, its dispose() method must be explicitly called.

> **dispose**()   Hides the widget and its children, and releases all associated operating system resources. In addition, it removes the widget from the children list of its parent. All references to other objects in the widget are set to null, facilitating garbage collection.[5]

SWT does *not* have a widget remove() method for the same reason that there is no add() method: It would leave the child in a state where it knows about its parent but the parent does not know about the child. Because widgets are alive for exactly the duration that they are referenced by their parents, implicit finalization (as provided by the garbage collector) does not make sense for widgets. Widgets are not finalized.[6]

Accessing a widget after it has been disposed of is an error and causes an SWTException ("Widget is disposed") to be thrown. The only method that is valid on a widget that has been disposed of is:

> **isDisposed**()   Returns *true* when the widget has been disposed of. Otherwise, returns *false*.

If you never dispose of a widget, eventually the operating system will run out of resources. In practice, it is hard to write code that does this. Programmers generally do not lose track of their widgets because they require them to present information to the user. Users generally control the life cycle of top-level windows—and the widgets they contain—by starting applications and clicking on "close boxes."

When a widget is disposed of, a dispose event is sent, and registered listeners are invoked in response. For more on this, see the section Events and Listeners.

---

5. Of course, your application has to have no references to the objects for them to be garbage collected.

6. This is covered in great detail in the article *SWT: The Standard Widget Toolkit—PART 2: Managing Operating System Resources* at Eclipse.org (see http://www.eclipse.org/articles/swt-design-2/swt-design-2.html).

1.1.4   Rules for Disposing of Widgets

There are only two rules that you need to know to determine when to dispose of a particular widget. Please excuse the references to specific classes and methods that have yet to be discussed. They will be described in detail later in the book. It is more important at this time that the "rules" are complete.

Rule 1:

If you created it, you dispose of it. SWT ensures that all operating system resources are acquired when the widget is created. As we have already seen, this happens in the constructor for the widget. What this means is that you are responsible for calling dispose() on SWT objects that you created using new. SWT will never create an object that needs to be disposed of by the programmer outside of a constructor.

Rule 2:

Disposing a parent disposes the children. Disposing of a top-level shell will dispose of its children. Disposing of a menu will dispose of its menu items. Disposing of a tree widget will dispose of the items in the tree. This is universal.

There are two extensions to Rule 2. These are places where a relationship exists that is not a parent-child relationship but where it also makes sense to dispose of a widget.

Rule 2a:

Disposing a MenuItem disposes the cascade Menu.

> **MenuItem.setMenu()**   Disposing of a MenuItem that has a submenu set with the setMenu() method disposes of the submenu. This is a natural extension of Rule 2. It would be a burden to the programmer to dispose of each individual submenu. It is also common behavior in most operating systems to do this automatically.[7]

Rule 2b:

Disposing a control disposes the pop-up Menu.

---

7. Windows and X/Motif dispose submenus when a cascading menu item is disposed. GTK and the Macintosh employ a reference-counting scheme that normally disposes of the menu, provided that there are no more references.

Control.setMenu()   Disposing of a control that has a pop-up menu assigned using the setMenu() method disposes the pop-up menu. Many application programmers expected this behavior, even though the operating systems do not do it automatically. We added this rule because too many application programs temporarily leaked pop-up menus.[8]

Another way to remember the extensions to Rule 2 is to notice that both extensions concern instances of the class Menu when used with the setMenu() method. For more information about menus, see Classes Menu and MenuItem in the ToolBars and Menus chapter.

1.2   Widget Hierarchy

The class Widget is the root of an *inheritance* hierarchy of diverse user interface elements such as buttons, lists, trees, and menus. Subclasses, both within the widgets package and outside it, extend the basic behavior of widgets by implementing events and adding API that is specific to the subclass. The inheritance hierarchy of the class Widget is static. For example, the class Button will always inherit from its superclass, Control.[9] Instances of Button will always respond to messages that are implemented in the class Control.

The *containment* hierarchy of a widget is defined by the parent/child relationship between widgets. It is built dynamically at runtime. For example, the parent of an instance of Button might be a group box or tab folder but instances of the class Button do not inherit from the classes that represent these widgets. As we have already seen, the containment hierarchy of a widget is defined when the widget is created, using the parent argument of the constructor.

1.2.1   *Subclassing in SWT*

Generally speaking, subclassing is not the safest way to extend a class in an object-oriented language, due to the *fragile superclass* problem.

The term *fragile superclass* comes from the C++ programming world. It normally refers to the fact that when a new method or field is added to a superclass, subclasses need to be recompiled or they might corrupt memory. Java solves the *static* or binary compatibility portion of the problem using a

---

8. The leak was only temporary because the pop-up menu was eventually disposed of when the top-level Shell was closed.

9. Controls are discussed in the section Controls, Composites, Shells, and the Display. Although we tend to use the terms widget and control somewhat interchangeably, there are differences. See the section Widgets That Are Not Controls for more on this.

name-lookup mechanism that is transparent to the programmer. However, there is also a *dynamic* portion of the problem where subclasses can inadvertently depend on the implementation of a superclass. For example, a subclass may depend on the fact that the internal implementation of the superclass calls a certain public method that is reimplemented in the subclass. Should the superclass be changed to no longer call this method, the subclass will behave differently and might be subtly broken. In SWT, where the implementation of most classes differs between platforms, the chances of this happening are increased. For this reason, subclassing in arbitrary places in the Widget class hierarchy is discouraged *by the implementation*.

In order to allow subclassing where it is normally disallowed, the Widget method checkSubclass() must be redefined.

checkSubclass()   Throws an SWTException("Subclassing not allowed") when the instance of the class is not an allowed subclass.

The protected method checkSubclass() is called internally by SWT when an instance of a widget is created. Subclasses can override this method to avoid the check and allow the instance to be created. The following code fragment defines an inner class that is a subclass of the class Label and reimplements the setText() method.

```
Label label = new Label(shell, SWT.NONE) {
    protected void checkSubclass() {
    }
    public void setText(String string) {
        System.out.println("Setting the string");
        super.setText(string);
    }
};
```

Why Aren't the Widget Classes "final"?

Java allows the programmer to tag a class as *final*, disallowing subclasses. In fact, in very early versions of SWT, classes that should not be subclassed were clearly marked as such using the *final* keyword. Unfortunately, this proved to be too inflexible. In particular, it meant that if a problem was found in an SWT class, only the SWT team could fix it. There was no way to temporarily "patch" the class by creating a subclass to override the problem method(s). Customers who needed to ship their product before a fix could be integrated into the next SWT release were willing to risk the dynamic fragile superclass problem in order to have the freedom to make this kind of patch. The checkSubclass() method is a compromise that allows them to do this without removing all constraints on subclassing.

It is important to note that this really is the only reason why the checkSubclass() method was added. Well-written SWT programs should *never* override checkSubclass().

In SWT, user interfaces are constructed by composition of widget instances. Event listeners (see Events and Listeners, below) are added to widgets to run application code when an event occurs, rather than overriding a method. Application programmers use listeners instead of subclassing to implement the code that reacts to changes in the user interface.

Subclassing *is* allowed in SWT but only at very controlled points, most notably, the classes that are used when implementing a custom widget: Composite or its subclass Canvas. To indicate this, the checkSubclass() method in Composite does not constrain the allowable subclasses. To create a new kind of widget in SWT, you would typically subclass Canvas, then implement and use event listeners to give it the required appearance and behavior. Note that you should still not reference internal details of the superclasses, because they may vary significantly between platforms and between subsequent versions of SWT. For an example of creating a custom widget, see MineSweeper in the Applications part of the book.[10]

1.2.2 Controls, Composites, Shells, and the Display

A *control* is a user interface element that is contained somewhere within a top-level window, called a *Shell*. Controls are common in all user interfaces. Buttons, labels, progress bars, and tables are all controls. Users are familiar with the standard set of controls that come with the operating system. In SWT, operating system controls are, by definition, instances of subclasses of the abstract class Control.

Taking a bottom-up view of the world, every control has a parent that is an instance of the class Composite or one of its subclasses. The class Shell, which represents the top-level windows of your application, is a subclass of Composite. Shells are created on a Display, which represents the "screen."

---

10. A good article that describes how to create custom widgets, entitled *Creating Your Own Widgets Using SWT*, can be found in the "articles" area at www.eclipse.org.

Stated another way, this time from the top down, a display contains a list of top-level shells, where each shell is the root of a tree composed of composites and controls. Composites can contain other composites, allowing the tree to have arbitrary depth. If the child of a shell is another shell, the child is commonly called a *dialog* shell. A dialog shell always stays in front of the parent shell.

1.2.3   Widgets That Are Not Controls

Unfortunately, the picture is not quite that simple. Some of the user interface elements that make up an SWT application are not represented by controls. In general, these are objects that are interesting enough to warrant being represented by instances of some class but do not have the operating system resource requirements of controls. For example, operating systems do not represent each of the items in a tree using other controls. Instead, to improve performance, the tree is responsible for drawing the items. Because the items no longer behave like controls, it would be a mistake to model them as such. The set of widgets that are not controls are exactly those that are not modeled as controls on all operating systems.[11]

1.3   Events and Listeners

An *event* is simply an indication that something interesting has happened. Events, such as "mouse down" and "key press," are issued when the user interacts with a widget through the mouse or keyboard. Event classes, used to represent the event, contain detailed information about what has happened. For example, when the user selects an item in a list, an event is created, capturing the fact that a "selection" occurred. The event is delivered to the application via a listener.

A *listener* is an instance of a class that implements one or more agreed-upon methods whose signatures are captured by an interface. Listener methods always take an instance of an event class as an argument. When something interesting occurs in a widget, the listener method is invoked with an appropriate event.

Most widgets track sequences of events and redraw based on them, sometimes issuing a higher-level event to indicate a state change. For example, a

---

11. Restrictions in Windows, for example, prevented us from making menus and scroll bars into controls.

button may track "mouse press," "move," and "release" in order to issue a "selection" event when the mouse is released inside the button.

Some widget methods generate events. For example, when you call setFocus() on a control, "focus" events are issued. The rules governing which methods cause events and which do not are largely historical, based on the behavior of the Windows and X/Motif operating systems. In order to be able to write portable applications, these rules have been standardized across platforms.

SWT has two kinds of listeners: untyped and typed.

1.3.1 *Untyped Listeners*

Untyped listeners provide a simple, generic, low-level mechanism to handle any type of event. There are only two Java types involved: a single generic interface called *Listener* and a single event class called *Event*. Untyped listeners are added using the method addListener().

> **addListener(int event, Listener listener)**   Adds the listener to the collection of listeners that will be notified when an event of the given type occurs. When the event occurs in the widget, the listener is notified by calling its handleEvent() method.

The type argument specifies the event you are interested in receiving. To help distinguish them from all the other SWT constants, type arguments are mixed upper- and lowercase by convention. All other constants in SWT are uppercase. The following code fragment uses addListener() to add a listener for SWT.Dispose.

```
widget.addListener(SWT.Dispose, new Listener() {
    public void handleEvent(Event event) {
        // widget was disposed
    }
});
```

When multiple listeners are added, they are called in the order they were added. This gives the first listener the opportunity to process the event and possibly filter the data before the remaining listeners are notified (see Event Filters in the chapter Display). Adding the same instance of a listener multiple times is supported, causing it to be invoked once for each time it was added.[12]

---

12. We can't think of any reason you would want to add the same listener multiple times but there is no restriction to stop you from doing this.

It is also possible to remove listeners using removeListener().

removeListener(int type, Listener listener) Removes the listener from the collection of listeners that will be notified when an event of the given type occurs.

In order for a listener to be removed, you must supply the *exact* instance of the listener that was added. If the same listener instance is added multiple times, it must be removed the same number of times it was added to remove it from the listener collection completely.

Generally speaking, removing listeners is unnecessary. Listeners are garbage collected when a control is disposed of, provided that there are no other references to the listener in the application program.

Application code can send events using notifyListeners().

notifyListeners(int type, Event event) Sets the type of the event to the given type and calls Listener.handleEvent() for each listener in the collection of listeners.

An important point to note is that notifyListeners() does not cause the corresponding operating system event to occur. For example, calling notifyListeners() with SWT.MouseDown on a button will not cause the button to appear to be pressed. Also, notifyListeners() does not ensure that the appropriate fields for the event have been correctly initialized for the given type of event. You can use notifyListeners() to invoke listeners that you define but it is probably easier simply to put the code in a helper method.

Class Event has a number of fields that are applicable only for a subset of the event types. These fields are discussed as each type of event is described. Table 1.1 shows the fields that are valid for all event types.

Table 1.1 Public Fields in Class Event That Are Applicable to All Untyped Events

Field	Description
display	the Display on which the event occurred
widget	the Widget that issued the event
type	the event type

Table 1.2 shows the type constants that describe all of the untyped events that SWT implements. More details are available in the descriptions of the individual widgets.

Table 1.2 Untyped Events

Event Type Constant	Description
SWT.KeyDown	A key was pressed
SWT.KeyUp	A key was released
SWT.MouseDown	A mouse button was pressed
SWT.MouseUp	A mouse button was released
SWT.MouseMove	The mouse was moved
SWT.MouseEnter	The mouse entered the client area of the control
SWT.MouseHover	The mouse lingered over a control
SWT.MouseExit	The mouse exited the client area of the control
SWT.MouseDoubleClick	A mouse button was pressed twice
SWT.Paint	A control was asked to draw
SWT.Move	The position of the control was changed
SWT.Resize	The size of the client area of the control changed
SWT.Dispose	The widget was disposed
SWT.Selection	A selection occurred in the widget
SWT.DefaultSelection	The default selection occurred in the widget
SWT.FocusIn	Keyboard focus was given to the control
SWT.FocusOut	The control lost keyboard focus
SWT.Expand	A tree item was expanded
SWT.Collapse	A tree item was collapsed
SWT.Iconify	The shell was minimized
SWT.Deiconify	The shell is no longer minimized
SWT.Close	The shell is being closed
SWT.Show	The widget is becoming visible
SWT.Hide	The widget is being hidden
SWT.Modify	Text has changed in the control
SWT.Verify	Text is to be validated in the control

Table 1.2   Untyped Events (continued)

Event Type Constant	Description
SWT.Activate	The control is being activated
SWT.Deactivate	The control is being deactivated
SWT.Help	The user requested help for the widget
SWT.DragDetect	A drag-and-drop user action occurred
SWT.MenuDetect	The user requested a context menu
SWT.Arm	The menu item is drawn in the armed state
SWT.Traverse	A keyboard navigation event occurred
SWT.HardKeyDown	A hardware button was pressed (handhelds)
SWT.HardKeyUp	A hardware button was released (handhelds)

If you are writing your own widget, you may want to use notifyListeners() to support the built-in untyped events in SWT since this allows your widget to behave like the native widgets with respect to the mapping between untyped and typed listeners. However, for events that are particular to your widget, you will also typically implement typed listeners.

1.3.2   Typed Listeners

A *typed listener* follows the standard JavaBeans listener pattern. Typed listeners and their corresponding event classes are found in the package *org.eclipse.swt.events*. For example, to listen for a dispose event on a widget, application code would use addDisposeListener().

> **addDisposeListener(DisposeListener listener)**   Adds the listener to the collection of listeners that will be notified when a widget is disposed. When the widget is disposed, the listener is notified by calling its widgetDisposed() method.

The following code fragment listens for a dispose event on a widget.

```
widget.addDisposeListener(new DisposeListener() {
    public void widgetDisposed(DisposeEvent event) {
        // widget was disposed
    }
});
```

DisposeListener is an interface. If there is more than one method defined by the listener, SWT provides an adapter class that contains no-op implementations of the methods.[13] For example, the interface SelectionListener has two methods, widgetSelected() and widgetDefaultSelected(), that take Selection-Events as arguments. As a result, the class SelectionAdapter is provided that provides no-op implementations for each method.

Typed listeners are removed using the corresponding remove method for the listener. For example, a listener for a dispose event is removed using removeDisposeListener().

removeDisposeListener(DisposeListener listener)   Removes the listener from the collection of listeners that will be notified when the widget is disposed.

Table 1.3 shows all of the typed events that SWT implements. These are described in more detail in the descriptions of the individual widgets.

Table 1.3   Typed Events

Event	*Listener*	*Methods*	*Untyped Event*
ArmEvent	ArmListener	widgetArmed(ArmEvent)	SWT.Arm
ControlEvent	ControlListener (and ControlAdapter)	controlMoved(ControlEvent) controlResized(ControlEvent)	SWT.Move SWT.Resize
DisposeEvent	DisposeListener	widgetDisposed(DisposeEvent)	SWT.Dispose
FocusEvent	FocusListener (and FocusAdapter)	focusGained(FocusEvent) focusLost(FocusEvent)	SWT.FocusIn SWT.FocusOut
HelpEvent	HelpListener	helpRequested(HelpEvent)	SWT.Help
KeyEvent	KeyListener (and KeyAdapter)	keyPressed(KeyEvent) keyReleased(KeyEvent)	SWT.KeyPressed SWT.KeyReleased
MenuEvent	MenuListener (and MenuAdapter)	menuHidden(MenuEvent) menuShown(MenuEvent)	SWT.Hide SWT.Show
ModifyEvent	ModifyListener	modifyText(ModifyEvent)	SWT.Modify
MouseEvent	MouseListener (and MouseAdapter)	mouseDoubleClick(MouseEvent) mouseDown(MouseEvent) mouseUp(MouseEvent)	SWT.MouseDoubleClick SWT.MouseDown SWT.MouseUp
MouseEvent	MouseMoveListener	mouseMove(MouseEvent)	SWT.MouseMove

---

13. Adapter classes are provided for convenience and to adhere to JavaBeans listener conventions.

Table 1.3 Typed Events (continued)

Event	Listener	Methods	Untyped Event
MouseEvent	MouseTrackListener (and MouseTrackAdapter)	mouseEnter(MouseEvent) mouseExit(MouseEvent) mouseHover(MouseEvent)	SWT.MouseEnter SWT.MouseExit SWT.MouseHover
PaintEvent	PaintListener	paintControl(PaintEvent)	SWT.Paint
SelectionEvent	SelectionListener (and SelectionAdapter)	widgetDefaultSelected(SelectionEvent) widgetSelected(SelectionEvent)	SWT.DefaultSelection SWT.Selection
ShellEvent	ShellListener (and ShellAdapter)	shellActivated(ShellEvent) shellClosed(ShellEvent) shellDeactivated(ShellEvent) shellDeiconified(ShellEvent) shellIconified(ShellEvent)	SWT.Activate SWT.Close SWT.Deactivate SWT.Deiconify SWT.Iconify
TraverseEvent	TraverseListener	keyTraversed(TraverseEvent)	SWT.Traverse
TreeEvent	TreeListener (and TreeAdapter)	treeCollapsed(TreeEvent) treeExpanded(TreeEvent)	SWT.Collapse SWT.Expand
VerifyEvent	VerifyListener	verifyText(VerifyEvent)	SWT.Verify

1.3.3 Why Are There Two Listener Mechanisms?

In early versions of SWT, there were only untyped listeners. After considerable discussion between the Eclipse implementers, the SWT user community, and the developers, it was decided to include a more "JavaBeans-like" listener mechanism. It was felt that this would ease the transition to SWT for developers who were already familiar with AWT/Swing. The untyped listeners remain as the implementation mechanism for event handling in SWT. The typed listeners are defined in terms of them.

We recommend that SWT applications always be implemented in terms of the typed listener mechanism, although this is largely based on the more familiar pattern they represent. Because of the simplicity of the untyped mechanism and our closeness to the implementation, we tend to use it in many of the small examples we write. To see a clear example of the typed mechanism in action, take a look at the FileExplorer example in the Applications part of the book.

Effectively, the trade-off between the two listener models is one of space versus ease of use and adherence to a standard pattern. Using untyped listeners, it is possible to minimize the number of classes and methods used to listen for events. The same listener can be used to listen for many different event types. For example, the following code fragment listens for dispose as well as mouse events.

```
Listener listener = new Listener() {
    public void handleEvent(Event event) {
        switch (event.type) {
            case SWT.Dispose: break;
            case SWT.MouseDown: break;
            case SWT.MouseUp: break;
            case SWT.MouseMove: break;
        }
        System.out.println("Something happened.");
    }
};
shell.addListener(SWT.Dispose, listener);
shell.addListener(SWT.MouseDown, listener);
shell.addListener(SWT.MouseUp, listener);
shell.addListener(SWT.MouseMove, listener);
```

In practice, unless space usage is the overwhelming constraint, we expect that most programmers will use the typed listener mechanism.[14] Note that typed events have very specific listener APIs, whereas the untyped events have only handleEvent(). Using untyped events can lead to switch logic that is more complicated. Refer to Table 1.3 to see the mapping between typed and untyped events.

1.3.4   Widget Events

SWT.Dispose (DisposeEvent)

Table 1.4 shows the dispose events that are provided by SWT.

Table 1.4   Dispose Events

Untyped Event	Description	
SWT.Dispose	The widget was disposed	
Typed Event	**Listener**	**Methods**
DisposeEvent	DisposeListener	widgetDisposed(DisposeEvent)

---

14. All of the typed listeners provided by the native widgets in SWT are found in the package *org.eclipse.swt.events*. When space is extremely limited, this package and all of the corresponding addXXXListener() and removeXXXListener() methods in *org.eclipse.swt.widgets* can be safely removed.

The SWT.Dispose event (typed event DisposeEvent) is sent when a widget is disposed of. Dispose events contain meaningful values in only the *display*, *widget*, and *type* fields.

1.4   Application Data

Using application data, you can associate arbitrary *named* and *unnamed* data with a widget. In some situations, this can be a useful alternative to subclassing. Given that subclassing at arbitrary places in the Widget hierarchy is strongly discouraged, if you are subclassing in order to add fields to a widget, application data can be used instead.

The setData() method is used to set application data. To allow any object to be associated with a widget, setData() and getData() accept and return objects.

setData(Object data)   Sets the unnamed application data. The *data* parameter is associated with the widget and stored in a single unnamed field. This field is for use by the application.

getData()   Answers the unnamed application data or null if none has been set.

setData(String key, Object data)   Sets the named application data. The *data* is stored as a "key/value" pair in the widget. These key/value pairs are for use by the application. The "value" can be any object. If the "key" is null, an IllegalArgumentException ("Argument cannot be null") is thrown.

getData(String key)   Answers the named application data. The *key* is used to find the key/value pair. If no such pair exists, null is returned.

The following code fragment associates an unnamed object (the string "Picard") with a widget. The string is then retrieved and the message "Found the captain!" is printed.

```
widget.setData("Picard");
if ("Picard".equals(widget.getData())) {
    System.out.println("Found the captain!");
}
```

The following code fragment associates the key "Android" with the object "Data" and the key "Captain" with the object "Picard". The key "Captain" is used to find the object "Picard", and the message "Found the captain again!" is printed.

```
widget.setData("Android", "Data");
widget.setData("Captain", "Picard");
if ("Picard".equals(widget.getData("Captain"))) {
    System.out.println("Found the captain again!");
}
```

Application data is optimized for space over speed. This means that storing keys and values is memory-efficient, with the result that adding, removing, and retrieving values is somewhat slower. In general, this is a good design trade-off, because most applications tend to store little or no data with their widgets. When data is stored with a widget, it is often a single named or unnamed value. When storing thousands of named values, if you experience performance problems, store a hash table or another data structure as data with the widget and look the values up in the table instead of in the widget.

1.5   Querying the Display

Widgets provide the method getDisplay() that is used to query the Display.

getDisplay()   Answers the display where the widget was created.

Display is such an important class in SWT that every widget knows on which Display it was created. Display is described in full detail in the chapter Display.

1.6   Summary

In this chapter, you have learned the fundamental behavior of widgets. Widgets are created using standard constructor patterns and explicitly disposed of when no longer needed. User interfaces are built in SWT by the composing instances of widgets to form containment hierarchies. Rather than subclassing and overriding methods, Listeners are used to notify an application when something interesting has happened. Methods of the class Widget were described as they relate to events, application data, and the Display.

CHAPTER 2

The Keyboard

This chapter describes keyboard and character input, covering topics such as focus, key events, traversal, mnemonics, and accelerators. The intent is to pull together everything you need to know about keyboard handling, rather than distributing it throughout the descriptions of the individual widgets. As such, there will be some forward references to classes, such as MenuItem, that will be covered in more detail later.

Implementing a portable API to provide access to the keyboard across multiple different operating systems is a difficult problem. Even on the same platform, depending on the version of the operating system and the locale, characters can be entered in a variety of ways.

The *input method*, sometimes called the *IM* or *IME*, is a custom character-processing engine that is provided by each operating system. It is responsible for converting sequences of key presses into characters from the user's national language. For example, on a Japanese locale, keystrokes are preprocessed by the IME to allow the user to enter Kanji characters. The GTK widget toolkit is even more flexible: Native applications provide a standard menu item on their context menus to configure the IME and assist in entering international text. Applications that do not provide the standard system menu look out of place. Applications that attempt to emulate this menu suffer from the problem that it can change between releases of the operating system, causing them to look out of date. In addition, a GTK-specific menu might look strange on another platform. Because SWT uses native controls, it displays the menu correctly.

Fortunately, most controls manage the keyboard without requiring program intervention. For example, when the user types Kanji characters in a text control, the control processes the characters and displays them. If there is a standard context menu, it is automatically provided. Nevertheless, you will need to understand how the keyboard support in SWT works in order to write your own widgets, process keys in other widgets, and specify accelerators and mnemonics.

2.1   When a Key Is Typed, Where Does It Go?

When a key is typed, the key is resolved by a subsystem in the following order.

1. Window system
2. Menu accelerators
3. Traversal
4. Focus control

In other words, each of these subsystems is given an opportunity to deal with the keystroke, in the order shown. Once one them has resolved (that is, dealt with) the keystroke, it is not delivered to any others. When a key is delivered to a control and resolved, we say that the key was *consumed*.

We will discuss each subsystem from the bottom up, starting with keyboard events and the focus control, because this is the likely order that you will need these concepts.

2.2   Keyboard Events and the Focus Control

Keyboard focus is the property that determines the target for keys that the user types. Normally, the control that has focus, called the *focus control*, receives all keyboard events until focus is assigned to another control. When a control has focus, it often draws in a different manner to give the user a visual cue. For example, a text widget might show a flashing I-beam caret; a list widget might draw a dotted rectangle; and so forth.

On some platforms, focus follows the mouse as it moves around the desktop from control to control. Keys go to the control that is under the mouse. On other platforms, the user must explicitly click in (or otherwise select) a control to give it focus. This policy is governed by the window manager and is not something that SWT programs need to worry about. That is, unless you deliberately override the behavior in your application, it will follow whatever the default is for the platform.

2.2.1   Setting the Focus Control

Focus is assigned to a control using Control.setFocus().

> **setFocus**()   Attempts to make this control be the one that receives keyboard events. If this control or a descendant takes focus, true is returned, indicating that the operation was successful. Composites attempt to assign focus to their children before taking focus themselves. Some controls, such as labels, do not normally take focus. A control will not take focus if it is disabled or hidden, or when input is blocked due to modality. If focus is not assigned for any reason, false is returned.

> **isFocusControl**()   Returns true if the control has focus, otherwise returns false.

You can find out which control has keyboard focus using Display.getFocusControl() (see Getting the Focus Control in the Display chapter).[1]

2.2.2   Forcing Focus to a Control

Under rare circumstances, you may want to force the keyboard focus to go to a control that does not normally take it. You can do this by calling forceFocus().

> **forceFocus**()   Forces the control to receive keyboard events. Controls that do not normally accept keyboard input will take focus using this method. If focus cannot be assigned for any reason, false is returned.

Most Programs Should Not Use forceFocus()

Generally speaking, forcing focus is something that you never want to do. For example, forcing focus to a label is not very useful because labels don't draw in a manner that indicates they can accept input. Forcing focus to a control that does not expect it can confuse users because they have no idea where their keystrokes are going. Application programs should always use setFocus() to assign focus.

---

1. Despite the fact that the focus control is a property of the Display, as of R3.0, SWT does *not* provide a Display.setFocusControl(Control control) method. The Control.setFocus() method is provided instead.

One occasion where forceFocus() might be necessary occurs when implementing your own controls. Normally, focus is not assigned to a composite that has children. For example, when focus is in an OK button in a dialog, if the user unintentionally clicks on the parent of the button, focus remains in the button. However, some composites have children and need to take focus themselves. For example, a "notebook" (a control that provides a strip of selectable tabs that are used to switch between pages) might need to take focus when the user clicks on a tab. Notebooks normally have children, one per page. If you were to implement a notebook, instead of using the native control provided by SWT, you would need to force focus to the notebook when the mouse was pressed over a tab.

2.2.3 Focus Events

Table 2.1 shows the focus-related events that are provided by SWT.

Table 2.1   Focus Events

Untyped Event		Description	
SWT.FocusIn		The control is now the focus widget	
SWT.FocusOut		The control is no longer the focus widget	
Typed Event	**Listener**		**Methods**
FocusEvent	FocusListener (and FocusAdapter)		focusGained(FocusEvent) focusLost(FocusEvent)

The SWT.FocusIn (typed event FocusEvent) and SWT.FocusOut (typed event FocusEvent) events can be used to track focus within a program. Focus events contain meaningful values in only the *display, widget,* and *type* fields.

Using SWT.FocusIn and SWT.FocusOut to Indicate Focus

The following example uses SWT.FocusIn and SWT.FocusOut to ensure that the class MyControl draws a focus indicator. The implementation of both events simply redraws the control. The SWT.Paint listener checks to see whether the MyControl has focus and draws a focus rectangle.[2] Figure 2.1 shows MyControl with focus in a Shell.

---

2. Note that the seemingly obvious approach of drawing and clearing the focus indicator inside the focus events will cause the widget to display incorrectly when there are outstanding paint events (see Painting in a Control in the Controls chapter). No matter where the focus indicator is drawn, paint listeners must always check for focus and draw accordingly.

```
static class MyControl extends Canvas implements Listener {
    String string = "";
    public MyControl(Composite parent, int style) {
        super(parent, style);
        addListener(SWT.Paint, this);
        addListener(SWT.FocusIn, this);
        addListener(SWT.FocusOut, this);
        addListener(SWT.KeyDown, this);
    }
    public void setText(String string) {
        checkWidget();
        this.string = string == null ? "" : string;
    }
    public void handleEvent(Event event) {
        switch (event.type) {
            case SWT.Paint:
                GC gc = event.gc;
                Rectangle rect = getClientArea();
                Point extent = gc.textExtent(string);
                int x = (rect.width - extent.x) / 2;
                int y = (rect.height - extent.y) / 2;
                gc.drawText(string, x, y);
                if (isFocusControl()) {
                    x -= 2; y -=2;
                    extent.x +=3; extent.y +=3;
                    gc.drawFocus(x, y, extent.x, extent.y);
                }
                break;
            case SWT.FocusIn:
            case SWT.FocusOut:
                redraw();
                break;
            case SWT.KeyDown:
                if (event.character == ' ') {
                    notifyListeners(SWT.Selection, null);
                }
                break;
        }
    }
}
```

Figure 2.1   The CH1a_MyControl example.

2.2.4 Key Events

When a key is pressed or released, a key event is normally created and delivered to your application. However, depending on the platform, the locale, and the keystroke, there are circumstances when this does not happen. For example, if the key is an accent character, the operating system key classification engine may temporarily consume it. When a caret character (^) is typed in a German locale followed by an *e*, the result is the accented character *ê*. Similarly, key events are not created for the intermediate keystrokes consumed by the IME when preprocessing sequences of keys into single Japanese characters. The reason for this is that these kinds of low-level key events are highly platform-specific and generally not useful to most programs.[3] SWT hides the underlying operating system events and issues a single key event when the operating system has finished classifying the keystroke.[4]

Table 2.2 shows the key events that are provided by SWT.

Table 2.2   Key Events

Untyped Event	Description	
SWT.KeyDown	A key was pressed	
SWT.KeyUp	A key was released	
Typed Event	**Listener**	**Methods**
KeyEvent	KeyListener (and KeyAdapter)	keyPressed(KeyEvent) keyReleased(KeyEvent)

The SWT.KeyDown (typed event KeyEvent) and SWT.KeyUp (typed event KeyEvent) events represent high-level key presses and key releases. They can be used to implement and intercept key processing. The relevant event fields during SWT.KeyDown and SWT.KeyUp are shown in Table 2.3.

---

3. The obvious exception would be programs that are trying to implement an IME. Because the appearance and behavior of the native IME are significantly different between operating systems and even between different releases of the same operating system, a nonnative implementation is guaranteed to look out of place.

4. On Windows, a single keystroke can result in multiple low-level Windows messages, such as WM_KEYDOWN, WM_SYSKEYDOWN, WM_CHAR, WM_SYSCHAR, WM_DEADCHAR, WM_SYSDEADCHAR, WM_IME_CHAR, and WM_IME_COMPOSITION. This makes the SWT keyboard implementation on Windows particularly troublesome.

Table 2.3 Public Fields of Class Event Valid during SWT.KeyDown and SWT.KeyUp

Field	Description
character	The Unicode value of the character (e.g., \u0041 for *A*)
keyCode	A constant indicating which key was pressed (e.g., SWT.PAGE_UP)
stateMask	The "state mask" representing keyboard modifiers (e.g., SWT.SHIFT)
doit	A boolean that can be used to cancel the key operation

2.2.5 Characters, Key Codes, and State Masks

For key events that represent characters found in the Unicode character set, the *character* field is set to the matching (Unicode) char value. For example, when the user presses the <a> key, an SWT.KeyDown event is issued. The *character* field in this event has the (char) value a.

Despite the fact that SWT characters are just Java char values, convenience constants are provided for most common control characters, even those that have standard escape sequences (such as '\n' for linefeed). Programmers are free to use the constants (found in Table 2.4) or their equivalents.

Table 2.4 Character Convenience Constants

Character Constant	Description
SWT.BS	The Backspace character ('\b')
SWT.CR	The Return character ('\r')
SWT.DEL	The Delete character ('\u007F')
SWT.ESC	The Escape character ('\u001B')
SWT.LF	The Linefeed character ('\n')
SWT.TAB	The Tab character ('\t')

The *character* field in a key event represents the *final character value* for the keystroke. Any *modifier* keys, such as <Shift> or <Ctrl>, that were held down when the key was pressed have been applied to the character. For example, when the user presses <Shift> and the <a> key, the *character* field contains A. Less obvious is the result of pressing <Ctrl> and the <a> key. This gives a Control+A character (with value '\u0001', known as *SOH* in the Unicode specification). Holding down <Ctrl> and pressing @, *a* to *z*, [, \,], ^, or _ results in the corresponding Unicode control characters in the range '\u0000' to '\u001F'.

Why Does SWT Generate Control Characters?

Programmers who are new to SWT sometimes find the fact that the *character* field contains the processed control character confusing. They expect to create the control character themselves based on the values in the *character* and *state-Mask* (see below) fields. Doing this is a source of programming errors on keyboards where the <Ctrl> key, in combination with other modifiers, is used to enter international characters. For example, on German Windows, the @ character is entered by holding down a special modifier key, <AltGr> (which is equivalent to pressing <Ctrl> and <Alt>), and typing the <q> key. SWT correctly creates a key event with the *character* field set to '@'. Application code that attempted to handle control characters itself by detecting when the <Ctrl> key was pressed would turn this sequence into the control character '\u0000' (called *NUL* in the Unicode spec), which is not the character that the user typed.

The *keyCode* field in the event is used to represent keystrokes that are not Unicode values. For example, pressing <F4> or <PageUp> causes the *keyCode* field to contain a corresponding key code value. All possible key code values are defined in the class SWT. For example, the key code value for the <PageUp> key is SWT.PAGE_UP. (There are simply too many constants to list here, see the Javadoc for class SWT for the complete list.)

Although, strictly speaking, there are Unicode values to represent almost every kind of key,[5] the *character* field in the key event is not always assigned. Normally, a key such as <PageUp> is intended to cause an action, not insert a character. Instead of attempting to draw a character, programs use the fact that the *character* field is unassigned to classify the keystroke.

The *keyCode* field has one further purpose. If the *character* field is assigned, the *keyCode* field is used to represent the key code of the "unaffected" character. For example, the *character* field will contain the plus character (+) when the <Add> key is pressed. It will also contain the plus when the numeric keypad <Add> key is pressed. Most programs process either <Add> key in the same manner, using the *character* field. However, some programs

---

5. Most notably, there are no standard Unicode characters for the function keys.

might want to differentiate between the two. In this case, the *keyCode* field will contain SWT.KEYPAD_ADD when the plus character originated from the numeric keypad.

The *stateMask* field is an integer bit-mask that captures that state of the keyboard and mouse **immediately prior to the event.**[6] This is an important point to understand. For example, at the time the <Shift> key is pressed, the <Shift> key is not down because you are in the process of pressing it. In this case, the *stateMask* field does not contain the SWT.SHIFT modifier. However, the *stateMask will* contain the SWT.SHIFT modifier when the next key is pressed because the <Shift> key is down at that time.

Table 2.5 shows the four[7] *specific* modifier masks supported by SWT.

Table 2.5   Specific Modifier Key State Masks

Modifier Mask	*Description*
SWT.CONTROL	The <Ctrl> key was down (same as SWT.CTRL)
SWT.SHIFT	The <Shift> key was down
SWT.ALT	The <Alt> key was down
SWT.COMMAND	The <Command> key was down

Modifier masks are also used to represent keystrokes when the modifier keys themselves are pressed. For example, when the user presses the <Shift> key and nothing else, a key down event is generated with the *character* field set to '\u0000', the *keyCode* field set to SWT.SHIFT, and the *stateMask* field set to zero. If the user were now to press the <a> key, another key event would be generated. This new event would have the *character* field set to A and the *stateMask* field set to SWT.SHIFT. This can be a little bit confusing at first because the same constant (SWT.SHIFT) is used to serve two different purposes in the two fields.

The specific modifier keys and state masks can be tricky to use portably. Most keyboards contain at least the <Shift>, <Ctrl>, and <Alt> keys but some platforms use more than just these three. To make things more complicated, plat-

---

6.   For those readers who are familiar with X Windows, the SWT *stateMask* field works the same way.

7.   The convenience constant SWT.CTRL is also provided that is identical to SWT.CONTROL. Applications can use these two interchangeably, although SWT.CTRL tends to be used to specify accelerators whereas SWT.CONTROL is used for listeners.

form-specific conventions exist that dictate which modifier keys should be used. For example, on the Macintosh, users expect to type Command+C to copy text to the clipboard. On Windows, the equivalent key combination is Control+C. Although it is possible to write code on a Macintosh that deliberately uses Control+C to copy text, any application that does this would be frustrating to use and would definitely not match the Macintosh user interface guidelines.

To solve this problem, SWT defines the *generic* modifier masks shown in Table 2.6.

Table 2.6   Generic Modifier Key State Masks

Modifier Mask	Description
SWT.MOD1	The first modifier was down (often SWT.CONTROL)
SWT.MOD2	The second modifier was down (often SWT.SHIFT)
SWT.MOD3	The third modifier was down (often SWT.ALT)
SWT.MOD4	The fourth modifier was down (often zero)
SWT.MODIFIER_MASK	Bitwise-OR of all valid modifiers

These generic modifier masks are initialized when SWT starts up on each platform. For example, SWT.MOD1 is set to SWT.CONTROL on Windows and to SWT.COMMAND on the Macintosh.

It is important to note that expecting to process a modifier key on a platform where the modifier does not exist is futile. For example, the SWT.COMMAND key can never be pressed on Windows because it does not exist on the keyboard.

The constant SWT.MODIFIER_MASK contains every valid modifier. It is generally used to test for an unmodified key. This constant ensures that when new modifier keys are added to SWT, code that tests for unmodified keys (or a key that is modified in any way) will continue to work. The following code fragment illustrates this point.

```
//WRONG — broken when new modifier masks are added
int bits = SWT.CONTROL | SWT.ALT | SWT.SHIFT | SWT.COMMAND;
if ((event.stateMask & bits) == 0) {
    System.out.println("No modifiers are down");
}

//CORRECT — works when new modifier masks are added
if ((event.stateMask & SWT.MODIFIER_MASK) == 0) {
    System.out.println("No modifiers are down");
}
```

Which Modifier Constants Should I Use?

Use the generic modifiers if you want the application to use the "expected" modifier keys for common actions on each platform.[8] Use the specific modifier constants if your application needs to handle the exact (named) modifiers the same way everywhere. For example, you would do this if you were building a terminal emulator that needed to pass the modifiers on to a remote host.

Eclipse uses the specific modifiers in its implementation but includes its own multiplatform, user-configurable key bindings mechanism to deal with them. The generic modifiers are definitely a simpler answer for most applications.

2.2.6 Using SWT.KeyDown to Print Key Events

The following program listens for key up and key down events and prints the *stateMask*, *keyCode*, and *character* values as keys are typed.

```
public static void main(String[] args) {
    Display display = new Display();
    Shell shell = new Shell(display);
    Listener listener = new Listener() {
        public void handleEvent(Event event) {
            String string =
                event.type == SWT.KeyDown ? "DOWN": "UP  ";
            string += ": stateMask=0x"
                + Integer.toHexString(event.stateMask);
            if ((event.stateMask & SWT.CTRL) != 0)
                string += " CTRL";
            if ((event.stateMask & SWT.ALT) != 0)
                string += " ALT";
            if ((event.stateMask & SWT.SHIFT) != 0)
                string += " SHIFT";
            if ((event.stateMask & SWT.COMMAND) != 0)
                string += " COMMAND";
            string += ", keyCode=0x"
                + Integer.toHexString(event.keyCode);
            string += ", character=0x"
                + Integer.toHexString(event.character);
            switch (event.character) {
                case 0: string += " '\\0'"; break;
                case SWT.BS: string += " '\\b'"; break;
                case SWT.CR: string += " '\\r'"; break;
                case SWT.DEL: string += " DEL"; break;
                case SWT.ESC: string += " ESC"; break;
```

---

8. Note that this mechanism maps only the modifier keys. It does not map all platform-specific key sequences. For example, it does *not* map the Macintosh Command+W (window close) key to the Windows equivalent, ALT+F4.

```
                    case SWT.LF: string += " '\\n'"; break;
                    case SWT.TAB: string += " '\\t'";
                        break;
                    default:
                        string += " '" + event.character + "'";
                        break;
                }
                System.out.println(string);
            }
        };
        shell.addListener(SWT.KeyDown, listener);
        shell.addListener(SWT.KeyUp, listener);
        shell.setSize(200, 200);
        shell.open();
        while (!shell.isDisposed()) {
            if (!display.readAndDispatch()) display.sleep();
        }
        display.dispose();
    }
```

Using SWT.KeyDown to Consume Keys

Occasionally under rare circumstances, it is necessary to consume key events before they are processed by a control. Because SWT is implemented using native controls, most of the processing behind each keystroke occurs in the operating system. For example, when the user types in a text control, the code that inserts and draws the characters runs in the operating system after the SWT.KeyDown listeners return. Using the *doit* field, you can consume the keystroke and stop the operating system from processing the character. The following example prevents the user from entering characters in a native text control by setting the *doit* field to false for every SWT.KeyDown event.

```
public static void main(String[] args) {
    Display display = new Display();
    Shell shell = new Shell(display);
    Text text = new Text(shell, SWT.SINGLE | SWT.BORDER);
    text.addListener(SWT.KeyDown, new Listener() {
        public void handleEvent(Event event) {
            event.doit = false;
        }
    });
    text.pack();
    shell.pack();
    shell.open();
    while (!shell.isDisposed()) {
        if (!display.readAndDispatch()) display.sleep();
    }
    display.dispose();
}
```

Sometimes programmers mistakenly attempt to use this feature to implement input validation for text controls. This is unnecessary and prone to error.[9] Input validation is provided in a platform-independent and portable manner for text controls using the SWT.Verify event (see Class Text in the Basic Controls chapter).

Note that setting the *doit* field to false will not stop the processing of keystrokes when this happens outside of the operating system, for example, in another SWT.KeyDown listener on the same control. In this case, because nothing is done with the keystroke in the operating system, there is nothing to cancel (although it is not harmful to set *doit* to false). A further problem arises when your listener is added after the other SWT.KeyDown listeners for the control. It runs after the processing has already happened. To solve this problem and intercept and cancel all key processing, no matter where and how the actual work is done, event filters can be used (see Event Filters in the Display chapter).

2.3   Traversal

Traversal keys move focus within the window and optionally invoke an action on a control. Traversal keys differ from accelerators and window system keys (which are discussed later in this chapter) in the following manner: It is up to the focus control to decide whether to perform the traversal operation or process the key. In the case of accelerators and window system keys, they are consumed before the control has a chance to see them. When a traversal operation is performed, the traversal key is consumed to stop further processing by the focus control.

There are two kinds of traversal: mnemonic and tab.

2.3.1   *Mnemonic Traversal*

Mnemonic traversal is supported on all platforms except the Macintosh, which does not have the concept.[10] Mnemonics are typically presented to the

---

9. Here are a few of the things that can go wrong when attempting to do input validation using the *doit* field. On Windows, the Control+V key sequence does not insert a Control V character. Instead, it pastes text from the clipboard. Programs that attempt to work around this either by consuming Control+V or validating the contents of the clipboard will fail on the Macintosh. The key sequence used to paste text on that platform is Command+V. Sometimes characters can be entered into a text control without typing, using a built-in context menu or some other input mechanism. These characters will bypass key listeners because a key was not pressed.

10. At least as of OS X 10.3, the Macintosh does not have mnemonics.

user as an underlined character in the label of a widget.[11] An action is invoked when the user presses a key sequence that matches the mnemonic, often by pressing the <Alt> key and the character. For example, when the user types Alt+F on Windows, the focus is moved to the File item in the menu bar, and the File menu is dropped down. Mnemonics are also found outside of menus. The underlined *Y* on the Yes button in a standard Yes/No/Cancel dialog (invoked by typing Alt+Y or just *y* on some platforms) is a mnemonic for a button.

Invoking a mnemonic is normally the keyboard equivalent of selecting the widget with the mouse. Controls that do not support selection, such as labels and group boxes, may still support mnemonics. Instead of invoking an action, they assign focus. The algorithm that detects and processes a mnemonic is platform-specific, but specifying a mnemonic character is not.

Specifying the Mnemonic Character

Table 2.7 shows some typical mnemonic strings and the resulting mnemonic characters.Mnemonics are indicated by an ampersand (&), which causes the next character to be the mnemonic character. The mnemonic indicator character can be escaped by doubling it in the string, causing a single ampersand to be displayed.

Table 2.7   Mnemonic Strings

String	*Result*
"&File"	File
"T&able"	Table
"This && That"	This & That

To use mnemonics, all you need to do is provide the appropriate strings. The controls themselves handle mnemonic processing and take the appropriate action. For example, setting the text of a menu item to "&File" causes *F* to be the mnemonic character for the menu item.

Using the SWT.Traverse event (see the Traversal Events section below), you can intercept mnemonics for built-in controls or implement mnemonics for the controls that you write.

---

11. On Windows XP, mnemonics are hidden until the user presses the <Alt> key. This is not the case in earlier versions of Windows.

2.3.2   Tab Traversal

Tab traversal is supported on all platforms. Unlike mnemonics, it is not indicated in any special manner by the controls. There is no need to do this because there are strict guidelines on each platform to define how focus moves between controls. For example, when the user presses the <Tab> key, it is expected that focus should go to the next control in the window. When focus reaches the last control, it cycles back to the first.

The name *tab traversal* is a misnomer, implying that traversal is done using only the <Tab> key. On some platforms the arrow keys also move focus. Other keys, such as the <Esc> key normally used to close a dialog, are considered to be tab traversal keys, as well.

As with mnemonic traversal, native controls do their own tab traversal processing. If your application **creates the controls in the order that you would like them traversed** within the parent control, nothing else is necessary to enable tab traversal.

Rules for Tab Ordering

By default, all controls in a containment hierarchy are traversable using the keyboard. The algorithm that ensures this is based on the concept of tab groups and tab items.

A *tab group* is either a single control or a composite. The <Tab> key is used to move focus between tab groups. For example, single-line text controls are tab groups. Users are familiar with tabbing between them in dialogs. When a composite is a tab group, it might take focus when the <Tab> key is pressed. For example, on some platforms, TabFolders take focus, allowing the user keyboard access the TabItems within the folder. However, most composites do not take focus; instead, they pass focus to their first tab item child, then to the remaining tab group children.[12]

A *tab item* is always a single control. The arrow keys are used to traverse between tab items. Typical tab items are radio and check buttons. When focus is on a tab item, in order to get to the next tab group, the <Tab> key is pressed.

There are also controls that are neither tab groups nor tab items. These are not traversable. For example, a label does not take part in traversal and does not take focus when either <Tab> or an arrow key is pressed.

---

12. By passing focus to the first tab item child, the algorithm ensures that every control is accessible when tab items and tab groups are mixed within the same composite. If the tab item children of a control are thought of as sharing a single invisible (and hypothetical) tab group parent, this invisible tab group is assigned focus before the other tab groups in the composite.

For native controls, the specifics as to whether a control is a tab group, tab item, or neither is part by the operating system.[13] Custom controls that use the SWT.NO_FOCUS style to avoid focus when the mouse is pressed also avoid focus during tab traversal. When a custom control listens for SWT. KeyUp or SWT.KeyDown, this indicates that it wants keyboard input, causing it to take focus when clicked with the mouse or during tab traversal.

Specifying the Tab Ordering

Sometimes an application program needs to explicitly set the order that the children are traversed when the user presses the <Tab> key. Generally speaking, applications should not do this for the following reasons.

❍ An incomplete tab list will make some controls inaccessible.

❍ Overriding the tab ordering disregards the operating system rules.

❍ The tab list must be kept up to date when new controls are created.

The Composite.setTabList() method is used to explicitly set tab ordering.

setTabList(Control [] tabList) Sets the array of the children to be used as the tab list. By default, tab traversal is performed in the order that the children are created. By setting the tab list, application programs can change the order to the order of the controls that are in the array. If tabList is null, the default tab ordering is restored.

getTabList() Returns an array of the children that make up the tab list. This is a copy of the array so that modifying this structure has no effect.

2.3.3   Traversal Events

If you are writing your own control, you *must* implement some form of traversal. If you do not, users will be able to traverse into your control but will be unable to traverse out.

---

13. For example, on X/Motif, push buttons are tab items, not tab groups. This leads to confusion when users expect to move between buttons such as the OK and Cancel buttons in a dialog using the tab key.

Why Isn't Traversal Implemented by Default for My Control?

In older versions of SWT, the default behavior for the <Tab>, <Esc>, and <Enter> keys was to perform a traversal operation and consume the key. However, programmers were confused when their key listeners did not see these keys. After one too many bug reports, we decided that default traversal was a bad idea. The fundamental problem is that it is not possible to determine in advance which keys the control expects to process and which ones it expects to traverse.

Table 2.8 shows the traversal events that are provided by SWT.

Table 2.8   Traversal Events

Untyped Event		Description
SWT.Traverse		A traversal key was pressed

Typed Event	Listener	Methods
TraverseEvent	TraverseListener	keyTraversed(TraverseEvent)

The SWT.Traverse (typed event TraverseEvent) event is issued when the user presses a traversal key sequence. It is used both to implement and to intercept keyboard traversal. Table 2.9 shows the relevant event fields during SWT.Traverse events.

Table 2.9   Public Fields of Class Event Valid during SWT.Traverse

Field	Description
detail	The traversal code
doit	Setting *doit* to false cancels the traversal operation. The default value indicates whether the particular traversal operation would normally be performed by the control. For controls that you write, *doit* is always false.

When a traversal key is pressed, the SWT.Traversal event is sent to the focus widget before any key event is issued. The *detail* field of the event contains a traversal code that describes the type of traversal. Table 2.10 shows the traversal codes defined in SWT.

Table 2.10   Keyboard Traversal Codes

Detail	Description
SWT.TRAVERSE_ESCAPE	Closes the dialog shell (if any)
SWT.TRAVERSE_RETURN	Invokes the "default button" (if any)
SWT.TRAVERSE_TAB_PREVIOUS	Moves focus to the previous "tab group"
SWT.TRAVERSE_TAB_NEXT	Moves focus to the next "tab group"
SWT.TRAVERSE_ARROW_PREVIOUS	Moves focus to the previous "tab item"
SWT.TRAVERSE_ARROW_NEXT	Moves focus to the next "tab item"
SWT.TRAVERSE_MNEMONIC	Invokes a "mnemonic control"
SWT.TRAVERSE_PAGE_PREVIOUS	Moves focus to the previous "notebook page"
SWT.TRAVERSE_PAGE_NEXT	Moves focus to the next "notebook page"
SWT.TRAVERSE_NONE	Performs no traversal action

Despite the fact that the traversal code constants include the words ESCAPE, RETURN, and TAB, there are no guarantees about which keystrokes cause traversal. However, the <Esc>, <Enter>, and <Tab> keys are very common across platforms.[14]

The *doit* field of the event is used either to implement or to stop traversal. Setting *doit* to true tells the control to perform the traversal operation that is described by the *detail* field. Performing the operation consumes the keystroke. Setting *doit* to false cancels the operation and allows a key event to be delivered to the control. For even more flexibility, the *detail* field can be assigned to change the type of traversal that will be performed.

Using SWT.Traverse to Manage Traversal

Traversal is an interesting and difficult area for which a portable, powerful, and flexible API has been provided. Unfortunately, this sort of generality can cause unwanted complexity. In this case, the fact that the SWT.Traverse event uses both the *detail* and *doit* fields makes it hard to understand.[15] Table 2.11 shows the resulting traversal action and key event for all combinations of the two fields.

---

14. On Windows CE running on the Smart Phone, the arrow keys are used for traversal.

15. Perhaps using a single field with bit field constants such as SWT.CONSUME and SWT.TRAVERSE would have been easier to understand.

Table 2.11   The *doit* and *detail* Fields

doit	detail	Traversal Performed	Key Event
true	Don't assign	Yes	No
false	Don't assign	No	Yes
true	SWT.TRAVERSE_NONE	No	No
false	SWT.TRAVERSE_NONE	No	Yes

Using SWT. Traverse to Implement Tab Group Traversal

The following example implements tab group traversal for a simple "drawing area" control called a *canvas* (see the chapter Canvas and Caret). Implementing this kind of traversal is simply a matter of setting *doit* to true to enable the traversal that is normally associated with <Esc>, <Enter>, <Tab>, and <Page> keystrokes. In the example, when the canvas gets focus, it changes its background color from blue to red. A key listener shows which keys are consumed and which are delivered. All of the traversal keys are consumed except <Esc>, which is delivered to the canvas. In this case, because the canvas is not part of a dialog Shell, the SWT.TRAVERSE_ESCAPE traversal is not performed, and the keystroke is delivered to the canvas.

   A button is used in this example to allow focus to be assigned elsewhere in the Shell.

```
public static void main(String[] args) {
   Display display = new Display();
   final Color red =
      display.getSystemColor(SWT.COLOR_RED);
   final Color blue =
      display.getSystemColor(SWT.COLOR_BLUE);
   Shell shell = new Shell(display);
   shell.setLayout(new RowLayout(SWT.VERTICAL));
   Button button = new Button(shell, SWT.PUSH);
   button.setBounds(10, 10, 100, 32);
   button.setText("Button");
   final Canvas canvas = new Canvas(shell, SWT.BORDER);
   canvas.setBackground(blue);
   canvas.addListener(SWT.Traverse, new Listener() {
      public void handleEvent(Event e) {
         switch (e.detail) {
            /* Do tab group traversal */
            case SWT.TRAVERSE_ESCAPE:
            case SWT.TRAVERSE_RETURN:
            case SWT.TRAVERSE_TAB_NEXT:
            case SWT.TRAVERSE_TAB_PREVIOUS:
            case SWT.TRAVERSE_PAGE_NEXT:
            case SWT.TRAVERSE_PAGE_PREVIOUS:
```

```
            e.doit = true;
            break;
        }
    }
});
canvas.addListener(SWT.FocusIn, new Listener() {
    public void handleEvent(Event e) {
        canvas.setBackground(red);
    }
});
canvas.addListener(SWT.FocusOut, new Listener() {
    public void handleEvent(Event e) {
        canvas.setBackground(blue);
    }
});
canvas.addListener(SWT.KeyDown, new Listener() {
    public void handleEvent(Event e) {
        System.out.println("Got a Key");
    }
});
shell.setDefaultButton(button);
shell.setSize(200, 200);
shell.open();
while (!shell.isDisposed()) {
    if (!display.readAndDispatch()) display.sleep();
}
display.dispose();
}
```

Using SWT.Traverse to Implement Text Traversal

A hypothetical custom text control could use the *doit* field to implement the
kind of traversal that is normally associated with text controls. When the control is editing a single line of text, the <Tab> and <Enter> keys need to perform
traversal. When the control is editing multiple lines, these keys need to
traverse but only when a modifier key such as <Ctrl> or <Shift> is pressed. The
following code fragment implements text traversal for such a hypothetical
text control.

```
Listener listener = new Listener() {
    public void handleEvent(Event e) {
        switch (e.detail) {
            case SWT.TRAVERSE_ESCAPE:
            case SWT.TRAVERSE_PAGE_NEXT:
            case SWT.TRAVERSE_PAGE_PREVIOUS:
                e.doit = true;
                break;
            case SWT.TRAVERSE_RETURN:
            case SWT.TRAVERSE_TAB_NEXT:
            case SWT.TRAVERSE_TAB_PREVIOUS:
                if ((getStyle() & SWT.SINGLE) != 0) {
                    e.doit = true;
                } else {
```

```
                            if ((e.stateMask & SWT.MODIFIER_MASK)
                                != 0) {
                                e.doit = true;
                            }
                        }
                        break;
                }
            }
        };
        text.addListener(SWT.Traverse, listener);
```

Using SWT.Traverse to Intercept Traversal

As previously stated, the <Esc> key normally cancels a dialog. <Esc> is also commonly used to cancel an in-line edit operation. For example, a text control can be used to edit the label of a tree or table item. When the table is created in a dialog shell, there is ambiguity: Should <Esc> close the in-line edit operation or the dialog shell? Most users agree that <Esc> should close the in-line editor when it is open but should close the dialog when it is not.[16] However, SWT has no way of knowing when a particular text control is being used as an in-line editor, so the dialog shell is closed.

It is easy to imagine how SWT.Traverse can be used to fix this problem. It can intercept traversal for the text control and cancel the SWT.TRAVERSE _ESCAPE. The following code fragment illustrates this strategy.

```
Listener listener = new Listener() {
    public void handleEvent(Event e) {
        switch (e.detail) {
            case SWT.TRAVERSE_ESCAPE:
                e.doit = false;
                /* Code to cancel edit goes here */
                break;
        }
    }
};
text.addListener(SWT.Traverse, listener);
```

Continuing with the example, consider what happens when the user presses <Enter>. On most platforms, this will select the default button. However, <Enter> is also commonly used during an in-line edit operation to accept the changed text. It seems on the surface that setting the *doit* flag to false would work, solving the problem in the same manner as <Esc>. However, there is one

---

16. The same kind of problem occurs when a drop-down combo box occurs in a dialog shell. The native combo box intercepts traversal to ensure that <Esc> will close the drop-down list, not the dialog.

further consideration: Text controls provide listeners that are activated when the user presses <Enter>. Setting *doit* to false will cancel the traversal operation but the key event is still delivered, invoking the listeners. If you created the text control, you can be sure that there are no listeners (by not adding any) but a better solution is to use both the *doit* and *detail* fields of the event.

Setting the *doit* field to true and *detail* to SWT.TRAVERSE_NONE tells the control to "go ahead and perform the traversal operation," but no traversal action is specified. As a result, the key is consumed, but no traversal occurs. The following revised code fragment consumes both <Esc> and <Enter>.

```
Listener listener = new Listener() {
  public void handleEvent(Event e) {
    switch (e.detail) {
      case SWT.TRAVERSE_ESCAPE:
        e.detail = SWT.TRAVERSE_NONE;
        e.doit = true;
        /* Code to cancel edit goes here */
        break;
      case SWT.TRAVERSE_RETURN:
        e.detail = SWT.TRAVERSE_NONE;
        e.doit = true;
        /* Code to accept edit goes here */
        break;
    }
  }
};
text.addListener(SWT.Traverse, listener);
```

2.4 Accelerators

A *menu accelerator,* also called a *keyboard shortcut,* is an application-defined key sequence that invokes a menu item. It gives the same result as though the user had selected the item with the mouse. Accelerators are always associated with menu items. In the same manner as items in the menu bar, accelerators are global to the window. When the user types an accelerator key, regardless of the focus control, a menu item is invoked. When an accelerator is triggered, the corresponding keystroke is consumed.[17]

---

17. Accelerators run before the key event is delivered to the control and on some platforms use the low-level window system keyboard classification engine to process the key, destructively modifying the key event in operating system event queue. This stops the focus control from ever seeing the keystroke.

2.4.1 Specifying an Accelerator

Accelerators are represented in SWT using an integer encoding. The encoding consists of zero or more modifiers and a single character or key code. An accelerator that contains only modifiers is invalid and cannot trigger a menu item.

Table 2.12 shows some sample accelerators.

Table 2.12 Sample Accelerators

Accelerator	Keystroke
SWT.CTRL + 'A'	The <Ctrl> and <A> keys
SWT.SHIFT + SWT.ARROW_UP	The <Shift> and <UpArrow> keys
SWT.MOD1 + 'S'	The primary modifier and <S> keys
SWT.MOD1 + SWT.MOD2 + 'B'	The primary and secondary modifier and <B> keys

Accelerators are assigned to menu items using the method MenuItem.setAccelerator(). The Tool Bars and Menus chapter contains a complete description of the MenuItem class.

setAccelerator(int accelerator)   Sets the accelerator for the item to be an integer that is composed of zero or more modifier masks and a key value. For example, the accelerator SWT.CTRL + 'A' causes the menu item to be invoked when the user presses a Ctrl+A key sequence. The accelerator SWT.MOD1 + 'A' is invoked when the user presses the primary modifier key and the <A> key. Setting the accelerator to zero removes it.

getAccelerator()   Returns the accelerator for the item. The integer encoding that was assigned in setAccelerator() is returned (or zero if an accelerator has never been set).

The following code fragment creates an accelerator for the primary modifier SWT.MOD1 and the 'A' character and associates it with a menu item.

```
item.setText("Select &All\tCtrl+A");
item.setAccelerator(SWT.MOD1 + 'A');
item.addListener(SWT.Selection, new Listener() {
    public void handleEvent(Event e) {
        System.out.println("The item was selected.");
    }
});
```

A perceptive reader should immediately notice a problem. The menu item text contains the string "Ctrl+A" but the accelerator is SWT.MOD1 + 'A'. Does this imply that this code fails on the Macintosh where the primary modifier is not the <Ctrl> key? To answer this question, you need to understand the difference between the accelerator and the accelerator text.

2.4.2   *Specifying the Accelerator Text*

To allow complete control over the label of a menu item, the accelerator text is specified independently of the accelerator.[18] An embedded \t character indicates that the following string is the *accelerator text*. On most platforms, the accelerator text is right-aligned within the menu.

When both an accelerator and accelerator text are provided, depending on the platform, SWT may override the accelerator text with more appropriate accelerator text. For example, on the Macintosh, the accelerator text "Ctrl+A" is ignored when the accelerator SWT.MOD1 + 'A' is specified. The correct accelerator text, a sequence of Macintosh specific glyphs, appears in the menu.

IMPORTANT:
You Must Provide Accelerator Text on Every Platform.

On every platform other than the Macintosh, the accelerator text is not overridden. This means that you need to provide the accelerator text, assuming that you are not on a Macintosh. It is possible that by the time this book goes to print, the Macintosh behavior will be implemented on the rest of the platforms, and this problem will be fixed.

2.5   Window System Keys

Keys that are processed by the window system never make it into your program. For example, Alt+F4 on many window systems closes the active window. The window manager invokes the appropriate action, and the key is consumed. The list of system key sequences is not only platform-specific; it is window manager-specific. Because there is no standard window manager API

---

18. Eclipse uses this feature to implement multiple accelerator key sequences (made popular by the Emacs text editor). These are not supported natively on any platform where SWT is implemented.

to query and intercept window system keys, there is generally nothing that can
be done to prevent this behavior. In any case, overriding system keys is not
something your application should do.

2.6   Summary

In this chapter, you have learned about the focus- and keyboard-handling
capabilities of SWT. When a key is typed, it is resolved as a window system
key, an accelerator key, a traversal key, or a key event. Except for window system keys and the preprocessing of international text, your program has the
opportunity to take part in any of these character-processing subsystems.

CHAPTER 3

The Mouse

All of the operating systems on which SWT is implemented support a pointing device. Usually this is a mouse, but it may be a trackball, trackpad, or some other type of hardware. On handheld computers, the pointing device is almost always a stylus. To keep things simple, we refer to the pointing device as the *mouse*, regardless of the type of physical device.

The position of the mouse is usually indicated by a small icon on the screen called the *cursor*. This is true on all SWT platforms except for Windows CE. Because Windows CE devices normally use a "direct" pointing device, such as a stylus, they do not need an on-screen representation of where the pointer is located.

Typical mice have up to three buttons[1] that are used among other things to point, click, drag, and select inside controls. They can also be used to request a context menu for a control. This can happen when the mouse is either pressed or released, depending on the platform.[2] The mouse gesture and button used to start a "drag-and-drop" operation are even more platform-specific.

As it moves across the screen, the cursor often changes shape, depending on the control that is underneath it. For example, a text widget changes the cursor to an I-beam to indicate that the user can type in the control. Within

---

1. On the Macintosh, the standard mouse has only one button, although mice with more buttons are supported.
2. On the Macintosh, the user requests a context menu by holding down the <Ctrl> key and pressing either the left mouse button or the single mouse button.

the cursor is a hotspot that indicates the x and y coordinates of the mouse when a mouse event occurs (for more on this, see the Cursors chapter).

As with the keyboard, most controls interact with the mouse without requiring program intervention.

3.1   Mouse Events

When a mouse button is pressed or the mouse is moved, a mouse event is created and normally delivered to the control that is beneath the cursor. However, when a mouse button is pressed and held, and the mouse is moved outside of the control (perhaps into another control or over the desktop), events are delivered to the original control that got the mouse press. When the mouse button is released, events are delivered normally. This temporary redirection of events is called *mouse capture* or *grabbing*. The control that receives the events is called the *grab control*. Mouse capture happens automatically in SWT. It is something that you need to be aware of but need not be concerned with. Most programmers simply expect the mouse to behave in this manner.[3]

3.1.1   *Mouse Buttons, Coordinates, and the State Mask*

When the mouse is pressed or released, the *button* field of the mouse event that is generated contains the *number* of the button that was pressed. Mouse buttons are numbered from left to right, using consecutive integer values starting from 1. For users who are left-handed (and configure the operating system for a left-handed person), the button numbering scheme remains the same but the buttons are arranged physically from right to left. This mapping for left-handed users is transparent to SWT and to your application.

When a mouse event occurs, the x and y coordinates are reported in the corresponding fields of the event. These coordinates are relative to the control that received the event **at the time the event occurred**.[4] Because the user may have moved the mouse between the time the event occurred and the time it was delivered, the physical location of the mouse can be different from the coordinates reported in the event.[5] Recording the position of the mouse in the

---

3.   On X Windows, grabbing is built into the operating system.

4.   Coordinate systems for controls and drawing are described in Control Fundamentals and Graphics Fundamentals.

5.   If you need the exact location of the mouse at any given moment, you can use Display.getCursorLocation() (see the Display chapter for more on this).

event prevents the system from being sensitive to these movements. You should always use the coordinates in the mouse event.

Mouse events use the *stateMask* field of the event to indicate the mouse state. In the same manner as key modifiers, the *stateMask* field contains the state of the mouse **immediately prior to the event**. For example, if no mouse buttons or keyboard modifier keys have already been pressed, when the left mouse button is pressed, a mouse down event is issued with the *button* field set to 1 and the *stateMask* set to zero. The *stateMask* field *does not* contain the "button 1" state mask. However, provided that the user holds the left button down, the *stateMask* field of subsequent mouse events *will* contain this mask.

Mouse state is represented by constants in the class SWT. Table 3.1 shows the mouse state mask values.

Table 3.1   Mouse State Masks

State Mask	Description
SWT.BUTTON1	Button 1 was down
SWT.BUTTON2	Button 2 was down
SWT.BUTTON3	Button 3 was down
SWT.BUTTON_MASK	Bitwise-OR of all valid button masks

The constant SWT.BUTTON_MASK contains every mouse mask and is used in a manner similar to SWT.MODIFIER_MASK:

```
//WRONG — broken when new mouse masks are added
int bits = SWT.BUTTON1 | SWT.BUTTON2 | SWT.BUTTON3;
if ((event.stateMask & bits) == 0) {
    System.out.println ("No mouse buttons are down");
}

//CORRECT — works when new mouse masks are added
if ((event.stateMask & SWT.BUTTON_MASK) == 0) {
    System.out.println ("No mouse buttons are down");
}
```

Why Is the Button Field an Integer Instead of a Button Constant?

Although it's pretty clear that the integer 1 can represent the first button on the mouse and so on, it would have been more consistent with the rest of SWT to reuse the button state masks. For example, the keyboard constant SWT.SHIFT is used to represent both the <Shift> key and the modifier mask. Unfortunately, this inconsistency was found too late in the release cycle, before 1.0. It was discovered that programmers were writing code such as "event.button == SWT.BUTTON1," which looks nice but is incorrect. Sadly, nothing can be done about this problem without breaking too many existing programs.

3.1.2 Mouse Events

Table 3.2 shows the mouse-related events that are provided by SWT.

Table 3.2   Mouse Events

Untyped Event	*Meaning*	
SWT.MouseDown	The mouse was pressed in a control	
SWT.MouseUp	The mouse was released in a control	
SWT.MouseMove	The mouse was moved in a control	
SWT.MouseEnter	The mouse entered a control	
SWT.MouseExit	The mouse exited a control	
SWT.MouseDoubleClick	The mouse was double-clicked in a control	
SWT.MouseHover	The mouse hovered in a control	
Typed Event	*Listener*	*Methods*
MouseEvent	MouseListener (and MouseAdapter)	mouseDoubleClick(MouseEvent) mouseDown(MouseEvent) mouseUp(MouseEvent)
MouseEvent	MouseMoveListener	mouseMove(MouseEvent)
MouseEvent	MouseTrackListener (and MouseTrackAdapter)	mouseEnter(MouseEvent) mouseExit(MouseEvent) mouseHover(MouseEvent)

The relevant event fields during mouse events are shown in Table 3.3.

Table 3.3   Public Fields of Class Event That Are Valid during the Mouse Events

Field	Meaning
button	The button that was pressed or released
x	The x coordinate where the mouse event occurred
y	The y coordinate where the mouse event occurred
stateMask	A bit-mask that indicates the mouse and keyboard state

The mouse up, down, and move events are self-evident, mapping directly to the operating system equivalents. It is important to note that only SWT.MouseDown and SWT.MouseUp use the *button* field. When the mouse is moved, even when a button is held down, this field is zero. This makes sense because the mouse can be moved while more than one button is pressed but the field can represent only a single button. In this case, the *stateMask* field is used to determine button state.

As expected, SWT.MouseEnter and SWT.MouseExit events occur when the user moves the mouse into and out of a control. SWT.MouseHover occurs when the mouse "lingers" within a control. The time period and exact criteria for SWT.MouseHover are platform-specific.

Double-Click Events

The SWT.MouseDoubleClick event is sent when the mouse is rapidly pressed and released twice. Once again, the exact time period and criteria for double-click are platform-specific. For example, on some platforms, the mouse must not only be pressed and released twice, but it must remain within a specific area that was determined by the first mouse press. The ordering of SWT.Mouse-Down, SWT.MouseUp, and SWT.MouseDoubleClick events is as follows.

1. SWT.MouseDown

2. SWT.MouseUp

3. SWT.MouseDown

4. SWT.MouseDoubleClick

5. SWT.MouseUp

The implications of this event ordering are subtle. When writing your own control, if it issues an SWT.Selection event on a single click and the SWT .DefaultSelection event on double-click, both these events need to be sent from SWT.MouseUp. Implementing   selection   the   obvious   way   by   sending

SWT.Selection from SWT.MouseDown and SWT.DefaultSelection from SWT .MouseDoubleClick means that when the user double-clicks on your control, you will send two SWT.Selection events and one SWT.DefaultSelection. Sending SWT.Selection from SWT.MouseUp has the further advantage that your control can implement "drag selection" and "scroll while selecting" behavior.

Displaying Mouse Events

The following example prints every mouse event that occurs in a shell.

```
public static void main(String[] args) {
    Display display = new Display();
    Shell shell = new Shell(display);
    Listener mouseListener = new Listener() {
        public void handleEvent(Event e) {
            String string = "UNKNOWN";
            switch (e.type) {
                case SWT.MouseDown: string = "DOWN"; break;
                case SWT.MouseUp: string = "UP"; break;
                case SWT.MouseMove: string = "MOVE"; break;
                case SWT.MouseDoubleClick:
                    string = "DOUBLE";
                    break;
                case SWT.MouseEnter: string="ENTER"; break;
                case SWT.MouseExit: string = "EXIT"; break;
                case SWT.MouseHover: string="HOVER"; break;
            }
            string += ": stateMask=0x"
                + Integer.toHexString(e.stateMask);
            if ((e.stateMask & SWT.CTRL) != 0)
                string += " CTRL";
            if ((e.stateMask & SWT.ALT) != 0)
                string += " ALT";
            if ((e.stateMask & SWT.SHIFT) != 0)
                string += " SHIFT";
            if ((e.stateMask & SWT.COMMAND) != 0)
                string += " COMMAND";
            if ((e.stateMask & SWT.BUTTON1) != 0)
                string += " BUTTON1";
            if ((e.stateMask & SWT.BUTTON2) != 0)
                string += " BUTTON2";
            if ((e.stateMask & SWT.BUTTON3) != 0)
                string += " BUTTON3";
            string += ", button=0x"
                + Integer.toHexString(e.button);
            string += ", x=" + e.x + ", y=" + e.y;
            System.out.println(string);
        }
    };
    shell.addListener(SWT.MouseDown, mouseListener);
    shell.addListener(SWT.MouseUp, mouseListener);
    shell.addListener(SWT.MouseMove, mouseListener);
    shell.addListener(SWT.MouseDoubleClick, mouseListener);
    shell.addListener(SWT.MouseEnter, mouseListener);
```

```
    shell.addListener(SWT.MouseExit, mouseListener);
    shell.addListener(SWT.MouseHover, mouseListener);
    shell.setSize(200, 200);
    shell.open();
    while (!shell.isDisposed()) {
        if (!display.readAndDispatch()) display.sleep();
    }
    display.dispose();
}
```

3.1.3   Detecting a Context Menu Request

To detect when the user has requested a context menu, SWT defines the SWT.MenuDetect event (Table 3.4).

Table 3.4   The MenuDetect Event

Untyped Event	Meaning
SWT.MenuDetect	The user requested a context menu

The relevant event fields during an SWT.MenuDetect event are shown in Table 3.5.

Table 3.5   Public Fields of Class Event That Are Valid during SWT.MenuDetect

Field	Meaning
x	The *x* coordinate where the menu should be displayed
y	The *y* coordinate where the menu should be displayed
doit	A boolean that is used to cancel the operation

The SWT.MenuDetect event is very flexible. Depending on the platform, some controls have a built-in context menu that the operating system provides.[6] Others have a context menu that was assigned by the application program. Some controls have no context menu at all. In any case, SWT.MenuDetect allows you to detect when a menu is requested and provide your own context menu at that time. You can either display it yourself by

---

6.   Windows XP and GTK do this, providing cut, copy, paste operations, as well as the ability to insert Unicode characters.

using the *x* and *y* coordinates in the event or assign the new menu using Control.setMenu(). The following example code does just that.

```
static int Count;
public static void main(String[] args) {
    Display display = new Display();
    final Shell shell = new Shell(display);
    shell.addListener(SWT.MenuDetect, new Listener() {
        public void handleEvent(Event event) {
            Menu menu = shell.getMenu();
            if (menu != null) menu.dispose();
            menu = new Menu(shell, SWT.POP_UP);
            MenuItem item = new MenuItem(menu, SWT.PUSH);
            item.setText("Menu " + Count++);
            shell.setMenu(menu);
        }
    });
    shell.pack();
    shell.open();
    while (!shell.isDisposed()) {
        if (!display.readAndDispatch()) display.sleep();
    }
    display.dispose();
}
```

Notice that a new menu with a different numbered menu item is created each time the MenuDetect event is received.

The *doit* field in the event is used to override the built-in context menu that is found in some controls or a menu that was supplied previously using setMenu(). Setting this field to false stops this menu from being displayed. You can provide your own menu (opening it in the listener code) or choose not to display a menu by setting this field to false.

One final note: SWT.MenuDetect is also sent when the user requests a context menu using the keyboard.

3.1.4 Detecting a Drag-and-Drop Request

To determine when a drag-and-drop operation should be initiated, the SWT.DragDetect event is used (Table 3.6).

Table 3.6 The DragDetect Event

Untyped Event	*Meaning*
SWT.DragDetect	The user requested a drag-and-drop operation

The relevant event fields during an SWT.DragDetect event are shown in Table 3.7.

Table 3.7 Public Fields of Class Event That Are Valid during SWT.DragDetect

Field	Meaning
x	The x coordinate where the mouse event occurred
y	The y coordinate where the mouse event occurred

Listening for SWT.DragDetect does not start a drag-and-drop operation. Rather, it detects the platform-specific mouse gesture used to indicate that a drag should start. On some platforms, drag operations are initiated using the middle mouse button. On others, the left mouse button is used. On some platforms, to distinguish a drag gesture from a mouse selection, the user moves the mouse a certain number of pixels while keeping it pressed.

Application programmers can listen for SWT.DragDetect and use it to decide when to move their own objects without requiring them to use the SWT drag-and-drop support.[7] The advantage over simply using an SWT .MouseDown to do this is that users are familiar with the standard mouse drag gesture from other applications on the desktop. By using SWT.DragDetect, the application will follow the platform conventions.

3.2 Selection

Selection is the *primary operation* that the user invokes on a widget. For example, when the user clicks on a button, chooses an item in a list, or drags a scroll bar, they are *selecting* the widget. Selection is normally performed when the user presses and releases the mouse but need not be initiated using the mouse at all. For example, pressing the space bar (on most platforms) while keyboard focus is on a push button will select the button. Every widget that interacts with the user provides selection, but some widgets provide additional operations. For example, a tree widget can be expanded or collapsed as well as selected.

---

7. The drag-and-drop support provided by SWT allows applications to plug into the native drag-and-drop mechanisms found on most modern platforms. It is an advanced topic that is not covered in this book but is touched on in the FileExplorer chapter. For more information, see the article *Drag and Drop—Adding Drag and Drop to an SWT Application* at www.eclipse.org and the Javadoc for the classes in the package *org.eclipse.swt.dnd*.

Default selection is the *secondary operation* (or sometimes the "default" operation) that the user invokes on a widget. When the user double-clicks in a list or presses the <Enter> key in a text control, the default selection operation is invoked.

Table 3.8 shows the selection-related events that are provided by SWT.

Table 3.8   The Selection Event

Untyped Event	Meaning	
SWT.Selection	The user selected a widget	
SWT.DefaultSelection	The user requested the default selection operation	

Typed Event	Listener	Methods
SelectionEvent	SelectionListener (and SelectionAdapter)	widgetDefaultSelected(SelectionEvent) widgetSelected(SelectionEvent)

The relevant event fields during a selection event are shown in Table 3.9.

Table 3.9   Public Fields of Class Event Valid during the Selection Events

Field	Meaning
item	The item that was selected
detail	The detail field describing the selection
x	The x coordinate where the selection occurred
y	The y coordinate where the selection occurred
width	The width of the selected area
height	The height of the selected area
stateMask	The state of the keyboard modifiers when the selection occurred
doit	A boolean that is used to cancel the operation

Depending on the widget, particular fields in the event may not be used. SWT reserves the right to make use of the unused fields in the future as the need arises. See the Javadoc for the particular widget and the Native Widgets chapters of this book for more details.

3.3   **Summary**

In this chapter, you learned about the mouse support in SWT. Included in the discussion were the SWT.MenuDetect and SWT.DragDetect events. Although strictly speaking they are not necessarily mouse events, they are almost always generated from the mouse. We ended on the important topic of selection, a concept that is critical and far reaching in SWT. You will run across selection again when you are studying the API of the individual SWT widgets.

CHAPTER 4

Control Fundamentals

We described the relationship between widgets and controls in the Widget Fundamentals chapter. In this chapter, we will look at a number of important concepts that are common to controls[1] but not found in widgets. These include the concepts of bounds and client area, as well as the support for moving, resizing, and painting.

4.1 Bounds

The rectangle that describes the location and size of a control within its parent is called the *bounds* of the control. The bounds of a control are expressed in pixels. For Shells, this is measured relative to the coordinate system of the Display; for all other controls it is relative to the parent. Figure 4.1 shows the bounds of a "group box."

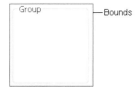

Figure 4.1 The bounds of a group box.

---

1. Remember that in SWT, controls are represented by instances of *subclasses* of class Control.

The bounds, location, and size of a control can be queried using get-Bounds(), getLocation(), and getSize().

getBounds()   Returns a rectangle[2] that describes the size and location of the control, relative to the parent. A new rectangle is returned so that modifying the rectangle will not affect the control.

getLocation()   Returns a point that describes the location of the control. A new point is returned so that modifying the point will not affect the control.

getSize()   Returns a point that describes the size of the control. A new point is returned so that modifying the point will not affect the control.

Why Is a Point Used to Represent the Size of a Control?

Because one of the design decisions of SWT is to minimize the number of classes in the toolkit, the Point class from *org.eclipse.swt.graphics* was chosen to represent the size of a control. The alternative would have been to define a Dimension class with width and height fields and no methods. We admit that using Point is a bit confusing (but not harmful).

4.2   Client Area

The *client area* of a Composite, List, or Text control[3] is a rectangle that describes the area within which content may be drawn. In this context, the term *client* refers to you, the programmer, viewed as a client of services offered by the control, so the client area is the area that you "own." Essentially, it is the area that is not covered by those parts of the control bounds that are considered to be "trimmings" such as borders, scroll bars, and the

---

2. Rectangle and Point are two SWT graphics classes that are commonly used by widgets. They are found in *org.eclipse.swt.graphics* and described in Graphics Fundamentals.

3. As of R3.0, *client area* is defined only for Composite, List, and Text controls but the concept is general enough to be applied to all Control subclasses. It is possible that future versions of SWT will address this issue by moving the client area API to class Control, which is why we are discussing it here.

menu bar.[4] Areas outside of the client area are off limits. Figure 4.2 shows the bounds and client area of a group box.

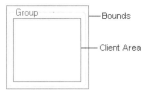

Figure 4.2   The bounds and client area of a group box.

The client area is expressed in pixels, this time in the coordinate system of the control (unlike the bounds that are in the coordinate system of the parent). Very often, the location of the client area within the control is (0, 0), but this is **not always the case**. Figure 4.3 shows the client area of two group boxes from different platforms, with Windows on the left and GTK on the right. On Windows, the location of the client area is (3, 13). On GTK, it is (0, 0).

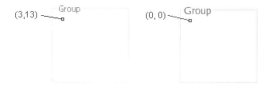

Figure 4.3   The location of the client area of a group box on Windows and GTK.

The concept of client area allows SWT to hide these kinds of platform differences neatly. You can determine the client area of a composite using getClientArea().

getClientArea()   Returns a rectangle that describes the area of the control that is capable of displaying data.

The client area of a control cannot be modified directly. Instead, moving or resizing the control or changing the trimmings indirectly resizes it. For example, hiding a scroll bar causes the client area to become larger.

---

4.   Both the need for a client area concept and the fact that the menu bar is considered part of the trimmings come from constraints imposed by Microsoft Windows. Modeling them explicitly in SWT was the only effective way to deal with them.

4.3   Moving and Resizing

Controls are moved or resized by changing their bounds. SWT provides the following methods to set the bounds of a control.

setBounds(int x, int y, int width, int height)   Sets the location and size of the control. The *x* and *y* coordinates are relative to the parent. If the *width* or *height* parameters are negative, zero is used instead.

setBounds(Rectangle bounds)   Sets the location and size of the control. Equivalent to *setBounds(bounds.x, bounds.y, bounds.width, bounds.height)*.

setLocation(int x, int y)   Sets the location of the control. The *x* and *y* coordinates are relative to the parent.

setLocation(Point location)   Sets the location of the control. Equivalent to *setLocation(location.x, location.y)*.

setSize(int width, int height)   Sets the size of the control. If the *width* or *height* parameters are negative, zero is used instead.

setSize(Point size)   Sets the size of the control. Equivalent to *setSize(size.x, size.y)*.

When a control is moved, an SWT.Move event is sent; when it is resized, an SWT.Resize event is sent.

4.3.1   *Move Events*

A control is *moved* when its location is changed relative to its parent (or for Shells, relative to the Display). Controls can be moved by calling setLocation(), setBounds() or, in the case of a shell, when the user repositions it on the desktop.

Table 4.1 shows the move-related events that are provided by SWT.

Table 4.1   Move Events

Untyped Event		Description	
SWT.Move		The position of the control was changed	
Typed Event	**Listener**		**Methods**
ControlEvent	ControlListener (and ControlAdapter)		controlMoved(ControlEvent) controlResize(ControlEvent)

The SWT.Move event (typed event ControlEvent) is sent whenever a control is moved, *after* its location has been changed. It is not sent to the control when the parent or any ancestor is moved. Move events contain meaningful values in only the *display*, *widget*, and *type* fields.

Using SWT.Move to Make a Shell Move with Its Parent

The following example uses the SWT.Move event to implement a dialog shell that "follows the parent," moving whenever the parent is moved. The code contains a subtle problem (actually, it overlooks a case), which we will discuss further in the Resize Events section.

```
public static void main(String[] args) {
    //NOTE — contains a problem (see SWT.Resize)
    Display display = new Display();
    final Shell shell1 = new Shell(display);
    shell1.pack();
    shell1.open();
    final Shell shell2 = new Shell(shell1, SWT.NONE);
    shell2.pack();
    shell2.open();
    Rectangle rect = shell1.getBounds();
    shell2.setLocation(rect.x + rect.width + 2, rect.y);
    shell1.addListener(SWT.Move, new Listener() {
        public void handleEvent(Event e) {
            Rectangle rect = shell1.getBounds();
            shell2.setLocation(
                rect.x + rect.width + 2, rect.y);
        }
    });
    while (!shell1.isDisposed()) {
        if (!display.readAndDispatch()) display.sleep();
    }
    display.dispose();
}
```

4.3.2 Resize Events

A control is *resized* whenever its client area is changed. This can occur explicitly, as the result of calls to setSize() or setBounds(), or implicitly, because of some operation that the user performs. For example, the user can often resize a shell by clicking and dragging one of its corners with the mouse.[5] In addition, on some operating systems, the width of the trimmings can be changed using the "control panel" or "theme manager." For example, when a scroll

---

5. Provided that the shell was created with the SWT.RESIZE style and the platform window manager supports resizing.

bar becomes wider because the theme has changed, the client area of a control is reduced, causing the control to receive an SWT.Resize event.

Table 4.2 shows the resize-related events that are provided by SWT.

Table 4.2   Resize Events

Untyped Event		*Description*	
SWT.Resize		The size of the client area of the control changed	
Typed Event	*Listener*	*Methods*	
ControlEvent	ControlListener (and ControlAdapter)	controlMoved(ControlEvent) controlResized(ControlEvent)	

The SWT.Resize event (typed event ControlEvent) is sent whenever a control is resized, *after* its size has been changed. It is not sent when the parent or any ancestor is resized. Resize events contain meaningful values in only the *display, widget,* and *type* fields.

Using SWT.Move and SWT.Size to Track a Parent Shell

The following example uses both SWT.Move and SWT.Resize events to implement a dialog shell that tracks its parent. This is a variant of the code from the previous section that adds the same listener for both SWT.Move and SWT .Resize. This fixes the problem that the previous example had: The tracking shell did not move when the user resized the bottom right corner of the parent.

```
public static void main(String[] args) {
    Display display = new Display();
    final Shell shell1 = new Shell(display);
    shell1.pack();
    shell1.open();
    final Shell shell2 = new Shell(shell1, SWT.NONE);
    shell2.pack();
    shell2.open();
    Rectangle rect = shell1.getBounds();
    shell2.setLocation(rect.x + rect.width + 2, rect.y);
    Listener listener = new Listener() {
        public void handleEvent(Event e) {
            Rectangle rect = shell1.getBounds();
            shell2.setLocation(
                rect.x + rect.width + 2, rect.y);
        }
    };
    shell1.addListener(SWT.Move, listener);
    shell1.addListener(SWT.Resize, listener);
    while (!shell1.isDisposed()) {
```

```
        if (!display.readAndDispatch()) display.sleep();
    }
    display.dispose();
}
```

Figure 4.4 shows the results of running the code. When *shell1* is moved or resized, *shell2* follows, remaining 2 pixels to the right.

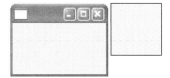

Figure 4.4

Using SWT.Resize to Move and Resize Children

Rather than calling setBounds(), most applications use layouts (as described in the Layout chapter) to position and resize controls. However, the SWT.Resize event is a useful alternative to layouts, allowing you precise control over the location and size of each child every time the parent is resized. You might choose to do this kind of positioning and resizing of controls inside an SWT.Resize event because you are unable to find a layout that suits your needs or because the code that is required to use the layout is simply too verbose. The alternative would be to implement a new Layout subclass that has the attributes you need, but for a single, special-purpose arrangement of widgets, this probably does not make sense.[6]

The following example uses an SWT.Resize event to position two buttons within a shell. The buttons are placed side by side, with an inset of 10 pixels surrounding them, as seen in Figure 4.5. When the shell is resized, the buttons grow or shrink in proportion to the new size of the shell.[7]

```
static final int INSET = 10;
public static void main(String[] args) {
    Display display = new Display();
    final Shell shell = new Shell(display);
    final Button b1 = new Button(shell, SWT.PUSH);
    final Button b2 = new Button(shell, SWT.PUSH);
```

---

6. The point here is that implementing a layout implies you are writing a general-purpose positioning algorithm, which is not the same as positioning a few controls in places that are specific to your application.

7. This exact behavior can be achieved using a FillLayout with the margin and spacing set to 10 pixels. For this simple case, using a FillLayout is the easier approach.

```
shell.addListener(SWT.Resize, new Listener() {
    public void handleEvent(Event event) {
        Rectangle rect = shell.getClientArea();
        int width = (rect.width - INSET * 3) / 2;
        b1.setBounds(
            INSET,
            INSET,
            width,
            rect.height - INSET * 2);
        b2.setBounds(
            width + INSET * 2,
            INSET,
            width,
            rect.height - INSET * 2);
    }
});
shell.setSize(200, 200);
shell.open();
while (!shell.isDisposed()) {
    if (!display.readAndDispatch()) display.sleep();
}
display.dispose();
}
```

Figure 4.5

4.4 Visibility

Every control has an associated property called its *visibility*. A control whose visibility is set to false is said to be *hidden,* and the act of setting the visibility to false is called *hiding* the control. A control whose visibility is set to true is said to be *visible* (not "shown"), and the act of setting the visibility to true is called *showing* the control.

If a control is visible, SWT will attempt to draw the control, allowing it to be seen by the user. However, it is important to note that being visible is only one of the requirements for a control to be seen. Circumstances that would prevent this include the following.

○ **The parent of the control may not be visible.**   Hiding a parent control hides the children of the control. Showing a parent control shows those children that were not explicitly hidden.

○ **The control may be clipped or obscured.**   If the control is positioned outside of the visible area of its parent (or outside the visible area of the Display) or some other control is drawn in front of the control, it will not be seen.

These circumstances are applied recursively so that if the parent of the control or any of the ancestors cannot be seen for one of the above reasons, the control will also not be seen.

With the exception of Shells, when a control is created, it is visible by default. Shells are invisible when created so that child controls can be created and configured without the user watching this process. The visibility of a control can be changed after creation using setVisible().

setVisible(boolean visible)   Shows or hides the control, depending on the boolean parameter. Based on the above rule for parent visibility, if the control is a Shell, dialog shells are shown and hidden as well.

Two methods are provided for checking the visibility state of a control.

getVisible()   Returns true if the control is visible and false if it is hidden.

isVisible()   Returns true if the control **and all ancestors** are visible or false if it or *any* of its ancestors are hidden.

Remember that these methods check only the value of the visibility property, so that even if isVisible() returns true, you may not be able to see the control.

The getVisible() and isVisible() Methods Are Not Equivalent

Despite their use of the JavaBeans naming convention, these methods are not equivalent. Programmers who are new to SWT often make the mistake of using these methods interchangeably.

4.5   Z-Order

The *z-order* of a control is the position of the control in the drawing order of its parent.[8] A control that is higher in the drawing order than some other control is said to be *above* the other control. Similarly, the lower control is said to be *below* the other control. When one control is above another and the controls overlap, the higher control is drawn on top, obscuring the overlapping part of the other control.

In SWT, the z-order matches the order that controls are stored in the children list of the parent. Controls that are on top occur earlier in the list. When a control is created, it is placed at the end of the children list, below the other siblings.

You can change the z-order of a control using moveAbove() and moveBelow().

moveAbove(Control control)   Moves the control that is sent this message above the control that is provided as the parameter. If the parameter is null, the control is moved to the top of the z-order, in front of every other control in the children list of the parent.

moveBelow(Control control)   Moves the control that is sent this message below the control that is provided as the parameter. If the parameter is null, the control is moved to the bottom of the z-order, behind every other control in the children list of the parent.

4.6   Enabling and Disabling

Every control has an associated property called its *enabled state.* A control whose enabled state is false is said to be *disabled,* and the act of setting the enabled state to false is called *disabling* the control. A control whose enabled state is true is said to be *enabled,* and the act of setting the enabled state to true is called *enabling* the control. When a control is enabled, it responds to mouse clicks, takes focus, and handles key presses. A disabled control is unresponsive to events and typically draws using a "grayed" look. When a parent control is disabled, all children of the control will behave as though they are disabled.

---

8.   The term *z-order* refers to the *z* axis of the standard mathematical XYZ coordinate system used to describe objects in three-dimensional space.

setEnabled(boolean enabled)   Enables or disables the control, depending on the boolean argument.

getEnabled()   Returns true if the control is enabled and false if it is disabled.

isEnabled()   Returns true if the control **and all ancestors** are enabled, or false if it or *any* of its ancestors is disabled.

The getEnabled() and isEnabled() Methods Are Not Equivalent

As is true of getVisible() and isVisible(), despite their JavaBeans naming convention, these methods are not equivalent.

Disabling a control causes the mouse events that were to be delivered to the control to be delivered to the parent instead. This makes sense because a disabled control should never process the mouse. Interestingly, this behavior can be used to intercept mouse events for a control.

4.6.1   Using setEnabled() to Intercept Mouse Events

The following example allows the user to drag a button by disabling the parent, causing mouse events to be delivered to the shell. Mouse listeners on the shell determine whether the mouse was pressed inside the button and drag the button when the mouse is moved.

```
public static void main(String[] args) {
    Display display = new Display();
    Shell shell = new Shell(display);
    shell.setLayout(new FillLayout());
    Composite composite = new Composite(shell, SWT.NULL);
    composite.setEnabled(false);
    final Button button = new Button(composite, SWT.PUSH);
    button.setText("Drag Me");
    button.pack();
    Listener listener = new Listener() {
        Point offset = null;
        public void handleEvent(Event e) {
            switch (e.type) {
                case SWT.MouseDown:
                    Rectangle rect = button.getBounds();
                    if (!rect.contains(e.x, e.y)) break;
                    Point pt = button.getLocation();
                    offset = new Point(e.x-pt.x, e.y-pt.y);
                    break;
```

```
                case SWT.MouseMove:
                    if (offset == null) break;
                    button.setLocation(
                        e.x - offset.x,
                        e.y - offset.y);
                    break;
                case SWT.MouseUp:
                    offset = null;
                    break;
            }
        }
    };
    shell.addListener(SWT.MouseDown, listener);
    shell.addListener(SWT.MouseUp, listener);
    shell.addListener(SWT.MouseMove, listener);
    shell.setSize(300, 300);
    shell.open();
    while (!shell.isDisposed()) {
        if (!display.readAndDispatch()) display.sleep();
    }
    display.dispose();
}
```

4.7   Preferred Size

Except for instances of class Shell,[9] when a control is created, its location and size are zero. It is your job to place controls where you want them and give them sizes that are appropriate for your application. Layouts (see the chapter Layout) use the concepts described in this section to position and resize their controls.

The *preferred size* of a control is the smallest possible size that best displays its content. For example, the preferred size of a button is large enough to show the label of the button but may be larger, according to the user interface design guidelines for the operating system. The preferred size of a composite that does not contain a layout is the smallest size that encloses its children. When a composite contains a layout, the layout computes the preferred size of the composite.

4.7.1   *Packing*

The simplest way to choose a reasonable size for a control is to *pack* it.

pack()   Causes the control to be resized to its preferred size; same as *pack(true)*.

---

9. Recall that the operating system chooses the initial position and size of a Shell.

pack(boolean changed)   Causes the control to be resized to its pre-ferred size. For a composite, this may involve computing the preferred size from its layout. If the layout has any cached state that was used to compute its preferred size, the *changed* parameter indicates that this cache should be flushed. The *changed* parameter is **used only by Layouts** and is described in detail in the Forcing a Layout section of the Layout chapter.

Packing a control is equivalent to computing the preferred size of a con-trol, then calling setSize() with the result.

4.7.2   *Computing the Preferred Size*

The method computeSize() is used to calculate the preferred size of a control.

computeSize(int wHint, int hHint)   Returns the preferred size of the control; same as *computeSize(wHint, hHint, true)*.

computeSize(int wHint, int hHint, boolean changed)   Returns the preferred size of the Control. The *wHint* and *hHint* parameters are positive integers that allow the caller to ask the Control questions such as, "Given a particular width, how high does the control need to be to show all its contents?" The special value SWT.DEFAULT is used to indicate that the dimension should not be constrained. Computing the preferred size of a composite may involve computing the preferred size from its Layout. If the Layout has any cached state that was used to compute its preferred size, the *changed* parameter indicates that this cache should be flushed. The *changed* parameter is used only by Layouts and is described in detail in Forcing a Layout.

The SWT.DEFAULT constant that is used in conjunction with compute-Size() is intended to be used with controls that wrap, such as labels (see Labels That Wrap).

4.8   Painting

Painting is the standard mechanism that the operating system uses to inform a control that it is time to draw. With the exception of class Canvas (see the section Class Canvas), whose function is to be a general-purpose "drawing area," controls are responsible for drawing themselves. This means that this section is mostly of interest to those programmers who are implementing their own controls or using canvases to draw arbitrary graphics.

4.8.1   Deferred Update Strategy

When it is time to draw a control, the windowing system issues one or more paint events for the control. Paint events are generated for a variety of reasons. For example, when a shell comes forward, replacing the topmost shell, areas within the shell that were obscured by the previous topmost shell need to be drawn. Similarly, when a control is moved, resized, or hidden, other controls within the shell can be uncovered or *exposed* and need to be drawn.

To minimize the number of paint events needed to draw a control, SWT uses a deferred update strategy. This strategy is implemented directly by most of the underlying windowing systems.[10] Each control maintains a graphics region called the *damaged region*. When a redraw is necessary, instead of issuing paint events immediately, the newly exposed area is added to the damaged region. When a paint event is finally issued, the damaged area is filled with the background color of the control,[11] and the damaged region is cleared to make it ready for the next redraw request. In this manner, multiple redraws are merged into a single paint event, which is delivered from the event loop.

4.8.2   Paint Events

An SWT.Paint event is sent when a control needs to be drawn. Controls listen for paint events to draw their contents. Table 4.3 shows the painting events that are provided by SWT.

Table 4.3   Paint Events

Untyped Event		Description	
SWT.Paint		A control was asked to draw	
Typed Event	**Listener**		**Methods**
PaintEvent	PaintListener		paintControl(PaintEvent)

---

10. X Windows provides only a partial implementation of this strategy. SWT uses the underlying X mechanism but augments it with an emulated version that provides the missing capabilities.
11. The background is *not* filled when SWT.NO_BACKGROUND is set. See Filling the Background in this section.

Table 4.4 shows the relevant event fields during a paint event.

Table 4.4   Public Fields of Class Event That Are Valid during SWT.Paint

Field	Meaning
gc	The GC (graphics context) that should be used to draw the control, configured with the font, foreground and background colors of the control, clipped to the damaged region (see Graphics Context)
x	The x coordinate of the largest rectangle surrounding the damaged region
y	The y coordinate of the largest rectangle surrounding the damaged region
width	The width of the largest rectangle surrounding the damaged region
height	The height of the largest rectangle surrounding the damaged region

Using SWT.Paint to Draw in a Canvas

The following example uses SWT.Paint to draw an oval in a shell.

```
public static void main(String[] args) {
    Display display = new Display();
    final Shell shell = new Shell(display);
    shell.addListener(SWT.Paint, new Listener() {
        public void handleEvent(Event event) {
            GC gc = event.gc;
            Rectangle rect = shell.getClientArea();
            gc.drawArc(0,0,rect.width,rect.height,0,360);
        }
    });
    shell.setSize(150, 150);
    shell.open();
    while (!shell.isDisposed()) {
        if (!display.readAndDispatch()) display.sleep();
    }
    display.dispose();
}
```

Notice that the example code uses getClientArea() to determine the bounds of the oval. Drawing occurs in the client area of a control, not the bounds.

Figure 4.6 shows the result of running the code. Although you cannot tell from the picture, only the area that needs to be painted is actually drawn, because the GC that is provided in the event is clipped to the damaged region. For more on clipping, regions, and class GC, see the Graphics Fundamentals chapter.

Figure 4.6

4.8.3 *Causing a Redraw*

As was previously stated, most controls are responsible for drawing themselves. However, for applications that draw their own content (on a canvas, for example), it is possible to exploit the deferred update strategy provided by the operating system to minimize the amount of drawing that is done. Calling one of the following methods indicates that a particular area of the control needs to be painted.

> **redraw()**   Causes the entire client area of the control to be added to the damaged region. The next time a paint event is issued, the control will be completely redrawn. The children of the control are not damaged.

> **redraw(int x, int y, int width, int height, boolean all)**   Causes a rectangular area of the control to be added to the damaged region. The next time a paint event is issued, the union of this rectangle and the previous damage will be drawn. The boolean flag indicates that the area that is the intersection of the specified rectangle and the children is added to the damaged regions of the children to be redrawn, as well.

The redraw() method can be used to get rid of multiple drawing operations, reducing flicker. For example, in a simple implementation of a control that just draws a string, if setting the string were to draw right away, the control would flash when the string was set multiple times. If instead, setting the string simply called redraw(), the control would draw the string once, in a paint event.

Normally, collapsing multiple drawing operations is a desirable behavior. However, there are circumstances when multiple draws are not only necessary but required for correctness. Consider this code fragment where a text control is used to show progress.

```
//WRONG — only draws last percentage
text.setText("0 %");
for (int i=1; i<=100; i++) {
    try {
        Thread.sleep(100);
    } catch (Throwable th) {}
    text.setText(i + " %");
}
```

You might expect that running this fragment would cause the text control to draw successive percentages, but this is not the case. Instead, only the last one is drawn. This happens because the text control uses the deferred painting strategy, merging the 100 paint requests into a single request that is delivered when your application returns to its event loop. Fortunately, SWT provides the ability to force paint events to happen outside of the event loop.

4.8.4   Forcing an Update

The update() method is used to force paint events for a control (see Updating the Display for information about forcing paint events for the Display).

update()   Forces all outstanding paint events for this control to be delivered before returning. The children of the control are unaffected. **Only paint events are dispatched.**

Using update(), the text control from the previous section can be forced to show each percentage as it occurs.

```
//CORRECT — draws every percentage
text.setText("0 %");
text.update();
for (int i=1; i<=100; i++) {
    try {
        Thread.sleep(100);
    } catch (Throwable th) {}
    text.setText(i + " %");
    text.update();
}
```

The update() Method Is Powerful and Dangerous

Using update() is generally unnecessary and can cause flickering and performance problems. This is true because update() defeats the merging of paint events implemented by the operating system.

4.8.5 *Turning off Redraw*

Although it is considered good practice and reduces the number of drawing operations, there is no guarantee that a control will always use the deferred update strategy. For example, to increase performance, many text editors draw each character immediately as it is typed, rather than calling redraw() with the area where the character should appear and drawing only inside paint events.

To further reduce the number of drawing operations for controls that draw outside of paint, setRedraw() can be used.

> **setRedraw(boolean redraw)** Turns drawing on or off for the control. If the *redraw* parameter is false, all subsequent drawing operations are *ignored*. No drawing of any kind will occur until this method is called again with true. At that time, the **entire client area** of the control will be redrawn, because there is no way for SWT to detect which areas of the control would have been changed by any interim drawing operations. Nested calls to setRedraw() stack, so setRedraw(true) must be called once for each call to setRedraw(false). Only after the last call with true will the control be redrawn.

Using setRedraw() in its intended role can be quite tricky. In particular, although the method is available on all platforms, it prevents drawing only on platforms that provide the underlying capability. Furthermore, turning redraw back on ensures that the entire control will redraw, which may look worse than allowing each of the individual graphics operations to occur.

Other Uses for setRedraw()

Despite its drawbacks, setRedraw() is often used by both the operating system and SWT to optimize operations that are unrelated to drawing. For example, on every platform, new items can be added more quickly to lists and tables when redraw is turned off. When many items are going to be added, turning redraw off and adding the items, then turning it back on and letting the widget redraw can be faster than adding and redrawing each separately.

4.9 **Repainting and Resizing**

When a control is resized to be larger, there is more space available for the control to display its content. Controls typically deal with this in two ways.

1. They "spread out" the existing content to cover the new area.

2. They leave the existing content where it was and draw more content in the new area.

If the control is going to spread out its contents, it needs to be notified that its entire client area must be repainted when the control is resized, either larger or smaller. This allows it to display all of its content in the new, correct places.

If the control is going to draw new content as it is resized to be larger but not change any of the previously visible content, it only needs to repaint the "backwards L" covering the newly visible area, as is shown by the white region in Figure 4.7. In this mode, when the control is resized to be smaller, no redrawing is required.

Figure 4.7

Because it is better for a control to display too much when it is repainted than it is for it to paint only part of the needed area, the default behavior in SWT is to cause the entire area of the control to be redrawn each time it is resized. However, drawing too much can cause a control to flicker.

If you specify the SWT.NO_REDRAW_RESIZE style when creating a control,[12] when the control is resized larger, a paint event is generated that contains a GC whose clipping region has been set to a Region containing only the newly visible area. If you resize the control to be smaller, a paint event is not generated at all.

---

12. SWT.NO_REDRAW_RESIZE and the other style bits that govern drawing are used with the classes Composite, Canvas, and Shell. All other classes use whatever strategy is implemented by the particular native control.

The following example code uses SWT.NO_REDRAW_RESIZE to generate Figure 4.7. The background color of the shell is set to gray before the shell is opened so that the first paint event will draw gray. After the shell is opened, an SWT.Paint listener is added that fills the entire client area in white. As you can see, when the shell is resized to be larger, the fill operation is clipped to the "backwards L."

```
public static void main(String[] args) {
    Display display = new Display();
    final Color white =
        display.getSystemColor(SWT.COLOR_WHITE);
    final Color gray =
        display.getSystemColor(SWT.COLOR_GRAY);
    int style = SWT.SHELL_TRIM | SWT.NO_REDRAW_RESIZE;
    final Shell shell = new Shell(display, style);
    shell.setBackground(gray);
    shell.setSize(200, 200);
    shell.open();
    shell.addListener(SWT.Paint, new Listener() {
        public void handleEvent(Event event) {
            GC gc = event.gc;
            gc.setBackground(white);
            gc.fillRectangle(shell.getClientArea());
        }
    });
    shell.setSize(250, 250);
    while (!shell.isDisposed()) {
        if (!display.readAndDispatch()) display.sleep();
    }
    display.dispose();
}
```

Why Isn't SWT.NO_REDRAW_RESIZE the Default?

Because there is no way of telling how a control will draw in advance, it is not possible to know whether the entire client area should be damaged when the control is resized. The choice is between drawing too much and possibly flickering or drawing too little, causing garbage to be drawn on the screen.

4.9.1   Using SWT.NO_REDRAW_RESIZE to Reduce Flicker

As was previously stated, if the graphics that you are drawing do not depend on the size of the control, redrawing the whole client area whenever the control is resized can cause areas that have not changed to flicker. For example, if your control draws a left-aligned list of strings, resizing the control to be

larger should draw only those strings that intersect with the "backwards L."
When the control is resized to be smaller, nothing needs to be drawn.

The following example uses SWT.NO_REDRAW_RESIZE to reduce the
amount of drawing for a list of strings. Note that this example is very simple
and could reduce the amount of drawing further by drawing only those strings
that intersect with the client area. Figure 4.8 shows the list of strings. Try
removing the SWT.NO_REDRAW_RESIZE to see the flicker.

```
public static void main(String[] args) {
    final String[] list = new String[128];
    for (int i = 0; i < list.length; i++) {
        list[i] = i + "-String-that-is-quite-long-" + i;
    }
    Display display = new Display();
    int style = SWT.SHELL_TRIM | SWT.NO_REDRAW_RESIZE;
    final Shell shell = new Shell(display, style);
    shell.addListener(SWT.Paint, new Listener() {
        public void handleEvent(Event event) {
            GC gc = event.gc;
            int height = gc.stringExtent("").y;
            for (int i = 0; i < list.length; i++) {
                gc.drawText(list[i], 2, i * height);
            }
        }
    });
    shell.setSize(200, 200);
    shell.open();
    while (!shell.isDisposed()) {
        if (!display.readAndDispatch()) display.sleep();
    }
    display.dispose();
}
```

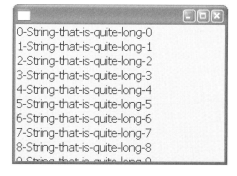

Figure 4.8

4.10   Filling the Background

By default, the background color of a control is filled before a paint event is sent. This allows you to concentrate on drawing the contents of the control. Generally, this approach works well unless you need to provide a custom background. For example, if you are implementing a control that draws a list of strings, alternating the background color between each line, then there are effectively two background colors. Sometimes, there is no notion of background color for a control. For example, a control that draws an image will fill the entire client area with the pixels that make up the image. For this control, filling the area to be drawn with the background color first is completely extraneous, because it will immediately be replaced with the image content. In both these cases, drawing the background can cause the control to flicker.

If you specify the SWT.NO_BACKGROUND style when a control is created, it will not fill the background before sending a paint event. Although this style can get rid of flicker, it means that the paint listener must draw every pixel. Failure to do so will leave the pixels that were on the screen before the paint event was issued untouched. The effect is unsettling, to say the least.

4.10.1   Using SWT.NO_BACKGROUND to Reduce Flicker

The following example first creates an image, then draws it in a paint event. SWT.NO_BACKGROUND is used to stop the background from drawing. When the control is resized to be larger than the image, the area that is not filled by the image (by coincidence, also a "backwards L" shape) is filled with the background color of the control, as shown in Figure 4.9.

```
public static void main(String[] args) {
    Display display = new Display();
    int style = SWT.SHELL_TRIM | SWT.NO_BACKGROUND;
    final Shell shell = new Shell(display, style);
    final Image image = new Image(display, 128, 128);
    GC gc = new GC(image);
    Rectangle rect = image.getBounds();
    gc.setBackground(
        display.getSystemColor(SWT.COLOR_RED));
    gc.fillArc(0, 0, rect.width, rect.height, 0, 360);
    gc.dispose();
    shell.addListener(SWT.Paint, new Listener() {
        public void handleEvent(Event event) {
            GC gc = event.gc;
            Rectangle rect = image.getBounds();
            Rectangle client = shell.getClientArea();
            gc.drawImage(image, 0, 0);
            int width =
                Math.max(0, client.width - rect.width);
```

```
                    int height =
                        Math.max(0, client.height - rect.height);
                    gc.fillRectangle(
                        rect.width,
                        0,
                        width,
                        client.height);
                    gc.fillRectangle(
                        0,
                        rect.height,
                        client.width,
                        height);
                }
            });
            shell.setSize(250, 250);
            shell.open();
            while (!shell.isDisposed()) {
                if (!display.readAndDispatch()) display.sleep();
            }
            image.dispose();
            display.dispose();
        }
```

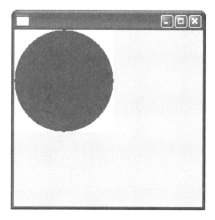

Figure 4.9

Why Isn't SWT.NO_BACKGROUND the Default?

Because there is no way of telling where the control will draw, it is not possible automatically to fill the areas that were not drawn. The choice is between drawing too much and possibly flickering or drawing too little, causing garbage to be drawn on the screen.

4.11   Summary

Controls are fundamental building blocks in SWT. They have bounds and a client area used for painting and positioning their children; they issue events when they are moved or resized; they support an enabled and visible state; and they offer interesting style bits to control painting. More details about individual control methods can be found in the chapter Controls, Composites, Groups, and Shells.

CHAPTER 5

Display

Instances of class Display manage the connection between SWT and the underlying window system.[1] Displays provide many other important capabilities, including API for the event loop, inter-thread communication, timers, and access to default system resources, such as fonts and colors. Displays also provide a number of utility functions that perform user interface thread-specific actions.

Displays do not model individual "computer screens" or monitors, but rather are the single point of contact for *all* the user interface capabilities the system provides (see the section Monitors, Bounds, and Client Area for more about monitors).

Sometimes criticized for being too generic, Display is actually a powerful and useful class, abstracting many different complicated operating system-level APIs and concepts.

Display Is Not a Widget

Display is not a subclass of Widget, although it shares many of the same concepts, such as life cycle, events, listeners, and application data (see the section Widget Fundamentals).

---

1. On X Windows, a display is a thin wrapper over an X Window display and serves much the same purpose.

5.1   Naming Your Application

Naming your application allows the operating system to distinguish it from
other applications built with SWT. The implications of this vary between platforms but can include changing the default label used when your application
windows are displayed as icons and controlling where window system-specific
resource files are found.

You can name your application using this *static* Display method.

setAppName(String name)   Sets the name of the application to the
argument.

On systems that use X resource files (notably, X Windows), the application name maps directly to an *X Application Name*. When set before creating
the display (see the section Display Life Cycle), the application name will be
used to find the X resources for your program, allowing you to change
attributes, such as fonts and colors. For example, to tell X Windows to search
for entries in its resource database of the form

```
Eclipse*<widget>.<resource>: <value>,
```

when creating the widgets for you application, you would use the following
statement.

```
Display.setAppName("Eclipse");
```

Configuring widgets using an X resource file is common for X Windows
applications and will not be further described here other than to say that SWT
does not ship with a prebuilt resource file. This is deliberate; it ensures that
SWT will use the default widget colors, fonts, and other properties configured
for the operating system, rather than overriding them to be something that is
unwanted.

If not specified, the default application name is *SWT*. It is worth changing
this for any application you create.

5.2   Display Life Cycle

Displays follow the same life cycle as widgets. They are explicitly created and
disposed of by the programmer. Before you can do anything useful with SWT,

you must create a display. When you are completely finished with the user interface for your application, call the dispose() method of Display.[2]

5.2.1   Creation

Normally, displays are singletons. On some platforms, it is possible to have multiple displays active at the same time but this generally is not a useful programming metaphor. Instances of class Display are constructed using a simple no-parameter constructor.

> **Display()**   Constructs a new display that allows access to the platform window system.

5.2.2   Destruction

Displays are disposed of in the same manner as widgets, by calling their dispose() method.

> **dispose()**   Disposes of all operating system resources associated with the display.

Calling the dispose() method causes all widgets that were created on the display to also be disposed of. Accessing a display after the dispose method has been called causes an SWTException ("Device is disposed"). Displays support the method isDisposed() that returns true when the display has been disposed of and false otherwise.

5.3   Events and Listeners

In the same manner as widgets, displays send events using *untyped* listeners.

> **addListener(int event, Listener listener)**   Adds the listener to the collection of listeners that will be notified when an event of the given type occurs. When the event occurs in the display, the listener is notified by calling its handleEvent() method.

---

2.   Strictly speaking, this is not necessary if your program exits. In this case, all memory, including window system resources, is released back to the operating system. You should call the dispose method anyway because it will allow third-party operating system leak detection tools to distinguish between leaks and resources that were automatically released on shutdown.

removeListener(int event, Listener listener)   Removes the listener from the collection of listeners that will be notified when an event of the given type occurs.

The following code fragment adds a listener that will be called when the Display is disposed of.

```
display.addListener(SWT.Dispose, new Listener() {
    public void handleEvent(Event event) {
        // the display is getting disposed
    }
});
```

5.3.1 Dispose and Close Listeners

The SWT.Dispose event is sent before the resources for the display and any widgets that were created on it are disposed. This makes a dispose listener a good place to save any data that is global to your application. For example, if your application allows the user to configure the default font to use when creating a certain kind of widget, saving the font name to a file here (to be read back when your program restarts) is a good idea.

In addition to SWT.Dispose, Displays support the SWT.Close event. This event is sent when the *user interface session* is ending, for example, when the window system is shutting down or the user is logging out. On some platforms, it is possible to cancel this operation by setting the *doit* field to false.

The following example uses SWT.Dispose and SWT.Close to save both global and window state when either the window is closed or the user interface session is ending.

```
public static void main(String[] args) {
    Display display = new Display();
    final Shell shell = new Shell(display);
    Listener listener = new Listener() {
        public void handleEvent(Event event) {
            int style =
                SWT.OK | SWT.CANCEL | SWT.APPLICATION_MODAL;
            MessageBox box = new MessageBox(shell, style);
            box.setMessage("Exit the application?");
            event.doit = box.open() == SWT.OK;
        }
    };
    display.addListener(SWT.Close, listener);
    display.addListener(SWT.Dispose, new Listener() {
        public void handleEvent(Event event) {
            System.out.println("Saving global state ... ");
        }
    });
    shell.addListener(SWT.Close, listener);
```

```
shell.addListener(SWT.Dispose, new Listener() {
    public void handleEvent(Event event) {
        System.out.println("Saving window state ... ");
    }
});
shell.setSize(200, 200);
shell.open();
while (!shell.isDisposed()) {
    if (!display.readAndDispatch())
        display.sleep();
}
display.dispose();
}
```

Note that if you run the above code on a platform that does not support
the ability to cancel the shutdown of the user interface session, the application
would exit, even if the user presses the Cancel button of the "Exit the application?" dialog. For this reason, it is best not to rely on being able to set the
doit flag of the SWT.Close event for the display. Generally speaking, stopping
the user interface session from shutting down is not something an application
program should do. Some operating systems kill your application if it does not
respond within a certain time interval and shut down anyway.

If you would like programmatically to cause the display to behave as
though a user interface session were ending, you can call its close() method.

close()   Causes the display to send an SWT.Close event to all listeners, then if the event *doit* flag is still true, dispose of the display.

In addition to listeners and events, Display supports *event filters* and *runnable "execs."*

5.4   Event Filters

An event filter is in essence a global untyped listener. Filtering an event is
equivalent to adding a listener to every widget on a display. Filters run before
the other event listeners, giving a filter the opportunity to modify the event or
even stop the other listeners from running. To add a filter, use the following
Display method.

addFilter(int eventType, Listener listener)   Adds the listener to the
collection of listeners that will be notified before any event of the
given type is sent to any widget.

The following code fragment throws away every key as it is typed and prevents all SWT.KeyDown listeners from running.[3]

```
display.addFilter(SWT.KeyDown, new Listener() {
    public void handleEvent(Event event) {
        event.type = SWT.None;
        event.doit = false;
    }
});
```

Setting the event *type* field to SWT.None cancels the event. Other listeners are stopped from running because they can no longer see the event; the event is no longer a key down, and processing is halted. Setting the *doit* field to false for a key event consumes the event and stops the native widget from processing it. It is important to note that the *doit* field is **consulted only for a subset of the events** (including SWT.KeyDown).

Filtering on an event type allows you to intercept every event of that type as it occurs and process the event before any listeners run. In the case of the SWT.KeyDown, we were able to set *doit* to false and consume the event before any listener had a chance to see it.

In the same manner as listeners, event filters run in the order they were added. If a filter that was added earlier cancels the event, filters that were added later will not see the event.

To remove a filter, use the following.

removeFilter(int eventType, Listener listener)   Removes the listener from the collection of listeners that will be notified before any event of the given type is sent to any widget. Note that listener must be the same instance that was passed to addFilter() in order to be successfully removed.

Filters Are Powerful and Dangerous

Event filters are generally very expensive and should be used sparingly. For example, putting a time-consuming calculation in an SWT.KeyDown filter will slow down typing for every keystroke in every widget.

---

3.   This would have the effect of making all widgets unresponsive to the keyboard.

5.5 Runnable "Execs"

In the same manner as listeners, *runnable execs* (referred to from now on simply as *runnables*) are application-defined blocks of code that are executed by the Display. However, there are several notable differences between listeners and runnables. Runnables are executed once, whereas listeners are typically invoked repeatedly, each time the event occurs. Runnables take no parameters and generally once they are added, they cannot be removed.

Runnables are used for timers (see the section Timers), executing code in the user interface thread (see the section Apartment Threading) and running code when a display is disposed.

5.5.1 Dispose Exec

The following method in class Display can be used to add a runnable that is executed when the display is disposed of.

> **disposeExec(Runnable runnable)**   Adds the runnable to the collection of Runnables that will be executed when the display is being disposed of. The runnable is executed after **all widgets on the display** have already been disposed of.

Notice that an important difference between disposeExec(Runnable) and the handling of the SWT.Dispose event is that dispose listeners run *before* any widgets have been disposed, whereas disposeExec() runnables run *afterward*. This means that disposeExec() can be used to free global resources, such as fonts that may be shared by many different widgets. For example, this code fragment adds a dispose runnable that releases the font used by the application after all the widgets have been disposed.

```
display.disposeExec(new Runnable() {
    public void run() {
        // dispose the shared font
        textFont.dispose();
    }
});
```

In this case, if you attempted to dispose of the font before the widgets that were using it were disposed of, exceptions would be generated. By putting it in a disposeExec() runnable, you are guaranteed that no widgets remain when the runnable is executed.

5.6   The Event Loop

Like most modern window systems, SWT supports an event-driven user interface. This requires an explicit event loop that repeatedly reads and dispatches the next user interface event from the operating system. When an event is *dispatched*, it is delivered to a widget for processing. For example, when the user moves the mouse, a mouse event is delivered to the control that is under the cursor.

When there are no events to be dispatched, the program "goes to sleep" waiting for the next event, yielding the CPU to other programs on the desktop.

The application stays in this loop until its exit conditions are met, for example, when the main application window is closed or when the "Quit..." menu item is selected.

Here is a typical event loop.

```
while (!shell.isDisposed()) {
    if (!display.readAndDispatch()) display.sleep();
}
```

5.6.1   Reading and Dispatching

The core of the event loop is the readAndDispatch() method in class Display.

> **readAndDispatch**()   Reads and dispatches the next available event from the operating system event queue. Returns true if an event was dispatched and false if no events were available. In either case, do not block in the operating system waiting for an event.

Programs will almost always call the sleep() method in class Display when readAndDispatch() returns false.

> **sleep**()   Causes the thread that called this method to stop executing until an event is available in the operating system event queue or some other thread calls the wake() method.

If you do not call sleep() in your main event loop, it will *busy wait* while dispatching events, never releasing the CPU to other programs on the desktop. For example, the following code fragment busy waits.

```
while (!done) display.readAndDispatch();  // Don't do this!
```

Operating systems time-slice threads and processes so that typically, the worst that will happen in this case is that overall system performance will degrade. However, busy waiting should **always be avoided.** If your application has other work to do when events are not being processed, it should use a separate thread for this work (see the section Multithreaded Programming).

Flushing the Event Queue

There is a specific situation where you would not call sleep() when readAnd-Dispatch() returns false.[4] This occurs when using readAndDispatch() to **flush the event queue** of all available events. The following code fragment dispatches events as long as any are available.

```
while (display.readAndDispatch());
```

Flushing the event queue is something an application might do **on rare occasions** to make sure that all outstanding events have been delivered before continuing.

Considerable care must be taken when using this approach, however. For example, if you wanted to ensure that all events have been delivered before doing some drawing operation, you might try flushing the event queue, then calling your drawing routines. The problem with this is that every kind of event is dispatched, not just drawing events. If the user closes the main shell and the event-flushing loop dispatches the dispose event, the shell will have been disposed of by the time your drawing code gets executed. Most of the time, this would not happen, but once in a while, when the timing was just right and the user closed the shell, your program would crash.

Any time you dispatch an arbitrary event in your code, you need to deal with the fact that assumptions you made beforehand (such as whether a particular widget has not been disposed of) may have been invalidated. Because it is difficult to handle these cases properly, API exists to flush only drawing events (see the section Updating the Display).

5.6.2   Sleeping and Waking

As was previously mentioned, when readAndDispatch() returns false, this is an indication that your program can suspend execution using the method sleep(). When an event becomes available, sleep() returns. Although the boolean return value of the sleep method is theoretically supposed to indicate whether an event actually became available, in practice, it will always be true.

---

4. As is always the case with these things, if you look hard, you can find other exceptions to the rule. One such exception is found in the section Detecting Inactivity in the Event Loop, where a single event is dispatched without calling sleep afterward.

Once the user interface has called the sleep() method, it is possible to awaken it even if no events are available by calling the wake() method:

wake()   If the thread that is running the event loop on the display is waiting in the sleep() method for an event to become available, this will immediately cause it to return from the method. This method can be called at any time; if the event loop thread is not sleeping, calling wake() has no effect.

To see why this method is required, consider the following code fragment.

```
// this code is running in the event loop thread
while (!done) {
    if (!display.readAndDispatch()) display.sleep();
}
```

It is clear that the event loop will run until the variable *done* becomes true. If *done* is set from within a listener, the exit condition for the loop will be tested, and sleep() will not get called because the listener was called from readAndDispatch(). This can be guaranteed because whenever readAndDispatch() invokes a listener, it will return true—an event has, by definition, been dispatched. Thus, sleep() is not called, and the loop returns to the *!done* test and exits.

When *done* is set from another thread, the result depends on what part of the event loop thread is being executed when the variable is set. For example, when the event loop thread is calling readAndDispatch(), if an event is dispatched, the loop does not sleep and *done* variable is checked. However, if the event loop thread is suspended inside sleep(), it will not wake up to check the variable until the next event occurs, perhaps when the user moves the mouse.

The Wiggly Mouse Problem

We call this sort of nondeterministic bug the *wiggly mouse problem*.[5] It can happen in code where a background thread is executing a long operation, periodically updating a progress bar or some other progress indicator. The symptom is that the progress bar goes all the way to the end and stays there, giving the user the impression that the operation is about to complete but is stuck in the final

---

5.   As a measure of how prevalent this is, the version of Microsoft Word that we are using to write this book exhibits the wiggly mouse problem when merging changes.

> stages. The user then moves the mouse, and the operation appears to complete. In reality, the operation has been finished for a while but the user interface thread was asleep.

The following code fragment, when executed from some other thread, guarantees that the event loop thread will check the *done* variable.

```
// this code is not running in the event loop thread
done = true;
display.wake ();
```

Here is a complete example that demonstrates the use of wake(). The event loop thread sleeps when no events are available. The other thread runs some arbitrary code (using System.out to "show progress" as each unit of work is completed), then calls wake() to wake the event loop thread from sleep().

```
public static void main(String[] args) {
    final Display display = new Display();
    Shell shell = new Shell(display);
    shell.pack();
    shell.open();
    final boolean[] done = new boolean[1];
    new Thread() {
        public void run() {
            for (int i = 0; i < 10; i++) {
                try {
                    Thread.sleep(500);
                } catch (Throwable th) {
                }
                System.out.print(".");
            }
            done[0] = true;
            display.wake();                     // wake the event loop
                                                // thread from sleep
        }
    }
    .start();
    System.out.print("Running ");
    while (!done[0]) {
        if (!display.readAndDispatch()) display.sleep();
    }
    System.out.print(" done.");
    display.dispose();
}
```

Note that wake() is useful only in multithreaded programs. In a single-threaded program, if the event loop thread is sleeping, it could not by definition be executing the wake() method. It turns out that issues involving threading, the Display, and the event loop are all tightly coupled.

5.7   Multithreaded Programming

In SWT, by definition, the thread that creates the display is called the *user interface thread*. This thread is responsible for reading and dispatching events from the operating system event queue and invoking listeners in response. You can find out which thread is the user interface thread for a particular display by calling the getThread() method on the display:

> **getThread**()   Returns the thread that is running the event loop on that display.

You can test whether your code is running in the user interface as follows.

```
if (display.getThread() == Thread.currentThread()) {
    // current thread is the user interface thread
}
```

Listener code is always executed in the user interface thread. This makes SWT applications generally quite responsive, behaving like most other native applications on the desktop. However, any long operation, when executed directly by a listener, will prevent the user interface thread from reading and dispatching other events. This gives the program the appearance of being *hung* while the operation is running.

If a listener has a large amount of work to perform, instead of doing the work in the user interface thread, it must fork a separate thread so that the user interface thread can continue dispatching events. If this other thread tries to execute code that accesses a widget, for example, to change the string in a label, there is a concurrency issue. Most operating systems do not support having multiple threads concurrently accessing the state of widgets. Typically, attempting to do this will cause crashes, hangs, or simply unpredictable behavior. Some kind of synchronization is necessary.

5.7.1   Apartment Threading

SWT implements a single-threaded user interface model that is typically called *apartment threading*. In this model, only the user interface thread can invoke user interface operations. This rule is strictly enforced. If you try to access an

SWT object from outside the user interface thread, you will get an SWTEx-
ception("Invalid thread access").

Different operating systems have diverse rules governing threads, widgets,
and synchronization. Some use an apartment-threaded model such as SWT.
Others allow any thread to invoke user interface operations but allow only
one thread at a time in the window system library, controlling access through
a global lock. This type of multithreaded user interface model is typically
called *free threading*. In order to be simple, efficient, and (most important)
portable, SWT is apartment-threaded. This is the only model that can be
implemented on all platforms.

To allow background threads to perform operations on objects belonging
to the user interface thread, the Display methods asyncExec() and syncExec()
are used.

asyncExec(Runnable runnable)   Causes the argument to be run by
the user interface thread of the display.

syncExec(Runnable runnable)   In addition to causing the argument
to be run by the user interface thread of the display, this method
causes the current thread (if it is different than the user interface
thread of the display) to wait for the runnable to finish.

Along with wake(), the asyncExec() and syncExec() methods are among a
handful of methods in the widgets package that can be called from any thread.

The syncExec() or asyncExec() Methods Do Not Create Threads

Beginning SWT developers sometimes get confused by the fact that syncExec()
and asyncExec() take a runnable as an argument. They expect these methods to
create a new thread or run in some other thread instead of executing the runnable in the user interface thread. This is *not* the case. If you perform a long operation inside a syncExec() or asyncExec(), you will temporarily hang the user
interface in the same manner as invoking the long operation from a listener.

Both asyncExec() and syncExec() cause their arguments to be run by the
user interface thread at the next "reasonable" opportunity. This occurs during readAndDispatch(), when no operating system events are available to be
processed. At this point, if there are runnables pending, they are removed
from the queue and sent the run() message. When run() returns, readAndDis-

patch() returns true, ensuring that it will be called again by the event loop to handle either any new events that are available or any other runnables that are pending.

Note that this process favors operating system events over code that is executed via asyncExec() and syncExec(). Because of this, the same caveat applies as was noted in the section Flushing the Event Queue: An arbitrary number of operating system events may be processed before your runnable is evaluated, so the state of the user interface may be different than you expect.

Using syncExec() to Run Code in the User Interface Thread

As noted above, when syncExec() is called from a background thread, the runnable is executed in the user interface thread, and the background thread waits for the result. Thus, runnables executed by syncExec() most closely match the equivalent "direct call" to the widget and should be used when you would like simply to call a widget method but cannot because of the apartment-threading model.

Here is a variation of the code from the section Sleeping and Waking that uses syncExec() to show progress from the background thread. In this case, the shell title is updated as each unit of work is completed, rather than simply writing to the console.

```java
public static void main(String[] args) {
    final Display display = new Display();
    final Shell shell = new Shell(display);
    shell.setSize(500, 64);
    shell.open();
    final boolean[] done = new boolean[1];
    new Thread() {
        public void run() {
            for (int i = 0; i < 10; i++) {
                try {
                    Thread.sleep(500);
                } catch (Throwable th) {
                }
                display.syncExec(new Runnable() {
                    public void run() {
                        if (shell.isDisposed()) return;
                        shell.setText(shell.getText()+".");
                    }
                });
            }
            done[0] = true;
            // wake the user interface thread from sleep
            display.wake();
        }
    }
    .start();
    shell.setText("Running ");
```

```
    while (!done[0]) {
        if (!display.readAndDispatch()) display.sleep();
    }
    if (!shell.isDisposed()) {
        shell.setText(shell.getText() + " done.");
        try {
            Thread.sleep(500);
        } catch (Throwable th) {
        }
    }
    display.dispose();
}
```

Note that using syncExec() ensures that the user interface thread and the background thread are synchronized at the time that the runnable is executed. In the example code, one period is used to represent 10% of work. For example, when the background thread has completed 70% of the work, it sets the title of the shell to seven periods, waiting for the user interface thread to update before proceeding with the other 30% of the work.

Using asyncExec() to Queue Code for the User Interface Thread

In the same manner as syncExec(), asyncExec() executes a runnable in the user interface thread. Instead of waiting for the result, asyncExec() queues the runnable and returns right away, allowing the background thread to keep running. Because asyncExec() does not wait, the user interface thread and the background thread execute independently.

The example in the section Using syncExec() to Run Code in the User Interface Thread can be recoded to use asyncExec() by simply changing the line

```
display.syncExec(new Runnable() {
```

to

```
display.asyncExec(new Runnable() {
```

Running this new version seems to give the same result as the original one, but there is a subtle difference.

When syncExec() is used, the user interface always shows the amount of work that the background thread has completed at the time the work is completed. This seems to be exactly what you want until you realize that the cost of this is that **no new work will be started** until the user interface thread can successfully indicate the completion of the current work. If the user interface thread is processing some long-running operation at the time syncExec() is called or if many operating system events are waiting to be dispatched, the background thread processing will be delayed.

Using asyncExec(), the background thread tells the user interface thread to indicate the progress but then continues immediately, executing the next element of work. This ensures that the background thread is not delayed by the user interface thread but leads to a new problem: If the background thread continues to finish work faster than the user interface thread can display the progress, more and more runnables will be queued. This situation is called *flooding* the user interface, which has several effects.

The user interface does not accurately display the amount of progress that has been made. The problem here is that the background thread may have completely finished its work before the user interface thread has reported the first amount of progress. What is worse, even though the task is complete by then, the user interface continues to display every interim progress state until all runnables have been processed.

The overall performance of the user interface is impacted. Time is wasted processing each of the runnables, even though they are no longer relevant. The importance of this should not be underestimated. Running code in the user interface thread can make the user interface thread slow to process operating system events, causing the user interface to become sluggish.

Consistency problems become more likely. Because runnables passed to asyncExec() (and syncExec()) are executed only when no operating system events are available, if there are many runnables to be processed, it becomes increasingly likely that something will have changed by the time the runnable is evaluated.

When to Use syncExec() and asyncExec()

Because it appears that both syncExec() and asyncExec() can potentially cause problems, which one should you use?

For most simple situations, use syncExec(). As long as the rest of your user interface is responsive, the cost of waiting for the runnable to be processed will be low enough that it will not impact the performance of your background thread significantly, particularly if you report progress (or whatever user interface painting you are doing) only after a certain minimum length of time has passed. For example, if you have reported progress in the last 0.01 of a second, you can probably avoid reporting it again now (unless intervals that short really are of interest in your particular application).

Unfortunately, there is another problem with syncExec() that can make it unusable in some situations: It can cause deadlock. Consider a multi-threaded application where access to some of the application resources is being managed by synchronization locks. In this situation, the following scenario could occur.

> The background thread acquires a lock. Meanwhile, the user pushes a button that causes the user interface thread to try to acquire the same lock. Next, the background thread does a syncExec() to execute code in the user interface. The background thread is left waiting for the user interface thread to process the syncExec() while the user interface is waiting for the background thread to release the lock. Neither thread will ever proceed, causing the application to be deadlocked.

If, however, the background thread had used asyncExec(), it would have continued running, eventually releasing the lock it held so that the user interface thread could acquire the lock, finish processing the button press event, and finally handle the runnable passed to it by the asyncExec() call.

It should be noted that deadlock problems are possible in any program that has multiple threads and more than one lock. As long as calls to syncExec() are treated as locks on the user interface thread, it is possible to code your application carefully so that it will not deadlock. This can be difficult for large systems though, particularly ones where the code is provided by many different developers and there is a large number of threads.[6]

It is relatively easy to prevent flooding by using variations of the pattern "Detect whether the last asyncExec has completed before scheduling another." Rather than providing (yet another) complete version of the code from the Sleeping and Waking section, here is just the relevant part, showing one way to implement the pattern.

```
...
final boolean[] reporting=new boolean[1];
final StringBuffer title=new StringBuffer("Running ");
new Thread() {
    public void run() {
        for (int i = 0; i < 10; i++) {
            try {
                Thread.sleep(500);
            } catch (Throwable th) {
            }
            title.append(".");
```

---

6. Of course, Eclipse is one such application. The prevailing wisdom in the Eclipse community is to use asyncExec() whenever possible for this very reason.

```
            if (reporting[0]) continue;
            reporting[0] = true;
            display.asyncExec(new Runnable() {
                public void run() {
                    if (shell.isDisposed()) return;
                    shell.setText(title.toString());
                    reporting[0] = false;
                }
            });
...
```

Notice that this code begins by building a single boolean state variable that will be true when the user interface is reporting progress and false otherwise. It then does its work as before (simulated by the Thread.sleep(500) call). After the work is completed, it checks whether there is already pending progress to be reported. If so, it simply continues doing its work. However, if progress is not currently being reported, it indicates that progress reporting has started (reporting[0]=true), then uses asyncExec, rather than syncExec, to queue the progress indication. When the runnable is eventually evaluated, it updates the shell title, then finally indicates that progress reporting has finished. In this way, there will never be more than one progress-reporting runnable pending at any given time.

One subtle point to notice about this version of the code is that it must keep track of the amount of progress that has been completed—in this case, the number of dots to display in the shell title—in a separate StringBuffer, rather than querying the old value from the shell, and adding a dot to it. This is required because there is no longer a one-to-one mapping between the number of times work is done, and progress is reported.

Normally, both syncExec() and asyncExec() are called from background threads. When syncExec() is called from the user interface thread, the runnable is executed immediately. There is no need to queue the runnable or lock anything because the current thread *is* the user interface thread. Calling syncExec() from the user interface thread is not very useful or harmful but is supported for completeness. It is interesting to note that asyncExec(), when called from the user interface thread, can be useful because it queues the work, causing it to happen at a later time.

Using asyncExec() from the User Interface Thread

Some operating systems have the concept of *idle handlers*, which allow you to execute code when the user interface becomes idle. As we noted in the Apartment Threading section, to make the user interface as responsive as possible, runnables queued by asyncExec() are evaluated only when there are no pending operating system events to be processed. This means that asyncExec(), when called from the user interface thread, will cause the runnable to be executed after readAndDispatch() has dispatched all outstanding events but before the event loop calls sleep(), making them equivalent to idle handlers.

The following code fragment calls asyncExec() from the user interface thread every time a key is pressed in a text control. To ensure that the text control has processed the key, before querying the contents of the control and setting it into a label, the code uses asyncExec().

```
public static void main(String[] args) {
    final Display display = new Display();
    Shell shell = new Shell(display);
    shell.setLayout(new FillLayout(SWT.VERTICAL));
    final Text text =
        new Text(shell, SWT.BORDER | SWT.SINGLE);
    final Label label = new Label(shell, SWT.BORDER);
    text.addListener(SWT.KeyDown, new Listener() {
        public void handleEvent(Event event) {
            display.asyncExec(new Runnable() {
                public void run() {
                    label.setText(
                        "\"" + text.getText() + "\"");
                }
            });
        }
    });
    shell.setSize(shell.computeSize(400, SWT.DEFAULT));
    shell.open();
    while (!shell.isDisposed()) {
        if (!display.readAndDispatch()) display.sleep();
    }
    display.dispose();
}
```

The call to asyncExec() in this example is critical, because the native text widget processes the keystroke only *after* all KeyDown listeners have been invoked. Thus, without the asyncExec() call, the key would not yet have been added to the text widget contents when the text.getText() call in the listener was made. This causes the contents of the label to be always one or more characters behind what the text control was showing. To see this bug, try changing the asyncExec() to a syncExec().

Of course, a runnable that calls asyncExec() on itself will run repeatedly, stopping the event loop from sleeping in the operating system.[7] Essentially, the program will never become idle because it is continually running an idle handler. This is equivalent in terms of CPU usage to busy waiting with readAndDispatch() (see the section Reading and Dispatching).

---

7. But not hanging the user interface, because readAndDispatch() will always dispatch any available operating system events before running the runnable again.

A better way to run code repeatedly is to use a timer.

5.8   Timers

Timers allow an arbitrary block of code to be run after waiting for a timeout interval. Timers are not implemented as interrupts. They are executed in the user interface thread like other operating system events. In fact, on some platforms, they are implemented as operating system events, coming in through the event queue like any other event. In any case, timers run before syncExec() and asyncExec() blocks, which run only when the user interface is idle.

The following method, on class Display, is used to create a timer.

timerExec(int milliseconds, Runnable runnable)   Causes the given Runnable to be evaluated after the specified number of milliseconds have elapsed.

This code fragment creates a timer to execute a runnable after waiting for 2 seconds.

```
display.timerExec(2000, new Runnable() {
    public void run() {
        System.out.println("Once, after 2 seconds.");
    }
});
```

Timers run only once. To run a timer repeatedly, queue the same runnable again, using the same time interval. This code fragment uses a timer to execute a runnable every 2 seconds.

```
display.timerExec(2000, new Runnable() {
    public void run() {
        System.out.println("Every 2 seconds.");
        display.timerExec(2000, this);
    }
});
```

To change the timeout period for a pending timer, timerExec() is called with the new interval and the original runnable. The following code fragment first sets a timer to run after 2 seconds, then resets the timer to run after 5 seconds, causing the timer to run once, after 5 seconds.

```
display.timerExec(2000, timer);
display.timerExec(5000, timer);
```

As you might expect, a pending timer can be forced to run right away by changing the timeout value to zero. A pending timer can also be removed by using a negative timeout interval. The following code fragment removes a pending timer.

```
display.timerExec(-1, timer);
```

5.8.1   Detecting Inactivity in the Event Loop

The following example uses a timer to detect 3 seconds of inactivity in the event loop.

```
public static void main(String[] args) {
    Display display = new Display();
    Shell shell = new Shell(display);
    shell.pack();
    shell.open();
    final int TIME_OUT = 3000;
    Runnable runnable = new Runnable() {
        public void run() {
            System.out.println(
                "Idle for "
                    + (TIME_OUT / 1000)
                    + " seconds");
        }
    };
    while (!shell.isDisposed()) {
        if (!display.readAndDispatch()) {
            display.timerExec(TIME_OUT, runnable);
            display.sleep();
            display.readAndDispatch();
            display.timerExec(-1, runnable);
        }
    }
    display.dispose();
}
```

Instead of simply sleeping right away when readAndDispatch() returns false, the example code first adds a timer. This ensures that sleep() will wake up after suspending execution for no more than 3 seconds. When sleep() wakes up, two things could have happened. Either the timer expired or an operating system event became available. To determine which occurred, readAndDispatch() is called. If the timer expired, readAndDispatch() executes the timer, and the system was idle for 3 seconds. Otherwise, readAndDispatch() dispatches the operating system event, and the system was not idle. In any case, the timer is removed so that it will not execute erroneously later on. It is not an error to attempt to remove a timer that has already expired, so no check for this case is necessary in the code.

There are many reasons why events are sent to an application. Even when the user is not clicking, moving the mouse, or typing on the keyboard, the event loop may not be idle. For example, another part of the program may register a timer. Even the operating system itself may generate events at arbitrary intervals.[8] A better way to detect inactivity is to monitor the keyboard.

5.8.2   Detecting Inactivity in the Keyboard

The following example uses a timer to detect inactivity in the keyboard after waiting 3 seconds.

```
public static void main(String[] args) {
    final Display display = new Display();
    Shell shell = new Shell(display);
    shell.pack();
    shell.open();
    final int TIME_OUT = 3000;
    final Runnable runnable = new Runnable() {
        public void run() {
            System.out.println(
                "Idle for "
                    + (TIME_OUT / 1000)
                    + " seconds");
            display.timerExec(TIME_OUT, this);
        }
    };
    display.addFilter(SWT.KeyDown, new Listener() {
        public void handleEvent (Event event) {
            display.timerExec(TIME_OUT, runnable);
        }
    });
    display.timerExec(TIME_OUT, runnable);
    while (!shell.isDisposed()) {
        if (!display.readAndDispatch()) display.sleep();
    }
    display.dispose();
}
```

The code works by adding the same timer (that fires once every 3 seconds) each time a key is pressed. Because the timer is added again each time, when the user types a key, the period is reset to be 3 seconds from that time. If 3 seconds pass without any keyboard events occurring, the timer will fire, then reschedule itself to run 3 seconds later. This causes the timer to fire every time there is a 3-second period of no keyboard activity. If you need to detect only

---

8.   This happens on Motif where the text widget uses a timer to blink the caret.

when it has been 3 seconds since the last time a key was pressed, you can leave out the display.timerExec(TIME_OUT, this) call in the body of the timer.

Similar code could be written to check for mouse events or any other combination of events.

5.9   Putting It All Together: Multithreading, Timers, Events, and the Event Loop

The event loop plays a critical role in synchronizing all of the user's actions, other operating system events, timers, and background threads with the user interface thread. This relationship can be summarized by the following description.

❍ Events are generated by the user and are read and dispatched from the event loop to widgets by the user interface thread.

❍ Application code registers interest in events by adding event listeners to widgets. This code is invoked in response to an event when it is dispatched. Thus, the event loop is running application code, as well as dispatching operating system events.

❍ If the user interface thread is busy running code and does not call readAndDipatch() when the user generates an event, the event is queued.

❍ When readAndDispatch() is called, outstanding events that the user has generated are delivered.

❍ If you do not call readAndDispatch(), events will never be delivered, your program will appear hung, and the user will eventually terminate it.

❍ Calling readAndDispatch() indicates that the user interface thread is at a clean point, ready to process an operating system event. At that time, by definition, the user interface thread is not busy running a widget operation or listener. Thus, it is ready to safely run timers that have expired or arbitrary code on behalf of other threads resulting from calls to syncExec() or asyncExec().

The fact that events from the user and operating system, timers, and syncExec() and asyncExec() runnables can be generated at any time but are delivered to your program only when you call readAndDispatch() makes your multithreaded program more deterministic.

Up to this point, we have been discussing listeners and the event loop. As mentioned previously, Display also provides many other utility functions.

5.10   Monitors, Bounds, and Client Area

Displays are connected to one or more physical monitors. Each monitor can have different dimensions and color characteristics. Figure 5.1 shows a display with three monitors.

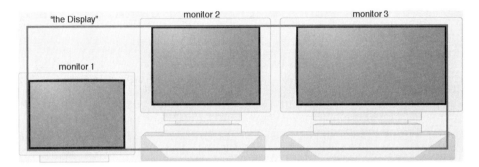

Figure 5.1   A display with three monitors.

Normally, users interact with one monitor (called the *primary monitor*) and use the other monitors to increase their desktop work area. The user generally expects new windows to open on the monitor where he or she is working and dialog windows to open on the same monitor as their parent. Windows do not usually straddle monitors unless the user arranges them that way.

SWT models the physical monitors that are connected to the display, using instances of class Monitor. Two methods are provided on class Display that return monitors.

getMonitors()   Returns an array containing all monitors that are attached to this Display.

getPrimaryMonitor()   Returns the monitor that the system is currently treating as the "main" monitor.

The following methods can be used to identify the area covered by each monitor.

getBounds()   Returns a rectangle containing the bounding box for the monitor. Note that in systems with multiple monitors, the location of the bounding box may be negative, depending on where it is positioned relative to the primary monitor. The location of the primary monitor is always (0, 0).

getClientArea()   Returns a rectangle containing the area of the monitor that should be accessed by client code. This is the area available to position shells. Note that in systems with multiple monitors, the location of the client area may be negative, depending on where the monitor is positioned relative to the primary monitor.

On any given monitor, some of the visible area may be reserved by the operating system. For example, on Windows the task bar is normally visible on the primary monitor, reducing the amount of space that is available to your application. To query the available space on a monitor, use getClientArea().

The support for describing multiple monitors was added in R3.0 of SWT. Previous to this, the best you could do was call the getBounds() method in class Display:

getBounds()   Returns a rectangle containing the bounding box for the display. For displays with multiple monitors this returns the union of the bounding boxes of the monitors.

The problem with using the getBounds() method of Display is that it includes areas that are not visible (see the gray rectangle marked "the Display" in Figure 5.1). You should always use getPrimaryMonitor() or getMonitors() to position your windows.

The following code fragment gets all the available monitors and prints their bounds as well as the bounds of the display.

```
Monitor[] list = display.getMonitors();
System.out.println(list.length + " monitors.");
for (int i = 0; i < list.length; i++) {
    String string = "\t" + i + " - " + list[i].getBounds();
    System.out.println(string);
}
System.out.println("Total bounds: " + display.getBounds());
```

5.10.1   Centering a Shell on the Primary Monitor

The following code fragment centers a shell on the primary monitor using getClientArea() to query the available space.

```
public static void main(String[] args) {
    Display display = new Display();
    Shell shell = new Shell(display);
    Monitor primary = display.getPrimaryMonitor();
    Rectangle bounds = primary.getBounds();
    Rectangle rect = shell.getBounds();
    int x = bounds.x
        + Math.max(0, (bounds.width - rect.width) / 2);
```

```
    int y = bounds.y
        + Math.max(0, (bounds.height - rect.height) / 2);
    shell.setBounds(x, y, rect.width, rect.height);
    shell.open();
    while (!shell.isDisposed()) {
        if (!display.readAndDispatch()) display.sleep();
    }
    display.dispose();
}
```

5.10.2 Positioning a Shell on a Monitor

As was previously noted, the origin of a monitor can be negative. This means
that a shell positioned at a negative location may be visible to the user. This is
a common source of programming errors. In other words, you cannot simply
position a shell at a negative offset to hide it. Code that attempts to position
a shell at a specific point needs to do so relative to the origin of the monitor,
not zero. The following example positions a shell at the current location of the
cursor within a monitor, ensuring that the shell is completely visible. If the
shell is larger than the monitor, it is left- and top-aligned.

```
public static void main(String[] args) {
    Display display = new Display();
    Shell shell = new Shell(display);
    shell.setSize(200, 200);
    Point pt = display.getCursorLocation();
    Point size = shell.getSize();
    Monitor [] monitors = display.getMonitors();
    for (int i= 0; i<monitors.length; i++) {
            if (monitors [i].getBounds().contains(pt)) {
                Rectangle rect = monitors [i].getClientArea();
                    pt.x =
                        Math.max(
                            rect.x,
                            Math.min(
                                Math.max(pt.x, rect.x),
                                rect.x + rect.width - size.x));
                    pt.y =
                        Math.max(
                            rect.y,
                            Math.min(
                                Math.max(pt.y, rect.y),
                                rect.y + rect.height - size.y));
                break;
            }
    }
    shell.setLocation(pt);
    shell.open();
    while (!shell.isDisposed()) {
        if (!display.readAndDispatch()) display.sleep();
    }
    display.dispose();
}
```

5.11   The Active Shell, All Shells, and Focus Control

Displays keep a list of all shells that were created, the active shell, and the focus control. This section discusses the methods in class Display that provide access to this state. Because the methods to set the active shell and focus control are implemented in the classes Shell and Control, they are discussed in the appropriate sections of the Controls, Composites, Groups, and Shells chapter.

5.11.1   Getting the Active Shell

At any given time, one shell at most is active on the desktop. Window systems often indicate the active shell by drawing the title bar in a different color or style. If the active shell was created on a particular display, it can be queried using the getActiveShell() method.

> **getActiveShell()**   Returns the active shell if it was created on this display. If there is no active shell or the active shell belongs to another application, getActiveShell() returns null.

On Windows, when the user clicks on the background of the desktop, no shell is active. In this case, getActiveShell() will return null.

The following code fragment finds and disposes of the active shell.

```
Shell shell = display.getActiveShell();
if (shell != null) shell.dispose();
```

5.11.2   Getting the List of Shells

The list of all shells for the display can be queried using the getShells() method.

> **getShells()**   Returns every shell that was created on the display, including shells that are children of other shells.

The following code fragment queries the list of shells and minimizes all but the active one.

```
Shell shell = display.getActiveShell();
if (shell != null) {
    while (shell.getParent() != null) {
        shell = shell.getParent().getShell();
    }
}
if (shell != null) {
```

```
Shell[] shells = display.getShells();
for (int i = 0; i < shells.length; i++) {
    if (shells[i].getParent() == null) {
        if (shells[i] != shell) {
            shells[i].setMinimized(true);
        }
    }
}
}
```

Notice that the code minimizes only the shells that have no parent. This works because minimizing a shell will cause all shells that are children of that shell to be hidden.

5.11.3 Getting the Focus Control

At most, one widget on the desktop can have *keyboard focus* (see the chapter The Keyboard). You can query the control that has keyboard focus using the following Display method.

> **getFocusControl**()   Returns the control that will receive keyboard events. If there is no widget that has keyboard focus or if the control that has keyboard focus belongs to some other application, null is returned. To set the focus control, use the method setFocus() in the class Control.

The following code fragment prints the focus control.

```
Control control = display.getFocusControl();
System.out.println("Focus control is " + control);
```

5.12 Cursor Control and Location

Displays provide API to identify the control that has the cursor and get and set the location of the cursor. Because there is only one cursor on the desktop, it is shared by all applications. Moving the cursor on the display will move the cursor for every application on the desktop.

5.12.1 Getting the Cursor Control

At any time, the cursor can be over a control or the desktop. Although it is possible to write code that gets the list of shells and recursively queries the bounds of their children to find the child that is under the cursor, this is inefficient and can be problematic. When the user clicks or moves the mouse, the operating system determines where the mouse operation occurred. This process is called *hit testing.* Normally, mouse events are delivered to the deepest child in the hierarchy[9] but this is not always the case. For example, a control that is disabled does not receive mouse clicks, even though it may contain the cursor. This prevents the control from acting on a mouse click while it is disabled.

To match the rules for operating system hit testing, you should use the get-CursorControl() method when you need to hit test your controls.

> **getCursorControl()**   Returns the control that would receive the SWT .MouseDown event if the mouse were clicked at the current cursor position or null if the event would not be sent to a control on this display.

The following example code uses getCursorControl() to detect when the mouse enters and exits the area covered by each control. Note that there are already events to do this for controls (see SWT.MouseEnter and SWT.Mouse-Exit in the chapter The Mouse), so this code does not have practical value beyond demonstrating the API.

```
public static void main(String[] args) {
    final Display display = new Display();
    final Control[] last = new Control[1];
    display.timerExec(100, new Runnable() {
        public void run() {
            Control control = display.getCursorControl();
            if (control != last[0]) {
                if (last[0] != null
                    && !last[0].isDisposed()) {
                    System.out.println("Exit:" + last[0]);
                }
                if (control != null
                    && !control.isDisposed()) {
                    System.out.println("Enter:" + control);
                }
            }
            last[0] = control;
            display.timerExec(100, this);
        }
    });
    Shell shell = new Shell(display);
    shell.pack();
    shell.open();
    while (!shell.isDisposed()) {
        if (!display.readAndDispatch()) display.sleep();
    }
    display.dispose();
}
```

---

9. In this case, we are talking about the *containment hierarchy* made up of controls and their children, so that the control that is returned would be the one that is under the cursor that does not have children that are also under the cursor.

The example checks the cursor control every 100 milliseconds; if it has changed, the previous focus control and the new one are printed.

5.12.2 *Setting and Getting the Cursor Location*

An application program can determine the location of the cursor using the Display method.

> **getCursorLocation()**   Returns the location of the cursor in coordinates that are relative to the display.

Note that the coordinates returned by getCursorLocation() differ from the coordinates reported in a mouse down event. The coordinates reported in mouse down events are relative to the control that received the event. In addition, because the mouse may have moved since the last mouse event was processed, the actual mouse location can be different. The getCursorLocation() method always returns the actual mouse location at the time it was called.

The following line of code queries the cursor location.

```
Point location = display.getCursorLocation();
```

Setting the location of the cursor is also supported using the following Display methods.

> **setCursorLocation(int x, int y)**   Moves the cursor to the location (x, y) relative to the origin of the display.

> **setCursorLocation(Point p)**   Equivalent to setCursorLocation(p.x, p.y).

It is considered bad user interface design to move the cursor using these methods because the user expects to be in control of the cursor location. If your application changes the location of the cursor programmatically, this expectation is broken. In fact, some windowing systems, such as GTK, do not support setting the cursor location. For both of these reasons, you should avoid calling setCursorLocation() unless it is absolutely necessary for your application.

5.13   Display Depth and DPI

SWT runs on many different display devices. These devices can be different sizes and support different numbers of colors. Application programmers can query the display in order to use the best possible colors for the device.

The bit depth of a graphics device is the number of bits it takes to represent each color on the device. It is also called *bits per pixel*. The bit depth of a device is usually one of 1, 8, 15, 16, 24, or 32. Application programmers can query the depth of a device using getDepth().

The physical size of a device is represented in *dots per inch* (DPI). The method getDPI() returns the number of dots, or pixels, per inch in both the horizontal and vertical direction. This can be used, for example, to allow the application to draw graphics the same size, regardless of the device.

Both getDepth() and getDPI() are covered further in the Graphics part of the book.

Some platforms restrict the number of colors that can be used for an icon separately from the number of colors available on the device. You can query the number of colors that are supported for icons using the getIconDepth() method.

getIconDepth()   Returns the maximum number of *bits per pixel* allowed for icons that are created on this display.

The primary use for this method is to choose the best icon for the display. For example, an application program could use the result of getIconDepth() to select one of several different icons, each representing the same picture but using different numbers of colors.

5.13.1   System Information

Display also provides system information and stock graphics objects or *system objects*. System objects are resources such as fonts and colors that are allocated by the operating system. They are available for use by every application but owned by the system and released on shutdown.

Do Not Call dispose() for System Objects

Do not attempt to dispose of system objects by calling dispose(). You did not allocate them, so you *must not* free them. If you do, depending on the platform and the object, the results will be unpredictable. For example, some operating systems (such as Microsoft Windows) guard against disposing of system objects, whereas others (such as Motif) do not.

5.13.2 System Colors

On every platform, no matter how many colors are available, the window system reserves a small number of colors. These are nominal enough to display the widgets on the desktop. If more colors are available, the desktop may make use of them, but the minimal set is always present and preallocated. These are called *system colors*.

In SWT, system colors are specified using constants with the prefix COLOR_. The following code fragment gets the color red from the system.

```
Color red = display.getSystemColor(SWT.COLOR_RED);
```

It is also possible to query standard system colors for things such as shadows, the background color of a text widget, and the gradient that should be used when drawing a title. These days, most platforms have *theme managers* that allow arbitrary code to be used to draw widgets. As long as your application uses the native widgets that SWT provides, it will take on the appearance generated by the theme manager. For custom widgets that you create, using the system colors will help the widget fit in with the appearance of the platform, but it is not sufficient to make them match exactly.

The SWT team is investigating the possibility of providing a "skinning" API that allows nonnative widgets to make direct use of the platform theme manager, but as of the writing of this book, this has not been implemented.

For a complete description of system colors, see the section System Colors in the Colors chapter.

5.13.3 System Font

The system font is the default font used by the window system on platforms that have this concept. The following code fragment queries the system font and sets it into a control.

```
Font font = display.getSystemFont();
control.setFont(font);
```

Note that it is best to avoid code like this. When a widget is created, the platform theme manager automatically assigns the appropriate font for the widget. Setting the font for a widget to null, rather than to the system font, restores the correct font for that widget.

The system font is covered further in the Fonts chapter.

5.14   Updating the Display

Sometimes an application program needs to flush outstanding paint events.[10] For example, when a Shell is disposed of, it is hidden, exposing other Shells underneath. Paint events are queued by the operating system, and the exposed areas are drawn when the application program calls readAndDispatch(). If readAndDispatch() is called right away, the events are dispatched, and the newly exposed areas are drawn immediately. However, if the program is busy running a long operation in the user interface thread, the redraw will be delayed until the operation is finished and the thread gets back to the event loop. Until that time, the exposed areas remain unpainted.

Typically, an application gets back to the event loop quickly so that the user will not notice the small delay. In addition, if more drawing events are created before previous ones are handled, the operating system will merge drawing events for overlapping areas into a single drawing event as an optimization. This reduces the amount of drawing that is done, gets rid of flicker, and allows the application to draw faster.

To handle the case where the program runs a long operation in the user interface thread or otherwise needs to force the screen to be redrawn, use the update() Display method.

> **update()**   Forces all outstanding *drawing* events to be dispatched before the method returns.

The following program creates two shells, then disposes of the second, using update() to force the first shell to draw before running the event loop.

```
public static void main(String[] args) {
    Display display = new Display();
    Shell shell1 = new Shell(display);
    shell1.setText("shell1");
    shell1.setBounds(50, 50, 200, 100);
    shell1.open();
    Shell shell2 = new Shell(display);
    shell2.setText("shell2");
    shell2.setBounds(60, 60, 200, 100);
    shell2.open();
    shell2.dispose();
    System.out.println("Waiting ... shell1 is not drawn.");
    try {Thread.sleep(5000);} catch (Throwable th) {};
    display.update();
    System.out.println("Waiting ... shell1 is drawn.");
```

---

10. To flush outstanding paint events for a single control, see Forcing an Update in the Control Fundamentals chapter.

```
    try {Thread.sleep(5000);} catch (Throwable th) {};
    System.out.println("Running the event loop.");
    while (!shell1.isDisposed()) {
        if (!display.readAndDispatch()) display.sleep();
    }
    display.dispose();
}
```

Instead of using update(), the example code could have flushed all out-standing events by using readAndDispatch() to run an event loop (see the section Reading and Dispatching). This would cause the first shell to draw but would also dispatch any other events that might be pending. In this simple example, the next thing the code does after the update() is to run the event loop, dispatching the events. However, flushing events instead of using update() in order to deliver outstanding redraws is generally disastrous. Consider the following code fragment.

```
shell2.dispose();
while (display.readAndDispatch());
Rectangle rect = shell1.getBounds();
```

Imagine that shell2 has an SWT.Dispose listener that runs a long opera-tion in the user interface thread. The user gets impatient and starts typing, clicking, and closing windows. None of these events is delivered until dis-pose() completes and readAndDispatch() runs, at which point they all come flooding in. Not only does shell1 redraw but the user may have closed it, causing getBounds() in the next line of code to issue SWTException("widget is dis-posed"). The worst part about all of this is that this behavior is nondetermin-istic. Sometimes the bug will happen, sometimes it will not, making it hard to recreate and debug.

The update() Method Is Powerful and Dangerous

Using update() is generally unnecessary and can cause flickering and perfor-mance problems. This is true because update() defeats the merging of drawing events by the operating system.

5.15 Application Data

Displays support setting and getting both named and unnamed data in the same manner as widgets, using the getData() and setData() methods (see the

Application Data section of the Widget Fundamentals chapter). For a typical application, these methods are less useful than their equivalent widget counterparts. Because there is only one display, the extra information that needs to be remembered can be stored anywhere. However, in large applications, where a framework of information about the display is created by one component and accessed by several others, it may make sense to use these methods to annotate the display.

5.15.1 Dismissal Alignment

On some platforms, such as Windows, in a dialog that contains both OK and Cancel buttons, the user interface guidelines specify that the OK button should be on the left. On other platforms, such as GTK and Mac OS X, the OK button is supposed to be on the right.[11] For native dialogs on these platforms, the implementations enforce the rules. For user-created dialogs, you would have to either write platform-specific code or have SWT provide a hint to indicate what the right order is in order to follow the guidelines.

In fact, this phenomenon is not peculiar to the OK and Cancel buttons. In most dialogs, there will be one button that performs the preferred action and dismisses the dialog. The platform user interface guidelines usually specify either that this default button should be **the first button found in "reading" order** (on the left) or that it should be **in the same position relative to the edge of the dialog** (on the right).

SWT provides the following API on class Display, which indicates how to align the button that performs the default action and dismisses the dialog.

> **getDismissalAlignment**() Returns either SWT.LEFT or SWT.RIGHT to indicate whether the button that performs the default action and dismisses a dialog with multiple buttons should be the leftmost or rightmost button.

The following code fragment creates two buttons and uses getDismissal-Alignment() to decide which button is the OK button and which is Cancel.

```
Button b1 = new Button(shell, SWT.PUSH);
Button b2 = new Button(shell, SWT.PUSH);
Button okButton = null, cancelButton = null;
if (display.getDismissalAlignment() == SWT.LEFT) {
    okButton = b1;
```

---

11. For bidirectional locales, where the dialog layouts are flipped left to right, the buttons also switch positions, as you would expect.

```
        cancelButton = b2;
} else {
        cancelButton = b1;
        okButton = b2;
}
okButton.setText("Ok");
cancelButton.setText("Cancel");
```

Later in the code, b1 and b2 can be positioned with b1 appearing before b2. In this manner, the application code does not care which button is actually the OK button and which is the Cancel button.

5.16   Coordinate Mapping and Mirroring

Display provides API to map points and rectangles from one control coordinate system to another. Coordinate mapping is useful when positioning controls with different parents in the same shell. Coordinate mapping is also needed to align controls between shells.

The map() method is used to map coordinates. There are several forms of this method.

> **map(Control from, Control to, int x, int y)**   Returns the equivalent point relative to the *to* control, of the point (x, y) relative to the *from* control. If either *from* or *to* is null, the associated point is treated as being relative to the display.

> **map(Control from, Control to, Point point)**   Equivalent to map(from, to, point.x, point.y).

> **map(Control from, Control to, int x, int y, int width, int height)**   Returns the equivalent rectangle relative to the *to* control of the rectangle located at (x, y) relative to the *from* control, with the same width and height. If either *from* or *to* is null, the associated rectangle is treated as being relative to the display.

> **map(Control from, Control to, Rectangle rectangle)**   Equivalent to map(from, to, rectangle.x, rectangle.y, rectangle.width, rectangle.height).

It is critical to use the map() method for transformations involving rectangles, rather than "doing the math" because of *mirroring*. When a coordinate system is mirrored, the origin, which is normally in the upper left corner of the control, is moved to the upper right. The *x* coordinates increase from right to left instead of left to right. Coordinate mirroring is used to support bidirectional languages, such as Hebrew and Arabic.[12]

Here is an example that attempts to align a shell below a push button when the user presses the button. The example does not use map() and fails because the shell is mirrored.

```
public static void main(String[] args) {
    final Display display = new Display();
    int style = SWT.SHELL_TRIM | SWT.RIGHT_TO_LEFT;
    final Shell shell = new Shell(display, style);
    final Button button = new Button(shell, SWT.PUSH);
    button.setText("Button");
    button.pack();
    button.addListener(SWT.Selection, new Listener() {
        public void handleEvent(Event event) {
            Shell dialog = new Shell(shell, SWT.ON_TOP);
            Rectangle rect = button.getBounds();
            // WRONG - Transforms the top corner of the
            // button (which is in the upper right) to
            // the coordinate system of the Display
            // which gives a point in the upper right
            // but in Display coordinates
            Point pt = shell.toDisplay (rect.x, rect.y);
            pt.y += rect.height;
            dialog.setBounds(pt.x, pt.y, rect.width, 200);
            dialog.setVisible(true);
        }
    });
    shell.pack();
    shell.open();
    while (!shell.isDisposed()) {
        if (!display.readAndDispatch()) display.sleep();
    }
    display.dispose();
}
```

Figure 5.2 shows the results of running this code. As you can see, the shell is in the wrong place.

---

12. A widget that is created with the style SWT.RIGHT_TO_LEFT is mirrored.

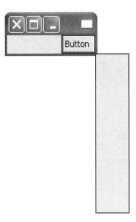

Figure 5.2 A Shell that is incorrectly aligned with a button.

The following code uses map() to correct the alignment problem, as shown in Figure 5.3.

```java
public static void main(String[] args) {
    final Display display = new Display();
    int style = SWT.SHELL_TRIM | SWT.RIGHT_TO_LEFT;
    final Shell shell = new Shell(display, style);
    final Button button = new Button(shell, SWT.PUSH);
    button.setText("Button");
    button.pack();
    button.addListener(SWT.Selection, new Listener() {
        public void handleEvent(Event event) {
            Shell dialog = new Shell(shell, SWT.ON_TOP);
            Rectangle rect = button.getBounds();
            // RIGHT - Transforms the bounds of button
            // (which is a rectangle with origin in the
            // upper right) to the coordinate system of
            // the Display.  This gives a rectangle that
            // is in the Display coordinates with origin
            // on the left
            rect = display.map (shell, null, rect);
            rect.y += rect.height;
            rect.height = 200;
            dialog.setBounds(rect);
            dialog.setVisible(true);
        }
    });
    shell.pack();
    shell.open();
    while (!shell.isDisposed()) {
        if (!display.readAndDispatch()) display.sleep();
    }
    display.dispose();
}
```

Figure 5.3 A Shell that is correctly aligned with a button.

5.17 Miscellaneous

This section contains a few Display methods that did not fit elsewhere.

5.17.1 Beep

Some platforms have a simple way to make a short "warning" noise, which is frequently used to indicate an exceptional condition of some kind. This method will cause the platform hardware to generate such a noise.

beep() Causes the platform hardware to generate a short beep if it supports this capability.

5.17.2 Double-Click Time

Normally, SWT detects double-click events for you and passes them to your application using an SWT.MouseDoubleClick event (see the Events and Listeners section of the Widget Fundamentals chapter). However, it is also possible to identify double-clicks manually by detecting whether the length of time between clicks is below some threshold. Because most operating systems allow users to set their preferred threshold for double-clicks, SWT provides API that returns the platform double-click time.

getDoubleClickTime() Returns the maximum length of time, in milliseconds, that can occur between two mouse clicks in order for the operating system to treat them as a double-click.

5.18 Summary

In this chapter, you learned about the class Display. This class has a rather large API devoted to many different operating system tasks. Two very complex and interrelated topics, the event loop and threading, were discussed in detail. The key point to remember from this discussion is that SWT is apartment-threaded, serializing access to the user interface through the methods syncExec() and asyncExec(). Runnables, queued by these two methods, are executed in the event loop when the user interface thread is idle. Timers were also introduced as another mechanism to queue work.

Much of the rest of the chapter dealt with miscellaneous API whose general theme was "one per application." For example, there is one list of monitors, one primary monitor, one list of Shells, one active Shell, one focus control, one cursor location, and so on. By studying dismissal alignment and coordinate mapping and mirroring, then using the code patterns described in those sections, your application will behave properly on platforms that are sensitive to these issues.

When designing the API for Display, we tried to make it as simple as possible, given the constraint that SWT had to be apartment-threaded. Display is really "the home of the operating system singleton."

CHAPTER 6

Native Widgets

Native widgets are the heart of SWT. We say *widget* here, rather than *control*, because this chapter and the ones that follow describe the subclasses of class Widget, which include controls but also menus, items, and other noncontrols. Because this is such a large topic, we will cover it across several chapters.

Basic Controls: the simplest controls in SWT

Tool Bars and Menus: controls that perform actions

Advanced Controls: tree, table, and tab folder controls

Range-Based Controls: controls that describe a numeric range

Controls, Composites, Groups, and Shells: the container controls

Canvas and Caret: drawing area controls

Draggable Controls: controls that can manipulate the user interface

These chapters are essentially a reference manual for the native widgets that are provided with SWT. For controls that have a particular item type[1] associated with them, the item is described with the control. For example, the section on the ToolBar control also describes the ToolItem widgets that are used with ToolBar.

You can certainly read through these chapters if you wish, but a better strategy might be to read just this overview, then skim over the following chapters the first time you read the book. Then go through the details of the

---

1. That is, a particular subclass of class Item (which is a subclass of class Widget).

sections that describe the widgets that your application will use (and their superclasses). As you work with the native widgets, you can use these chapters as a reference. Each section contains the following.

1. One or more example screenshots showing what the widget looks like

2. A picture showing the class hierarchy for the widget

3. A table of the style constants supported by the widget

4. A table of the events implemented by the widget[2]

5. Several sections that describe the usage and API of the widget

Note that in the interest of brevity, the two tables describe only the styles and event types that are *added* by the widget. To see the full list of supported styles and events, you need to follow the class hierarchy up to class Widget.

The usage sections describe the API for the widget but in addition frequently contain useful hints about the more subtle usage patterns.

6.1   Native Widgets Summary

Figure 6.1 shows the class hierarchy for all of the native widgets provided by SWT. Four abstract classes define the basic structure (these are denoted by a small letter *A* beside the class icon in Figure 6.1).

Widget   This is the root of the widget hierarchy. It defines the life cycle and event-handling API.

Control   Controls are user interface elements that have operating system windows associated with them. These are typically called *heavyweight* widgets.

Scrollable   The superclass of any control that has scroll bars.[3]

Item   Items are user interface elements that typically do not have operating system resources associated with them. These are typically called *lightweight* widgets.

---

2. The table in the Typed Listeners section of the Widget Fundamentals chapter shows the mapping between untyped and typed events for all widgets.

3. Note that this is *not* an interface, despite the name.

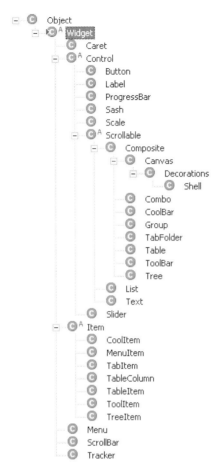

Figure 6.1   Class hierarchy showing all native widgets.

Note that there is an additional class, Decorations, that is treated as an abstract class, although it is not marked as such.[4] This class was intended to be a placeholder for work in SWT to support the multiple-document interface (MDI) API found in Microsoft Windows. As such, the implementation of the Shell API is actually split between Shell and Decorations but is always described as though it were found in class Shell.

What follows are capsule descriptions of the concrete widget classes provided by SWT. As was already noted, these are described in detail in the next

---

4.   This was an oversight that could not be corrected once SWT 1.0 had shipped. You should *never* create an instance of the class Decorations or reference this class anywhere in your code.

few sections that contain images of each widget. This will help if you are having trouble identifying them from their descriptions.

Caret   Caret is an insertion point for text, sometimes called an *I-beam*. This class is useful only in conjunction with class Canvas.

Button   Buttons represent all the buttonlike controls that are normally found in a widget system (push buttons, radio buttons, etc.).

Label   Labels are static, passive controls capable of displaying either text or images. Labels are also used to display "separators" between other controls.

ProgressBar   ProgressBar is used to display activity or degree of completion.

Sash   Sashes are placed between controls and can be positioned by dragging. Note that moving Sash does not automatically reposition the controls that it separates, although you would typically add listeners to do this.

Scale   Scale is a linear potentiometer that is used to measure either discrete or continuous quantities (such as the volume controls on a mixer).

Canvas   Canvas is a general-purpose drawing surface.

Shell   Shell represents all top-level windows on the desktop, including dialog boxes.

Combo   Combo is a combination of Text and List controls used to display a selection of choices in a compact area.

CoolBar and CoolItem   CoolBar displays moveable instances of CoolItem that can contain arbitrary widgets. These are almost exclusively used to position tool bars.

Group   Group is a static control that draws a border around a set of other controls and optionally displays a title.

TabFolder and TabItem   TabFolder displays a row of tab items that have the appearance of pages in a notebook.

Table, TableColumn, and TableItem   Table is used to display tabular data, which can contain both text and images. Each column in the table is represented by TableColumn, and each row is described by TableItem.

ToolBar and ToolItem   ToolBar is used to display one or more rows of buttonlike tool items.

Tree and TreeItem   Tree is used to display hierarchical information, represented by multiple instances of TreeItem that can contain both text and graphics.

List   List displays a single column of tabular data that can contain only text.

Text   Text controls are single- or multiple-line text editors.

Slider   Slider is a kind of scroll bar that can be placed anywhere in a composite.

Menu and MenuItem   Menu allows an action to be chosen from a list of menu items. Menu bars, pull-down menus, and pop-up menus are all represented by instances of class Menu.

ScrollBar   ScrollBar is used to scroll the contents of a control and is automatically positioned along the bottom and right[5] edges of the control.

Tracker   Tracker is used to allow the user to move or resize one or more rectangles on the screen. This kind of action is sometimes called *rubber banding*.

---

5.   On BIDI (bidirectional) locales, this can be the bottom and left edges.

CHAPTER 7

Basic Controls

The simplest controls commonly used in application programs are labels, buttons, texts, lists, and combo boxes. These controls are most often found in dialogs but may also appear in top-level windows. For this reason, studying them is important and a good place to start learning SWT.

Many of the concepts that are introduced in this section also apply to the more complex controls. For example, the "item" classes, associated with trees and tables, often provide API that is very similar to class Button. As well, in this chapter you will encounter some of the fundamental design philosophies of SWT. A firm understanding of the simplest controls in SWT will allow you to move forward to more complex topics.

7.1 Class Label

7.1.1 Example

This is a text label. Below is a separator and a label with an image.

7.1.2 Label Hierarchy

7.1.3 Label Styles

Style	Description
SWT.WRAP	Wrap the text to fit the visible area
SWT.LEFT	Left-align the label
SWT.CENTER	Center-align the label
SWT.RIGHT	Right-align the label
SWT.SEPARATOR	Draw a separator instead of text or an image
SWT.HORIZONTAL	Draw the separator horizontally
SWT.VERTICAL	Draw the separator vertically
SWT.SHADOW_IN	Draw the separator with a "shadow in" effect
SWT.SHADOW_OUT`	Draw the separator with a "shadow out" effect

7.1.4 Label Events (none)

Event	Description

Labels are static widgets that draw text, images, or separators. A *static* control neither takes focus nor participates in tab traversal. Clicking on a static control with the mouse has no effect.

Labels are common, and most programs make use of them. For example, to provide descriptive text, a label is placed in front of a "text entry" field in a dialog. Often a label, acting as a separator, appears in a "wizard" as the line between the wizard content and a row of navigation buttons.

Although it is possible to use SWT graphics operations to draw text, images, and separators, using Label instead ensures that the appropriate operating system theme and colors are used. In addition, because Label is implemented using the underlying native label control, platform-specific automated testing tools and screen readers (used to facilitate computing for the visually impaired) will deal with them correctly.[1]

The following code fragment creates a label using the SWT.NONE style. This is used to indicate that the label will display either text or an image.

```
Label label = new Label(parent, SWT.NONE);
label.setText("User Name:");
```

It is interesting to note that Label does not support events other than those inherited from Control. This is a feature of all static controls in SWT, not just Label.

7.1.5   Text and Images

Labels allow you to set the text or image that they display. If you do not set either, the label is empty. An empty label displays the background color or draws using the operating system theme.

setText(String string)   Sets the text of a label. If the label is a separator, no action is taken. The string can include mnemonic characters (see Specifying the Mnemonic Character) and line delimiters. When the user presses a key sequence that matches the mnemonic, focus is assigned to the "next" control that follows the label. This is usually the next child in the children list of the parent. If no such child exists, a platform-specific algorithm is applied that finds the closest control.

getText()   Returns the label text. This is an empty string if the label is a separator or if the text has never been set.

setImage(Image image)   Sets the image for a label. If the label is a separator, no action is taken.

getImage()   Returns the label image. This is null if the label is a separator or if the image has never been set.

---

1.   This is just another of the many good reasons to "go native," even for very simple controls.

Text or Image But Not Both

As of R3.0, a label can display either a string or an image but not both at the same time.[2] When you set a string and an image, the label displays the last object that you set. This behavior is currently undocumented, so don't rely on it. It is quite possible that a future release of SWT will provide the ability to display both objects. If you need to display both a string and an image in a static control, you can use a CLabel, found in the *org.eclipse.swt.custom* package.

7.1.6 Wrapping

When a label is created with the SWT.WRAP style, it will wrap strings that are too long to fit within the control. If you embed a linefeed character '\n' in the string, the label will always wrap the string at this location. Because the rules for wrapping strings are operating system- and locale-specific and because labels implement these rules correctly, you should use a label to display text that might wrap, rather than writing the code to wrap and draw it yourself.

The following code fragment creates a label and ensures that it will wrap its text. This is achieved by computing the width required to show the string without wrapping, then setting the width of the label to be half of that value.

```
Label label = new Label(parent, SWT.WRAP);
label.setText("This is a label with text that wraps.");
Point size = label.computeSize(SWT.DEFAULT, SWT.DEFAULT);
label.setSize(size.x / 2, 200);
```

Sometimes, even though the SWT.WRAP style is set, when used within Layout (see the Layout chapter), the text does not appear to wrap. For an in-depth discussion of this issue, see Forcing Controls to Wrap in the Layout chapter.

7.1.7 Alignment

If you create a label with one of the SWT.LEFT, SWT.CENTER, or SWT.RIGHT[3] styles, it will horizontally align the text or image. As well as

---

2. This is a platform limitation on X/Motif and Microsoft Windows.

3. As of R3.0, the convenience constants SWT.LEAD and SWT.TRAIL were added to support bidirectional (BIDI) languages. These have the same value as SWT.LEFT and SWT.RIGHT. Because SWT uses *coordinate mirroring* to support BIDI, the use of these convenience constants can make code clearer but is not a requirement. For example, when you left-align a label that was created with the style SWT.RIGHT_TO_LEFT, the result is right-aligned.

using the style bits, the setAlignment() method can be used to change the label alignment after the control has been created.[4]

setAlignment(int alignment)   Sets the alignment of the control to be left-, center-, or right-aligned, depending on the argument, which must be one of SWT.LEFT, SWT.CENTER, or SWT.RIGHT.

getAlignment()   Returns the alignment of the control.

The default alignment for Label is SWT.LEFT. The alignment of a label is typically a property that most programs will not change. Instead, the control itself is often aligned with its siblings using setBounds() or Layout.

7.1.8   Separators

Labels are capable of behaving like separators. A *separator* is a "line" that is drawn by a widget.[5] The number and position of the lines as well as their shading and color are operating system-dependent. Sometimes nothing is drawn at all, depending on the operating system theme.

To create a label that draws a separator, use the SWT.SEPARATOR style. Note that once the label has been created with this style, it will not draw text or an image. Attempts to set and get either of these properties are ignored.

The orientation of the separator is controlled using style bits SWT .HORIZONTAL and SWT.VERTICAL.

The style bits SWT.SHADOW_IN or SWT.SHADOW_OUT are used to specify the appearance of a shadow for the separator on platforms that support this. Because the appearance of the separator is platform-specific and not all platforms support shadows, these style bits will have no effect on some platforms.

One common use for separators, as was described earlier, is to create the line that separates content from buttons in a wizard dialog. The following code fragment creates this kind of separator.

```
Label separator =
    new Label(parent, SWT.SEPARATOR | SWT.SHADOW_OUT);
```

---

4.   This is an example of a method that can change a widget style after the widget has been created.

5.   The separator concept also occurs in MenuItem and ToolItem.

7.2   Class Button

7.2.1   Examples

7.2.2   Button Hierarchy

7.2.3   Button Styles

Style	Description
SWT.ARROW	Draw an arrow instead of text or an image
SWT.CHECK	Create a check button
SWT.PUSH	Create a push button
SWT.RADIO	Create a radio button
SWT.TOGGLE	Create a toggle button
SWT.FLAT	Draw the button with a flat look
SWT.UP	Draw an up arrow
SWT.DOWN	Draw a down arrow
SWT.LEFT	Left-align the button (or draw a left arrow)
SWT.RIGHT	Right-align the button (or draw a right arrow)
SWT.CENTER	Center align the button

7.2.4   Button Events

Event	Description
SWT.Selection	The button was selected

Buttons are simple controls that are commonly found in desktop applications. Aside from their appearance, buttons are fundamentally different from labels: Unlike labels, buttons are active. They react when the user clicks on them and issue events.

> **Where Are All the Button Classes?**
>
> Most widget toolkits provide a hierarchy of Button classes that map to the various kinds of operating system buttons. SWT provides one Button class and uses style bits to specify the appearance and behavior of Button instances. This same approach is used by the native button control on Windows, but more important, it reduces the number of classes needed to represent a similar concept. Reducing the number of classes in the toolkit is one of the design goals of SWT. Fewer classes lead to faster startup times and a smaller memory footprint. There are also fewer classes for you to learn.

7.2.5   *Text and Images*

Buttons support text and images using methods with the same signatures as Label. One interesting difference between strings in Button versus Label is that Button does not support SWT.WRAP or the linefeed character. This means that more than one line of text cannot be displayed in a button. Like labels, buttons can display either text or an image but not both at the same time (see the Text or Image but Not Both box earlier in this chapter for details).

> **setText(String string)**   Sets the text of the button. This string may include mnemonic characters (see Specifying the Mnemonic Character) but *cannot* include line delimiters.

> **getText()**   Returns the button text. This is an empty string if the text has never been set.

> **setImage(Image image)**   Sets the image for a button.

> **getImage()**   Returns the button image. This is null if the image has never been set.

Despite the fact that images are supported, buttons that display images are generally uncommon. Tool bars are almost always used instead (see Classes ToolBar and ToolItem).

7.2.6 *Alignment*

You can horizontally align the button text or the image using one of the SWT .LEFT, SWT.CENTER, or SWT.RIGHT style bits, or the setAlignment() method.

> **setAlignment(int alignment)**   Sets the alignment of the control to be left-, center-, or right-aligned, depending on the argument, which must be one of SWT.LEFT, SWT.CENTER, or SWT.RIGHT.

> **getAlignment()**   Returns the alignment of the control.

Button alignment is something that is rarely used in programs. Normally, you should not override the default alignment of a button because the default matches the standard appearance for the operating system. If you change the alignment of the buttons in your application, it may look out of place.

7.2.7 *Push Buttons*

Push buttons are created using the style SWT.PUSH. They are often used within a program to launch an action. For example, programs often use push buttons to allow the user to move forward in a wizard dialog, choose Yes in a message box, or to get more details in an error dialog.

When pushed, buttons draw in a pressed state. The user normally releases it at once, causing it to return to an unpressed state. If the mouse is released inside a button, an SWT.Selection event is issued. Application programs use this event to launch an action. Unlike other buttons, push buttons do not maintain their selected or unselected state between SWT.Selection events. They are considered to be always unselected.

The following code fragment creates a push button and sets the text to the string "Ok".

```
Button button = new Button(parent, SWT.PUSH);
button.setText("Ok");
```

7.2.8 *Check Buttons*

Check buttons are created with the style SWT.CHECK. They differ from push buttons in that they maintain a boolean selection state.[6] The user toggles the selection state of a check button using the mouse or the keyboard.

---

6. Outside of SWT, the selection state of a check button is more commonly called the *checked* or *unchecked* state.

The appearance of a selected check button varies between platforms. For example, on some platforms, a check button draws an *x* when selected, whereas on others it draws a diamond.

You can set the selection state of a check button using the setSelection() method.

setSelection(boolean selection)   Sets the selection state for the button. If the button is a check, radio, or toggle button, the new selection is assigned.

getSelection()   Returns a boolean that is the selection for the button.

The following code fragment creates a check button, sets the text to the string "Overwrite when typing", then selects the button, causing it to be checked.

```
Button button = new Button(parent, SWT.CHECK);
button.setText("Overwrite when typing");
button.setSelection(true);
```

Calling setSelection() Does Not Cause an SWT.Selection Event

Programmers new to SWT often find this behavior confusing. After a long and arduous debate within the SWT community, it was decided that sending the event caused more problems than it solved. For example, if the SWT.Selection event were to be sent from setSelection(), multiple calls to this method would cause the listeners to run for each call, causing potential performance problems. As a result, it was decided that in SWT, setSelection() would *not* cause an SWT.Selection event.

Check buttons are mainly used to represent boolean state in a program. Very often, check buttons can be found in "preference" dialogs. Preference dialogs show the user the options available in a program and those that are selected. Although check buttons issue the SWT.Selection event when the user selects them, unlike push buttons, this event is generally not used to invoke an action. In the case of the preferences dialog, the action that accompanies the change in selection is performed when the dialog is closed (or when an *apply* push button in the dialog is pressed).[7]

---

7. On the Macintosh, well-behaved programs do not do this. Instead, options are applied as the user selects them in the dialog. If you want to implement the Macintosh behavior, you can do so by watching for SWT.Selection events and invoking the action right away.

When a group of check buttons appears together, selecting one check button in the group does *not* affect the selection state of others.

7.2.9   Radio Buttons

Radio buttons, created using the SWT.RADIO style, are common user interface elements. Like check buttons, they maintain a boolean state between selections. However, when multiple radio buttons have the same parent, only one button can be selected at a time. When the user selects another radio button, the previous radio button loses its selection state. This is called *radio behavior*.[8]

The following code creates three radio buttons that allow the user to configure the word wrap state of a hypothetical text editor.

```
Button button1 = new Button(parent, SWT.RADIO);
button1.setText("Don't wrap");
button1.setSelection(true);
Button button2 = new Button(parent, SWT.RADIO);
button2.setText("Wrap to window");
Button button3 = new Button(parent, SWT.RADIO);
button3.setText("Wrap to ruler");
```

Radio buttons typically represent enumerations in a program. For example, in the code fragment above, they could be used to indicate three possible word wrap states of a text editor. Although not necessarily the case, in the source code for the editor, there would probably be an enumeration for the three wrap states and a variable to keep track of the current state. If this were the case, the following code fragment could be used to initialize the state of each radio button.

```
button1.setSelection(wrap == WRAP_NONE);
button2.setSelection(wrap == WRAP_WINDOW);
button3.setSelection(wrap == WRAP_RULER);
```

When to Use a Radio Button

Using a single radio button is almost certainly an error. Given that only one radio button in a group can be selected, the button will always be selected. In this case, a check button should be used instead.

---

8. It is very likely that the term *radio* refers to the row of buttons that were found on the car radios of the '50s and '60s. These buttons also exhibited the behavior that only one could be pressed at a time.

Two radio buttons can be replaced by one check button. This is because a boolean and an enumeration with two states are equivalent. Of course, there are cases where it makes more sense to use two radio buttons instead of a single check button. For example, two radio buttons that offer a choice between *"Red"* or *"Green"* make more sense than a single check button to turn *"Red"* on or off.

Unfortunately, radio buttons can use lots of screen space. For example, an enumeration that contains 10 states will require 10 radio buttons. To minimize the required screen space, sometimes a read-only combo box is used in place of multiple radio buttons (see the Combo section).

If for some reason you need radio buttons that do not have radio behavior, the SWT.NO_RADIO_GROUP style, when specified **on the parent**, allows you to disable it. This style is almost never used because radio buttons without radio behavior are confusing to the user.

7.2.10   Toggle Buttons

Toggle buttons are push buttons that remain pressed when selected. They are created with the style SWT.TOGGLE.

```
Button button = new Button(parent, SWT.TOGGLE);
button.setText("Play");
button.setSelection(true);
```

Toggle buttons should generally be avoided. Before tool bars were invented, toggle buttons and push buttons were sometimes used to implement tool bar behavior. Programs that do this today look dated.

Because toggle buttons maintain their selection, every place you might use a toggle button, a check button can be used instead. Probably the only place where a toggle button might be useful is to model a physical button that is expected to stay pressed. For example, a toggle button would look better than a check button when implementing a software DVD player.

7.2.11   Arrow Buttons

Arrow buttons are buttons that draw a small, arrow-shaped icon. The arrow shape is platform-specific and is not guaranteed to match the arrow part of a scroll bar, although it is often similar.

Arrow buttons are created with the style SWT.ARROW. They can be made to point in one of four directions using the constants SWT.LEFT, SWT.RIGHT, SWT.UP, and SWT.DOWN.

```
Button button = new Button(parent, SWT.ARROW);
button.setAlignment(SWT.RIGHT);
```

Arrow buttons are uncommon. Occasionally, they are used to allow users to navigate through data one page at a time. More often, operations such as "next page" and "previous page" are presented to the user as icons on a tool bar.

7.2.12   Button Events

SWT.Selection (SelectionEvent)

The SWT.Selection event (typed event SelectionEvent) is sent when the user clicks on a button with the mouse or activates it with the keyboard. The space bar or <Enter> key usually activates a button (but this is not guaranteed on all platforms). The selection event for Button contains meaningful values in only the *display*, *widget*, and *type* fields.

The following code fragment prints "Ok Pressed" when a button is selected.

```
button.addListener(SWT.Selection, new Listener() {
    public void handleEvent(Event event) {
        System.out.println("Ok Pressed");
    }
});
```

Sometimes programmers are confused by the fact that SWT.Selection is sent whenever the user causes the state of a button to change. The rationale should be obvious with some reflection, but the result has subtle implications for radio buttons.

Using SWT.Selection with Radio Buttons

First of all, SWT.Selection is rarely used with radio buttons. Like check buttons, radio buttons often appear in dialogs. On most operating systems, programs do not take action until the dialog is closed.

Surprisingly, when the user selects a radio button in a group of radio buttons, two SWT.Selection events are sent. The previously selected radio button receives an SWT.Selection event indicating that the selection state has been changed to false. The newly selected radio button gets an SWT.Selection event to indicate that its selection state is now true. It sometimes helps to understand why there are two SWT.Selection events if you imagine for a moment that radio buttons did not support radio behavior. Hypothetically, the first event would be generated when the user clicked to "turn off" the first radio button, and the second event would be generated when the user clicked to "turn on" the second button.

If you want to perform an action when the user selects a radio button, you almost always need to get the selection before performing the action. The following code fragment uses getSelection() to ensure that the arriving message is printed once each time the user selects a radio button.

```
Listener listener = new Listener() {
    public void handleEvent(Event event) {
        Button button = (Button) event.widget;
        if (!button.getSelection()) return;
        System.out.println(
"Arriving " + button.getText());
    }
};
Button land = new Button(shell, SWT.RADIO);
land.setText("By Land");
land.addListener(SWT.Selection, listener);
Button sea = new Button(shell, SWT.RADIO);
sea.setText("By Sea");
sea.addListener(SWT.Selection, listener);
sea.setSelection(true);
```

Figure 7.1 shows this code fragment running within Shell.

Figure 7.1   Using SWT.Selection with two radio buttons.

7.3   Class Text

7.3.1   Example

This is a text widget

7.3.2 Text Hierarchy

7.3.3 Text Styles

Style	Description
SWT.SINGLE	Allow a single line to be edited
SWT.MULTI	Allow multiple lines to be edited
SWT.READ_ONLY	Make the control noneditable
SWT.WRAP	Allow strings to wrap instead of scrolling
SWT.LEFT	Left-align the contents of the control
SWT.CENTER	Center-align the contents of the control
SWT.RIGHT	Right-align the contents of the control

7.3.4 Text Events

Event	Description
SWT.DefaultSelection	Default selection occurred (user pressed <Enter>)
SWT.Modify	Text has changed in the control
SWT.Verify	Text is to be validated in the control

Text controls are common user interface elements that allow the user to edit strings. Text controls are selectable. The selection in a text control is the insertion point for characters. If the selection extends over one or more characters, the text control indicates this by drawing the selected characters in a different manner than the unselected characters. If the selection does not extend over any characters, it is indicated by a caret (also called an *I-beam*). A *caret* is a thin vertical line that appears between characters. The caret provides a visual cue for the user, indicating where keystrokes will go. On some platforms, the caret blinks to get attention.

Text controls support only "plain" text. This means that all characters in the control are the same font and color. Applications that need a more flexible text editing control can use *org.eclipse.swt.custom.StyledText*, which was designed for use by Eclipse. Note that StyledText is *not* a native widget.

It is common for an application program to detect when a text control has changed or to filter characters as they are typed. For example, a program may want to prompt the user to save changes when the shell is closed or ensure that only digits can be entered. To do this, programs listen for the SWT.Modify and SWT.Verify events, described later in this section.

There are two kinds of text controls: those that can contain only a single line of text and those that can contain multiple lines of text.

7.3.5 Single-Line and Multiline Text Controls

The SWT.SINGLE style is used to create single-line text controls. The following code fragment creates a single-line text control with a border, then sets the contents of the control to the string "Texan".

```
Text text = new Text(parent, SWT.SINGLE | SWT.BORDER);
text.setText("Texan");
```

Multiline text controls are created with the style SWT.MULTI. Unlike their single-line counterparts, they can include scroll bars. Scroll bars are created when you specify the SWT.H_SCROLL or SWT.V_SCROLL styles. The following code fragment creates a multiline text control with a border and scroll bars.

```
int style =
    SWT.MULTI | SWT.BORDER | SWT.V_SCROLL | SWT.H_SCROLL;
Text text = new Text(parent, style);
```

In the following sections, some concepts apply to one or both kinds of text controls. When a concept applies to only one type of text control, this is indicated in the discussion.

7.3.6 String Operations

Text controls support setting and getting their text in the same manner as Button, Label, and many other widgets in SWT.

setText(String string)   Sets the contents of the text control to the specified string. The previous contents are cleared, the new string inserted, and the I-beam is placed just before the first character. If the text control has the style SWT.SINGLE and the string contains line delimiters, the behavior is undefined. For more information about line delimiters, see Line Delimiters in this section. Mnemonic characters are not supported in Text controls.

getText()   Returns a string that is the contents of the text control. If the string has never been set, an empty string is returned.

getText(int start, int end)   Returns a substring of the text that is contained in the text control. The substring includes characters in the range from *start* to *end*, including both the start and end indices. Indexing starts from zero. If the indices are out of range, as many characters as possible that are within the range are returned.

Indexing and Range Operations in SWT

To be consistent with the indexing model used by Java, indexing operations in SWT start from zero. Unfortunately, ranges in SWT include both the start and the end of the interval and do not follow the Java standard. For example, Text.getText(int, int) includes the last character, whereas substring(int, int) does not. This was simply a mistake on our part.

Ranges in SWT are consistent but different from the Java standard. Unfortunately, we can't fix this problem due to backward compatibility issues, even though the Java standard is arguably better (it admits the possibility of an empty range). At this point, any new API in SWT will also have to follow the SWT range convention. The issue here is that we believe consistency to be more important than being "correct" in some places and "wrong" in others. Some people don't agree with this philosophy, but nonetheless, it is one of the fundamental SWT design decisions.

getCharCount()   Returns the number of characters in the text control. It is much faster to use this method than to use getText() to get the contents, then ask the resulting string for its length().

7.3.7 Passwords and the Echo Character

Single-line text controls can be used to obtain a password from the user. As the user types, a specific character (called the *echo character*) is displayed instead of the one that was typed. The SWT.PASSWORD style is used to create text controls that display in this fashion. The following code fragment uses SWT.PASSWORD to create a single-line text control capable of acquiring a password from the user.

```
int style = SWT.SINGLE | SWT.BORDER | SWT.PASSWORD;
Text text = new Text(parent, style);
text.setText("fred54"); //this text won't be displayed
```

Note that the echo character is platform-specific and can change between themes and even between releases of the operating system.[9] To force the echo character to be the same on every platform, the setEchoChar() method can be used.

> **setEchoChar(char echo)**   Sets the character that will be displayed as the user types. If the *echo* character is '\0', the control no longer hides characters, and the current text is displayed.

> **getEchoChar()**   Returns the character that was set by setEchoChar(). If an echo character was not set, '\0' is returned, indicating that the control is drawing characters normally. When the SWT.PASSWORD style is used, the result of getEchoChar() is undefined.

Generally speaking, it is unwise to set the echo character because it is part of the platform look and feel.

7.3.8   *Lines and Line Height*

You can query the number of lines in a text control and the height of each line using getLineCount() and getLineHeight().

> **getLineCount()**   Returns the number of lines in the control. If the control is a single-line text control, the integer 1 is returned.

> **getLineHeight()**   Returns the height of a line in the control in pixels. This value can be different from the height of the font that is in use by the control because some platforms include extra space between lines.

The getLineHeight() method is used mainly when computing the initial size of a text control. The following program uses getLineHeight() and Font-

---

9.   This is exactly what happened between releases of Windows 2000 and XP. The asterisk charac-
      ter, echoed on Windows 2000, was changed to a large dot on Windows XP.

Metrics (see Class FontMetrics in the Fonts chapter) to set the size of a multi-line text control so that it displays about five rows of text and is about ten characters wide.

```
public static void main(String[] args) {
    Display display = new Display();
    Shell shell = new Shell(display);
    Text text = new Text(shell, SWT.H_SCROLL|SWT.V_SCROLL);
    int rows = 5, columns = 10;
    GC gc = new GC(text);
    FontMetrics fm = gc.getFontMetrics();
    gc.dispose();
    int height = rows * text.getLineHeight();
    int width = columns * fm.getAverageCharWidth();
    text.setSize(text.computeSize (width, height));
    shell.pack();
    shell.open();
    while (!shell.isDisposed()) {
        if (!display.readAndDispatch()) display.sleep();
    }
    display.dispose();
}
```

Figure 7.2 shows the result of running this example and typing three lines of text into the control.

Figure 7.2

7.3.9 Line Delimiters

Different operating systems use different line delimiters to separate lines in multiline text controls.[10] Because SWT uses the native text control and cannot

---

10. Note that we are talking about the delimiters used by *text controls* here: On Windows, the line delimiter is "\r\n". On X/Motif and GTK, the delimiter is "\n". On the Macintosh, it is "\r". This should not be confused with the line delimiter used when storing text files on disk, which may be different, as it is on Mac OS X.

change the delimiter that it uses, strings are processed by SWT text controls using these platform-specific line delimiters.[11]

Using the line delimiter for one platform when running on another can cause portability problems. To ensure that you always use the right delimiter, you can use the constant Text.DELIMITER or the method getLineDelimiter().

getLineDelimiter()   Returns the line delimiter for the text control.

The following code fragment sets the contents of a multiline Text control to contain three lines of text.

```
String lf = Text.DELIMITER;
text.setText("Line 1" + lf + "Line 2" + lf + "Line 3");
```

As a convenience, multiline text controls can also accept text that is delimited using "\n" on every platform. This means that using the text control line delimiter is not absolutely necessary when *setting* text into a text control. However, when text is queried back, the string that is returned uses the platform delimiter. Thus, making use of this convenience is problematic for all but the simplest uses of the control. For example, if your code computes string offsets in a string delimited by "\n", these offsets will not match character positions in the text control on Microsoft Windows. The best way to avoid this kind of error is to ensure that the source string also uses the operating system delimiter. Because the text control will accept "\n" as a delimiter, one possible way to convert the string is using setText() and getText(), like the following.

```
String string = "Line 1\nLine 2\nLine 3\nLine 4";
text.setText(string);
string = text.getText();
```

7.3.10   The Selection

Substrings within a text control can be selected using the setSelection() method. This method takes a selection range. Indices are zero-based and describe a range of integer selection positions anywhere from *0* to *N*, where *N* is the number of characters in the control.

At first glance, it might seem that including the *N*th "character" in the selection range is an error. However, this makes sense because selection indices address caret positions, not characters. Caret positions occur between charac-

---

11. This was a necessity. Because the delimiters can be different lengths, attempting to convert the delimiters automatically would have required either continuous linear scans of the contents or impossible amounts of internal bookkeeping.

ters. Given *N* characters, there are *N+1* possible caret positions. To address *N+1* positions, the indices *0* to *N* are needed.

Figure 7.3 shows the caret positions in a string that is five characters long:

Figure 7.3   Caret positions in a string within a text control.

When the start of the selection is the same as the end, the selection range is empty, and an I-beam is displayed.

> **setSelection(int start, int end)**   Sets the selection in the text control. All characters between the *start* and *end* **caret positions** are selected. When *start* and *end* are the same, the selection becomes an I-beam. If any of the indices are out of range, as much text as possible that is within the bounds of the text is selected. The text control is scrolled to ensure that the user sees the new selection.

> **setSelection(int start)**   Sets the selection in the text control. This method is the same as calling setSelection(start, start).

> **setSelection(Point selection)**   Sets the selection in a text control. This method is the same as calling setSelection(selection.x, selection.y).

Why Is Point Used to Represent the Selection in a Text Control?

The earliest versions of SWT represented selection in a text control using an integer array. Subsequently, it was decided that the integer array was too confusing, and a Range class was introduced. The Range class had *start* and *end* fields. Then it was decided that the Range class added little value because it provided only two fields and had no operations. Because one of the design decisions of SWT is to minimize the number of classes, the Range class was removed and Point was used instead. We admit it's a bit confusing (but not harmful).

> **selectAll()**   Selects all the text in the text control. This method is the same as calling setSelection(0, text.getCharCount()) but is slightly faster because it avoids getting the number of characters in the control.

clearSelection()   Clears the selection, causing it to draw as an I-beam.

Is the clearSelection() Method Necessary?

It seems on the surface that setting the start of the selection equal to the end should be equivalent to calling clearSelection(). The problem with this is determining where the I-beam should be placed. There are two possibilities: either the start or the end of the previous selection. It turns out that choosing one over the other is not straightforward. Among other factors, the position of the I-beam within the selection depends on the direction that the user has selected text with the mouse. For example, when the user selects from left to right, the I-beam is placed at the end of the selection. If the user selects from right to left, the I-beam is at the start. Using clearSelection() ensures that the I-beam does not move when the selection is cleared, making it a necessary API for text controls.

---

getSelection()   Returns a point that represents the selection. The x coordinate is the start index, and the y coordinate is the end index of the selection range.

The following code fragment uses setSelection(int, int) to select the word *There* in a text control.

```
text.setText("Hello There Fred!");
text.setSelection(6, 11);
```

The following program creates a shell and a text control and initializes it, then uses setSelection(int, int) to select the first occurrence of the string "word" in the control. Figure 7.4 shows the result of running this example.

```
public static void main(String[] args) {
    Display display = new Display();
    Shell shell = new Shell(display);
    shell.setLayout(new FillLayout());
    int style = SWT.V_SCROLL | SWT.H_SCROLL | SWT.BORDER;
    Text text = new Text(shell, style);
    text.setText("Here is\na word that\nneeds selecting.");
    shell.setSize(200, 200);
    shell.open();
    String string = "word";
    int index = text.getText().indexOf(string);
    if (index != -1) {
        text.setSelection(index, index + string.length());
    }
    while (!shell.isDisposed()) {
```

```
            if (!display.readAndDispatch()) display.sleep();
        }
        display.dispose();
}
```

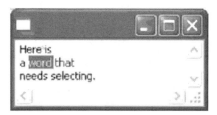

Figure 7.4   Selecting a word in a text control.

7.3.11   Inserting and Appending

Characters are inserted into a text control using the insert() method. Insertion always happens at the selection. It is not possible to insert text at an arbitrary location within a text control without first moving the selection to the new location.[12]

If the selection is an I-beam, the new text is inserted, as you would expect. If the selection is a range, the characters within the range are deleted, making the selection an I-beam and inserting the new characters. If you think about it, the insert() method behaves as though the characters were typed into the control.

> **insert(String string)**   Inserts a string into the text control. The new string replaces the current selection. The control is scrolled to show the new string, and the I-beam is placed at the end of the string.

The following code fragment first selects *There*, then replaces it with the string "New Text".

```
text.setText("Hello There Fred!");
text.setSelection(6, 11);
text.insert("New Text");
```

Inserting a string at the end of a text control is very a common operation. For this reason, the convenience operation append() is provided.

---

12. This fact of life was dictated by the native Windows text control that does not provide API to insert characters anywhere else.

append(String string)   Inserts a string at the end of the text control. The control is scrolled to show the new string, and the I-beam is placed at the end of the control.

Appending a string is equivalent to setting the selection to the end of the control, inserting the new string, then setting the selection to the end once more. The following code fragment uses append() to append the string "New Text". It then performs the equivalent operation with the string "More New Text" using the methods setSelection() and insert().

```
text.append("New Text");
text.setSelection (text.getCharCount());
text.insert("More new text");
text.setSelection(text.getCharCount());
```

7.3.12   *Wrapping*

When a multiline text control is created with the SWT.WRAP style, it will wrap any line that cannot be fully displayed in the control.

If you provide both the SWT.WRAP and SWT.H_SCROLL styles, SWT.H_SCROLL is ignored (i.e., the control will not create a horizontal scroll bar). A horizontal scroll bar is used to allow text lines that are wider than the width of the control to be fully seen so that, given that this cannot happen if the text is wrapped, the scroll bar is unnecessary.

For more information about wrapping, see Labels That Wrap.

7.3.13   *Clipboard Operations*

Text controls provide the copy(), cut(), and paste() clipboard operations. Text controls also support platform-specific keystrokes to perform these operations within the control.

Some platforms provide a built-in Cut/Copy/Paste context menu. The clipboard operation methods are useful whenever you want to build your own context menu that contains these operations.

cut()   Cuts the selection to the clipboard. The characters within the selection range are placed on the clipboard, then deleted from the text control.

copy()   Copies the selection to the clipboard. The characters within selection range are placed on the clipboard. The text control is unaffected.

paste()   Pastes text from the clipboard. The characters within selection range are replaced with the contents of the clipboard.

7.3.14 *Scrolling*

Text controls, along with the other controls that scroll in SWT, use the concept of *top index* to determine where to scroll. The top index of a text control is the zero-relative index of the **topmost visible line** in the control. For single-line text controls, the top index is always zero. The top index is set using the setTopIndex() method.

> **setTopIndex(int index)**   Scrolls by positioning the line indicated by the index at the top of the control. Indexing starts at zero. If the index is out of range, the control scrolls to show the closest index that is within the text contents. Depending on the platform and the number of lines, it may not be possible for the particular line to be placed at the top of the control. This can happen when the platform does not allow the control to scroll so that white space follows that last line.

> **getTopIndex()**   Returns the index of the line that is at the top of the control. The top index can change for many reasons other than calling setTopIndex(). For example, as the user enters new lines of text, the control may scroll, changing the top index.

Sometimes you might need to bring the selection to the attention of the user. The showSelection() method is used to scroll the control so that the selection is visible. Note that calling showSelection() after setSelection() is unnecessary because setSelection() already scrolls to show the new selection. However, there are circumstances where the selection may have changed and scrolled out of view.

> **showSelection()**   Scrolls to show the selection. The selection is made visible somewhere inside the control. If the selection is already visible, nothing happens.

7.3.15 *Text Limits*

Some programs, particularly those that interact with databases, might need to restrict the amount of text that can be entered into a text control. For example, they do this to ensure that they do not attempt to store more characters in a database field than it will accept.

setTextLimit(int limit)   Sets the text limit. This is the number of characters that the control can contain. If the user attempts to type in more characters than the control can hold, the new characters are discarded. When this happens, the control issues a platform-specific warning, usually in the form of a short beep. You can limit the number of characters that a text control can contain using setTextLimit().

getTextLimit()   Returns the text limit. If no limit has been set, this is the maximum number of characters that the control can contain.

7.3.16   Text Events

SWT.DefaultSelection (SelectionEvent)

The SWT.DefaultSelection event (typed event SelectionEvent) is sent whenever the user presses the <Enter> key for *single-line* text controls or uses a platform-specific mechanism to cause the event. Multiline text controls do not send the event, instead using the <Enter> key to insert a new line. The default selection event for a text control contains meaningful values in only the *display, widget,* and *type* fields.

SWT.Modify (ModifyEvent)

Table 7.1 shows the modify event for text controls.

Table 7.1   Modify Event

Untyped Event	Description	
SWT.Modify	Text has changed in the control	
Typed Event	**Listener**	**Methods**
ModifyEvent	ModifyListener	modifyText(ModifyEvent)

The SWT.Modify event (typed event ModifyEvent) is sent *after* characters have been inserted or deleted from a text control. The event is sent both when the user types and when the program changes the characters in the control. Modify events contain meaningful values in only the *display, widget,* and *type* fields.

Using SWT.Modify to Check Changes before Closing a Shell

The following example uses the SWT.Modify event to track the modified state of a text control. In the example, the text control is considered modified when characters have been entered that have not been saved. When the shell is closed, the user is prompted to save the changes, as shown in Figure 7.5. Note that when the program modifies the text control by setting the initial string, the modified flag must be cleared. This is necessary because SWT.Modify is sent *any* time the characters within the text control are changed.

```
public static void main(String[] args) {
    Display display = new Display();
    final Shell shell = new Shell(display);
    shell.setText("ModifyExample");
    shell.setLayout(new FillLayout());
    int style = SWT.V_SCROLL | SWT.H_SCROLL | SWT.BORDER;
    Text text = new Text(shell, style);
    final boolean[] modified = new boolean [1];
    text.addListener(SWT.Modify, new Listener() {
        public void handleEvent(Event e) {
            modified[0] = true;
        }
    });
    shell.addListener(SWT.Close, new Listener() {
        public void handleEvent(Event e) {
            if (!modified[0]) return;
            int style = SWT.PRIMARY_MODAL |
            SWT.YES | SWT.NO | SWT.CANCEL;
            MessageBox box = new MessageBox(shell, style);
            box.setText(shell.getText());
            box.setMessage("Save changes?");
            switch (box.open()) {
                case SWT.YES:
                    System.out.println ("Saving ...");
                    // if (!saveText()) break;
                    //FALL THROUGH
                case SWT.NO :
                    break;
                case SWT.CANCEL :
                    e.doit = false;
                    break;
            }
        }
    });
    text.setText("Initial text.");
    modified[0] = false;
    shell.setSize(200, 200);
    shell.open();
    while (!shell.isDisposed()) {
        if (!display.readAndDispatch()) display.sleep();
    }
    display.dispose();
}
```

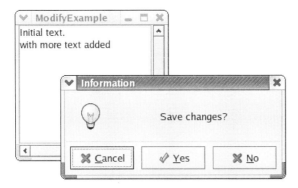

Figure 7.5

This example is simple. It does not include the code that loads or saves the contents of the text control to a file. As well as performing the appropriate operation, code that loaded or saved the contents of the text control would need to clear the modified flag. This is necessary to allow the flag to be reset the next time the user types a character.

Using SWT.Modify to Warn the User of Invalid Input

Sometimes a program will warn the user with an error message when an invalid character is typed. This allows users temporarily to enter invalid input and fix it at their leisure. The SWT.Modify event is perfect for this task, because it is sent after the characters have been entered.

The following example warns the user when a character that is not a letter or a digit is typed into a text control. The warning message is displayed in a label that appears underneath the text control. To ensure that the warning message is valid, it is updated after every character. This ensures that when the user fixes the error, the warning message disappears.

```
public static void main(String[] args) {
    Display display = new Display();
    final Shell shell = new Shell(display);
    shell.setLayout(new RowLayout(SWT.VERTICAL));
    final Text text = new Text(shell, SWT.BORDER);
    text.setLayoutData(new RowData(250, SWT.DEFAULT));
    final Label label = new Label(shell, SWT.NONE);
    text.addListener(SWT.Modify, new Listener() {
        public void handleEvent(Event event) {
            String string = text.getText();
            int index = 0;
            while (index < string.length()) {
                char ch = string.charAt(index);
                if (!Character.isLetterOrDigit(ch)) break;
                index++;
```

```
            }
            if (index != string.length()) {
                label.setText(
                    "Must contain only letters and digits");
            } else {
                label.setText("");
            }
            shell.layout();
        }
    });
    shell.pack();
    shell.open();
    while (!shell.isDisposed()) {
        if (!display.readAndDispatch()) display.sleep();
    }
    display.dispose();
}
```

Figure 7.6 shows this example running after the user has typed the string "Hello?".

Figure 7.6

SWT.Verify (VerifyEvent)

Table 7.2 shows the verify event for a text control.

Table 7.2   Verify Event

Untyped Event		Description
SWT.Verify		Text is to be validated in the control
Typed Event	**Listener**	**Methods**
VerifyEvent	VerifyListener	verifyText(VerifyEvent)

The SWT.Verify event (typed event VerifyEvent) is sent *before* characters are inserted or deleted from a text control. The event is sent both when the user types and when the program changes the characters in the control. The relevant event fields during a verify event for a text control are as follows.

Public Fields of Class Event That Are Valid during SWT.Verify

Field	Description
doit	Setting *doit* to false cancels the operation
text	The text that is about to be inserted
start	The start of the selection that will be replaced
end	The end of the selection that will be replaced

In contrast to the SWT.Modify event, because SWT.Verify is sent before the text control is changed, the program can filter the string that is about to be entered or cancel the operation. The following example uses the SWT.Verify event to allow only digits to be entered into a single-line text control:

```
public static void main(String[] args) {
    Display display = new Display();
    Shell shell = new Shell(display);
    Text text = new Text(shell, SWT.BORDER | SWT.SINGLE);
    text.setSize (text.computeSize (128, SWT.DEFAULT));
    text.addListener(SWT.Verify, new Listener() {
        public void handleEvent(Event e) {
            String text = e.text;
            char[] chars = new char[text.length()];
            text.getChars(0, chars.length, chars, 0);
            for (int i = 0; i < chars.length; i++) {
                if (!('0' <= chars[i] && chars[i] <= '9')){
                    e.doit = false;
                    return;
                }
            }
        }
    });
    shell.pack();
    shell.open();
    while (!shell.isDisposed()) {
        if (!display.readAndDispatch()) display.sleep();
    }
    display.dispose();
}
```

The SWT.Verify event contains sufficient information to maintain a copy of the contents of a text control. The following example implements a text control that emulates the SWT.PASSWORD style, inserting an asterisk for every character the user types or pastes into the text, as shown in Figure 7.7. The actual string that the user entered is stored in the variable *string*.

```
static String string = "";
public static void main(String[] args) {
    Display display = new Display();
    Shell shell = new Shell(display);
    Text text = new Text(shell, SWT.BORDER | SWT.SINGLE);
    text.setSize(text.computeSize(128, SWT.DEFAULT));
    text.addListener(SWT.Verify, new Listener() {
        public void handleEvent(Event e) {
            String prefix = string.substring(0, e.start);
            String suffix =
                string.substring(e.end, string.length());
            string = prefix + e.text + suffix;
            int length = e.text.length();
            e.text = "";
            for (int i = 0; i < length; i++) e.text += '*';
        }
    });
    shell.pack();
    shell.open();
    while (!shell.isDisposed()) {
        if (!display.readAndDispatch()) display.sleep();
    }
    System.out.println("String is " + string + ".");
    display.dispose();
}
```

Figure 7.7

7.4   Class List

7.4.1   Example

7.4.2   List Hierarchy

7.4.3   List Styles

Style	Description
SWT.MULTI	Create a list that can have multiple items selected
SWT.SINGLE	Create a list that can have only one item selected

7.4.4   List Events

Event	Description
SWT.Selection	The user selected an item
SWT.DefaultSelection	The user double-clicked on an item

Lists allow the user to select one or more strings from a collection of strings. The strings are presented to the user in a single column.

Lists provide a rich API to manipulate their contents. Because List allows duplicates, the most useful methods in the class are index-based, because using indices allows you to specify exactly which item in the list will be referenced.

Where Do I Use a List?

At one time, before icons ruled the user interface, lists were ubiquitous. Programs used them to show most kinds of data. These days, lists are uncommon. For example, lists are sometimes used to show key words in a Help dialog, but tables are used for almost everything else. If your application needs to display a list of strings, use a list. Otherwise, you should consider using a table (see the section Classes Table, TableItem, and TableColumn). In particular, you should use a table if you want to display an icon beside each item.

In the descriptions that follow, the term *item* is used interchangeably with *string*. This is done on purpose because some of the concepts and behaviors that are first mentioned in class List, which uses String, also apply to class Table, which uses TableItem.

7.4.5 Single- and Multiselect Lists

There are two kinds of lists in SWT: single-select and multiselect. Lists that allow only a single item to be selected at a time are called *single-select* lists. They are constructed by using the style SWT.SINGLE. Similarly, lists that allow multiple items to be selected are called *multiselect* lists and can be constructed by specifying the style constant SWT.MULTI.

Just like text controls, lists can include scroll bars and borders. The following code fragment creates a single-select list that has a border and vertical and horizontal scroll bars.

```
List list = new List (SWT.SINGLE | SWT.BORDER |
    SWT.V_SCROLL | SWT.H_SCROLL);
```

7.4.6 Setting Items

Typically, the contents of a list are initialized using setItems(). To change a single item, use setItem(). Indexing operations that get and set items throw an exception when an index is out of bounds.

setItems(String[] items)   Sets the items. This method removes the previous items from the list and replaces them with the new items. The selection is cleared, and the list is scrolled to the top.

setItem(int index, String string)   Sets the item at an index. This method replaces the previous item with the new string. If the index is out of range, an IllegalArgumentException ("Index out of bounds") is thrown.

getItems()   Returns the items, which is an array of strings. The array that is returned is a *copy* of the contents. Modifying this array will not affect the control.

getItem(int index)   Returns the item at an index. If the index is out of range, an IllegalArgumentException ("Index out of bounds") is thrown.

getItemCount()   Returns the number of items in the control.

It is much more efficient to reset the contents of a list using setItems(), rather than updating each individual item using setItem(). The setItem() method is intended for those times when you have a list whose contents are mostly correct and you need to change only a few items.

7.4.7   Item Height

You can find out the height of an item within a list using getItemHeight().

> **getItemHeight()**   Returns the height in pixels of an item in the control. This value can be different from height of the font that is in use by the control, because some platforms include spacing between items.

The getItemHeight() method is mostly used to compute the initial size of a list. Refer to Lines and the Line Delimiter in Class Text for an example that computes the initial size of a text control. The code to do this for List is equivalent but uses getItemHeight() instead.[13] Here are the relevant changes:

```
int height = rows * list.getItemHeight();
int width = columns * fm.getAverageCharWidth();
list.setSize(list.computeSize(width, height));
```

7.4.8   Adding Items

Items can also be added to a list one at a time using the add() method. Methods that add items throw an exception when an index is out of bounds.

> **add(String string)**   Adds an item at the end of the list. This is the same as add(string, list.getItemCount()) but is slightly faster on some platforms.

> **add(String string, int index)**   Adds the item to the list at the given index. The operation is equivalent to performing the following steps.

1. The size of the list is increased by one.

2. All items in the list between the index and the original end of the list are shifted one position toward the end.

3. The new string is stored at the index (i.e., setItem(index, string)).

---

13. Actually, the getItemHeight() method is defined in the classes List, Tree, and Table. It is functionally equivalent to getLineHeight() in class Text. All of these methods are normally used to compute the preferred height of their respective controls.

In other words, the string is inserted into the list immediately *before* the item that was originally at the given index. For example, add("New Item", 5) causes "New Item" to become the fifth item in the list; the item that *was* the fifth item becomes the new sixth item, and so forth. The valid range for the index parameter is *0..N*, where *N* is the number of items in the list. Using an index of zero makes the string the first element in the list. Using an index of *N* makes the string the last element in the list. If the index is out of range, an IllegalArgumentException ("Index out of bounds") is thrown.

Note that adding all of the items one at a time is much slower than setting all of the items at once. Of course, if you are adding only a couple of items to a preexisting list, using add() is more efficient than resetting the entire contents.

7.4.9   Removing Items

Items are removed using remove() or removeAll(). As was true for the add() methods, methods that remove items throw an exception when an index is out of bounds.

remove(int index)   Removes the item at the index. If the index is out of range, an IllegalArgumentException ("Index out of bounds") is thrown.

remove(int start, int end)   Removes items from start to end, inclusive. If an index is out of range, an IllegalArgumentException ("Index out of bounds") is thrown.

remove(int[] indices)   Removes items using an array of indices. If an index is out of range, an IllegalArgumentException ("Index out of bounds") is thrown.

remove(String string)   Removes the first occurrence of the string from the list. Note that the string must be an exact, case-sensitive match for one of the elements of the list. If the string is not found, an IllegalArgumentException ("Argument not valid") is thrown.

removeAll()   Removes all the items from the list.

The following code fragment initializes a list to contain the strings "Red", "Green", and "Blue", then removes the item "Green".

```
list.setItems(new String[] {"Red", "Green", "Blue"});
list.remove("Green");
```

It is much faster to remove a range of items than to remove items one at a time. Note that removeAll() and setItems(new String[0]) are equivalent operations.

7.4.10 The Selection

Lists provide many different methods to set the selection. Most of these methods are index-based, and all of them scroll to show the new selection. Unlike methods that add and remove items, methods that set the selection ignore indices that are out of bounds.

Why Do Some SWT Operations Check "bounds" and Others Do Not?

Early versions of SWT attempted to be consistent with respect to bounds checking for methods that took indices by always checking bounds and throwing an exception. The result was a disaster. It was discovered that many programs routinely expected to be able to pass indices that were out of range for certain kinds of operations. As a result, we ended up taking a rather pragmatic approach to bounds checking, throwing exceptions only where the consistency of the list would be affected. For example, *selection* and *range* operations (such as setting the thumb of a scroll bar) do not throw exceptions, instead attempting to do something reasonable when a value is out of range. Operations that *add*, *get*, *set*, or *remove* items can throw "Index out of bounds" exceptions.

---

setSelection(int index)   Selects the item at the given index. Indices that are out of range are ignored. Any previous selection is cleared. The control is scrolled to bring the new selection to the attention of the user. If the control has a focus indicator, the focus indicator is assigned to the new selection.

Methods That "set" the Selection Do More Than Just Set the Value

As you might expect, methods that set properties first clear the old value, then set the new one. In addition, any action that is necessary to bring the new value to the attention of the user is performed. For example, when setSelection() is called for a list control, not only is the old selection cleared and the new selection assigned but the control is also scrolled so that the new selection can be seen. The select() method (described later in this section) simply selects the item without scrolling or affecting the previous selection.

setSelection(int start, int end)   Selects all items in the range *start* to *end*, inclusive. If the control is single-select and the range contains more than one item, all of the indices are ignored. Once the previous selection has been cleared and the new items have been selected, the control is scrolled to show the new selection, and the focus indicator is assigned.

setSelection(int[] indices)   Selects items using an array of indices. If the array is empty, the selection is cleared. If the control is single-select and the array contains more than one item, all of the indices are ignored. Once the previous selection has been cleared and the new items have been selected, the control is scrolled to show the new selection, and the focus indicator is assigned.

setSelection(String[] strings)   Selects items using an array of items. This method behaves the same as though setSelection(indices) were called using an array of indices computed by determining the index within the control of each item in the array of strings.

getSelection()   Returns the selection as an array of items. Note that this is an array of strings for a list control. This is a *copy* so that modifying the array has no effect on the control.

getSelectionCount()   Returns the number of selected items.

getSelectionIndex()   Returns the index of the item that is selected, based on the following rules.

1. If no items are selected, –1 is returned.

2. If the item that has the focus indicator is selected, that index is returned.

3. Otherwise, the index of the first selected item is returned.

getSelectionIndices()   Returns the selection as an array of indices. This is a *copy* so that modifying the array has no effect on the control.

isSelected(int index)   Returns true if the item at the index is selected. If the item is not selected or the index is out of range, false is returned.

7.4.11   *Deselecting and Selecting Items*

The methods in this section differ from the setSelection() methods in two significant ways.

1. They do not clear the previous selection before acting.

2. They do not cause the control to scroll.

Because these methods are operations on the selection, when an index is out of range, an exception is *not* thrown.

deselect(int index)   Deselects the item at the given index. Indices that are out of range are ignored.

deselect(int start, int end)   Deselects items in the range *start* to *end*, inclusive. Indices that are out of range are ignored.

deselect(int[] indices)   Deselects items using an array of indices. Indices that are out of range are ignored.

deselectAll()   Deselects all items in the control.

select(int index)   Selects the item at the given index. Indices that are out of range are ignored.

select(int start, int end)   Selects items in the range *start* to *end*, inclusive. Indices that are out of range are ignored. If the control is single-select and the range contains more than one item, all of the indices are ignored.

select(int[] indices)   Selects items using an array of indices. Indices that are out of range are ignored. If the control is single-select and the array contains more than one item, all of the indices are ignored.

selectAll()   Selects all items in the control. If the control is single-select, the selection is not changed.

7.4.12   *Scrolling*

Scrolling in a list has the same API as scrolling in a text control. Instead of the top index being the index of a line of text, it is the index of an item in List.

setTopIndex(int index)   Scrolls to show the item indicated by the *index* parameter at the top of the control. Indexing starts at zero. If the index is out of range, the control scrolls to show the closest index that is within range. Depending on both the platform and the number of items, it may not be possible for the particular item to be displayed at the top of the control; this can happen if the platform does not allow the control to scroll so that white space follows the last item.

getTopIndex()   Returns the line that is at the top of the control. The top index can change for many reasons other than calling setTopIndex(). For example, setSelection() can scroll the control to show the new selection, or the user can scroll the control.

showSelection()   Scrolls to show the selection. If the selection is already visible, nothing happens. Because the control may be scrolled, this method is useful to bring the selection to the attention of the user. If multiple items are selected, the control is scrolled so that at least part of the selection is visible.

7.4.13   Searching

Lists provide a number of searching operations that allow you to find the index of a string within a list.

indexOf(String string)   Returns the zero-based index of the string. This is the same as calling indexOf(string, 0).

indexOf(String string, int start)   Returns the zero-based index of the string, starting at the start index. If the string is not found, –1 is returned.

7.4.14   List Events

SWT.Selection (SelectionEvent)

The SWT.Selection event (typed event SelectionEvent) is sent whenever the user selects an item with the mouse or the keyboard. The selection event for List contains meaningful values in only the *display, widget,* and *type* fields.

SWT.DefaultSelection (SelectionEvent)

The SWT.DefaultSelection event (typed event SelectionEvent) is sent whenever the user performs the platform-specific operation that indicates default selection. On most platforms, default selection occurs when the user double-clicks on an item or presses the <Enter> key. The default selection event for List contains meaningful values in only the *display, widget,* and *type* fields.

Using SWT.Selection to Print the Current Selection

The following example uses SWT.Selection to print the current selection of the list when the user selects items. The example uses add() instead of setItems() because the number of items is small.

```
public static void main(String[] args) {
    Display display = new Display();
    Shell shell = new Shell(display);
    int style =
        SWT.MULTI|SWT.BORDER|SWT.H_SCROLL|SWT.V_SCROLL;
    final List list = new List(shell, style);
    for (int i=0; i<128; i++) {
        list.add("Item " + i);
    }
    list.addListener(SWT.Selection, new Listener() {
        public void handleEvent(Event event) {
            String[] selection = list.getSelection();
            System.out.print("{");
            for (int i = 0; i < selection.length; i++) {
                System.out.print(selection[i]);
                if (i < selection.length - 1) {
                    System.out.print(" ");
                }
            }
            System.out.println("}");
        }
    });
    list.setSize(200, 200);
    shell.pack();
    shell.open();
    while (!shell.isDisposed()) {
        if (!display.readAndDispatch()) display.sleep();
    }
    display.dispose();
}
```

7.5   Class Combo

7.5.1   Example

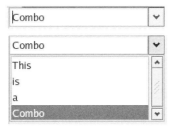

7.5.2 Combo Hierarchy

7.5.3 Combo Styles

Style	Description
SWT.READ_ONLY	Make the control noneditable
SWT.DROP_DOWN	The list drops down when needed
SWT.SIMPLE	The list is always visible

7.5.4 Combo Events

Event	Description
SWT.Selection	The user selected an item
SWT.DefaultSelection	Default selection occurred (user pressed <Enter>)
SWT.Modify	Text has changed in the control

A combo control, also called a *combo box*, is the *combination* of a single-line text and a single-select list control.[14] The user can type characters into the text control or choose an item from the list, causing it to appear in the text control. The text control can be read-only, in which case the user can select only an item from the list. Normally, combo controls include a small drop-down indicator that is used to hide and show the list. On some platforms when the SWT.SIMPLE style is specified, the list is always visible. Other platforms do not support this hint.

---

14. Most platforms actually implement combo controls this way, except for Microsoft Windows. On Windows, when a combo box is not editable, the text is drawn in the combo box control instead of using an embedded single-line text control. This means that SWT cannot provide an API that exposes the underlying controls. Nevertheless, describing the API in terms of these two controls makes it easier to explain.

A combo control that is created with the style SWT.READ_ONLY causes the text portion of the combo box to be noneditable, just like a read-only text control.

> **When to Use a Combo**
>
> Any place where a single-select list could be used, a drop-down read-only combo can be used instead. This will conserve screen real estate. Drop-down read-only combos can also be used in places where you might use a group of radio buttons. In this case, the text field portion of the combo is analogous to the currently selected radio button. The disadvantage of using combos this way occurs when the list needs to be accessed frequently. Also, it is not possible to see at a glance the options that are available because they are hidden in the list.
>
> A drop-down editable combo can be used instead of a single-line text control. To save the user typing, commonly used strings are made available in the drop-down list. Sometimes a program will update the list to include the last string that the user typed.

Combo boxes support the SWT.Selection and SWT.DefaultSelection events. The selection event behaves just like selection for lists, whereas default selection behaves like default selection in a text control.

7.5.5   Combo Is a Combination of API

Combo is more than just a combination of Text and List. The API provided by Combo in SWT is also a combination of the API provided by those two classes. Combo reuses names and concepts from them, so knowing the API of List and Text means that you already know the naming and the major concepts for combos. The downside of this is that it is possible to confuse methods that operate on the text control with methods that operate on the list, and vice versa.

7.5.6   Text Methods

The following methods apply to the text control portion of a combo control and behave in a manner that is similar to methods with the same name in the class Text.

- ○ clearSelection()
- ○ copy()
- ○ cut()
- ○ getSelection()
- ○ getText()
- ○ getTextHeight()
- ○ getTextLimit()
- ○ paste()
- ○ setSelection(Point)
- ○ setText(String)
- ○ setTextLimit(int)

7.5.7 List Methods

The following methods apply to the list control portion of a combo. These behave in a manner that is similar to methods of the same name in class List.

- ○ add(String)
- ○ add(String, int)
- ○ deselect(int)
- ○ deselectAll()
- ○ getItem(int)
- ○ getItemCount()
- ○ getItemHeight()
- ○ getItems()
- ○ getSelectionIndex()
- ○ indexOf(String)
- ○ indexOf(String, int)
- ○ remove(int)
- ○ remove(int, int)
- ○ remove(String)
- ○ removeAll()
- ○ select(int)
- ○ setItem(int, String)
- ○ setItems(String[])

Notice that although the select() and deselect() methods apply to the list control portion of the combo, the setSelection() method applies to the text control.

7.5.8 Resizing a Drop-Down Combo

Drop-down combo boxes have the interesting property of having a very specific preferred height. This is the height of the text field plus any extra trimming that the combo might have added. For this reason, some platforms refuse to resize a combo to be smaller than its preferred height.[15] SWT enforces this behavior on every platform in order to be consistent across platforms.

7.5.9 Combo Events

SWT.Selection (SelectionEvent)

The SWT.Selection event (typed event SelectionEvent) is sent whenever the user selects a list item with the mouse or the keyboard. The selection event for Combo contains meaningful values in only the *display*, *widget*, and *type* fields.

SWT.DefaultSelection (SelectionEvent)

The SWT.DefaultSelection event (typed event SelectionEvent) is sent whenever the user performs the platform-specific operation that indicates default selection. On most platforms, default selection occurs when the user presses the <Enter> key. The default selection event for Combo contains meaningful values in only the *display*, *widget*, and *type* fields.

Using SWT.DefaultSelection to Keep a "Recently Typed" List

The following example code (results shown in Figure 7.8) uses the SWT.DefaultSelection event to add the strings that the user types in the text control to the list portion of the combo control. Combo controls allow duplicate items. This means that we need to check that the string is not already present before adding it. To stop the list from growing without bound, a limit on the number of strings is enforced. When the limit is reached, the oldest string is deleted from the list.

```
static final int LIMIT = 10;
public static void main(String[] args) {
    Display display = new Display();
```

---

15. Microsoft Windows has this behavior.

```
Shell shell = new Shell(display);
final Combo combo = new Combo(shell, SWT.DROP_DOWN);
combo.pack();
Point size = combo.getSize();
combo.setSize(200, size.y);
combo.addListener(SWT.DefaultSelection,new Listener() {
    public void handleEvent(Event event) {
        String text = combo.getText();
        if (combo.indexOf(text) == -1) {
            if (combo.getItemCount() >= LIMIT) {
                combo.remove(0);
            }
            combo.add(text);
        }
    }
});
shell.pack();
shell.open();
while (!shell.isDisposed()) {
    if (!display.readAndDispatch()) display.sleep();
}
display.dispose();
}
```

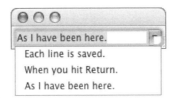

Figure 7.8

When to Use SWT.Selection and SWT.DefaultSelection

When a combo is read-only, the text field can be changed by the user only through the list, causing the SWT.Selection event. This means that for a read-only combo, it is appropriate to invoke an action from SWT.Selection. It is also reasonable (but not necessary) to invoke the same action from the SWT.DefaultSelection event, rather than forcing the user to reselect the item.

When a combo is editable, the case for using the SWT.Selection event to invoke an action is less clear. For example, when the string in the text control matches an item in the list, there is ambiguity. The user may have entered the string or selected the item. In the case of a Web browser that uses a combo to get a URL, the SWT.Selection event should navigate to the Web page. When a combo is prompting for a file name, perhaps to run a program, the SWT.Selection event should probably not invoke the program. In both cases, it is appropriate to use SWT.DefaultSelection to invoke the action.

SWT.Modify (ModifyEvent)

Table 7.3 shows the modify event for the combo control.

Table 7.3   Modify Event

Untyped Event		Description
SWT.Modify		Text has changed in the control
Typed Event	**Listener**	**Methods**
ModifyEvent	ModifyListener	modifyText(ModifyEvent)

The SWT.Modify event (typed event ModifyEvent) is sent *after* characters have been inserted or deleted from a combo control. The event is sent both when the user types and when the program changes the control. Modify events contain meaningful values in only the *display*, *widget*, and *type* fields.

The SWT.Modify event for combo controls is used in the same manner as SWT.Modify for text controls. The SWT.Modify example in the Text Events section can easily be changed to use an editable combo instead of a text control. The implementation is left as an exercise for the reader.

7.6   Summary

In this chapter, you have learned to use some of the simplest controls in SWT. Along the way, important widget properties, such as text, image, and alignment, were introduced. These properties, along with the separator concept from class Label, will appear again when we discuss the item classes in SWT. From class Button, we encountered selection and learned that SWT uses style bits to minimize the number of classes in the toolkit. Text controls provided the concepts of single- and multiline, read-only, and scrolling. Lists, although no longer very popular controls, are index-based and bear close resemblance to the advanced controls Table and Tree. Ideas introduced in List can be applied to those classes.

Understanding the basic controls and the concepts they introduce is essential to understanding the more complicated controls and the general philosophies of SWT.

CHAPTER 8

Tool Bars and Menus

Tool bars and menus are widgets that are primarily used to invoke actions in a program. Users expect the text and icons that they display and their placement in an application to be intuitive. In fact, in the best-case scenario, they can be intuitive enough to teach people how to use a program without resorting to the manual. For that reason, an understanding of tool bars and menus in SWT is important.

8.1 Classes ToolBar and ToolItem

8.1.1 Example

8.1.2 ToolBar and ToolItem Hierarchies

8.1.3   ToolBar Styles

Style	Description
SWT.WRAP	Wrap the buttons to fit the visible area
SWT.FLAT	Draw the tool bar with a flat look
SWT.HORIZONTAL	Layout buttons from left to right
SWT.VERTICAL	Layout buttons from top to bottom
SWT.RIGHT	Place the text in each item to the right in the item
SWT.SHADOW_OUT	Draw a separator above the tool bar

8.1.4   ToolBar Events (none)

Event	Description

8.1.5   ToolItem Styles

Style	Description
SWT.PUSH	Create a push button tool item
SWT.CHECK	Create a check button tool item
SWT.RADIO	Create a radio button tool item
SWT.SEPARATOR	Create a separator tool item
SWT.DROP_DOWN	Create a drop-down tool item

8.1.6   ToolItem Events

Event	Description
SWT.Selection	The tool item was selected

Tool bars are used to display horizontal or vertical rows of tool bar buttons represented by instances of the class ToolItem. Tool bars are often placed just below the main menu bar at the top of the shell.[1] When resized, tool bars are responsible for automatically positioning and resizing their tool items.[2] Creating a tool bar with the style SWT.HORIZONTAL causes the items to be displayed in rows. The SWT.VERTICAL style is used to display the items in columns.

Tool items are analogous to push buttons and menu items, supporting similar creation styles and listeners. They are automatically added to the list of items in a tool bar when they are created. The position index parameter in the ToolItem constructor can be used to create an item at a specific index, relative to the other items in the tool bar. If a position index is not provided, the item is added to the end of the list. ToolBar *does not* implement a remove() or setVisible() operation. Items are removed and hidden when their dispose() method is called.

Tool items, like buttons, can display strings and images. Surprisingly, tool items are also used to represent the spacing between items, behaving as separators. Separators cannot be selected and do not draw strings or images.

A drop-down tool item is a special kind of item that behaves similar to a combo, allowing the user to select a small drop-down indicator. Often, a program will display a menu or list when the indicator is selected.

The following fragment creates a horizontal tool bar and adds three tool items. One item represents a *cut* operation, one a *copy* operation, and the last, a *paste* operation:

```
ToolBar toolBar = new ToolBar(parent, SWT.HORIZONTAL);
ToolItem cutItem = new ToolItem(toolBar, SWT.PUSH);
cutItem.setImage(cutImage);
ToolItem copyItem = new ToolItem(toolBar, SWT.PUSH);
copyItem.setImage(copyImage);
ToolItem pasteItem = new ToolItem(toolBar, SWT.PUSH);
pasteItem.setImage(pasteImage);
```

Tool items often provide quick access to actions that also appear somewhere on the main menu. When first introduced and used in this capacity, they were sometimes called *smart icons*. When used as smart icons, tool items play

---

1. Of course, on the Macintosh, the main menu bar is not in the shell.

2. ToolBar is often used in conjunction with the classes CoolBar and CoolItem (see Classes CoolBar and CoolItem). This combination allows the user to rearrange tool bars dynamically with the mouse. Tool bars by themselves do not provide this capability.

the same role as accelerators, providing quick access to menu operations. However, access is provided using the mouse instead of the keyboard.

Tool Tips to the Rescue!

A funny thing happened when smart icons were introduced. When too many were used within a program, some people found them overwhelming. The problem was that users couldn't immediately figure out which operations they performed. Despite valiant attempts by user interface designers, pictures can be ambiguous. (In this case, a picture is not worth 1,000 words.)

Contrast this with menus. New users often spend time examining (but not invoking) the menus in a program to see what the program can do. Fortunately, tool tips were invented to allow new users to do the same thing with tool bars. When the mouse is hovered over a tool item, a short descriptive message roughly equivalent to the text that might have appeared in a menu item is displayed.

See the section Tool Item Tool Tips to make sure that the tool items you create provide tool tips. Otherwise, your smart icons might frustrate the user.

8.1.7 *Tool Items That Act Like Buttons*

Tool items that support text and images use the same API as buttons. Just like the Button class, ToolItem does not support wrapping or SWT.WRAP (although the ToolBar class *does* support SWT.WRAP to wrap the tool items). More than one line of text in a tool item is not supported.

setText(String string)   Sets the text for the item. The string may include mnemonic characters but *cannot* include line delimiters. Setting the text of the item causes the tool bar to reposition its items.

getText()   Returns the text for the item. This is an empty string if the text has never been set or if the tool item is a separator.

setImage(Image image)   Sets the image for the item. Setting the image of a tool item causes the tool bar to reposition its items.

The First Image Defines the Size of All Images in the Control

Many of the controls in SWT that support multiple images scale all of the images they display to be the same size. By definition, this is the size of the first image inserted into the control. This restriction is a direct result of a limitation of Microsoft Windows and cannot be worked around in SWT. The controls that are affected are ToolBar, TabFolder, Tree, and Table.

getImage()   Returns the image for the item. This is null if the image has never been set or if the item is separator.

ToolItem supports the SWT.PUSH, SWT.CHECK, and SWT.RADIO styles. When a tool item is created with one of these styles, it behaves in the same manner as a button with the equivalent style.

Tool items created with the SWT.CHECK style stay selected after the user has clicked on them. Tool items created with SWT.RADIO, when grouped together, behave like radio buttons. Check or radio tool items allow you to set their selection state using setSelection().

setSelection(boolean selection)   Sets the selection state for the item.

getSelection()   Returns a boolean that is the selection state of the item.

The following example creates six tool items with the styles SWT.CHECK, SWT.PUSH, and SWT.RADIO. The result is shown in Figure 8.1.

```
public static void main(String[] args) {
    Display display = new Display();
    Shell shell = new Shell(display);
    ToolBar toolBar = new ToolBar(shell, SWT.HORIZONTAL);
    for (int i = 0; i < 2; i++) {
        ToolItem item = new ToolItem(toolBar, SWT.CHECK);
        item.setText("Check " + i);
    }
    for (int i = 0; i < 2; i++) {
        ToolItem item = new ToolItem(toolBar, SWT.PUSH);
        item.setText("Push " + i);
    }
    for (int i = 0; i < 2; i++) {
        ToolItem item = new ToolItem(toolBar, SWT.RADIO);
        item.setText("Radio " + i);
    }
    toolBar.pack();
    shell.pack();
    shell.open();
    while (!shell.isDisposed()) {
        if (!display.readAndDispatch()) display.sleep();
    }
    display.dispose();
}
```

Figure 8.1

A radio group of tool items is formed when one radio tool item is placed next to another. It is possible to create multiple groups of radio items in one tool bar by separating radio items with items that do not have the SWT.RADIO style.[3] This differs from the behavior of radio buttons in composites, where there is only ever one radio group, no matter how the buttons are separated.[4] ToolBar supports the SWT.NO_RADIO_GROUP style to allow you to disable radio behavior but application programs rarely use it.

8.1.8 Tool Items That Act Like Separators

Tool items with the style SWT.SEPARATOR serve two purposes. The most obvious use is to provide spacing between items. However, they are also used to position *any* control within a tool bar, as seen below. In both cases, the width of the separator tool item is specified using setWidth().

setWidth(int width)   Sets the width of the separator item and causes the tool bar to reposition the items to take into account the new width.

getWidth()   Returns the width of the tool item.

The following example creates a tool bar with a combo control, followed by two separators and two push button tool items. Because it is not an instance of ToolItem, a combo cannot truly be an item in a tool bar. Instead, it is placed on top of the first separator tool item using setControl(). The result is shown in Figure 8.2.

```
public static void main(String[] args) {
    Display display = new Display();
    Shell shell = new Shell(display);
    ToolBar toolBar = new ToolBar(shell, SWT.HORIZONTAL);
    Combo combo = new Combo(toolBar, SWT.READ_ONLY);
    ToolItem comboItem =
        new ToolItem(toolBar, SWT.SEPARATOR);
```

---

3. Multiple radio groups are supported in menus in the same manner, using menu items created with SWT.RADIO.

4. We actually tried to change this behavior to be consistent with tool items between SWT 1.0 and 2.0 but it broke Eclipse.

```
comboItem.setControl(combo);
comboItem.setWidth(64);
new ToolItem(toolBar, SWT.SEPARATOR);
for (int i = 0; i < 2; i++) {
    ToolItem item = new ToolItem(toolBar, SWT.PUSH);
    item.setText("Push " + i);
}
toolBar.pack();
shell.pack();
shell.open();
while (!shell.isDisposed()) {
    if (!display.readAndDispatch()) display.sleep();
}
display.dispose();
}
```

Figure 8.2

Placing a combo on top of a tool item seems a little strange but is the direct result of the fact that tool items are not controls. It is not possible to include them in the items list of a tool bar because that list can contain only tool items.[5]

The setControl() method is used to associate a control with a tool item.

setControl(Control control)   Sets the control that will be positioned on top of the tool item when it has the SWT.SEPARATOR style. When the tool bar positions the separator item, the control is moved and resized accordingly.

getControl()   Returns the control that will be positioned on top of the tool item when the item has the style SWT.SEPARATOR.

8.1.9   Tool Items That Drop Down

Tool items, when created with the style SWT.DROP_DOWN, provide a "drop-down arrow" that can be selected by the user like a combo control. One big difference between a combo and a drop-down tool item is the fact that the drop-down list is not provided automatically by the tool item. This allows the application code to display any kind of control for the item.

_____

5.   Ah, the joys of strongly typed languages.

When the user selects the drop-down arrow, an SWT.Selection event is issued. The detail field of the event is set to SWT.ARROW to indicate that the arrow was pressed. A drop-down tool item can also be selected outside of the drop-down arrow indicator. In this case, the detail field is zero.

The following example code displays a menu using a drop-down tool item, as shown in Figure 8.3.

```
public static void main(String[] args) {
    final Display display = new Display();
    Shell shell = new Shell(display);
    final ToolBar toolBar =
        new ToolBar(shell, SWT.HORIZONTAL);
    final Menu menu = new Menu(shell, SWT.POP_UP);
    for (int i = 0; i < 8; i++) {
        MenuItem item = new MenuItem(menu, SWT.PUSH);
        item.setText("Item " + i);
    }
    final ToolItem item =
        new ToolItem(toolBar, SWT.DROP_DOWN);
    item.setText("Drop Down");
    item.addListener(SWT.Selection, new Listener() {
        public void handleEvent(Event event) {
            if (event.detail == SWT.ARROW) {
                Point point = new Point(event.x, event.y);
                point = display.map(toolBar, null, point);
                menu.setLocation(point);
                menu.setVisible(true);
            }
        }
    });
    toolBar.pack();
    shell.pack();
    shell.open();
    while (!shell.isDisposed()) {
        if (!display.readAndDispatch()) display.sleep();
    }
    display.dispose();
}
```

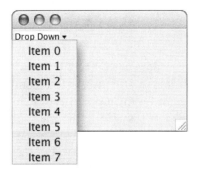

Figure 8.3

The *x* and *y* coordinates provided in the event should be used to position the widget that you create. By using these coordinates, your widget will appear at the correct location, relative to the tool item.

8.1.10   Tool Item Bounds

Sometimes you might need to query the bounds of a tool item, possibly to determine whether it is visible in a tool bar. When a tool bar is resized to be too small to show all the items, they are clipped. The bounds of each item can be compared against the client area of the tool bar to see which items are clipped.

To find out the bounds of a tool item, the getBounds() method is used.

getBounds()   Returns a rectangle that describes the location and size of the item, relative to its parent.

8.1.11   Tool Item Tool Tips

Tool tips are short, descriptive messages that appear when the user hovers the mouse over a widget. Tool tips are supported for tool items using the setTool-TipText() method.

setToolTipText(String string)   Sets the tool tip text for the item. This string is displayed when the user hovers with the mouse over the item.[6] Setting this string to null removes the tool tip.

getToolTipText()   Returns the tool tip text.

Note that the duration, location, and mouse gesture that triggers the tool tip are all platform-specific.

8.1.12   Enabling and Disabling Tool Items

Even though they are not controls, tool items can be enabled and disabled, just like controls. If you consider that tool items behave a lot like buttons and menu items, then the ability to enable and disable a tool item is an important feature.

---

6.   The user doesn't actually hover in the "flying carpet" sense of the word!

setEnabled(boolean enabled)   Enables or disables the item, depending on the boolean argument. A disabled item is not selectable in the user interface and draws using a "grayed" look.

getEnabled()   Returns the enabled state of the item.

isEnabled()   Returns true if the item is enabled, the tool bar that contains it is enabled, and all of the ancestors of the tool bar are enabled; otherwise, it returns false.

8.1.13   Disabled and Hot Images

The ToolItem class supports three different types of images. The first type of image, which was described in the section Tool Items That Act Like Buttons, is called the *normal image*. This image is assigned using setImage() and behaves as you might expect.

The second type of image is called the *disabled image*. This image is displayed whenever a tool item is disabled by a call to setEnabled(false).

setDisabledImage(Image image)   Sets the image to be displayed in a tool item when the tool item is disabled. Setting this image to null causes the tool item to use the normal image, graying it appropriately when the item is disabled.

getDisabledImage()   Returns the disabled image.

The disabled image can be very useful when the platform-specific algorithm that is used to gray the normal image behaves poorly, producing a "gray but mangled" image. This can happen when the graying algorithm is sensitive to the colors in your image. Setting the disabled image overrides the algorithm, ensuring that a disabled tool item draws using an image that looks good because it uses an image that you constructed.

The third type of image is called the *hot image*. The hot image is displayed when the mouse enters a tool item. When the mouse exits, the normal image is restored.

setHotImage(Image image)   Sets the image to be displayed in the tool item when the mouse is inside the item. Setting this image to null causes the tool item to use the normal image.

getHotImage()   Returns the hot image.

Hot images are generally less useful than disabled images. They represent a particular user interface look made popular by Windows 98, which is now generally abandoned, even on Windows.

Is the Tool Item Disabled?

Windows 98 and versions of Internet Explorer at the time used hot images to draw attention to the fact that the mouse had entered a tool item. The hot images were typically full color, whereas the normal images were grayscale. The problem with this approach was that the grayscale images looked too much like disabled images. Users couldn't tell when a tool item was disabled. It was this kind of ambiguity that probably caused hot images in tool bars to be abandoned.

8.1.14   *Tool Bars That Wrap*

When a tool bar is created with the style SWT.WRAP, it will wrap tool items when there is insufficient space to fit the items on a single row. The algorithm that is used to wrap tool items is platform-specific.[7] When a tool bar wraps, the number of rows in the tool bar increases. You can query the number of rows in a tool bar using getRowCount().

> **getRowCount**()   Returns the number of rows in a tool bar. This method normally returns the integer 1, but it will return an integer between 2 and the number of items in the tool bar if the items are wrapped.

Sometimes, even though the tool bar was created with the SWT.WRAP style, when the tool bar is positioned by a layout (see the chapter Layout), the tool items do not seem to wrap. For a detailed discussion of this issue, see Forcing Controls to Wrap.

8.1.15   *Tool Bars That Are Flat*

To create a tool bar that draws with a "flat look," use the style SWT.FLAT. A flat tool bar generally does not draw push button borders for the items until

---

7. For example, Windows keeps certain kinds of items together, most notably radio items. Separators are used as hints to indicate when to wrap to the next item.

the mouse moves over an item. The flat look of a tool bar is defined by the operating system theme.

These days, most programs use flat tool bars. Unfortunately, SWT.FLAT is not the default style in SWT. This is regrettable because applications that do not use flat tool bars can look dated.[8]

The Flat Look Is Back?

User interface fads come and go. Early versions of X/Motif sported a Romanesque, "chiseled" look. Menus resembled slabs of stone. Lists had huge, beveled borders. The first Macintoshes and Windows 2.0 had a "sheet of paper" look with oval buttons that were filled and flashed when you selected them. OS/ 2 and Windows 3.0 introduced 3D buttons and scroll bars. This was sometimes called the "2 $\frac{1}{2}$ D" look because only some controls were 3D. By the time Windows 95 was released, chiseling and the 3D look were back. But then, users began to realize that excess borders and chiseling took up too much space. With the advent of the World Wide Web, the flat look is back. Who knows what will happen in the future? Perhaps antialiasing and transparency will become prevalent, giving birth to the "smeared look."

8.1.16   *The Separator above the Tool Bar*

Many applications include a tool bar that is positioned at the top of the window, under the menu bar. Visually, the tool bar is often separated from the menu bar by a separator. Early SWT programs emulated this behavior by placing a label with the styles SWT.SEPARATOR and SWT.SHADOW_OUT between the two widgets. This approach worked reasonably well on Windows but failed elsewhere. On the Macintosh, where the desktop provides a single menu bar that is shared by every application, the separator looked particularly strange.

To get around this platform difference, the SWT.SHADOW_OUT style was defined for ToolBar. This style causes tool bars to draw the appropriate separator. On the Macintosh and platforms that do not support this look, the separator is not drawn.

---

8. We could possibly have fixed this problem by defining a new constant, such as SWT.RAISED or SWT.NOT_FLAT, and changing the default. Unfortunately, this kind of change would break too many application programs.

8.1.17   Searching and Hit Test Operations

The ToolBar class provides a number of searching and "hit test" operations that allow you to find items and indices.

getItem(int index)   Returns the item at the index, which is zero-based. If the index is out of range, an IllegalArgumentException ("Index out of bounds") is thrown.

getItem(Point point)   Returns the item under a point. The point is relative to the origin of the control.

getItemCount()   Returns the number of items in the tool bar.

getItems()   Returns an array of the items. This is a *copy* so that modifying it has no effect on the control.

indexOf(ToolItem item)   Returns the zero-based index of the item. If the item is not found, –1 is returned.

8.1.18   ToolItem Events

SWT.Selection (SelectionEvent)

The SWT.Selection event (typed event SelectionEvent) is sent whenever the user selects an item with the mouse or the keyboard. The event fields relevant during a selection event for an instance of ToolItem are as follows.

Public Fields of Class Event That Are Valid during SWT.Selection

Field	Description
detail	This field contains SWT.ARROW if the drop-down indicator of a drop-down tool item was selected.
x	The *x* coordinate to be used when positioning a widget for a drop-down tool item. Note that this value is in the coordinate system of the tool bar.
y	The y coordinate to be used when positioning a widget for a drop-down tool item. Note that this value is in the coordinate system of the tool bar.

Note that the *x* and *y* coordinates almost always need to be translated to the coordinate system of the display. This is because the drop-down widget that you display is usually a shell or menu. See the map() method described in the chapter Display.

Using SWT.Selection to Implement a Drop-Down Toolltem

A good example that uses the SWT.Selection event with a drop-down tool item can be found in the section Tool Items That Drop Down.

8.2 Classes Menu and MenuItem

8.2.1 Example

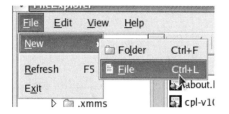

8.2.2 Menu and MenuItem Hierarchies

8.2.3 Menu Styles

Style	Description
SWT.BAR	Create a menu bar
SWT.DROP_DOWN	Create a drop-down menu
SWT.POP_UP	Create a pop-up menu
SWT.NO_RADIO_GROUP	Disable radio button behavior
SWT.LEFT_TO_RIGHT	Force the menu orientation to be left to right
SWT.RIGHT_TO_LEFT	Force the menu orientation to be right to left

8.2.4 Menu Events

Event	Description
SWT.Hide	The menu is being hidden
SWT.Show	The menu is being shown
SWT.Help	The user requested help for the menu

8.2.5 MenuItem Styles

Style	Description
SWT.PUSH	Creates a push button menu item
SWT.CHECK	Creates a check button menu item
SWT.RADIO	Creates a radio button menu item
SWT.SEPARATOR	Creates a separator menu item
SWT.CASCADE	Creates a cascade menu item

8.2.6 MenuItem Events

Event	Description
SWT.Selection	The menu item was selected
SWT.Arm	The menu item is drawn in the armed state
SWT.Help	The user requested help for the menu item

Menus are very common user interface elements used to display a list of choices. Menus are represented in SWT by the classes Menu and MenuItem.[9] Menus are not controls.[10]

There are three kinds of menus: *Menu bars,* also called *main menus,* are created using the SWT.BAR style and appear as part of the shell trimming[11]

---

9. The fact that a single Menu class is used to create every kind of menu is another example of the "minimize the number of classes" design philosophy of SWT.

10. It seems strange but menus in Windows are not modeled in the operating system as controls. This forced us to model SWT menus the same way. The alternative is the tedious, thankless, and error-prone task of providing an implementation of every method they would inherit from control.

11. This is not true on the Macintosh where there is a single menu bar shared by all applications on the desktop.

below the shell title. *Drop-down* menus,[12] sometimes called *submenus* or *cascade menus*, are created with the SWT.DROP_DOWN style. They are displayed when the user selects a menu item from the menu bar or an item from another menu that contains a drop-down indicator. *Pop-up* or context menus, created using the SWT.POP_UP style, are displayed when the user requests a menu in a control using the mouse or the keyboard.

One way to think about the relationship between the different kinds of menus is to consider that menu bars and pop-up menus are always the root of a containment hierarchy, composed of drop-down menus. This containment hierarchy is displayed whenever the user clicks on a menu item in the menu bar or requests a context menu.

The MenuItem class is analogous to the Button and ToolItem classes, supporting similar creation styles and listeners. Like instances of the other "item" classes, menu items are automatically added when created and are positioned similarly in the children list of the parent, using the location constructor parameter. Menu items are removed from a menu when they are disposed.

Like ToolItem and Button, instances of the MenuItem class support text and images. They also support separators and cascade items. A *cascade item* is a menu item that allows a drop-down menu to appear. Cascade items display the drop-down indicator.

8.2.7 *Menu Items That Behave Like Buttons*

The MenuItem class supports styles and listeners similar to the ToolItem and Button classes. For example, check and radio menu items are provided using the styles SWT.CHECK and SWT.RADIO. Text and images, mnemonics, and enabling and disabling are supported using Button and ToolItem API naming conventions. Like buttons and tool items, menu items do not wrap their text or support more than one line of text. One interesting difference between MenuItem and the other "buttonlike" classes is that MenuItem supports accelerators and accelerator text.

> **setText(String string)** Sets the text for the item. This string may include mnemonic characters but *cannot* include line delimiters. The special character '\t' separates the menu text from the accelerator text. Accelerator text is the string used to inform the user that the menu

---

12. On many platforms, the operating system makes no distinction between drop-down and pop-up menus, allowing them to be used interchangeably in either role. Unfortunately, Motif does not allow this, forcing SWT to make the same distinction. The alternative would have been to violate the rule that operating system resources are acquired when a widget is created.

item can be triggered using a key sequence. On platforms that support accelerator text, the string that follows the '\t' character is presented to the user, often right-aligned in the menu. Note that setting the accelerator text does not actually install an accelerator key. This is done using setAccelerator(). Accelerator text allows the application program complete control over the string that is displayed in the menu item, independent of the accelerator keystroke that invokes it. See Specifying the Accelerator Text in the chapter The Keyboard for further discussion and examples.

getText()   Returns the item text. This is an empty string if the item text has never been set or if the item is a separator.

setImage(Image image)   Sets the item contents to an image.

getImage()   Returns the item image. This is null if the image has never been set or if the item is a separator.

setEnabled(boolean enable)   Enables or disables the item, depending on the boolean argument. A disabled item is not selectable in the user interface and draws using a grayed look.

getEnabled()   Returns the enabled state of the item.

isEnabled()   Returns true if the item is enabled and all ancestors are enabled, otherwise returns false. Ancestors of a menu item do not follow the regular parent-child definition. Rather, the ancestors are traced from the menu item to the menu of the cascade menu item. This process continues all the way to the root menu, which is a either a menu bar or a pop-up menu.

8.2.8   *Menu Items That Behave Like Separators*

Menu items with the style SWT.SEPARATOR are used to reserve space between items in a menu. Sometimes the space is simply left blank between the items or an "etched line" is drawn. Even on the same operating system, the menu separator look can change between releases.[13]

---

13. This happened between the Jaguar and Panther releases of Macintosh OS X.

8.2.9   Menu Items That Show Other Menus

Menu items with the style SWT.CASCADE are used to connect menus together. When the user selects the menu item, a drop-down menu cascades into view. Drop-down menus are connected to the menu bar, pop-up menus, or other drop-down menus using setMenu().

> **setMenu(Menu menu)**   Sets the menu for the item, connecting the drop-down menu to the cascade item. The item must have been created with the style SWT.CASCADE and the menu with the style SWT.DROP_DOWN, or an IllegalArgumentException is thrown. Setting the menu to null disconnects the menu from the item.

> **getMenu()**   Returns the menu for the item. This value is null when no menu has been set into the item.

8.2.10   Menu Items with Accelerators

Accelerators are keyboard shortcuts that allow the user to invoke menu items using the keyboard instead of the mouse. The section Accelerators in the chapter The Keyboard describes accelerators in detail, so they will not be discussed here.

8.2.11   Main Menus

To create a main menu, you need to create a menu with the style SWT.BAR. You can create many different menu bars, but only one can be displayed at a time. The setMenuBar() method in class Shell is used to show the menu bar (see Setting the Menu Bar in the Class Shell).

The following example program creates a shell and a menu bar with the classic "File" and "Edit" menus:

```
public static void main(String[] args) {
    Display display = new Display();
    Shell shell = new Shell(display);
    Menu menuBar = new Menu(shell, SWT.BAR);
    shell.setMenuBar(menuBar);
    MenuItem fileItem = new MenuItem(menuBar, SWT.CASCADE);
    fileItem.setText("File");
    MenuItem editItem = new MenuItem(menuBar, SWT.CASCADE);
    editItem.setText("Edit");
    Menu fileMenu = new Menu(shell, SWT.DROP_DOWN);
    fileItem.setMenu(fileMenu);
    String [] fileStrings = {"New", "Close", "Exit"};
    for (int i=0; i<fileStrings.length; i++) {
```

```
            MenuItem item = new MenuItem(fileMenu, SWT.PUSH);
            item.setText(fileStrings [i]);
    }
    Menu editMenu = new Menu(shell, SWT.DROP_DOWN);
    String [] editStrings = {"Cut", "Copy", "Paste"};
    editItem.setMenu(editMenu);
    for (int i=0; i<editStrings.length; i++) {
            MenuItem item = new MenuItem(editMenu, SWT.PUSH);
            item.setText(editStrings [i]);
    }
    shell.pack();
    shell.open();
    while (!shell.isDisposed()) {
        if (!display.readAndDispatch()) display.sleep();
    }
    display.dispose();
}
```

Although this example program is a good vehicle to show how menus and menu items are created and wired together, application programs that use menus generally do not create their menu items from an array of strings. This is because menu items, like tool items and buttons, need more properties than just text in order to be really useful in a program.

8.2.12   Pop-Up Menus

To create a pop-up menu, you create a menu with the style SWT.POP_UP. Pop-up menus can be displayed automatically by the control (using the method Control.setMenu()) when the user requests a menu or they can be displayed programmatically using the setVisible() method.

> **setVisible(boolean visible)**   Shows or hides the menu. If a location was not specified and the menu is being shown, it is displayed at the current mouse location.

To show a menu at a particular location, setLocation() is used.

> **setLocation(int x, int y)**   Sets the location of the menu. The x and y coordinates are in the coordinate system of the display.

> **setLocation(Point location)**   Sets the location of the menu using a point. This is equivalent to setLocation(location.x, location.y).

Note that if you are showing a pop-up menu using setVisible() and setLocation(), you need to show it at the right time and the right place. The mouse movements and keyboard sequence used to request a pop-up menu are platform-specific. If you guess wrong, your pop-up menus will frustrate the user.

The easiest way to avoid this problem is to let SWT pop the menu up for you using Control.setMenu() or to implement the control event SWT.MenuDetect (see Detecting a Context Menu Request).

The following example creates a pop-up menu and assigns it to a list control.

```
public static void main(String[] args) {
    Display display = new Display();
    Shell shell = new Shell(display);
    List list = new List(shell, SWT.BORDER | SWT.V_SCROLL);
    list.setItems(new String [] {"A", "B", "C", "D"});
    list.setSize(200, 200);
    Menu menu = new Menu(shell, SWT.POP_UP);
    for (int i=0; i<8; i++) {
            MenuItem item = new MenuItem(menu, SWT.PUSH);
            item.setText("Item " + i);
    }
    list.setMenu(menu);
    shell.pack();
    shell.open();
    while (!shell.isDisposed()) {
        if (!display.readAndDispatch()) display.sleep();
    }
    display.dispose();
}
```

8.2.13 Index-Based Operations for Menus

Menus provide a number of index and location operations that allow application programs to query items and indices from a menu.

getItem(int index)   Returns the item at the index, which is zero-based. If the index is out of range, IllegalArgumentException("Index out of bounds") is thrown.

getItemCount()   Returns the number of items in the menu.

getItems()   Returns the items in the menu. This is a copy of the array that is used to hold the items so that modifying this structure will not affect the menu.

indexOf(MenuItem item)   Returns the zero-based index of the item in the menu. If the item is not found, −1 is returned.

8.2.14   Menu Events

SWT.Show (MenuEvent)

Table 8.1 shows the show event for Menu.

Table 8.1   Show Event

Untyped Event		Description	
SWT.Show		The widget is becoming visible	

Typed Event	Listener		Methods
MenuEvent	MenuListener (and MenuAdapter)		menuHidden(MenuEvent)
			menuShown(MenuEvent)

The SWT.Show event (typed event MenuEvent) is sent whenever a pull-down or pop-up menu is shown. The happens when the user requests the menu or the application program makes the menu visible using setVisible(). Show events contain meaningful values in only the *display*, *widget*, and *type* fields.

The SWT.Show event for Menu is one of the most useful events in SWT. It is often used to run the application code that enables or disables menu items. Because it occurs just before a menu is shown, modifications to the menu, including adding and removing menu items, are not visible to the user. The real benefit of SWT.Show is that it allows you to keep the code that maintains menu item state in one place. Without this event, the code would need to be distributed throughout your application in order to keep the menu up to date as state changes within your program. This kind of distributed code is error-prone. Note that you *cannot* use this approach for pull-down menus whose items contain accelerators. When the user types an accelerator, the menu is not shown, so SWT.Show will not be sent. The main disadvantage of using SWT.Show to update your menus is that the state of every menu item needs to be calculated, even if it has not changed since the last time the menu was shown. This is true because the menu item state is *not* maintained elsewhere in your program. If the application code that computes this state is slow, the user will be forced to wait for the menu to appear. Slow menus make the entire application appear to be slow.

The following example program uses SWT.Show to enable and disable menu items that correspond to the selected items in a list. If an item is selected, it is enabled.

```
public static void main(String[] args) {
    Display display = new Display();
    Shell shell = new Shell(display);
    final List list =
        new List(shell, SWT.BORDER | SWT.MULTI);
    for (int i=0; i<8; i++) list.add("Item " + i);
    list.setSize(200, 200);
    final Menu menu = new Menu(shell, SWT.POP_UP);
    for (int i = 0; i < list.getItemCount(); i++) {
        MenuItem item = new MenuItem(menu, SWT.PUSH);
        item.setText(list.getItem(i));
    }
    list.setMenu(menu);
    menu.addListener(SWT.Show, new Listener() {
        public void handleEvent(Event event) {
            MenuItem[] items = menu.getItems();
            for (int i = 0; i < items.length; i++) {
                MenuItem item = items[i];
                item.setEnabled(list.isSelected(i));
            }
        }
    });
    shell.pack();
    shell.open();
    while (!shell.isDisposed()) {
        if (!display.readAndDispatch()) display.sleep();
    }
    display.dispose();
}
```

SWT.Hide (MenuEvent)

Table 8.2 shows the hide event for Menu.

Table 8.2 Hide Event

Untyped Event	Description	
SWT.Hide	The widget is being hidden	

Typed Event	Listener	Methods
MenuEvent	MenuListener (and MenuAdapter)	menuHidden(MenuEvent)
		menuShown(MenuEvent)

The SWT.Hide event (typed event MenuEvent) is sent whenever the menu is hidden. The can happen when the user selects a menu item or dismisses the menu, or when the application program makes a menu invisible using setVisible(false). Hide events contain meaningful values in only the *display, widget,* and *type* fields.

SWT.Help (HelpEvent)

Table 8.3 shows the help event for Menu.

Table 8.3 Help Event

Untyped Event	Description	
SWT.Help	The user requested help for a widget	

Typed Event	Listener	Methods
HelpEvent	HelpListener	helpRequested(HelpEvent)

The SWT.Help event (typed event HelpEvent) is sent whenever the user asks for help in a widget. Typically, the <F1> key is used for help but some platforms, such as the Macintosh, have a dedicated Help key. If no help is found for the menu, the request is forwarded to the shell. Help events contain meaningful values in only the *display, widget,* and *type* fields.

8.2.15 MenuItem Events

SWT.Selection (SelectionEvent)

The SWT.Selection event (typed event SelectionEvent) is sent whenever the user selects a menu item with the mouse or the keyboard. The event fields relevant during a selection event for a menu item are as follows.

Public Fields of Class Event That Are Valid during SWT.Selection

Field	Description
stateMask	A bitwise OR of modifier masks, indicating the state of the keyboard when the item was selected

The following code fragment prints "Menu item selected" when an item is selected.

```
item.addListener(SWT.Selection, new Listener() {
    public void handleEvent(Event event) {
        System.out.println("Menu item selected");
    }
});
```

SWT.Arm (ArmEvent)

Table 8.4 shows the arm event for Menu.

Table 8.4   Arm Event

Untyped Event		Description
SWT.Arm		A menu item is drawn in the armed state
Typed Event	**Listener**	**Methods**
ArmEvent	ArmListener	widgetArmed(ArmEvent)

The SWT.Arm event (typed event ArmEvent) is sent whenever the user causes the menu item to draw highlighted but does not select the item. This can happen using either the mouse or the keyboard. Arm events contain meaningful values in only the *display, widget,* and *type* fields.

Using SWT.Arm to Update a Status Line

The SWT.Arm event is often used to show a short help message in the status line of a window while the user browses through menu items without selecting them. Used in this capacity, it provides functionality that is analogous to tool tips.

By itself, the SWT.Arm event is not particularly useful. It allows you to set the status line text when the item is armed but there is no obvious MenuItem event that can be used to clear the text when the user closes the last menu. Fortunately, the Menu event SWT.Hide can be used to do this. However, from inside the SWT.Hide event, it is not possible to tell the difference between a menu that is hidden because the user is dragging the mouse across the menu bar and the user closing the last menu on the menu bar. In the former case, the SWT.Hide from the menu happens before the SWT.Arm for the menu item. The solution is to use the Menu event SWT.Show to set the status line text, as well.

The following example program uses SWT.Arm to implement a simple menu status line.

```
public static void main(String[] args) {
    Display display = new Display();
    Shell shell = new Shell(display);
    FormLayout layout = new FormLayout();
    shell.setLayout(layout);
    final Label label = new Label(shell, SWT.BORDER);
    Listener armListener = new Listener() {
        public void handleEvent(Event event) {
            MenuItem item = (MenuItem) event.widget;
```

```
                    label.setText(item.getText());
            }
        };
        Listener showListener = new Listener() {
            public void handleEvent(Event event) {
                Menu menu = (Menu) event.widget;
                MenuItem item = menu.getParentItem();
                if (item != null) {
                    label.setText(item.getText());
                }
            }
        };
        Listener hideListener = new Listener() {
            public void handleEvent(Event event) {
                label.setText("");
            }
        };
        FormData labelData = new FormData();
        labelData.left = new FormAttachment(0);
        labelData.right = new FormAttachment(100);
        labelData.bottom = new FormAttachment(100);
        label.setLayoutData(labelData);
        Menu menuBar = new Menu(shell, SWT.BAR);
        shell.setMenuBar(menuBar);
        MenuItem fileItem = new MenuItem(menuBar, SWT.CASCADE);
        fileItem.setText("File");
        fileItem.addListener(SWT.Arm, armListener);
        MenuItem editItem = new MenuItem(menuBar, SWT.CASCADE);
        editItem.setText("Edit");
        editItem.addListener(SWT.Arm, armListener);
        Menu fileMenu = new Menu(shell, SWT.DROP_DOWN);
        fileMenu.addListener(SWT.Hide, hideListener);
        fileMenu.addListener(SWT.Show, showListener);
        fileItem.setMenu(fileMenu);
        String[] fileStrings = { "New", "Close", "Exit" };
        for (int i = 0; i < fileStrings.length; i++) {
            MenuItem item = new MenuItem(fileMenu, SWT.PUSH);
            item.setText(fileStrings[i]);
            item.addListener(SWT.Arm, armListener);
        }
        Menu editMenu = new Menu(shell, SWT.DROP_DOWN);
        editMenu.addListener(SWT.Hide, hideListener);
        editMenu.addListener(SWT.Show, showListener);
        String[] editStrings = { "Cut", "Copy", "Paste" };
        editItem.setMenu(editMenu);
        for (int i = 0; i < editStrings.length; i++) {
            MenuItem item = new MenuItem(editMenu, SWT.PUSH);
            item.setText(editStrings[i]);
            item.addListener(SWT.Arm, armListener);
        }
        shell.open();
        while (!shell.isDisposed()) {
            if (!display.readAndDispatch()) display.sleep();
        }
        display.dispose();
    }
```

The result of running this code with the "Copy" menu item selected is shown in Figure 8.4.

Figure 8.4

SWT.Help (HelpEvent)

Table 8.5 shows the help event for MenuItem.

Table 8.5   Help Event

Untyped Event		Description	
SWT.Help		The user requested help for a widget	
Typed Event	**Listener**		**Methods**
HelpEvent	HelpListener		helpRequested(HelpEvent)

The SWT.Help event (typed event HelpEvent) is sent whenever the user asks for help in a widget. Typically, the <F1> key is used for help but some platforms, such as the Macintosh, have a dedicated Help key. If no help is found in the menu item, the request is forwarded to the menu. Help events contain meaningful values in only the *display, widget,* and *type* fields.

8.3   Summary

Tool bars and menus build on the basic widgets of SWT. Their items both share "buttonlike" behavior and the separator style that was first encountered in class Label. Unfortunately, tool bars suffer from the "first image defines the item size" limitation (forced on SWT by Microsoft Windows). The advanced control classes Tree, Table, and TabFolder share this limitation.

One criticism of the ToolBar and Menu API in SWT is that it is too verbose. Some native toolkits provide helper or "factory" methods in an attempt to lessen the burden.[14] We have thought long and hard about this problem and have come to the conclusion that, although helper API allows you to get something coded quickly, in real-world applications you need to specify most menu and tool item properties anyway, causing the helper code to be just as verbose. Helper methods suffer from the problem that they tend to become outdated when new functionality is added to the classes they wrap. In Java, the problem of defining helper methods that really help is further exacerbated by the verbose nature of inner classes and the fact that the use of reflection to transform data into something executable is frowned on by the Java community.

---

14. GTK provides "Item Factories." Motif provides the "Simple Menu" API.

CHAPTER 9

Advanced Controls

Basic controls, menus, and tool bars go only so far when creating commercial-quality applications. Most programs make use of at least one tree, table, or tab folder. These widgets are called the *advanced controls*. Why are they advanced? Early versions of the operating systems were missing them, possibly making them "advanced." For example, Windows 3.11 did not provide API for an operating system tree or table control, despite the fact that the desktop was clearly using both. Motif version 1.2 was also missing these controls. The tab folder has a rich history dating back to the notebook control of OS/2 but was not introduced officially on Windows (along with the tree and table) until Windows 95.

It is unlikely that any application you build in SWT will not make use of the advanced controls. For that reason, it is important that you study this section. Despite the fact that it is long, there are surprisingly few new concepts for you to learn. For example, if you already understand the scrolling and indexing operations from List, you are already familiar with the equivalent operations for tables.

9.1   Classes Tree and TreeItem

9.1.1   Example

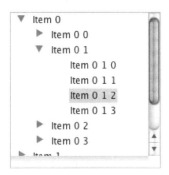

9.1.2   Tree and TreeItem Hierarchies

9.1.3   Tree Styles

Style	Description
SWT.SINGLE	Create a single-select tree
SWT.MULTI	Create a multiselect tree
SWT.CHECK	Create a tree with check boxes

9.1.4   Tree Events

Event	Description
SWT.Selection	A tree item was selected
SWT.DefaultSelection	A tree item was default selected
SWT.Expand	A tree item was expanded
SWT.Collapse	A tree item was collapsed

9.1.5   *TreeItem Styles (none)*

Style	Description

9.1.6   *TreeItem Events (none)*

Event	Description

Trees are selectable controls that are capable of displaying hierarchies of nodes. Each node in a tree is represented by an instance of the class TreeItem. A tree item can be expanded or collapsed, showing or hiding other tree items. When an item is collapsed, a small "plus" indicator is displayed. An expanded item shows a "minus" indicator. These indicators are platform-specific and may not resemble plus or minus characters.[1] Tree items can draw a string, an icon, or both at the same time.

Users are familiar with tree controls because they are often used to implement the desktop file system browser. File systems are hierarchical. This makes Tree the ideal choice for a visual representation of a file system. However, it is prohibitively time-consuming to construct a tree item for every directory in a file system. When there are potentially too many items in a tree, programs often create the tree items on demand. The best time to do this is when items are expanded. If the user does not expand an item, child items are not created (see the section Using SWT.Expand to Fill a Tree Lazily).

Like lists and tables, when a tree is created with the SWT.MULTI style, users can select more than one tree item at the same time. Unlike List and Table, Tree is *not* indexed-based. For example, you cannot query the fifth row in a tree because the fifth row can change when the fourth row is expanded.

Tree items by themselves do not support any styles or listeners. Instead, listeners and styles are associated with the tree.

Why Doesn't TreeItem Support SWT.Selection?

Sometimes it's hard to remember exactly how responsibilities are divided among the various classes in SWT, particularly when item classes are involved. For example, ToolItem and Button both support SWT.Selection. Why doesn't

---

1.   They are often triangles on GTK and the Macintosh but can change with the operating system theme.

TreeItem? Although it might be easy enough to define rules such as "always put the event on the item," dogma can get in the way of pragmatics. For example, it makes sense for ToolItem to support the SWT.Selection event because tool items behave like buttons. However, it does not make sense for TreeItem to support SWT.Selection because if this were the case, to listen for selection in a tree, programs would need to add a selection listener to every instance of TreeItem. Selection is really better served as a property of the tree, despite the fact that the user actually selects a tree item with the mouse.

In SWT, we try to organize class responsibilities pragmatically, rather than just mechanically following a pattern.

Sometimes a tree is used to represent a hierarchy of boolean options. These kinds of trees, called *check box trees,* are created with the style SWT.CHECK.[2] Check box trees draw check boxes next to each item. These check boxes often resemble check buttons.

Trees Always Have scroll bars

Due to a Microsoft Windows limitation, trees on every platform will always have scroll bars,[3] even if you do not create them with SWT.H_SCROLL or SWT.V_SCROLL.

9.1.7 Creating a Hierarchy

Creating a hierarchy of tree items is straightforward in SWT. The constructors in the class TreeItem allow the parent of an item to be the tree or another tree item. When the parent of an item is a tree, the tree item is a root. Otherwise, it is an interior node in the hierarchy. For greater flexibility, the position parameter of the TreeItem constructor allows a tree item to be inserted at an index, relative to the other tree items in the items list of the parent.

---

2. Although it would have been more consistent to support the SWT.CHECK for TreeItem rather than Tree, Windows forced the issue. Check box behavior on Windows is a property of the tree, specified when the tree is created.

3. In early versions of SWT, this rule was not enforced. Programs that were written on Windows relied on this behavior, failing on other platforms. As a result, we were forced to include this Windows limitation as part of SWT.

The following program creates a tree that is three levels deep with four nodes on each level. The result is shown in Figure 9.1.

```java
public static void main(String[] args) {
    Display display = new Display();
    Shell shell = new Shell(display);
    Tree tree = new Tree(shell, SWT.BORDER);
    for (int i = 0; i < 4; i++) {
        TreeItem itemI = new TreeItem(tree, SWT.NULL);
        itemI.setText("Item " + i);
        for (int j = 0; j < 4; j++) {
            TreeItem itemJ = new TreeItem(itemI, SWT.NULL);
            itemJ.setText("Item " + i + " " + j);
            for (int k = 0; k < 4; k++) {
                TreeItem itemK =
                    new TreeItem(itemJ, SWT.NULL);
                itemK.setText(
                    "Item " + i + " " + j + " " + k);
            }
        }
    }
    tree.setSize(200, 200);
    shell.pack();
    shell.open();
    while (!shell.isDisposed()) {
        if (!display.readAndDispatch()) display.sleep();
    }
    display.dispose();
}
```

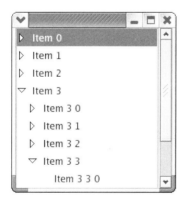

Figure 9.1

9.1.8   Text and Images

TreeItem supports the standard API to assign text and images to a widget. Like Button, TreeItem does not support mnemonics, wrapping, the SWT.WRAP style, or more than one line of text in an item.

setText(String string)   Sets the text for the tree item. The string cannot contain line delimiters or mnemonic characters.

getText()   Returns the tree item text. This is an empty string if the text has never been set.

setImage(Image image)   Sets the image for the tree item.

The First Image Defines the Size of All Images in the Control

Due to the same Windows limitation that is shared by ToolBar, TabFolder, and Table, Tree scales the images it displays to be the same size. By definition, this is the size of the first image that was inserted into the control.

---

getImage()   Returns the TreeItem image. This is null if the image has never been set.

9.1.9   *Expanding and Collapsing*

At any particular time, a tree item that has children is in either one of two states: expanded or collapsed. A tree item that is *expanded* shows its children. When a tree item is *collapsed*, it does not show its children. Tree items that do not have any children are called *leaf items* and do not have an expanded or collapsed state.[4]

To expand or collapse TreeItem, use setExpanded(). Calling setExpanded() on a leaf item does nothing.

setExpanded(boolean expanded)   Sets the expanded state of the item. This method does nothing if the item is already expanded or is a leaf item.

getExpanded()   Returns the expanded state of an item. Leaf items return false to indicate that they are not expanded.

When a tree item is either expanded or collapsed by the user, a corresponding SWT.Expand or SWT.Collapse event is issued. If the setExpanded() method is used to expand or collapse the item, an event is *not* issued.

---

4.   Strictly speaking, a leaf item is not expanded because getExpanded() returns false for a leaf. However, if SWT had defined a getCollapsed() method, it would also return false.

On some platforms, such as Windows, when the tree item is collapsed, the selection can change as a result of the collapse operation. For example, if the selection is in an item belonging to the subtree that is about to be collapsed, the selection is assigned elsewhere in the tree (usually to the item that is being collapsed). In this case, an SWT.Selection event *is* issued, regardless of whether the user collapsed the tree item or the program collapsed it using setExpanded(false).

Why Can setExpanded() Cause SWT.Selection?

At first, this seems to break the rules. On the surface, you might think that the user, not the program, should be the source of SWT.Selection events. After all, calling setSelection() doesn't cause them. In this case, the difference is that when collapsing an item changes the selection, the program has no simple way to detect the change. It doesn't matter that the user didn't collapse the item; the selection was changed without calling setSelection(). This makes the change unexpected. To be consistent, an SWT.Selection event is issued when this happens. This means that a program that tracks the selection will not get out of step when calling setExpanded(). For a similar reason, when setSelection() expands tree items to show a new selection, SWT.Expand events are sent.

9.1.10   *Hierarchical Operations*

Tree and TreeItem provide a number of hierarchical operations that allow you to determine the parent–child relationship between items. The methods to do this are found in *both* the Tree and TreeItem classes. Because Tree is not an index-based control, these methods are not index-based.

getParentItem()   Returns the parent item of the tree item. If the item is a root item, null is returned. This method is included in Tree for completeness only. It always returns null when called on a tree.

getItemCount()   Returns the number of items in a tree or a tree item.

getItems()   Returns an array of the child items in a tree or a tree item. This is a copy of the array that is used to hold the items so that modifying this array has no effect.

The following code fragment prints a text representation of a tree by visiting every node and printing it indented by its depth in the tree.

```
static void traverse(TreeItem[] items) {
    for (int i = 0; i < items.length; i++) {
        TreeItem item = items[i];
        String string = item.toString();
        while (item.getParentItem() != null) {
            string = "\t" + string;
            item = item.getParentItem();
        }
        System.out.println(string);
        traverse(items[i].getItems());
    }
}
```

This code is simple and was written to show the use of getParentItem()
and getItems(). A better implementation would avoid the string concatenation
and include a *level* parameter that was incremented with every recursive call.
This would allow us to get rid of the loop that computes depth.

At first, this implementation of traverse() might seem a little strange.
Good programming practice dictates that recursive traversal code should perform the operation on the item, then make the recursive call on each child of
the item. However, our traverse() method takes an array of items. This implementation of traverse(), although unorthodox, is correct. Its implementation
was forced by the fact that although Tree.getItems() and TreeItem.getItems()
have the same method signature, there is no interface to capture the commonality. Without resorting to casting, it is not possible to write a version of the
traverse() method that takes a single object.

Here is an alternate implementation of traverse() that uses two methods:
one that takes a tree item and another that takes a tree. It does not cast but
contains two identical loops.

```
static void traverse(TreeItem item) {
    String string = item.toString();
        TreeItem temp = item.getParentItem();
    while (temp != null) {
        string = "\t" + string;
        temp = temp.getParentItem();
    }
    System.out.println(string);
    TreeItem[] items = item.getItems();
    for (int i = 0; i < items.length; i++) {
        traverse(items[i]);
    }
}

static void traverse(Tree tree) {
    TreeItem[] items = tree.getItems();
    for (int i = 0; i < items.length; i++) {
        traverse(items[i]);
    }
}
```

As of R3.0, interfaces are not defined in SWT to capture commonality between classes. The rationale for this design decision is beyond the scope of this book.

9.1.11   Checked and Grayed Tree Items

Trees support a checked and grayed state for tree items. As was previously described, in order to check or gray the check box for a tree item, the tree must have been created with the SWT.CHECK style. Figure 9.2 shows a check box tree running on Windows.

Figure 9.2

setChecked(boolean checked)   Sets the checked state of the item. The checked state of an item usually takes the form of a small check box, located before the icon or text of the item. If the tree was not created with the SWT.CHECK style, nothing is checked.

getChecked()   Returns the checked state of the item. If the tree was not created with the SWT.CHECK style, false is returned.

setGrayed(boolean grayed)   Sets the grayed state of the item. When the grayed state is true, the *check box portion* of the item draws using a "grayed" look. Note that the item is *not disabled* and can still be selected by the user. If the tree was not created with the SWT.CHECK style, nothing is grayed.

getGrayed()   Returns the grayed state of the item. If the tree was not created with the SWT.CHECK style, false is returned.

The checked state of a tree item is independent of the checked state of its parent or child items. This means that when an item is checked or unchecked, other items are unaffected. However, many users expect that when an item is checked or unchecked, its child items are also automatically checked or unchecked. Grayed tree items are often used to indicate that some of the items below a checked item are not checked. Because neither of these features is implemented by default, you will need to write the code to make this happen.

The following program maintains the checked state and grayed state of the tree items in a tree, as described above. An SWT.Selection listener is used to compute the two states when the user selects a check box. The result, with some items checked, is shown in Figure 9.3.

```
static void checkPath(
    TreeItem item,
    boolean checked,
    boolean grayed) {
    if (item == null) return;
    if (grayed) {
        checked = true;
    } else {
        int index = 0;
        TreeItem[] items = item.getItems();
        while (index < items.length) {
            TreeItem child = items[index];
            if (child.getGrayed()
                || checked != child.getChecked()) {
                checked = grayed = true;
                break;
            }
            index++;
        }
    }
    item.setChecked(checked);
    item.setGrayed(grayed);
    checkPath(item.getParentItem(), checked, grayed);
}

static void checkItems(TreeItem item, boolean checked) {
    item.setGrayed(false);
    item.setChecked(checked);
    TreeItem[] items = item.getItems();
    for (int i = 0; i < items.length; i++) {
        checkItems(items[i], checked);
    }
}

public static void main(String[] args) {
    Display display = new Display();
    Shell shell = new Shell(display);
    Tree tree = new Tree(shell, SWT.BORDER | SWT.CHECK);
    tree.addListener(SWT.Selection, new Listener() {
        public void handleEvent(Event event) {
            if (event.detail == SWT.CHECK) {
                TreeItem item = (TreeItem) event.item;
                boolean checked = item.getChecked();
                checkItems(item, checked);
```

```
                    checkPath(
                        item.getParentItem(),
                        checked,
                        false);
                }
            }
        });
        for (int i = 0; i < 4; i++) {
            TreeItem itemI = new TreeItem(tree, SWT.NULL);
            itemI.setText("Item " + i);
            for (int j = 0; j < 4; j++) {
                TreeItem itemJ = new TreeItem(itemI, SWT.NULL);
                itemJ.setText("Item " + i + " " + j);
                for (int k = 0; k < 4; k++) {
                    TreeItem itemK =
                        new TreeItem(itemJ, SWT.NULL);
                    itemK.setText(
                        "Item " + i + " " + j + " " + k);
                }
            }
        }
        tree.setSize(200, 200);
        shell.pack();
        shell.open();
        while (!shell.isDisposed()) {
            if (!display.readAndDispatch()) display.sleep();
        }
        display.dispose();
    }
```

The checkItems() method recursively checks or unchecks the item and all child items. As you would expect, regardless of the new checked state, all items are ungrayed. This is done because items in the subtree are all either checked or unchecked.

The checkPath() method is used to ensure that when the checked state of an item changes, its ancestors in the tree are either checked, grayed, or unchecked to match the new state of their children. This method is initially called with the *parent* of the item whose state has changed, the new checked state, and the desired grayed state. While processing the ancestors of an item, if any child is either grayed or checked, the item must become both grayed and checked.

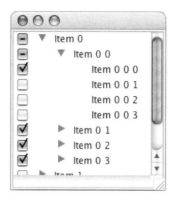

Figure 9.3

9.1.12   TreeItem Foreground, Background, and Font

TreeItem supports the ability to set the foreground color, background color, and font used by an individual item.

setForeground(Color color)   Sets the foreground color of the item. If the color is null, the default foreground color for the item is restored.

getForeground()   Returns the foreground color of the item. If the color has not been set, the default foreground color is returned.

setBackground(Color color)   Sets the background color of the item. If the color is null, the default background color of the item is restored.

getBackground()   Returns the background color of the item. If the color has not been set, the default background color is returned.

setFont(Font font)   Sets the font that is used to draw the text in the item. If the font is null, the default font is restored.

getFont()   Returns the font that is used to draw text in the item. If the font has not been set, the default font is returned.

9.1.13   The Selection

Application programs often need to work with the selection in a tree. Once again, because trees are not index-based controls, selection is specified using tree items. The following methods are used to manipulate the selection in a tree:

setSelection(TreeItem[] selection)   Sets the selection to be the array of items. The previous selection is cleared, and the tree is scrolled and expanded so that the new selection becomes visible. If the tree is single-select and the array contains more than one item, the first item is selected.

getSelection()   Returns an array of the selected items. This is a *copy* so that modifying the array has no effect on the control. When no items are selected, this array is empty.

getSelectionCount()   Returns the number of items that are selected in the tree.

selectAll()   Selects all the items in a tree. If the tree is single-select, no action is taken.

deselectAll()   Deselects all items in the tree.

9.1.14   *Scrolling*

Tree controls provide the ability to scroll a tree by getting and setting the top item. The *top item* of a tree is the tree item that is displayed at the *top* of the control. The top item is set using the setTopItem() method.

setTopItem(TreeItem item)   Scrolls to show the new item at the top of the tree control. Depending on the platform and the number of items in the tree, it may not be possible for the particular item to become the top item. This can happen when the platform does not allow the control to scroll so that white space follows that last item.

getTopItem(TreeItem item)   Returns the item that is at the top of the tree. The top item can change when items are added, deleted, scrolled, expanded, or collapsed.

Generally speaking, application programs rarely need to scroll a tree to show the selection. This is because setSelection() automatically makes the selection visible to the user. However, there are circumstances where you might need to show the selection. In these cases, the showSelection() method can be used.

showSelection()   Scrolls to show the selection. The selection is made visible somewhere inside the control. If the selection is already visible, nothing happens. Because the control may be scrolled, this method is used to bring the selection to the attention of the user.

showItem(TreeItem item) Scrolls to show the item. As with show-Selection(), the item is made visible but the exact location of the item in the tree is unspecified.

9.1.15 Removing Items

Tree items are removed using the TreeItem method dispose(). When an item is disposed, child items are also disposed. One way to remove all the tree items in a tree is to dispose of all the roots. This can be time-consuming and cause too many redraws, especially when there are many items in the tree. The recommended way to dispose all items in a tree is to use the Tree method removeAll().

removeAll() Disposes all the items in a tree and redraws once after all the items have been disposed.

9.1.16 Tree Events

SWT.Selection (SelectionEvent)

The SWT.Selection event (typed event SelectionEvent) is sent whenever the user selects an item with the mouse or the keyboard or when the selection changes because of the tree being expanded or collapsed (see the Why Can set-Expanded() Cause SWT.Selection? box). The relevant event fields during a selection event for Tree are as follows.

Public Fields of Class Event That Are Valid during SWT.Selection

Field	Description
detail	Set to SWT.CHECK when the user selected the check box portion of the item
item	The item that was affected when the selection changed. Typically, this item is selected but can be unselected when the detail is SWT.CHECK or in a multiselect tree, when the user changes the selection by deselecting the item.

SWT.DefaultSelection (SelectionEvent)

The SWT.DefaultSelection event (typed event SelectionEvent) is sent whenever the user performs the platform-specific operation that is treated as a default selection. On most platforms, default selection occurs when the user double-clicks on an item or presses the <Enter> key. The relevant event fields during a default selection event for Tree are as follows.

Public Fields of Class Event That Are Valid during SWT.DefaultSelection

Field	Description
detail	Set to SWT.CHECK when the user selected the check box part of the item
item	The primary item that was affected when the selection changed

SWT.Expand (TreeEvent)

Table 9.1 shows the expand event for tree controls.

Table 9.1 Expand Event

Untyped Event	Description	
SWT.Expand	A tree item was expanded	
Typed Event	**Listener**	**Methods**
TreeEvent	TreeListener (and TreeAdapter)	treeCollapsed(TreeEvent) treeExpanded(TreeEvent)

The SWT.Expand event (typed event TreeEvent) is sent whenever the user expands a tree item with the mouse or the keyboard or when the item is expanded as the result of any method other than setExpanded(). The relevant event fields during an expand event for Tree are as follows.

Public Fields of Class Event That Are Valid during SWT.Expand

Field	Description
item	The item that was expanded

Using SWT.Expand to Fill a Tree Lazily

Building a tree that contains thousands of items is time-consuming. For example, a tree used to represent a large hierarchical file system would need not only to create thousands of tree items but also to visit every directory on the file system. Fortunately, the SWT.Expand event can be used to create tree items lazily, as the user expands the tree.

The following example uses an SWT.Expand listener to fill a tree with directories and files as the user expands the tree. This involves creating a dummy item to force the tree to show the plus indicator. This dummy item does not have a file or directory associated with it. When a real item is created, the setData() method is used to store the file or directory.

The roots of the tree, which are always directories, are initialized to contain dummy items. When a tree item is expanded for the first time, the dummy item is deleted, and the real items are created. If any of the real items are directories, a dummy child item is created for each one, allowing the lazy filling process to continue the next time the user selects one of these items. Figure 9.4 shows the result open to an arbitrary place in a file system.

```
public static void main(String[] args) {
    Display display = new Display();
    Shell shell = new Shell(display);
    shell.setText("Lazy Tree");
    Tree tree = new Tree(shell, SWT.BORDER);

    /* Initialize the roots of the tree */
    File[] roots = File.listRoots();
    for (int i = 0; i < roots.length; i++) {
        TreeItem root = new TreeItem(tree, SWT.NULL);
        root.setText(roots[i].toString());
        root.setData(roots[i]);

        /* Use a dummy item to force the '+' */
        new TreeItem(root, SWT.NULL);
    }

    /* Use SWT.Expand to lazily fill the tree */
    tree.addListener(SWT.Expand, new Listener() {
        public void handleEvent(Event event) {

            /*
             * If the item does not contain a
             * dummy node, return. A dummy item
             * is a single child of the root that
             * does not have any application data.
             */
            TreeItem root = (TreeItem) event.item;
            TreeItem[] items = root.getItems();
            if (items.length != 1) return;
            if (items[0].getData() != null) return;
            items[0].dispose();

            /* Create the item children */
            File file = (File) root.getData();
            File[] files = file.listFiles();
            if (files == null) return;
            for (int i = 0; i < files.length; i++) {
                TreeItem item =new TreeItem(root,SWT.NULL);
                item.setText(files[i].getName());
                item.setData(files[i]);
```

```
                    /* Use a dummy item to force the '+' */
                    if (files[i].isDirectory()) {
                        new TreeItem(item, SWT.NULL);
                    }
                }
            }
        });

        /* Set size of the tree and open the shell */
        tree.setSize(300, 300);
        shell.pack();
        shell.open();
        while (!shell.isDisposed()) {
            if (!display.readAndDispatch()) display.sleep();
        }
        display.dispose();
}
```

Figure 9.4

Note that a better implementation would sort the items, show icons, and include only directories as nodes in the tree.

SWT.Collapse (TreeEvent)

Table 9.2 shows the collapse event for tree controls.

Table 9.2   Collapse Event

Untyped Event	Description	
SWT.Collapse	A tree item was collapsed	

Typed Event	Listener	Methods
TreeEvent	TreeListener (and TreeAdapter)	treeCollapsed(TreeEvent) treeExpanded(TreeEvent)

The SWT.Collapse event (typed event TreeEvent) is sent whenever the user collapses an item with the mouse or the keyboard or when the item is collapsed as the result of any method other than setExpanded(). The relevant event fields during a collapse event for Tree are as follows.

Public Fields of Class Event That Are Valid during SWT.Collapse

Field	Description
item	The item that was collapsed

9.2 Classes Table, TableItem, and TableColumn

9.2.1 Example

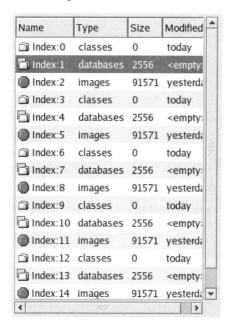

9.2.2 Table, TableItem, and TableColumn Hierarchies

9.2.3   Table Styles

Style	Description
SWT.SINGLE	Create a single-select table
SWT.MULTI	Create a multiselect table
SWT.CHECK	Create a table with check boxes
SWT.FULL_SELECTION	The selection is expanded to fill an entire row
SWT.HIDE_SELECTION	The selection is hidden when focus is lost

9.2.4   Table Events

Event	Description
SWT.Selection	A table item was selected
SWT.DefaultSelection	A table item was default selected

9.2.5   TableItem Styles (none)

Style	Description

9.2.6   TableItem Events (none)

Event	Description

9.2.7   TableColumn Styles

Style	Description
SWT.LEFT	The table column is left-justified
SWT.RIGHT	The table column is right-justified
SWT.CENTER	The table column is centered

9.2.8   TableColumn Events

Event	Description
SWT.Selection	The table column was selected
SWT.Move	The table column was moved
SWT.Resize	The table column was resized

Tables are selectable controls that are capable of displaying vertical rows of items. Each row is represented by an instance of TableItem. Table items are automatically added when created and are positioned in the parent using the location constructor parameter.

Tables are analogous to lists but are more flexible. Although lists can contain only strings, tables can contain strings and images. Tables are also capable of displaying multiple columns. A table that is displaying columns uses instances of TableColumn to represent each column.

Tables can optionally include headers and grid lines. The *header* portion of a table resembles a row of push buttons displayed at the top of the control. Each button in the header is the width of the corresponding table column. *Grid lines* refer to a horizontal and/or vertical pattern that is drawn to accentuate the rows and columns. This pattern is often composed of a matrix or grid of lines drawn between the items or by alternating the background color of the rows.[5]

Table shares many of the same concepts, limitations, and behaviors of List and Tree.

Tables Always Have Scroll Bars

Due to the same limitation that affects trees and for the same reasons, tables always have scroll bars (see Classes Tree and TreeItem for a full explanation).

Like List and Tree, Table can allow either a single item or multiple items to be selected at a time and supports scroll bars and borders. If you are famil-

---

5. This is the case on GTK where the native table control does not draw lines. Because the native control is used to draw the table, grid lines are drawn using the native support. If the native control does not have this capability, grid lines will not be drawn.

iar with the sections Classes Tree and TreeItem and Class List, you will find
the material in this section easy to follow. The API of class Table is very similar
to those classes.

   Users are familiar with tables because they are used everywhere on the
desktop. For example, the Windows XP Task Manager uses a table with multiple columns to show tasks and their status.

A Table Is Not a Spreadsheet

Despite the fact that tables have rows and columns, Table is not a general-
purpose spreadsheet class. If you are expecting the features and capabilities of
something like Microsoft Excel, you will be disappointed. Native tables just aren't
that sophisticated. Nevertheless, they are useful in many contexts. The class
TableEditor, found in the package *org.eclipse.swt.custom*, provides the rudimentary capability to place a control within a Table cell. This can be used to do "in-
place editing," for example, as we do in the FileExplorer example in Part III.

9.2.9   Full Row Selection

When the user selects a table item, some platforms require the user to select
either the text or icon in order to select the item.[6] On other platforms, the user
can select anywhere within the same row. This behavior is platform-specific
but can be configured by creating a table with the style SWT.FULL
_SELECTION. When this style is provided, selecting any column on the same
row as a table item selects the item. Tables often indicate SWT.FULL
_SELECTION by drawing the selection highlight over the entire row. It is
important to note that SWT.FULL_SELECTION is a hint and may not be
honored on some platforms.

9.2.10   Hiding the Selection

When a table loses focus, the selection is either unchanged or draws in some
manner to indicate that focus is no longer in the control. The SWT.HIDE
_SELECTION style causes a table to hide its selection when focus is lost,
drawing as though it were not selected. The SWT.HIDE_SELECTION style is
a hint that may not be honored on some platforms.

---

6. For example, Microsoft Windows forces you to do this, whereas the Macintosh does not.

9.2.11   Tables in List Mode

When you create table items but *do not* create any table columns, Table acts like List. This kind of table is said to be operating in "list mode." However, even though you did not create a table column, the user still sees a column of items, just like the column of strings that is displayed by a list. This can be a bit confusing at first because there is clearly a column of items on the screen but a table column was not created. It helps in this case to think of the table as a fancy kind of list, one that is capable of displaying both icons and strings. List does not require you to create a list column in order to display strings, so neither does Table.

The following program creates a table with 1,000 items but does not create a table column.

```
public static void main(String[] args) {
    Display display = new Display();
    Shell shell = new Shell(display);
    Table table = new Table(shell, SWT.BORDER);
    for (int i = 0; i < 1000; i++) {
        TableItem item = new TableItem(table, SWT.NULL);
        item.setText("Item " + i);
    }
    table.setSize(200, 200);
    shell.pack();
    shell.open();
    while (!shell.isDisposed()) {
        if (!display.readAndDispatch()) display.sleep();
    }
    display.dispose();
}
```

9.2.12   Getting the Items

Using getItems(), you can retrieve the items that you created in a table.

getItems()   Returns the items, which is an array of table items. The array that is returned is a copy so that modifying this array will not affect the control.

getItem(int index)   Returns the item at an index. If the index is out of range, an IllegalArgumentException ("Index out of bounds") is thrown.

getItemCount()   Returns the number of items in the control.

Where Is the setItems() Method?

The reason that there isn't a setItems() method for Table is a direct result of the rule that widgets are always created with a parent. When a table item is created, it is already inserted into the table. When a table item is disposed, it is removed from the table and is no longer valid. Given these two conditions and the fact that an item can have only one parent, there are no possible items for hypothetical setItems() method to insert.

9.2.13 Headers and Grid Lines

Headers and grid lines are properties of tables. Although it is possible to show both when a table is in list mode, it generally is not very useful. You will use both when we describe Tables with Multiple Columns later in this chapter.

setHeaderVisible(boolean visible)   Sets the visibility state of the header.

getHeaderVisible()   Returns the visibility state of the header.

getHeaderHeight()   Returns the height of the header. If the header is not visible, the height is zero. On all platforms, the header is considered to be within the client area of the table.[7] This means that you may need to get the height of the header in order to compute the preferred size of a table.

setLinesVisible(boolean visible)   Sets the visibility state of the grid lines.

getLinesVisible()   Returns the visibility state of the grid lines.

9.2.14 Item Height

You can find out the height of an item within a table control using getItem-Height().

---

7. Although table headers seem as though they should be "trimming," the underlying implementation of tables on many platforms uses a native header control. This control is a child of the table and is positioned within the client area of the table. Because SWT answers the client area by querying the operating systems, the header is not part of the trim.

getItemHeight()   Returns the height of an item in the control. This value can be different from the height of the font that is used by the control, because some platforms include spacing between items.

The getItemHeight() method is often used to compute the initial size of a control, in this case, a table. Refer to the section Lines and the Line Delimiter in Class Text for an example of this. The code to compute the initial size for a table is equivalent but uses getItemHeight() and getHeaderHeight() instead of getLineHeight().

```
int height =
    rows * table.getItemHeight() + table.getHeaderHeight();
int width = columns * fm.getAverageCharWidth();
table.setSize(table.computeSize(width, height));
```

9.2.15 *Tables with Multiple Columns*

To have multiple columns in a table, you must create instances of TableColumn to represent each column. As soon as you create the first table column, the table is no longer operating in list mode. This means that you are responsible for setting the widths of the columns so that the user can see the data that they will contain.

The following program creates a table with 1,000 items and creates a single table column. The table column is set to be 100 pixels wide so the user can see the strings. Otherwise, the code is identical to the example code in Tables in List Mode.

```
public static void main(String[] args) {
    Display display = new Display();
    Shell shell = new Shell(display);
    Table table = new Table(shell, SWT.BORDER);
    TableColumn column = new TableColumn(table, SWT.NONE);
    column.setWidth(100);
    for (int i = 0; i < 1000; i++) {
        TableItem item = new TableItem(table, SWT.NULL);
        item.setText("Item " + i);
    }
    table.setSize(200, 200);
    shell.pack();
    shell.open();
    while (!shell.isDisposed()) {
        if (!display.readAndDispatch()) display.sleep();
    }
    display.dispose();
}
```

A table that has one table column is not particularly useful (although were the header to be visible, a program could use it to invoke a sort operation). On some platforms, tables use the column width to determine when scroll bars are needed. This means that in the above example, if a table item were to contain a string that was wider than 100 pixels, it would be clipped. This does not happen to a table that is operating in list mode. Because there are no table columns, there is nothing to clip.

When you use a table that has multiple columns, often you will decide to show the table header. By default, the header is not visible. Showing the header allows the user to resize the columns.

Here is a more realistic example that creates a table with a header and multiple columns. To ensure that the table and table columns are a reasonable size, the table columns are packed after all of the items have been created. Figure 9.5 shows the result running on Macintosh OS X.

```
static final int COLUMNS = 8, ROWS = 8;
public static void main(String[] args) {
    Display display = new Display();
    Shell shell = new Shell(display);
    Table table = new Table(shell, SWT.BORDER);
    table.setHeaderVisible(true);
    table.setLinesVisible(true);
    for (int i = 0; i < COLUMNS; i++) {
        TableColumn column=new TableColumn(table,SWT.NONE);
        column.setText("Column " + i);
    }
    for (int i = 0; i < ROWS; i++) {
        TableItem item = new TableItem(table, SWT.NULL);
        for (int j = 0; j < COLUMNS; j++) {
            item.setText(j, "Item " + i + "-" + j);
        }
    }
    for (int i = 0; i < COLUMNS; i++) {
        TableColumn column = table.getColumn(i);
        column.pack();
    }
    table.pack();
    shell.pack();
    shell.open();
    while (!shell.isDisposed()) {
        if (!display.readAndDispatch()) display.sleep();
    }
    display.dispose();
}
```

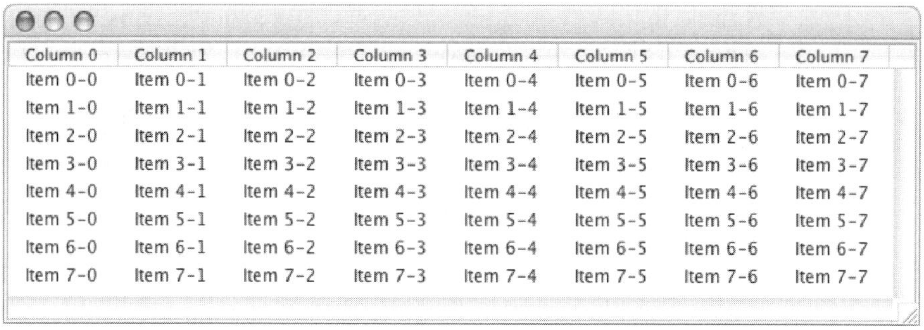

Figure 9.5

9.2.16 Text and Images in a Table Column

TableColumn, like many other widgets in SWT, supports the standard API to set and get text and images. TableColumn supports mnemonic characters in strings but does not wrap or support the SWT.WRAP style.

setText(String string)   Sets the text for the column. The string cannot contain line delimiters. Mnemonics characters, indicated by '&', are supported.

getText()   Returns the text. This is an empty string if the text has never been set.

setImage(Image image)   Sets the image for the column.

getImage()   Returns the item image. This is null if the image has never been set.

9.2.17 The Width of a Table Column

When a table column is created, like the other widgets in SWT, its width is zero. You can use setWidth() or pack() to resize a table column.

setWidth(int width)   Sets the width of the column.

getWidth()   Returns the width of the column.

pack()   Sets the width of the column to be wide enough to show the maximum of the contents of the header item and the column of data in the table. For very large tables, this method can be time-consuming because it may need to measure all the data in the column.

When to Set the Width of a Table Column

Generally, it's a bad idea to set the width of a table column after the table has been displayed. The problem with doing this is that the user can resize the same column, leading to a situation where you and the user are fighting over the width. A friendly user interface always lets the user win.

9.2.18   Alignment in a Table Column

When a table column is created, the alignment of the column can be configured using one of the styles SWT.LEFT, SWT.CENTER, or SWT.RIGHT, just like Label and Button. Alignment in TableColumn differs from alignment in the other widgets because it applies to the entire column, not just the text or image in the header.

After the column has been created, the setAlignment() method can be used to change alignment.

setAlignment(int alignment)   Sets the alignment for the column to be either left-, center-, or right-aligned, depending on the argument.

getAlignment()   Returns the alignment for the column.

The default alignment style for a table column is SWT.LEFT. Unlike Button alignment, TableColumn alignment is not part of the platform look and feel, so you should feel free to change it to suit your needs.

The First Column in a Table Is Always Left-Aligned

Due to a restriction in Microsoft Windows, the alignment of the first column in a table cannot be changed. To create programs that are portable to other platforms, this restriction is enforced by SWT on every platform. To work around this problem, application programs can create a zero-sized first column.

9.2.19   Text and Images in a Table Item

TableItem, like TreeItem and other widgets, supports the standard API to set text and images. Unlike TreeItem, when the table has multiple columns, you can set the text and image for each individual cell. TableItem does not support mnemonics, wrapping, or the SWT.WRAP style.

setText(String string)   Sets the text for the table item. This is the same as setText(0, string).

setText(int index, String string)   Sets the text that will be displayed in the column (of the table item) that is specified by the given column index. The string cannot contain line delimiters or mnemonics characters.

getText()   Returns the table item text. This is the same as getText(0).

getText(int index)   Returns the text of the column (of the table item) that is specified by the given column index. This is an empty string if the text has never been set.

setImage(Image image)   Sets the image for the item. This is the same as setImage(0, image).

The First Image Defines the Size of All Images in the Control

Due to a Windows limitation, just like ToolBar, TabFolder, and Tree, Table scales the images it displays to be the size of the first image inserted into the control.

setImage(int index, Image image)   Sets the image that will be displayed in the column (of the table item) that is specified by the given column index.

getImage()   Returns the TableItem image. This is the same as getImage(0).

getImage(int index)   Returns the image of the column (of the table item) that is specified by the given column index. This is null if the image has never been set.

TableItem provides two convenience methods that allow you to set multiple strings and images at the same time. They are currently no faster than setting the individual properties but may be optimized in the future.

setText(String[] strings)   Sets the text for each column of the table item to the corresponding string in the array.

setImage(Image[] images)   Sets the image for each column of the table item to the corresponding image in the array.

9.2.20   Checked and Grayed Table Items

Like Tree, Table supports checked and grayed check boxes. In order to check or gray the check box for an item, Table must have been created with the SWT.CHECK style.

setChecked(boolean checked)   Sets the checked state of the item. The checked state of an item usually takes the form of a small check box, located before the icon or text for the item. If the table was not created with the SWT.CHECK style, nothing is checked.

getChecked()   Returns the checked state of the item. If the table was not created with the SWT.CHECK style, false is returned.

setGrayed(boolean grayed)   Sets the grayed state of the item. When the grayed state is true, the check box portion of the item draws using a grayed look. Note that the item is not disabled and can still be selected by the user. If the table was not created with the SWT.CHECK style, nothing is grayed.

getGrayed()   Returns the grayed state of the item. If the table was not created with the SWT.CHECK style, false is returned.

9.2.21   TableItem Foreground, Background, and Font

Table supports the ability to set the foreground color, background color, and font of a table item. Unlike TreeItem (which does not support columns), TableItem allows you to set the color and font of an individual cell.

setForeground(Color color)   Sets the foreground color of the item. This method sets the color for the every cell in the item.

setForeground(int index, Color color)   Sets the foreground color of the item at a column index. If the color is null, the default foreground color of the item is restored.

getForeground()   Returns the foreground color of the item.

getForeground(int index)   Returns the foreground color of the item at a column index. If the color has not been set, the foreground color for the item is returned. If the item does not have a foreground color, the foreground color for the table is returned.

setBackground(Color color)   Sets the background color of the item. This method sets the color for the every cell in the item.

setBackground(int index, Color color)   Sets the background color of the item at a column index. If the color is null, the default background color of the item is restored.

getBackground()   Returns the background color of the item.

getBackground(int index)   Returns the background color of the item at a column index. If the color has not been set, the background color for the item is returned. If the item does not have a background color, the background color for the table is returned.

setFont(Font font)   Sets the font that is used to draw the text in the item. If the font is null, the default font is restored.

setFont(int index, Font font)   Sets the font of the item at a column index. If the font is null, the default font of the item is restored.

getFont()   Returns the font that is used to draw text in the item. If the font has not been set, the default font is returned.

getFont(int index)   Returns the font of the item at a column index. If the font has not been set, the font for the item is returned. If the item does not have a font, the font for the table is returned.

9.2.22   *Removing Table Items*

Table items are removed using the remove() and removeAll() methods.[8] Removing a table item has the same affect as disposing of it. However, it is *much* faster to remove a range of table items rather than dispose of them one at a time. For this reason, and because tables are index-based controls, it makes sense for Table to define remove() operations.

---

8. By now, you should be familiar with the conventions of SWT, so it should not seem strange to you that Table has remove() methods but no add() methods. The reason that Table does not define add() methods is because table items are added when they are created. (See the Where Is the setItems() Method? box.)

remove(int index)   Removes the item at an index. If the index is out of range, an IllegalArgumentException ("Index out of bounds") is thrown.

remove(int start, int end)   Removes items from start to end, inclusive. If an index is out of range, an IllegalArgumentException ("Index out of bounds") is thrown.

remove(int[] indices)   Removes items using an array of indices. If an index is out of range, an IllegalArgumentException ("Index out of bounds") is thrown.

remove(TableItem item)   Returns the item at an index. This method removes the item from the control.

removeAll()   Removes all the items from the control.

9.2.23   The Selection

Table supports the same kind of selection API as List, with the significant difference that parameters that are Strings in class List are TableItems in class Table. Tables cannot, by definition, contain duplicate instances of TableItem.[9] As you would expect, the strings and icons within different instances of TableItem can be the same, causing the two objects to look the same, despite the fact that they are not identical.

setSelection(int index)   Selects the item at an index. Indices that are out of range are ignored. Any previous selection is cleared. The control is scrolled to bring the new selection to the attention of the user. If the control has a focus indicator, the focus indicator is assigned to the new selection.

setSelection(int start, int end)   Selects all items in the range *start* to *end*, inclusive. If the control is single-select and the range contains more than one item, all of the indices are ignored. Once the previous selection has been cleared and the new items have been selected, the control is scrolled to show the new selection, and the focus indicator is assigned.

setSelection(int[] indices)   Selects items using an array of indices. If the array is empty, the selection is cleared. If the control is single-select

---

9.   This just is not possible, because there is no add() operation.

and the array contains more than one item, all of the indices are ignored. Once the previous selection has been cleared and the new items have been selected, the control is scrolled to show the new selection, and the focus indicator is assigned.

setSelection(TableItems[] items) Selects items using an array of items. This method behaves the same as though setSelection(indices) were called using an array of indices composed of the indices of each item in the control.

getSelection() Returns the selection as an array of items. This is a *copy* so that modifying the array has no effect on the control.

getSelectionCount() Returns the number of selected items.

getSelectionIndex() Returns the index of the item that is selected, based on the following rules.

1. If no items are selected, −1 is returned.

2. If the item that has the focus indicator is selected, that index is returned.

3. Otherwise, the index of the first selected item is returned.

getSelectionIndices() Returns the selection as an array of indices. This is a *copy* so that modifying the array has no effect on the control.

isSelected(int index) Returns true if the item at the index is selected. If the item is not selected or the index is out of range, false is returned.

9.2.24 Deselecting and Selecting Items

To manipulate the selection of individual items without affecting the current selection, Table defines the equivalent List API. The methods in this section differ from the setSelection() methods in Table in the same significant ways.

1. They do not clear the previous selection before acting.

2. They do not cause the table to scroll.

deselect(int index) Deselects the item at an index. Indices that are out of range are ignored.

deselect(int start, int end) Deselects items in range *start* to *end*, inclusive. Indices that are out of range are ignored.

deselect(int[] indices)   Deselects items using an array of indices. Indices that are out of range are ignored.

deselectAll()   Deselects all items in the control.

select(int index)   Selects the item at an index. Indices that are out of range are ignored.

select(int start, int end)   Selects items in range *start* to *end*, inclusive. Indices that are out of range are ignored.

select (int[] indices)   Selects items using the array of indices. This method behaves the same as though select(index) were called from a loop, using *indices*. Indices that are out of range are ignored.

selectAll()   Selects all items in the control. If the control is single-select, the selection is not changed.

9.2.25   *Scrolling*

Because Table and List are index-based, scrolling in a table is equivalent to scrolling in a list. Both use the "top index" concept.

setTopIndex(int index)   Scrolls to show the item indicated by the *index* parameter at the top of the control. Indexing starts at zero. If the index is out of range, the control scrolls to show the closest index that is within range. Depending on the platform and the number of items, it may not be possible for the particular item to become placed at the top of the control. This can happen when the platform does not allow the control to scroll so that white space follows the last item.

getTopIndex()   Returns the line that is at the top of the control. The top index can change for many reasons other than calling setTopIndex(). For example, setSelection() can scroll the control to show the new selection.

Tables, lists, trees, and text controls all define showSelection(). Tables define the method showItem() that has an equivalent method in class Tree.

showSelection()   Scrolls to show the selection. The selection is made visible somewhere inside the control. If the selection is already visible, nothing happens. Because the control may be scrolled, this method is used to bring the selection to the attention of the user.

showItem(TableItem item)   Scrolls to show the item. As with showSelection(), the item is made visible but exact location of the item in the table is unspecified.

9.2.26   *Search and Hit Test Operations*

Tables provide a number of search operations that allow you to find the index of an item and determine the item that is underneath a point. The term *hit testing* is used to describe this kind of operation. Hit testing for controls was discussed in Getting the Cursor Control in the Display chapter.

indexOf(TableItem item)   Returns the zero-based index of the item. If the item is not found, –1 is returned.

getItem(Point point)   Returns the item under a point. The point is in the coordinate system of the control. If the table supports the SWT.FULL_SELECTION style, the search includes every column of the table. Otherwise, only the first column is searched.

9.2.27   *Implementing Your Own Hit Test Operations*

Sometimes you might need to find out the row and column of the item where the mouse was pressed in a table with multiple columns. Unfortunately, the getItem(Point point) method does not do what you want. For tables that are not created with SWT.FULL_SELECTION, only the first column is searched. Fortunately, table items allow you to determine their bounds. Using this, you can write your own hit test operation.

getBounds(int index)   Returns the rectangle covered by the cell in the given column of the table item. The result is relative to the origin of the table.

getImageBounds(int index)   Returns the rectangle covered by the *image* in the cell in the given column of the table item. The result is relative to the origin of the table.

The following fragment adds an SWT.MouseDown listener to a table. This listener uses getBounds() and Rectangle operations to determine the row and column in the table where the mouse was pressed.

```
table.addListener(SWT.MouseDown, new Listener() {
    public void handleEvent(Event event) {
        Rectangle rect = table.getClientArea();
```

```
int itemCount = table.getItemCount();
int columnCount = table.getColumnCount();
int i = table.getTopIndex();
while (i < itemCount) {
    TableItem item = table.getItem(i);
    for (int j = 0; j < columnCount; j++) {
        Rectangle bounds = item.getBounds(j);
        if (bounds.y > rect.height) return;
        if (bounds.contains(event.x, event.y)) {
            System.out.println(item.getText(j));
            return;
        }
    }
    i++;
}
}
});
```

9.2.28 *Working with Large Tables*

Tables that are *virtual* allow you to configure table items on demand. When the data for each table item is required, the table requests it from your program. The advantage of virtual tables is that they request only the data that they need. Performance is improved by putting the cost of configuring items where it is unnoticed and not bothering to configure items that are unreferenced.

SWT Under Construction

At the time of writing of this book, extensive investigation is being performed to determine whether *native* virtual table support can be made available via the SWT API. Until that investigation is complete, you can use the coding patterns described in this section to get some of the same benefits.

There is also a movement within the community to write an emulated Table class, which could provide virtual support as well as remove some of the other restrictions of native tables.

The following program creates a large table and fills it with strings, one page of data at a time. While Table is being filled, a progress bar shows the number of table items that have been created. The function that fills the table is called *fillTable()*. Several alternate implementations of the fillTable() method follow the main body of the code.

```
static final int COLUMNS = 3, ROWS = 100000, PAGE = 100;
static final String[][] DATA = new String[ROWS][COLUMNS];
static {
    for (int i = 0; i < ROWS; i++) {
        for (int j = 0; j < COLUMNS; j++) {
            DATA[i][j] = "Item " + i + "-" + j;
        }
    }
}

public static void main(String[] args) {
    Display display = new Display();
    Shell shell = new Shell(display);
    RowLayout layout = new RowLayout(SWT.VERTICAL);
    layout.fill = true;
    shell.setLayout(layout);
    final Table table = new Table(shell, SWT.BORDER);
    table.setLayoutData(new RowData(400, 400));
    table.setHeaderVisible(true);
    for (int i = 0; i < COLUMNS; i++) {
        TableColumn column=new TableColumn(table,SWT.NONE);
        column.setText("Column " + i);
        column.setWidth(128);
    }
    final ProgressBar progress =
        new ProgressBar(shell, SWT.NONE);
    progress.setMaximum(ROWS - 1);
    shell.pack();
    shell.open();
    fillTable(table, progress, PAGE);
    while (!shell.isDisposed()) {
        if (!display.readAndDispatch()) display.sleep();
    }
    display.dispose();
}
```

Performance Improvements in Table in R3.0

Even though R3.0 will not have shipped by the time this book is completed, many performance improvements have already been made in the Table class. If you try to run any of the examples in this section in R2.1.x, you will be disappointed.

Using setRedraw() When Creating Table Items

The simplest way to improve performance when filling a table is to use setRedraw(). Many operating systems use setRedraw() to optimize drawing and defer expensive calculations when adding (the native equivalent of) table items. For a complete description of setRedraw(), see Turning off Redraw in the Control Fundamentals chapter.

Here is an implementation of fillTable() that uses setRedraw() to turn off drawing while the table items are created.

```
static void fillTable(
    final Table table,
    final ProgressBar progress,
    final int page) {
    table.setRedraw(false);
    for (int i = 0; i < ROWS; i++) {
        TableItem item = new TableItem(table, SWT.NULL);
        for (int j = 0; j < COLUMNS; j++) {
            item.setText(j, DATA[i][j]);
        }
        if (i % page == 0) progress.setSelection(i);
    }
    table.setRedraw(true);
    progress.setSelection(0);
}
```

Creating TableItems in an Idle Handler

One technique that avoids making the user wait for a large table is to create table items in an "idle handler" (see Using asyncExec() from the User Interface Thread in the chapter Display). Because asyncExec() runnables are executed when the event loop is idle, priority is given to the user interface thread.

Creating table items this way is somewhat slower than the equivalent code that fills the table in the user interface thread. This is due to the overhead of the runnables and the fact that setRedraw() cannot be used without causing the table to flash. However, this approach has the advantage that the user can browse the items that have been created so far while the table is still being filled. A smarter version of fillTable() could also allow the user to cancel the operation.

This implementation of fillTable() uses asyncExec() to create a table item when the event loop is idle.

```
static void fillTable(
    final Table table,
    final ProgressBar progress,
    final int page) {
    final Display display = table.getDisplay();
    Runnable runnable = new Runnable() {
        int index = 0;
        public void run() {
            if (table.isDisposed()) return;
            int end = Math.min(index + page, ROWS);
            while (index < end) {
```

```
            TableItem item =
                new TableItem(table, SWT.NULL);
            for (int j = 0; j < COLUMNS; j++) {
                item.setText(j, DATA[index][j]);
            }
            index++;
        }
        if (end == ROWS) end = 0;
        progress.setSelection(end);
        if (index < ROWS) display.asyncExec(this);
    }
};
display.asyncExec(runnable);
}
```

Creating Table Items in Another Thread

This approach is similar to using asyncExec() from the user interface thread. It has similar behavior and performance characteristics. However, the approach differs because it uses syncExec() and does not favor the user interface thread. If asyncExec() were to be used instead, the table-filling thread would never be blocked waiting on the user interface thread because asyncExec() does not wait. Threading, syncExec(), and asyncExec() are discussed in great detail in the Multithreaded Programming section of the chapter Display.

The following fillTable() implementation uses syncExec() to create items, a page at a time, in the user interface thread.

```
static void fillTable(
    final Table table,
    final ProgressBar progress,
    final int page) {
    final Display display = table.getDisplay();
    Thread thread = new Thread() {
        public void run() {
            int index = 0;
            while (index < ROWS) {
                if (table.isDisposed()) return;
                final int start = index;
                final int end=Math.min(index + page, ROWS);
                display.syncExec(new Runnable() {
                    public void run() {
                        if (table.isDisposed()) return;
                        for (int i = start; i < end; i++) {
                            TableItem item =
                             new TableItem(table,SWT.NULL);
                            for (int j=0; j<COLUMNS; j++) {
                                item.setText(j,DATA[i][j]);
                            }
                        }
                        int value = end == ROWS ? 0 : end;
                        progress.setSelection(value);
                    }
```

```
                        });
                        index = end;
                    }
                }
            };
            thread.start();
        }
```

Each of the above strategies will be applicable in some situation. Even when the virtual table support becomes available in SWT, these solutions are still applicable for data that is streamed.

9.2.29   Table Events

SWT.Selection (SelectionEvent)

The SWT.Selection event (typed event SelectionEvent) is sent whenever the user selects an item with the mouse or the keyboard. The relevant event fields during a selection event for Table are as follows.

Public Fields of Class Event That Are Valid during SWT.Selection

Field	Description
detail	Set to SWT.CHECK when the user selected the check box part of the item
item	The primary item that was affected when the selection changed. Typically, this item is selected but can be unselected when the detail is SWT.CHECK or in a multiselect table when the user changes the selection by deselecting the item.

SWT.DefaultSelection (SelectionEvent)

The SWT.DefaultSelection event (typed event SelectionEvent) is sent whenever the user performs the platform-specific operation that indicates default selection. On most platforms, default selection occurs when the user double-clicks on an item or presses the <Enter> key. The relevant event fields during a default selection event for Table are as follows.

Public Fields of Class Event That Are Valid during SWT.DefaultSelection

Field	Description
detail	Set to SWT.CHECK when the user selected the check box part of the item
item	The item that was affected to change the selection. Typically, this item is selected but can be unselected when the detail is SWT.CHECK or in a multiselect table when the user changes the selection by deselecting the item.

9.2.30   Using SWT.Selection with a Check Box Table

The following program uses the SWT.Selection event along with the *item* and *detail* fields to detect when a table item has been either checked or unchecked.

```
public static void main(String[] args) {
    Display display = new Display();
    Shell shell = new Shell(display);
    Table table = new Table(shell, SWT.CHECK | SWT.BORDER);
    for (int i = 0; i < 32; i++) {
        TableItem item = new TableItem(table, SWT.NULL);
        item.setText("Item " + i);
    }
    table.setSize(200, 200);
    table.addListener(SWT.Selection, new Listener() {
        public void handleEvent(Event event) {
            if (event.detail == SWT.CHECK) {
                TableItem item = (TableItem) event.item;
                System.out.println(
                    item + " checked " + item.getChecked());
            }
        }
    });
    shell.pack();
    shell.open();
    while (!shell.isDisposed()) {
        if (!display.readAndDispatch()) display.sleep();
    }
    display.dispose();
}
```

9.2.31   TableColumn Events

SWT.Selection (SelectionEvent)

The SWT.Selection event (typed event SelectionEvent) is sent whenever the user selects a column header with the mouse or the keyboard. Selection events contain meaningful values in only the *display, widget,* and *type* fields.

Using SWT.Selection to Sort Items in a Table

Sorting items in a table using a table column selection to initiate the sort is a very common user interface metaphor. The following program creates a table with two columns of data. Each item of data is stored in the class MyData.

```
static class MyData {
    String string1, string2;
    public MyData(String string1, String string2) {
        this.string1 = string1;
        this.string2 = string2;
    }
}
```

When the table is created, the setData() method is used to associate instances of MyData with TableItem. The sort() method sorts data by column in either ascending or descending order. The first part of the method creates an array of MyData using getData() to retrieve instances of MyData from the items in the table. The column parameter indicates the column in the table that should be sorted. After the data has been sorted, it is assigned back to each table item, and the string for the item is updated.

```
static void sort(
    Table table,
    final int column,
    final boolean descend) {

    int count = table.getItemCount();
    MyData[] list = new MyData[count];
    for (int i = 0; i < count; i++) {
        Object data = table.getItem(i).getData();
        list[i] = (MyData) data;
    }
    Arrays.sort(list, new Comparator() {
        public int compare(Object a, Object b) {
            MyData d1 = (MyData) (descend ? b : a);
            MyData d2 = (MyData) (descend ? a : b);
            switch (column) {
                case 0 :
                    return d1.string1.compareTo(d2.string1);
                case 1 :
                    return d1.string2.compareTo(d2.string2);
            }
            return 0;
        }
    });
    for (int i = 0; i < list.length; i++) {
        TableItem item = table.getItem(i);
        item.setText(0, list[i].string1);
        item.setText(1, list[i].string2);
        item.setData(list[i]);
    }
}
```

The main program creates the table and two table columns. The current sorting order (ascending or descending) is stored as a boolean in each column using setData(). When a column is selected, the index of the column that was selected is computed and the sorting retrieved. Finally, the column is sorted by inverting the current sorting order.

```
static int ROWS = 10000;
public static void main(String[] args) {
    Display display = new Display();
    Shell shell = new Shell(display);
    final Table table = new Table(shell, SWT.BORDER);
```

```
table.setHeaderVisible(true);
for (int i = 0; i < 2; i++) {
    TableColumn column =
        new TableColumn(table, SWT.NONE);
    column.setText("Column " + i);
    column.setData(new Boolean(false));
}
Random r = new Random();
table.setRedraw(false);
for (int i = 0; i < ROWS; i++) {
    TableItem item = new TableItem(table, SWT.NULL);
    MyData data =
        new MyData(
            "A" + r.nextInt(1000),
            "B" + r.nextInt(1000));
    item.setText(0, data.string1);
    item.setText(1, data.string2);
    item.setData(data);
}
sort(table, 0, false);
table.setRedraw(true);
for (int i = 0; i < table.getColumnCount(); i++) {
    final TableColumn column = table.getColumn(i);
    column.pack();
    column.addListener(SWT.Selection, new Listener() {
        public void handleEvent(Event event) {
            int index = table.indexOf(column);
            if (index != -1) {
                Boolean b = (Boolean) column.getData();
                boolean value = b.booleanValue();
                sort(table, index, !value);
                column.setData(new Boolean(!value));
            }
        }
    });
}
table.setSize(200, 200);
shell.pack();
shell.open();
while (!shell.isDisposed()) {
    if (!display.readAndDispatch()) display.sleep();
}
display.dispose();
}
```

SWT.DefaultSelection (SelectionEvent)

The SWT.DefaultSelection event (typed event SelectionEvent) is sent whenever the user performs the platform-specific operation that indicates default selection. On most platforms, default selection occurs when the user double-clicks on a column header. Default selection events contain meaningful values in only the *display, widget,* and *type* fields.

SWT.Move (ControlEvent)

The SWT.Move event (typed event MoveEvent) is sent whenever a column is moved. Move events contain meaningful values in only the *display*, *widget*, and *type* fields.

SWT.Resize (ControlEvent)

The SWT.Resize event (typed event ControlEvent) is sent whenever a column is resized. Resize events contain meaningful values in only the *display*, *widget*, and *type* fields.

9.3   Classes TabFolder and TabItem

9.3.1   Example

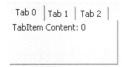

9.3.2   TabFolder and TabItem Hierarchies

9.3.3   TabFolder Styles

Style	Description
SWT.TOP	Items are placed at the top of the tab folder
SWT.BOTTOM	Items are placed at the bottom of the tab folder

9.3.4   TabFolder Events

Event	Description
SWT.Selection	A tab item was selected

9.3.5   TabItem Styles (none)

Style	Description

9.3.6   TabItem Events (none)

Event	Description

Sometimes called *notebooks*, tab folders provide a very simple "pages-in-a-book" user interface metaphor. Tabs in the book, represented by instances of the class TabItem, provide random access to the pages. When the user selects a tab item, the item comes to the front, and the client area of the tab folder is filled with the controls that represent the page. Tab items can contain text, icons, or both.

Tab folders operate in one of two paging modes: automatic and manual. In *automatic* mode, the application program creates each page when the tab folder is created. When the user selects a tab, pages are shown automatically. In *manual* mode, the application program listens for selection events on the tab folder and provides the contents of each page on demand. Most programs do not use manual mode because it is somewhat more complicated to use than automatic mode. Manual mode provides the most benefit when pages are expensive to create, allowing you to delay the creation of pages until they are needed.

The following example program creates a tab folder in automatic mode, filling each page with a push button. Figure 9.6 shows the result.

```
public static void main(String[] args) {
    Display display = new Display();
    Shell shell = new Shell(display);
    TabFolder folder = new TabFolder(shell, SWT.NONE);
    for (int i = 0; i < 4; i++) {
        TabItem item = new TabItem(folder, SWT.NONE);
        item.setText("Item " + i);
        Button button = new Button(folder, SWT.PUSH);
        button.setText("Button " + i);
        item.setControl(button);
    }
    folder.setSize(400, 400);
    shell.pack();
    shell.open();
    while (!shell.isDisposed()) {
        if (!display.readAndDispatch()) display.sleep();
    }
    display.dispose();
}
```

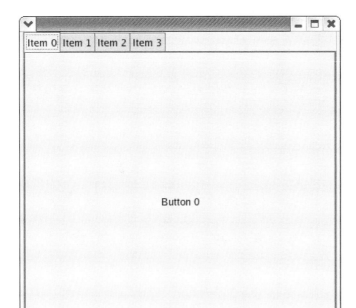

Figure 9.6

Tab folders are often used in dialogs that allow the user to set program preferences. Before the advent of the tab folder, users often had to navigate several levels of dialogs to set all the preferences for a particular area. This was cumbersome. Sometimes when navigating through the chain of dialogs, users would forget from which dialog they had come and the preferences they were trying to change. The nice thing about tab folders is that they are compact and allow fast access to any of the pages. The tabs themselves also give a quick summary of the operations that are available.[10]

9.3.7   Text and Images

TabItem supports the standard API for text and images. TabItem supports mnemonics but does not support wrapping or more than one line of text in an item.

---

10. Another technique to avoid nested dialogs is to use a tree of options instead of a tab folder. When the user selects an item in the tree, a page is displayed. The advantage of this approach over tab folders is that options can be presented to the user hierarchically.

setText(String string)   Sets the text for the item. The string cannot contain line delimiters. Mnemonics characters, indicated by '&', are supported.

getText()   Returns the item text. This is an empty string if the text has never been set.

setImage(Image image)   Sets the image for the item.

> ### The First Image Defines the Size of All Images in the Control
>
> Just like ToolBar, Tree, and Table, TabFolder scales the image it displays to be the size of the first image inserted into the control. Thanks Microsoft!

getImage()   Returns the item image. This is null if the image has never been set.

9.3.8   Tool Tips

TabItem supports tool tips in a manner that is similar to ToolItem.

setToolTipText(String string)   Sets the tool tip text for the item. This string is displayed when the mouse hovers within the bounds of the item. Setting this string to null removes the tool tip.

getToolTipText()   Returns the tool tip text.

9.3.9   Automatic Paging

Automatic paging is implemented for tab folders using page controls. A *page control* is the control that will fill the client area of a tab folder when the user selects a tab. The previous page control, belonging to another tab, is automatically hidden after the new page has been displayed.

Page controls are properties of tab items, even though the control itself must be a child of the tab folder. This can be a little confusing at first. Because tab items are not controls, the page control cannot be a child of a tab item, as you might expect.[11]

---

11. Strong typing prevents this.

Page controls are assigned using setControl().

setControl(Control control)   Sets the page control for the tab item. The page control is automatically resized to fit the client area of the tab folder when the tab is selected. The tab folder hides the previous page control that belongs to another tab item.

getControl()   Returns the page control. If no control has been set, null is returned.

9.3.10   The Selection

Application programs sometimes need to manipulate the selection in a tab folder, either querying it or setting it. For example, some programs remember the last tab item that was selected in a dialog that contains a tab folder and restore the selection to that tab item when the user reopens the dialog.

Tab folders are index-based controls, so the selection can be specified in terms of indices. Tab folders are always single-select. There can never be more than one tab item selected at a time. Despite this fact, to be consistent with other controls that contain items, methods that get and set the selection in terms of items use arrays.[12]

The following methods are used to manipulate the selection in a tab folder.

getSelection()   Returns an array of the selected items. When there are no selected items, the array is empty. Because tab folders are always single-select, this array is either of size zero or size 1.

getSelectionIndex()   Returns the index of the item that is selected. If no items are selected, –1 is returned. On some platforms, it is not possible to have a tab folder with no selection. In this case, –1 can never be returned.

setSelection (int index)   Sets the selection to the item at the index. If the index is out of range, it is ignored. If the current tab item has a page control, it is hidden before the new tab item and page control are shown.

setSelection(TabItem[] items)   Sets the selection to items in the array. If the array is empty and the platform allows a tab folder to have no

---

12. By the time you read this, methods may have been defined that take single items for R3.0.

selection, the selection is cleared. Otherwise, the selection is set to the first item in the array. Page controls are hidden and shown in the same manner as setSelection(int).

9.3.11 Searching Operations

TabFolder provides a number of index and locating operations that allow an application program to find items and indices.

getItem(int index)   Returns the item at the index that is zero-based. If the index is out of range, an IllegalArgumentException ("Index out of bounds") is thrown.

getItemCount()   Returns the number of items in the tab folder.

getItems()   Returns an array of the items. This is a *copy* so that modifying the array has no effect.

indexOf(TabItem item)   Returns the zero-based index of the item in the tab folder. If the item is not found, −1 is returned.

9.3.12 TabFolder Events

SWT.Selection (SelectionEvent)

The SWT.Selection event (typed event SelectionEvent) is sent whenever the user selects an item with the mouse or the keyboard. The relevant event fields during a selection event for TabItem are as follows.

Public Fields of Class Event That Are Valid during SWT.Selection

Field	Description
item	The item that was selected

Using SWT.Selection to Implement Manual Paging

Under certain circumstances, you may wish to implement manual paging in a tab folder. For example, it may be too expensive to create all of the page controls up front. Sometimes the pages are mostly the same between tabs. Manual paging allows you to reuse controls between pages by changing the contents of the client area when the user selects a tab, instead of hiding and showing a single page control.

The following example implements a manual and automatic paging hybrid. Pages are created lazily. Once a page has been created, it becomes automatically displayed the next time the user selects the tab.

```java
public static void main(String[] args) {
    Display display = new Display();
    Shell shell = new Shell(display);
    final TabFolder folder = new TabFolder(shell,SWT.NONE);
    folder.addListener(SWT.Selection, new Listener() {
        public void handleEvent(Event event) {
            TabItem item = (TabItem) event.item;
            if (item.getControl() != null) return;
            Button button = new Button(folder, SWT.PUSH);
            button.setText("Button "+folder.indexOf(item));
            item.setControl(button);
        }
    });
    for (int i = 0; i < 4; i++) {
        TabItem item = new TabItem(folder, SWT.NONE);
        item.setText("Item " + i);
    }
    folder.setSize(400, 400);
    shell.pack();
    shell.open();
    while (!shell.isDisposed()) {
        if (!display.readAndDispatch()) display.sleep();
    }
    display.dispose();
}
```

9.4 Summary

The advanced controls in SWT build on the standard concepts and API names of the toolkit. For that reason, although these controls define lots of API, they do not add many new names or concepts, making them easy to learn. Trees and tab folders support the lazy creation of items and controls using very different techniques. Trees requires a dummy item, whereas tab folders use the selection event. Although not done lazily, TableItem creation can be performed in a background thread or idle handle, freeing up the user interface.

CHAPTER 10

Range-Based Controls

Range-based controls in SWT provide at the very least a minimum, a maximum, and a value that is somewhere between the two. They are special-purpose controls that some applications may require. For example, if you are implementing scrolling, you will almost certainly need to use a scroll bar. Many applications display a progress bar when they are busy performing a computation. Some applications use a scale to query the user for numeric values. All of these controls are range-based and have a very specific function.

10.1 Class ProgressBar

10.1.1 Example

10.1.2 ProgressBar Hierarchy

ⓒᴬ Widget
   ⓒᴬ Control
      ⓒ ProgressBar

10.1.3   ProgressBar Styles

Style	Description
SWT.SMOOTH	Fill the progress bar instead of showing steps
SWT.HORIZONTAL	Create a horizontal progress bar
SWT.VERTICAL	Create a vertical progress bar
SWT.INDETERMINATE	Show progress bar activity

10.1.4   ProgressBar Events (none)

Event	Description

Progress bars are static user interface controls that inform the user of the *progress* of an operation. Sometimes they draw a rectangle and gradually fill it. When the rectangle is full, the operation is done.

Like Label, ProgressBar is static. Clicking on a progress bar does not invoke an action. Like Slider, Scale, and ScrollBar (described later in this chapter), ProgressBar is range-based. It has a minimum, maximum, and selection.[1] The selection is always between the minimum and the maximum.

The following example creates a shell with a progress bar and simulates a program that does some arbitrary processing in another thread. To simulate the work, the thread runs a loop that repeatedly sleeps for 100 milliseconds, then sets the progress bar selection. The thread uses asyncExec() (described in the Display chapter) to update the progress bar from a non-user-interface thread.

```
public static void main(String[] args) {
    final Display display = new Display();
    Shell shell = new Shell(display);
    final ProgressBar bar =new ProgressBar(shell,SWT.NONE);
    bar.setSize(200, 32);
    shell.pack();
    shell.open();
    final int maximum = bar.getMaximum();
    new Thread() {
        public void run() {
            for (int i = 0; i <= maximum; i++) {
```

---

1. "Selection" is a misnomer. The user can't select anything. This name was chosen to be consistent with the other range-based classes in SWT.

```
                    try {
                        Thread.sleep(100);
                    } catch (Throwable th) {
                    }
                    final int index = i;
                    display.asyncExec(new Runnable() {
                        public void run() {
                            bar.setSelection(index);
                        }
                    });
                }
            }
        }.start();
        while (!shell.isDisposed()) {
            if (!display.readAndDispatch()) display.sleep();
        }
        display.dispose();
    }
```

10.1.5   Range Operations

ProgressBar provides a number of range operations to allow you to define the units of work.

setMinimum(int minimum)   Sets the minimum. If this value is negative or greater than or equal to the maximum, the value is ignored. The selection is adjusted to fit within the new range.

getMinimum()   Returns the minimum. If this value has never been set, the default value is zero.

setMaximum(int maximum)   Sets the maximum. If this value is negative or less than or equal to the minimum, the value is ignored. The selection is adjusted to fit within the new range.

getMaximum()   Returns the maximum. If this value has never been set, the default value is 100.

10.1.6   The Selection

The selection within a progress bar is an integer that represents the extent of the "fill rectangle." It is always a value between the minimum and maximum.

setSelection(int value)   Sets the selection. If the selection is out of range, it is adjusted to fit within the range. Note that setSelection() draws right away, allowing it to show progress in the user interface thread without returning to the event loop to paint the control.

getSelection()   Returns the selection. The default value is zero.

10.1.7 Indeterminate Progress Bars

Sometimes it is not possible to determine the amount of time an operation will take. In this case, using an indeterminate progress bar rather than guessing is appropriate. Indeterminate progress bars are created with the style SWT.INDE-TERMINATE. They display a platform-specific animation to show activity.

Indeterminate Progress Bars Do Not Use Threads

Indeterminate progress bars do not use threads to run their animation. If you are doing a lot of work in the user interface thread, an indeterminate progress bar will not update until your return to the event loop. This is in contrast to a regular progress bar that draws every time you call setSelection(). This means that inde-terminate progress bars are suitable only for use with background operations (work that is not performed by the user interface thread).

10.2   Class Scale

10.2.1 Example

10.2.2 Scale Hierarchy

- C^A Widget
  - C^A Control
    - C Scale

10.2.3 Scale Styles

Style	Description
SWT.HORIZONTAL	Create a horizontal scale
SWT.VERTICAL	Create a vertical scale

10.2.4 Scale Events

Event	Description
SWT.Selection	The scale was selected

Scales are user interface elements that allow the user to select from a series of integer values. Scales often draw a small draggable box, called the *thumb*, which is dragged by the user within a "trough." The trough is surrounded on either side by a succession of short lines called *ticks*.

Unlike ProgressBar, Scale is *not* static. The following example code creates a scale in a shell.

```
public static void main(String[] args) {
    Display display = new Display();
    Shell shell = new Shell(display);
    Scale scale = new Scale(shell, SWT.HORIZONTAL);
    scale.pack();
    shell.pack();
    shell.open();
    while (!shell.isDisposed()) {
        if (!display.readAndDispatch()) display.sleep();
    }
    display.dispose();
}
```

Scales are often used to implement sliding "volume controls."

10.2.5   Range Operations

Scale provides the following range operations.

setMinimum(int minimum)   Sets the minimum. If this value is negative or greater than or equal to the maximum, the value is ignored. The selection is adjusted to fit within the new range.

getMinimum()   Returns the minimum. If this value has never been set, the default value is zero.

setMaximum(int maximum)   Sets the maximum. If this value is negative or less than or equal to the minimum, the value is ignored. The selection is adjusted to fit within the new range.

getMaximum()   Returns the maximum. If this value has never been set, the default value is 100.

10.2.6   The Selection

The selection within a scale refers to the position of the thumb. Although the thumb takes up space on the screen, it does not affect the range. This means that the selection can vary from the minimum value to the maximum.

setSelection(int value)   Sets the selection. If the selection is out of range, it is adjusted to fit within the range.

getSelection()   Returns the selection. The default is zero.

10.2.7   Increment and Page Increment

Scale provides API that allows you to set the *increment* and *page increment*. These are the values the scale uses to increment the selection when the user drags the thumb or clicks inside the trough. The user can also manipulate the thumb using the keyboard. In this case, typically the arrow keys move the thumb using the increment, and the <Page Up> and <Page Down> keys move it using the page increment.

Setting the increment and page increment does not affect the minimum, maximum, and selection. The following methods are used to set the two kinds of increment.

setIncrement(int increment)   Sets the increment value. If this value is less than or equal to zero, the value is ignored.

getIncrement()   Returns the increment. If this value has never been set, the default value is 1.

setPageIncrement(int pageIncrement)   Sets the page increment value. If this value is less than or equal to zero, the value is ignored.

getPageIncrement()   Returns the page increment. If this value has never been set, the default value is 1.

10.2.8   Scale Events

SWT.Selection (SelectionEvent)

The SWT.Selection event (typed event SelectionEvent) is sent whenever the user changes the scale using the mouse or the keyboard. Selection events contain meaningful values in only the *display, widget,* and *type* fields.

10.3 Classes ScrollBar and Slider

10.3.1 Example

10.3.2 ScrollBar and Slider Hierarchy

10.3.3 ScrollBar and Slider Styles

Style	Description
SWT.HORIZONTAL	Create a horizontal slider
SWT.VERTICAL	Create a vertical slider

10.3.4 ScrollBar and Slider Events

Event	Description
SWT.Selection	The widget was selected

ScrollBar and Slider are analogous to Scale. Like Scale, they allow the user to select from a continuous series of integer values. Unlike Scale, they provide a programmable thumb that is often used to show the proportion of the visible area of a document, compared with the total area needed to display it.

ScrollBar and Slider are range-based classes, allowing the user to select a value between the minimum and maximum, less the size of the thumb. Both controls draw in a similar manner, have the same API, and are manipulated in the same manner by the user.

Instances of the class Slider are controls, whereas instances of ScrollBar are not. Sliders are created and manipulated like any other control. Scroll bars, on the other hand, are part of the trim, normally appearing to the right and bottom of a control, outside the client area. When the control is resized, the scroll bars are moved and resized with the rest of the trim.

Why Are Two Classes Needed to Represent Scroll Bars?

The distinction between a scroll bar and a slider is one that was forced by Microsoft Windows. Back in the early days of Windows, even before 3.0, possibly in an attempt to conserve system resources, the scroll bars that appeared as part of the trim of a control were *not* controls. This meant that they could not be children of other controls, had no operating system resources, and could not be resized or positioned. Windows called these trim scroll bars *Standard Scroll Bars*. Windows also provided another kind of scroll bar that *was* a control. This scroll bar was called a *Scroll Bar Control*.

Unfortunately, we were forced to model scroll bars in SWT after Windows in order to implement both kinds of scroll bars on that platform correctly. An alternative implementation would have been to pretend that Standard Scroll Bars were real Windows controls and implement everything they would inherit from Control. Another possibility would be to use Scroll Bar Controls everywhere and not use Standard Scroll Bars at all. Both of these approaches were considered to be too error-prone. The first is a great deal of work for very little benefit. The second risks getting the Windows look and feel wrong. In the end, we went with the simplest approach and defined the two classes.

The following example code creates a horizontal and a vertical scroll bar and a horizontal slider in a shell.

```
public static void main(String[] args) {
    Display display = new Display();
    int style = SWT.SHELL_TRIM|SWT.H_SCROLL|SWT.V_SCROLL;
    Shell shell = new Shell(display, style);
    Slider slider = new Slider(shell, SWT.H_SCROLL);
    slider.pack();
    slider.setLocation(20, 20);
    shell.setSize(300, 300);
    shell.open();
    while (!shell.isDisposed()) {
        if (!display.readAndDispatch()) display.sleep();
    }
    display.dispose();
}
```

10.3.5 Scroll Bars

Scroll bars are created when their parent is created. Unlike other widgets in SWT, the SWT.H_SCROLL and SWT.V_SCROLL styles are given to the parent, causing the parent to create the scroll bar. We have already seen these styles used to indicate horizontal and vertical scroll bars in the classes Text, List, Tree, and Table. Once the scroll bar has been created, it is queried from its parent.[2] You cannot create a scroll bar using a ScrollBar constructor.

getHorizontalBar()   Returns the horizontal scroll bar if there is one, otherwise returns null.

getVerticalBar()   Returns the vertical scroll bar if there is one, otherwise returns null.

10.3.6 *Range Operations*

ScrollBar and Slider provide the following range operations.

setMinimum(int minimum)   Sets the minimum value. If this value is negative or greater than or equal to the maximum, the value is ignored. If necessary, first the thumb and then the selection are adjusted to fit within the new range.

getMinimum()   Returns the minimum. If this value has never been set, the default value is zero.

setMaximum(int maximum)   Sets the maximum. If this value is negative or less than or equal to the minimum, the value is ignored. If necessary, first the thumb and then the selection are adjusted to fit within the new range.

getMaximum()   Returns the maximum. If this value has never been set, the default value is 100.

10.3.7 *The Selection and the Thumb*

The selection refers to the position of the thumb, which is the current integer value in a scroll bar or a slider. The thumb, unlike the thumb portion of a scale, has a size that affects the available range, which is defined as minimum to maximum minus the thumb size.

---

2. Despite the fact that a scroll bar has a parent, it does not appear in the children list of the parent. This happens because children are arrays of controls, and scroll bars are not controls. Because scroll bars are part of the trim, it's not clear that returning them as part of the children list would have value.

setSelection(int value)   Sets the selection. If the value is out of range, it is adjusted to fit within the range.

getSelection()   Returns the selection.

setThumb(int value)   Sets the size of the thumb. If the value is less than 1 or larger than the minimum minus the maximum, it is ignored. The selection is adjusted to fit within the new range that will change when any of the thumb, maximum, or minimum is changed.

getThumb()   Returns the size of the thumb. If this value has never been set, the default value is 10.

10.3.8   *Increment and Page Increment*

Just like Scale, Slider and ScrollBar support increment and page increments. The API works in exactly the same manner.

setIncrement(int increment)   Sets the increment value. If this value is less than 1, the value is ignored.

getIncrement()   Returns the increment. If this value has never been set, the default value is 1.

setPageIncrement(int pageIncrement)   Sets the page increment value. If this value is less than 1, the value is ignored.

getPageIncrement()   Returns the page increment. If this value has never been set, the default value is 1.

10.3.9   *Configuring Operations*

ScrollBar and Slider perform range checks when setting the selection, thumb, minimum, maximum, increment, and page increment. Sometimes the order in which these properties are set determines the success of the operation. For example, if the minimum is zero and the maximum is 100, this code fails.

```
//fails when minimum is 0 and maximum is 100
slider.setMinimum(120);
slider.setMaximum(140);
```

This code, on the other hand, works.

```
//works when minimum is 0 and maximum is 100
slider.setMaximum(140);
slider.setMinimum(120);
```

Setting the maximum before the minimum does not work every time either. For example, when the minimum is 120, the maximum is 140, and the desired minimum and maximum are to be zero and 100, the minimum must be set before the maximum or the code will fail. The setValues() method avoids problems of this kind and can be more efficient, depending on the platform.

setValues(int selection, int minimum, int maximum, int thumb, int increment, int pageIncrement)   Sets the selection, minimum, maximum, thumb, increment, and page increment all at once. The minimum and maximum must be greater than zero, and the minimum must be less than the maximum. The thumb must be greater than or equal to 1 and less than or equal to the maximum minus the minimum. The increment and page increment must be greater than or equal to 1. If any one of these conditions is not satisfied, none of the values are set.

10.3.10   ScrollBar and Slider Events

SWT.Selection (SelectionEvent)

The SWT.Selection event (typed event SelectionEvent) is sent whenever the user changes the value of a scroll bar or a slider using the mouse or the keyboard. The relevant event fields during a selection event for ScrollBar or Slider are as follows.

Public Fields of Class Event That Are Valid during SWT.Selection

Field	Description
detail	One of SWT.DRAG, SWT.HOME, SWT.END, SWT.ARROW_UP, SWT.ARROW_DOWN, SWT.PAGE_UP, or SWT.PAGE_DOWN indicating the action that caused the selection to change

Using SWT.Selection to Scroll a List of Strings

The following example implements a very simple scrolling list of strings. It shows you how to create a control with scroll bars and listen for SWT.Selection.

First, a shell is created with both horizontal and vertical scroll bars. We make use of the fact that Shell is a subclass of Composite and can have scroll bars. The SWT.NO_BACKGROUND and SWT.NO_REDRAW_RESIZE style bits are used to minimize flashing when the shell is painted and resized.

Next, an SWT.Selection listener is created and added to each scroll bar. This listener redraws the entire list when the scroll bar is selected. A more efficient scrolling implementation would probably use Canvas.scroll() to copy and damage the client area.

An SWT.Paint listener uses the current position of each scroll bar to draw the strings. The horizontal scroll bar scrolls in pixel units. The *x* coordinate of each visible item in the list is the current location of the horizontal scroll bar (negated). The vertical scroll bar scrolls the list in index units. The *y* coordinate of each visible item is computed using the current location of ScrollBar to get the first visible index. Note that the SWT.Paint listener uses gc.fillRectangle() to ensure that every pixel is drawn, a requirement of SWT.NO _BACKGROUND.

To configure the horizontal scroll bar, an SWT.Resize listener computes the pixel width of the widest item and uses this value as the horizontal scroll bar maximum. The thumb is the minimum of the client area and the widest item. This gives a range from zero to the widest item, less the client area width, which is exactly the amount that needs to be scrolled to show the widest item.

The vertical scroll bar maximum is the number of items in the list. The thumb is the number of completely visible items, which is computed by dividing the height of the client area by the height of an item. The page increment is assigned to be one less than the thumb, causing <Page Down> and <Page Up> always to show one item from the previous page. Because of the SWT.NO_RESIZE_REDRAW style, when the shell becomes larger and the scroll bars are configured, either scroll bar selection can change. This causes the location of the entire list to change, creating a problem because only the exposed areas were damaged. To avoid drawing garbage on the screen, the shell is completely redrawn whenever this happens.

```
public static void main(String[] args) {
    final String[] list = new String[128];
    for (int i = 0; i < list.length; i++) {
        list[i] = i + "-String-that-is-quite-long-" + i;
    }
    Display display = new Display();
    int style = SWT.SHELL_TRIM|SWT.H_SCROLL|SWT.V_SCROLL;
    style |= SWT.NO_BACKGROUND | SWT.NO_REDRAW_RESIZE;
    final Shell shell = new Shell(display, style);
    Listener scrollListener = new Listener() {
        public void handleEvent(Event event) {
            shell.redraw();
        }
```

```
        };
        final ScrollBar hBar = shell.getHorizontalBar();
        final ScrollBar vBar = shell.getVerticalBar();
        hBar.addListener(SWT.Selection, scrollListener);
        vBar.addListener(SWT.Selection, scrollListener);
        final Color listForeground =
            display.getSystemColor(SWT.COLOR_LIST_FOREGROUND);
        final Color listBackground =
            display.getSystemColor(SWT.COLOR_LIST_BACKGROUND);
        shell.addListener(SWT.Paint, new Listener() {
            public void handleEvent(Event event) {
                GC gc = event.gc;
                gc.setForeground(listForeground);
                gc.setBackground(listBackground);
                Rectangle rect = shell.getClientArea();
                gc.fillRectangle(rect);
                int x = -hBar.getSelection();
                int height = gc.stringExtent("").y;
                int start = vBar.getSelection();
                int end =
                    Math.min(
                        list.length - 1,
                        start + rect.height / height);
                for (int i = start; i <= end; i++) {
                    gc.drawText(
                        list[i],
                        x + 2,
                        (i - start) * height + 2);
                }
            }
        });
        shell.addListener(SWT.Resize, new Listener() {
            public void handleEvent(Event event) {
                int hSelection = hBar.getSelection();
                int vSelection = vBar.getSelection();
                Rectangle rect = shell.getClientArea();
                GC gc = new GC(shell);
                int width = 0;
                for (int i = 0; i < list.length; i++) {
                    width =
                        Math.max(
                            width,
                            gc.textExtent(list[i]).x);
                }
                width += 4;
                hBar.setMaximum(width);
                hBar.setThumb(Math.min(width, rect.width));
                hBar.setPageIncrement(hBar.getThumb());
                int height = gc.stringExtent("").y;
                vBar.setMaximum(list.length);
                int page = Math.max(1, rect.height / height);
                vBar.setThumb(Math.min(page, list.length));
                vBar.setPageIncrement(vBar.getThumb() - 1);
                gc.dispose();
                if (hSelection != hBar.getSelection()
                    || vSelection != vBar.getSelection()) {
```

```
                    shell.redraw();
                }
            }
        });
        shell.setSize(200, 200);
        shell.open();
        while (!shell.isDisposed()) {
            if (!display.readAndDispatch()) display.sleep();
        }
        display.dispose();
    }
```

10.4 Summary

Range-based controls are very simple, special-purpose controls that are easy
to use and understand.

CHAPTER 11

Controls, Composites, Groups, and Shells

Containment (sometimes called *nesting*) is a valuable technique that allows one control to be placed inside another. Composites and shells support nesting of controls, allowing you to build complex containment hierarchies. Group boxes are composites that support nesting, often containing radio buttons.

Although many of the concepts related to containment, shells, and controls have been discussed elsewhere, the classes themselves are described here. In particular, shells provide a rich API to interact with the window manager.

11.1   Class Control

11.1.1   *Example (none—class is abstract)*

11.1.2   *Control Hierarchy*

11.1.3 Control Styles

Style	Description
SWT.BORDER	Draw the control with the appropriate border
SWT.LEFT_TO_RIGHT	Force the control orientation to be left to right
SWT.RIGHT_TO_LEFT	Force the control orientation to be right to left

11.1.4 Control Events

Event	Description
SWT.DragDetect	The user requested a drag and drop operation
SWT.FocusIn	The control is now the focus control
SWT.FocusOut	The control is no longer the focus control
SWT.Help	The user requested help for the control
SWT.KeyDown	A key was pressed
SWT.KeyUp	A key was released
SWT.MenuDetect	The user requested a context menu
SWT.MouseDoubleClick	A mouse button was pressed twice
SWT.MouseDown	A mouse button was pressed
SWT.MouseEnter	The mouse entered the client area of the control
SWT.MouseExit	The mouse exited the client area of the control
SWT.MouseHover	The mouse lingered over the control
SWT.MouseUp	A mouse button was released
SWT.MouseMove	The mouse was moved
SWT.Move	The position of the control was changed
SWT.Paint	The control was asked to draw
SWT.Resize	The size of the client area of the control changed

Controls are one of the most basic building blocks in SWT. As such, they have already been described in great detail in the chapters Widget Fundamentals, The Keyboard, The Mouse, and Control Fundamentals. Topics that have been covered in those chapters will not be covered again here.

11.1.5   *Parent, Shell, and Monitor*

You can query the parent of a control, the shell that contains a control, and the monitor that contains a control using getParent(), getShell(), and getMonitor().

> **getParent**()   Returns the parent of the control. If the control is a shell, the parent can be either null, indicating a "top-level" window, or another shell, when the control is a "dialog" window.

> **getShell**()   Returns the shell that contains the control. If the control is a shell, the control is returned. Use getParent() to get the parent shell of a dialog shell.

> **getMonitor**()   Returns the monitor that contains the control. If the control straddles monitors, a platform-specific algorithm is used to determine the "best" monitor, which is the one that contains the majority of the control.

11.1.6   *Context Menus*

Every control can contain a single context menu that is displayed when the user requests it. The context menu, as described in the section Classes Menu and MenuItem, must be created with the style SWT.POP_UP.

> **setMenu(Menu menu)**   Sets the context menu for the control. When the user performs the default action for the platform to request a context menu, this menu is displayed. To override this behavior or compute the context menu for a control dynamically, see Detecting a Context Menu Request in the chapter The Mouse.

> **getMenu**()   Returns the context menu for the control. This value is null when no menu has been set into the control.

11.1.7   *Foreground, Background, and Font*

Controls support the ability to set the foreground and background colors, as well as the font. On some platforms, the theme manager may refuse the color or font change.

> **setForeground(Color color)**   Sets the foreground color of the control. If the color is null, the default foreground color for the control is restored.

getForeground()   Returns the foreground color of the control. If the foreground color has not been set, the default foreground color for the control is returned.

setBackground(Color color)   Sets the background color of the control. If the color is null, the default background color for the control is restored.

getBackground()   Returns the background color of the control. If the background color has not been set, the default background color for the control is returned.

setFont(Font font)   Sets the font that is used to draw text in the control. If the font is null, the default font for the control is restored.

getFont()   Returns the font that is used to draw text in the control. If the font has not been set, the default font for the control is returned.

11.1.8 Tool Tips

Tool tips are short descriptive messages that appear when the mouse lingers within a control. Tool tips are supported for controls using the setToolTip-Text() method.

setToolTipText(String string)   Sets the tool tip text for the control. This string is displayed when the mouse hovers within the bound of the control. Setting this string to null removes the tool tip.

getToolTipText()   Returns the tool tip text. If the tool tip text has never been set, the default value is null, indicating that no tool tip text should be displayed.

Note that the duration, location, and mouse gesture that trigger the tool tip are platform-specific. Tool tips can also be found in the classes ToolItem and TabItem.

11.1.9 Cursors

Setting the cursor for a control is supported using the setCursor() method.

setCursor(Cursor cursor)   Sets the cursor for the control. The cursor is displayed immediately if the mouse is inside the control. Otherwise, it is displayed whenever the mouse enters the control. If the cursor is null, the default cursor for the control is restored. For example, a text control might restore the cursor to an I-beam, rather than an arrow.

If a cursor is not defined for a control, it is inherited. This means that setting the cursor for a parent implicitly defines the cursor for the child, provided that the child does not explicitly set its own cursor. When a child is disabled, the cursor is inherited. This makes sense, given that mouse events for a disabled control are delivered to the parent. For example, a disabled text control will not respond to mouse clicks, take focus, or show an I-beam.

Some controls use more than one cursor. For example, a table may show a resize cursor when the mouse is moved over a column. In this case, setCursor() is called from an SWT.MouseMove listener for the table to set the appropriate cursor.

See the Cursors chapter for more on working with cursors.

11.2   Class Composite

11.2.1   Example

11.2.2   Composite Hierarchy

11.2.3   Composite Styles

Style	Description
SWT.H_SCROLL	Create a horizontal standard scroll bar
SWT.V_SCROLL	Create a vertical standard scroll bar
SWT. NO_BACKGROUND	Do not fill the background when painting
SWT. NO_REDRAW_RESIZE	Do not damage the entire client area when resizing
SWT. NO_MERGE_PAINTS	Do not merge damage rectangles when painting
SWT.NO_FOCUS	Do not take focus
SWT.NO_RADIO_GROUP	Disable radio button behavior

11.2.4   Composite Events (none)

Event	Description

Composites are most often used to construct containment hierarchies, as described in the chapter Widget Fundamentals. Note that topics that have already been described in other sections of the book will not be described again here.

Composites support arbitrary SWT graphics. In fact, the subclass Canvas (designated as the class to be used as a "drawing area") inherits its graphics support from Composite. This means that a composite can be used for drawing anywhere a canvas is used.

11.2.5   Getting the Children

The children of a composite are queried using getChildren(). Children are always instances of Control.

getChildren()   Returns an array of the children. This is a *copy* of the array that is used to hold the children so that modifying it has no effect. The z-order of each child is captured by its position in the array. The first child in the array is above the second, and so on.

The following code fragment implements a traversal function that prints out each control in a hierarchy, using tab characters to indent the level.

```
static void traverse(Control control, int level) {
    for (int i = 0; i < level; i++) {
        System.out.print("\t");
    }
    System.out.println(control);
    if (!(control instanceof Composite)) return;
    Composite composite = (Composite) control;
    Control[] children = composite.getChildren();
    for (int i = 0; i < children.length; i++) {
        traverse(children[i], level + 1);
    }
}
```

11.2.6   Tab Traversal

Sometimes an application program needs to set the traversal order of the children explicitly when the user presses the <Tab> key. See the section Tab Traversal in the chapter The Keyboard for details.

11.2.7   Layout

Composites support Layout to assist in positioning and sizing their children. See the chapter Layout for more details.

11.3   Class Group

11.3.1   Example

11.3.2   Group Hierarchy

11.3.3   Group Styles (none)

Style	Description

11.3.4   Group Events (none)

Event	Description

Groups, sometimes called *group boxes* or *frames*, are controls that are used to provide a "title" and a "border" that surrounds their children. Group is a static control (like Label and ProgressBar) that does not interact with the user.

The following example creates a group of radio buttons.

```
public static void main(String[] args) {
    Display display = new Display();
```

```
Shell shell = new Shell(display);
shell.setLayout(new RowLayout());
Group group = new Group(shell, SWT.NONE);
group.setText("Group");
group.setLayout(new RowLayout(SWT.VERTICAL));
for (int i=0; i<4; i++) {
     Button button = new Button(group, SWT.RADIO);
     button.setText("Button " + i);
}
group.pack();
shell.pack();
shell.open();
while (!shell.isDisposed()) {
    if (!display.readAndDispatch()) display.sleep();
}
display.dispose();
}
```

11.3.5 Setting the Text of a Group

Groups support the standard SWT API for setting and getting text, which is the title of the group. Mnemonic characters are supported in the title. Wrapping, the SWT.WRAP style, and more than one line of text are not supported.

setText(String string)   Sets the text for the item. The string cannot contain line delimiters. Mnemonic characters, indicated by '&', are supported.

getText()   Returns the item text. This is an empty string if the text has never been set.

11.4   Class Shell

11.4.1   Example

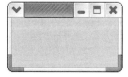

11.4.2 Shell Hierarchy

11.4.3 Shell Styles

Style	Description
SWT.BORDER	Provide a dialog border
SWT.CLOSE	Provide a close box
SWT.MIN	Provide a minimize box
SWT.MAX	Provide a maximize box
SWT.RESIZE	Provide a resizable border
SWT.TITLE	Provide a title bar
SWT.NO_TRIM	Force the shell to have no trim
SWT.ON_TOP	Stay on top of other shells
SWT.TOOL	Make the a shell be a "tool window"
SWT.SHELL_TRIM	Same as SWT.TITLE | SWT.CLOSE | SWT.MIN | SWT.MAX | SWT.RESIZE
SWT.DIALOG_TRIM	Same as SWT.TITLE | SWT.CLOSE | SWT.BORDER
SWT.PRIMARY_MODAL	Make the shell primary modal
SWT.APPLICATION_MODAL	Make the shell application modal
SWT.SYSTEM_MODAL	Make the shell system modal

11.4.4 Shell Events

Event	Description
SWT.Activate	The shell is being activated
SWT.Deactivate	The shell is being deactivated
SWT.Close	The shell is being closed
SWT.Iconify	The shell is being minimized
SWT.Deiconify	The shell is no longer minimized

Shells are used to represent windows that are managed on the desktop by the window manager.[1] Shells that are parented under the display are called *top-level shells*. Shells that are parented under another shell are called *dialog shells*. Top-level shells and dialog shells have standard window *trimmings*, provided by the window manager. The menu bar, borders, and other decorations, such as resize handles, are included in the window trim.[2] The window manager also provides *modality*, a property that blocks input from the mouse and keyboard. Window trimming and modality are hints that may not be granted, depending on the particular window manager.

If you do not specify a location or size for a shell, the window manager will choose both for you. It is a good idea to let this happen, especially when multiple monitors are involved. For more information about positioning a shell, see Centering a Shell on the Primary Monitor.

11.4.5 Setting the Text and Image

Shells support the standard SWT methods for text and images. To display the best possible image on the desktop, some platforms allow you to specify more that one image for a shell. These images represent the same icon at different resolutions.[3] When both a single image and an array of images are provided,

---

1. The window manager is an X Windows concept. It refers, among other things, to an operating system process that reparents X windows as they are created on the desktop. The window manger provides the shell trimmings and modality, and interacts with the desktop, minimizing and maximizing windows.

2. On some platforms, such as X/Motif on Japanese Solaris, space in the trimming is reserved for the Input Method Editor.

3. The method Display.getIconSizes() returns a list of the recommended icon sizes for the platform.

the last one "wins," allowing you easily to override the images used by a shell that you did not create.[4]

setText(String string) Sets the text for the shell. The text is used as the title of the shell and is normally displayed by the window manager in the title bar portion of the window trimming. It cannot contain delimiters and does not support mnemonics.

getText() Returns the shell text. This is an empty string if the text has never been set.

setImage(Image image) Sets the image for the shell. Some window managers use the image as an icon in the task bar. Others use it in the title bar on a button that invokes the system menu. This image may also appear in the Alt+Tab list used by some window managers to allow quick access to any window on the desktop with the keyboard.

getImage() Returns the image for the shell. This is null if the image has never been set. When an image has not been set for a shell, the window manager may display nothing or choose a "stock application" image to use for the shell.

setImages(Image[] image) Sets the images for the shell. This allows the window manager to choose the best image for the task bar, title bar, system menu, Alt+Tab list, or any other place where an image is needed.

getImages() Returns the images for the shell. This is an empty array if the images have never been set. When an image has not been set for a shell, the window manager may display nothing or choose a "stock application" image to use for the shell.

11.4.6 *Opening a Shell*

Shells are distinguished from other controls because they have an active state. A shell that is *active* contains the focus control. At any given time, the window manager ensures that only one shell from any application on the desktop is active. The window manager sometimes indicates this by drawing the shell

---

4. An alternative strategy would have been to provide both the single image and the array of images to the window manager. This approach is flawed because the single image might be a totally different icon, causing a different icon to be shown for the same window in some places on the desktop.

trim in a different style using different colors. Normally, the active shell is also the topmost shell on the desktop, but this is not necessarily the case. Some window managers support the "focus follows pointer" mode where the shell that is underneath the pointer is made active when the pointer moves over it. In this mode, the shell is not brought to the front.

Unlike other controls, shells are invisible when created. This means that at the very least, setVisible() needs to be called to present a shell to the user. Usually, open() is called instead. When a shell is opened, it becomes the active shell.

> **open()**   Opens the shell. The shell is made visible and becomes the active shell. Focus is assigned to a control within the shell. Depending on the window manager, the shell might become the topmost shell on the desktop. Shells are usually opened only once, although it is not harmful to call open() multiple times on the same shell.

If a shell is already visible, it might not be active. In that case, it can be made to be the active shell using setActive().

> **setActive()**   Makes the shell become the active shell. This method is similar to open() but does not explicitly assign focus. If the shell is already active, this method does nothing.

When a shell is made active, some window managers make the shell the topmost shell within the application but do not bring the shell to the top on the desktop unless the application program that owns the shell is the foreground process. In this case, the shell that was made active will become the active shell when the application program becomes the foreground process. This solves the classic user interface problem, typified by the statement, "I was typing in a window, and another window opened and stole my keystrokes." Sometimes it is necessary to override this behavior, forcing a shell to become active despite the fact that it might steal focus, by using forceFocus().

> **forceActive()**   Forces the shell to be the active shell. This method is similar to setActive() but forces the window manager to make the shell active when it otherwise might not. Even then, the window manager may choose to ignore this request.

Most Programs Should Never Need to Use forceActive()

Forcing a shell to be active should be reserved for those occasions when you *must* get the attention of the user (which is almost never). After all, do you like it when another window steals your keystrokes?

11.4.7   Closing a Shell

By clicking on the close box of the shell, the user indicates that the shell should be disposed of. Application programs can simulate this behavior using the close() method.

> **close()**   Closes the shell in the same manner it would be closed had the user clicked on the close box or performed some other platform-specific keyboard or mouse operation that indicates the shell should be disposed of. If the close box is disabled for any reason, close() will not dispose of the shell.

What's the Difference Between close() and dispose()?

The close() method allows the SWT.Close event to run before attempting to dispose of the shell. Application programs can use the SWT.Close event to prompt the user, prevent the shell from being closed, or run any arbitrary code. This means that calling close() may not actually dispose of the shell, depending on the close listeners. Calling dispose() guarantees that the shell will be disposed of before the method returns.

11.4.8   Setting the Menu Bar

In SWT, the main menu bar is part of the shell trimming.[5] This means that menu bars cannot be accessed until they have been included in the shell trim. The setMenuBar() method is used to add and remove menus from the main menu bar.

> **setMenuBar(Menu menu)**   Sets the menu to be the main menu bar for the shell. Before the new menu is assigned, the previous menu is removed. If the new menu is null, the shell does not have a main menu, and space is not reserved for a menu bar.

> **getMenuBar()**   Returns the menu that is the main menu bar for the shell.

---

5.   On Windows, where there is no window manager, the menu bar is natively part of the window trim. On almost every other platform, this is not the case. Although it might have been possible to fake this on Windows, the fact that menus are not controls on Windows makes this approach unworkable.

11.4.9   Creating Shells with Standard Trim

Very often, top-level shells and dialog shells have a standard look for the platform. The class Shell provides two constructors that do not take style bits. These constructors create shells that have standard trim. If you use these constructors, it will ensure that the shells you create do not look out of place on the desktop.

Shell(Display display)   Creates a new shell on the display. The new shell has the appropriate trim for a top-level shell.

Shell(Shell shell)   Creates a new dialog shell with a given parent. The new shell has the appropriate trim for a dialog shell.

11.4.10   Creating Shells with Nonstandard Trim

To create shells with nonstandard trim, style bits are used to choose the particular decoration. The term *decoration* is used to describe a window trim feature, such as the close box or resize handles.

Shell(Display display, int style)   Creates a new shell on the display using the style bits. If the SWT.SHELL_TRIM style is specified, a shell with the standard top-level window trimmings is created.

Shell(Shell shell, int style)   Creates a new dialog shell with the given parent shell, using the style bits. If the SWT.DIALOG_TRIM style is specified, a shell with the standard dialog trimmings is created.

The styles SWT.BORDER, SWT.RESIZE, SWT.CLOSE, SWT.MIN, and SWT.MAX indicate that the shell should have a dialog border, resize handles, close box, minimize button, and maximize button. Shells that are created with the style SWT.NONE have the default trim for the platform, which is a thin black border. Some platforms have a particular look that should be used for a "tool window." The SWT.TOOL style is used to create tool windows.[6]

The convenience constants SWT.SHELL_TRIM and SWT.DIALOG_TRIM allow you to create the standard shell trim for top-level and dialog shells.

---

6. On Windows, a tool window has a title bar that is about half the height of a regular title bar.

> **Shell Trim Is a Hint**
>
> It is up to the window manager whether a particular window trimming combi-
> nation will be honored. For example, some window managers force all windows
> to have resize handles. This means that there is no way to create a shell that is
> not resizable.

11.4.11   Creating Shells without Trim

The SWT.NO_TRIM style ensures that the shell you create has no trimmings.
This constant instructs the window manager that the shell is not under the
control of the window manager and should not be made the active shell. The
SWT.ON_TOP style ensures that the shell stays on top of every other shell on
the desktop.

Both these styles are often used to implement tool tips and code assist
whose shells need to pop up but not take focus or change the active shell.

The following example implements a simple hover help window using
SWT.ON_TOP and SWT.MouseHover. All of the work is done in tipListener.
This listener is rather complicated because it includes the methods createTool-
Tip() and handleEvent(). The createToolTip() method creates the hover help
shell, using the style SWT.ON_TOP. When the mouse is moved or a key is
pressed, handleEvent() disposes of the current hover help shell. When a mouse
hover event occurs, handleEvent() creates the hover shell, positions it, and
makes it visible.

```
public static void main(String[] args) {
    final Display display = new Display();
    final Shell shell = new Shell(display);
    shell.setLayout(new FillLayout());
    Listener tipListener = new Listener() {
        Shell tip = null;
        Label label = null;
        void createToolTip() {
            tip = new Shell(shell, SWT.ON_TOP);
            tip.setLayout(new FillLayout());
            label = new Label(tip, SWT.NONE);
            Listener listener = new Listener() {
                public void handleEvent(Event event) {
                    tip.dispose();
                }
            };
            label.addListener(SWT.MouseExit, listener);
            Color foreground =
                display.getSystemColor(
                    SWT.COLOR_INFO_FOREGROUND);
            label.setForeground(foreground);
```

```
                    Color background =
                        display.getSystemColor(
                            SWT.COLOR_INFO_BACKGROUND);
                    label.setBackground(background);
                    label.setText("ToolTip");
                    tip.pack();
                }
                public void handleEvent(Event e) {
                    switch (e.type) {
                        case SWT.KeyDown:
                        case SWT.MouseMove:
                            if (tip != null) tip.dispose();
                            tip = null;
                            break;
                        case SWT.MouseHover: {
                            if (tip != null) break;
                            createToolTip();
                            Rectangle rect = tip.getBounds();
                            rect.x = e.x;
                            rect.y = e.y + 22;
                            tip.setBounds(
                                display.map(shell, null, rect));
                            tip.setVisible(true);
                        }
                    }
                }
            };
            shell.addListener(SWT.KeyDown, tipListener);
            shell.addListener(SWT.MouseHover, tipListener);
            shell.addListener(SWT.MouseMove, tipListener);
            shell.pack();
            shell.open();
            while (!shell.isDisposed()) {
                if (!display.readAndDispatch()) display.sleep();
            }
            display.dispose();
        }
```

Figure 11.1 shows the hover help window open over the shell. Note that the cursor is hidden in the screenshot.

Figure 11.1

11.4.12   Modality

Modality is a property of a shell that blocks input to one or more other shells in the same application program or the entire desktop. A shell that is not blocking input is said to be *modeless*. In a typical application program, most top-level shells are modeless. A shell that blocks input to its parent is *primary modal*. Primary modal shells are created with the style SWT.PRIMARY_MODAL. When a shell blocks input to every other shell in the application, the shell is said to be *application modal*. Application modal shells are created with the style SWT.APPLICATION_MODAL. Finally, a shell that blocks input to the desktop is *system modal* and is created with the style SWT.SYSTEM_MODAL.

Shells are created with a single modality style that cannot be changed after the shell has been created. When the shell is made visible, the modality style takes effect. When the shell is hidden or disposed of, modality is cleared.

Modality Is a Hint

Modality styles are treated as hints, because not all types of modality are supported on every platform for every kind of shell. If a modality style is not supported, it is upgraded to a more restrictive modality that *is* supported. For example, if SWT.PRIMARY_MODAL were not supported, it would be upgraded to SWT.APPLICATION_MODAL. If a more restrictive style does not exist, it may also be downgraded to the next restrictive style. For example, most operating systems no longer support SWT.SYSTEM_MODAL because it has the ability to bring the desktop to a halt. Most application programs are aware of this and no longer ask for system modality. For those that do, SWT.SYSTEM _MODAL is almost always downgraded to SWT.APPLICATION_MODAL.

11.4.13   Minimizing, Maximizing, and Restoring a Shell

At any given time, a top-level shell is in one of three states: *minimized*, *normal*, or *maximized*. When a shell is minimized (also called *iconified*), the window manager removes it from the screen. A minimized window usually appears on the desktop as an icon in the task bar. A shell that is *normal* draws using the trimming specified by the style constants. It can be moved and resized by the user. When a shell is maximized, the window manager resizes it to fill the entire screen and may temporarily disallow moving and resizing until it is no longer maximized.

Shells are minimized using setMinimized() and maximized using setMaximized().

setMinimized(boolean minimized)   Sets the minimized state of the shell. If minimized is true, the shell is iconified to the task bar. If false, the shell is restored to its previous state, either normal or maximized.

getMinimized()   Returns true if the shell is minimized, otherwise returns false.

setMaximized(boolean maximized)   Sets the maximized state of the shell. If maximized is true, the shell is resized to fit the screen. If false, the shell is restored to the previous state, either normal or minimized.

getMaximized()   Returns true if the shell is maximized, otherwise returns false.

11.4.14   The Default Button

The *default button* is the button that is selected when the user presses <Enter> in a shell, no matter which control has the focus. Default buttons are often used in dialog shells to allow the user quickly to accept or dismiss the window.

setDefaultButton(Button button)   Sets the default button for the shell. When the user presses <Enter>, the button is selected, no matter which control has focus. A thick black line surrounding the button or some other kind of platform-specific emphasis is used to distinguish the default button from other buttons in the shell. At any given time, there can be at most one default button. This button is a descendent of the shell but does not need to be a direct child.

getDefaultButton()   Returns the default button for the shell. On some platforms, when a button gets focus, it becomes the default button. When focus moves to another control that is not a button, the default button status is cleared. At that time, the original default button that was set using setDefaultButton() is restored. If there is no current or original default button, the shell does not have a default button, and this method returns null.

11.4.15   Nonrectangular Shells

Very rarely, an application program needs to create a shell that is nonrectangular. Nonrectangular shells cannot have window trimmings.

setRegion(Region region)   Sets the region that is used to define the shape of the shell. If the region is null, the default rectangular shape for the shell is restored. To specify a region, the shell must be created with the style SWT.NO_TRIM.

getRegion()   Returns the region that is used to define the shape of the shell. If one has not previously been set, null is returned, indicating that the shell is rectangular.

The following example program creates a nonrectangular shell using a region constructed from the radial pattern described in Line and Figure Drawing from Graphics Fundamentals. Because the shell has no trim, SWT.Mouse-Down and SWT.MouseMove are used to allow the user to move the shell on the desktop. When the user types any key, the shell is disposed of. The result is shown in Figure 11.2.

```
static final int POINTS = 11;

public static void main(String[] args) {
    final Point center = new Point(0, 0);
    final int[] radial = new int[POINTS * 2];
    final Display display = new Display();
    final Color black =
        display.getSystemColor(SWT.COLOR_BLACK);
    final Shell shell = new Shell(display, SWT.NO_TRIM);
    shell.setBackground(black);
    shell.setSize(200, 200);
    Rectangle bounds = shell.getClientArea();
    center.x = bounds.x + bounds.width / 2;
    center.y = bounds.y + bounds.height / 2;
    int pos = 0;
    for (int i = 0; i < POINTS; ++i) {
        double r = Math.PI * 2 * pos / POINTS;
        radial[i*2] = (int)((1 + Math.cos(r)) * center.x);
        radial[i*2+1] = (int)((1 + Math.sin(r))*center.y);
        pos = (pos + POINTS / 2) % POINTS;
    }
    Listener listener = new Listener() {
        int offsetX = 0, offsetY = 0;
        public void handleEvent(Event e) {
            switch (e.type) {
                case SWT.MouseDown:
                    if (e.button == 1) {
                        offsetX = e.x;
                        offsetY = e.y;
                    }
                    break;
                case SWT.MouseMove:
                    if ((e.stateMask & SWT.BUTTON1) != 0) {
                        Point pt=shell.toDisplay(e.x, e.y);
                        pt.x -= offsetX;
                        pt.y -= offsetY;
                        shell.setLocation(pt);
                    }
```

```
                        break;
                    case SWT.KeyDown :
                        shell.dispose();
                        break;
                }
            }
        };
        shell.addListener(SWT.MouseDown, listener);
        shell.addListener(SWT.MouseMove, listener);
        shell.addListener(SWT.KeyDown, listener);
        Region region = new Region(display);
        region.add(radial);
        shell.setRegion(region);
        shell.open();
        while (!shell.isDisposed()) {
            if (!display.readAndDispatch()) display.sleep();
        }
        region.dispose();
        display.dispose();
    }
```

Figure 11.2

11.4.16   Shell Events

SWT.Close (ShellEvent)

Table 11.1 shows the close event for Shell.

Table 11.1   Close Event

Untyped Event		Description	
SWT.Close		The shell is being closed	
Typed Event	Listener		Methods
ShellEvent	ShellListener (and ShellAdapter)		shellActivated(ShellEvent) shellClosed(ShellEvent) shellDeactivated(ShellEvent) shellDeiconified(ShellEvent) shellIconified(ShellEvent)

The SWT.Close event (typed event ShellEvent) is sent whenever the user closes the shell or the close() method is called. The relevant event fields during a close event for Shell are as follows.

Public Fields of Class Event That Are Valid during SWT.Close

Field	Description
doit	Setting *doit* to false cancels the close operation. The default is true.

Using SWT.Close to Prevent a Shell from Closing

The following example prompts the user with a "yes/no/cancel" message box before closing the shell. If the user cancels the close operation, the shell is not closed. Otherwise, the shell is closed in the normal manner.

```
public static void main(String[] args) {
    Display display = new Display();
    final Shell shell = new Shell(display);
    shell.setText("Close Example");
    shell.addListener(SWT.Close, new Listener() {
        public void handleEvent(Event event) {
            int style = SWT.YES | SWT.NO | SWT.CANCEL;
            style |= SWT.APPLICATION_MODAL;
            MessageBox box = new MessageBox(shell, style);
            box.setText(shell.getText());
            box.setMessage("Save changes?");
            switch (box.open()) {
                case SWT.YES: break;
                case SWT.NO: break;
                case SWT.CANCEL :
                    event.doit = false;
                    break;
            }
```

```
        }
    });
    shell.setSize(200, 200);
    shell.open();
    while (!shell.isDisposed()) {
        if (!display.readAndDispatch()) display.sleep();
    }
    display.dispose();
}
```

SWT.Activate (ShellEvent)

The SWT.Activate event (typed event ShellEvent) is sent whenever the shell becomes active. Activate events contain meaningful values in only the *display*, *widget*, and *type* fields.

SWT.Deactivate (ShellEvent)

The SWT.Deactivate event (typed event ShellEvent) is sent whenever the shell becomes inactive. Deactivate events contain meaningful values in only the *display*, *widget*, and *type* fields.

SWT.Iconify (ShellEvent)

The SWT.Iconify event (typed event ShellEvent) is sent whenever the shell becomes iconified. Iconify events contain meaningful values in only the *display*, *widget*, and *type* fields.

SWT.Deiconify (ShellEvent)

The SWT.Deiconify event (typed event ShellEvent) is sent whenever the shell becomes no longer iconified. Deiconify events contain meaningful values in only the *display*, *widget*, and *type* fields.

11.5 Summary

In this chapter, you have learned about the properties that are shared by all controls. These include font, foreground, and background color. The simple container classes, Composite and Group, were described. These allow you to build complex containment hierarchies. Finally, Shell was described. It is the fundamental class that represents top-level windows, supports menu bars, interacts with the window manager, and provides modality. It is hard to imagine an SWT application that does not contain at least one shell. For this reason, knowledge of class Shell is essential.

CHAPTER 12

Canvas and Caret

Much of the capability to draw graphics within a control has already been described in Control Fundamentals. This section covers those topics that have not already been discussed, specifically, support for carets in SWT.

12.1 Class Canvas

12.1.1 Example

12.1.2 Canvas Hierarchy

12.1.3   Canvas Styles (none)

Style	Description

12.1.4   Canvas Events (none)

Event	Description

Canvases are controls that are specifically built to support SWT graphics. They inherit a number of interesting style bits from their superclass Composite that govern the way they draw. Styles such as SWT.NO_BACKGROUND are often used to reduce redraws at the cost of more complicated code.

Because Canvas is a subclass of Composite, it can contain scroll bars. Canvas provides support for a caret and the ability to call methods that scroll the client area, neither of which is supported by Composite. It is important to note that a canvas with scroll bars does *not* automatically scroll the client area.[1] You will need to write the code that does this.

12.1.5   Painting in a Canvas

For a complete discussion of the styles that govern redraw, paint events, and drawing graphics in a canvas, see Painting in the Control Fundamentals chapter. The graphics chapters in this book are also essential.

12.1.6   Carets

By definition, at any given time, there is exactly one caret visible at a time. This makes sense because the caret is used to indicate focus and give the user a visual cue that typing is permitted.

If you create more than one caret, you can change the caret that the canvas is displaying using setCaret().

> **setCaret(Caret caret)**   Sets the caret. If there is a previous caret, it is removed before the new caret is assigned. Canvases hide and show the caret automatically when getting and losing focus, resizing, or painting.

---

1. The class org.eclipse.swt.custom.ScrolledComposite provides this capability and is worth investigating.

getCaret()   Returns the caret. If this value was never set, the default value null is returned.

12.1.7   Scrolling

Scrolling is so common that many operating systems provide native support for the operation. Normally, it involves copying an area of a control to another location, then damaging the area that was just copied.[2]

scroll(int destX, int destY, int x, int y, int width, int height, boolean all)   Scrolls a rectangular area in the control using a platform-specific scrolling mechanism. The area specified by the source rectangle is copied to the location specified by the destination point, then damaged to cause a paint event. Before the source can be copied, all outstanding paint events are flushed to ensure that the source bits are up to date. Children intersecting the source rectangle are optionally moved during the operation.

When you call scroll(), the method does the equivalent of calling update() on the canvas before copying the source rectangle. This can lead to subtle pixel corruption[3] problems in programs that keep scrolling state that is independent of the scroll bars. For example, consider the following code fragment.

```
// FAILS - copies bits using new origin, then damages
originX = newOriginX;
originY = newOriginY;
canvas.scroll(destX, destY, 0, 0, width, height, false);
```

The important variables are *originX* and *originY*. These fields are set when scrolling and used by a hypothetical paint listener to draw the contents of the canvas at a scrolled offset. Setting the fields and calling scroll() forces outstanding paints to be delivered. If there are no pending paints, this code will work. If there are any pending paint events, the paint listener will draw them at the new origin. This origin has yet to be scrolled, so pixel corruption will result. The correct way to use scroll() is to set the variables after the call to scroll().

2. In future, this may not always be the case. For example, when a control is transparent, copying an area does not give the correct result. One alternative is to copy nothing and damage both areas instead.

3. This is called *cheese* by the SWT team. Nobody knows why.

```
//WORKS - copies bits at the old origin, then damages
canvas.scroll(destX, destY, 0, 0, width, height, false);
originX = newOriginX;
originY = newOriginY;
```

12.2 Class Caret

12.2.1 Example

12.2.2 Caret Hierarchy

12.2.3 Caret Styles (none)

Style	Description

12.2.4 Caret Events (none)

Event	Description

A caret, sometimes called an *I-beam*, indicates the target for keys that are typed by the user. On some platforms, the caret blinks. Carets are used exclusively with canvases.[4] They are not controls but provide the standard SWT API for visibility, positioning, and resizing.

12.2.5 Bounds, Size, and Location

The size and location of a caret is configured using setBounds(), setLocation(), and setSize().

---

4. The text control for each platform also appears to have a caret. On platforms that do not have a native caret, the caret is implemented by code within the text control. For this reason, the text control caret cannot be accessed directly.

setBounds(int x, int y, int width, int height)   Sets the location and size of the caret. The *x* and *y* coordinates are relative to the parent. If the *width* or *height* parameters are negative, zero is used instead.

setBounds(Rectangle bounds)   Sets the location and size of the caret. Equivalent to setBounds(bounds.x, bounds.y, bounds.width, bounds.height).

getBounds()   Returns a rectangle that describes the size and location of the caret, relative to the parent. A new rectangle is returned so that modifying the rectangle will not affect the caret.

setLocation(int x, int y)   Sets the location of the caret. The *x* and *y* coordinates are relative to the parent.

setLocation(Point location)   Sets the location of the caret. Equivalent to setLocation(location.x, location.y).

getLocation()   Returns a point that describes the location of the caret. A new point is returned so that modifying the point will not affect the caret.

setSize(int width, int height)   Sets the size of the caret. If the *width* or *height* parameters are negative, zero is used instead.

setSize(Point size)   Sets the size of the caret. Equivalent to setSize(size.x, size.y).

getSize()   Returns a point that describes the size of the caret. A new point is returned so that modifying the point will not affect the caret.

12.2.6   *Visibility*

Despite the fact that carets can draw and be resized, they are not clipped. This means that you need to be careful when you draw in a canvas to avoid drawing over the caret. When a canvas is painting or scrolling, in either SWT.Paint or Canvas.scroll(), the caret is automatically hidden and shown again when the operation completes. If you draw outside of a paint event, you will need to explicitly hide and show the caret. A caret is hidden or shown using setVisible().

setVisible(boolean visible)   Shows or hides the caret, depending on the boolean parameter.

getVisible()   Returns true if the caret is visible and false if it is hidden.

isVisible()   Returns true if the caret and *all* ancestors are visible or false if it or *any* of its ancestors are hidden.

It is not possible to show a caret in a canvas that does not have focus. Calling setVisible() indicates that when the canvas gets focus, the caret will be shown.

12.2.7   The Input Method Editor Font

Carets, as you might expect, provide the location for the input method (described in the chapter The Keyboard). When editing "in place," the Input Method Editor (IME) uses the location of the caret to position a preprocessing window. By default, the IME uses the font for the canvas for characters displayed in this window. The setFont() method of Caret is used to override the default font for the IME (something a multifont editor might decide to do).

setFont(Font font)   Sets the font that is used to draw text in the IME. If the font is null, the font for the canvas is used.

getFont()   Returns the font that is used to draw text in the IME. If the font has not been set, the default font for the canvas is returned.

12.2.8   Using a Caret to Write a Single-Line Text Editor

The following complete example implements a very simple single-line text editor that allows the user to type characters and move the caret within the text using the arrow keys, the <Home> key, and the <End> key. The code is quite simplistic. For example, selection and clipboard operations are not implemented.

```
static int ibeam = 0;
static String text = "0123456789";

public static void main(String[] args) {
    Display display = new Display();
    final Shell shell = new Shell(display);
    shell.setLayout(new FillLayout());
    final Caret caret = new Caret(shell, SWT.NONE);
    GC gc = new GC(shell);
    Point size = gc.stringExtent("");
    caret.setSize(1, size.y);
    gc.dispose();
    shell.addListener(SWT.Paint, new Listener() {
        public void handleEvent(Event e) {
```

```
                    e.gc.drawString(text, 0, 0);
            }
    });
    shell.addListener(SWT.KeyDown, new Listener() {
        public void handleEvent(Event e) {
            int length = text.length();
            if (e.character == 0) {
                switch (e.keyCode) {
                    case SWT.HOME: ibeam = 0; break;
                    case SWT.END: ibeam = length; break;
                    case SWT.ARROW_LEFT: --ibeam; break;
                    case SWT.ARROW_RIGHT: ibeam++; break;
                }
                ibeam = Math.min(Math.max(0,ibeam),length);
            }
            String left = text.substring(0, ibeam);
            String right = text.substring(ibeam, length);
            switch (e.character) {
                case SWT.CR:
                case SWT.LF:
                case SWT.TAB: break;
                case SWT.BS:
                    ibeam = Math.max(0, ibeam - 1);
                    left = text.substring(0, ibeam);
                    break;
                case SWT.DEL:
                    int pos =
                        Math.min(ibeam + 1, length);
                    right = text.substring(pos, length);
                    break;
                default:
                    if (e.character < ' ') break;
                    ibeam = Math.min(length + 1,ibeam + 1);
                    left = left + e.character;
            }
            GC gc = new GC(shell);
            Point size = gc.stringExtent(left);
            caret.setLocation(size.x, 0);
            gc.dispose();
            if (e.character != 0) {
                text = left + right;
                shell.redraw();
            }
        }
    });
    shell.addListener(SWT.MouseDown, new Listener() {
        public void handleEvent(Event e) {
            GC gc = new GC(shell);
            int length = text.length();
            int width = 0, lastWidth = 0;
            ibeam = 0;
            while (ibeam <= length) {
                lastWidth = width;
                String string = text.substring(0, ibeam);
                width = gc.stringExtent(string).x;
                if (width >= e.x)  break;
```

```
                    ibeam++;
                }
                int offset = (width - lastWidth) / 2;
                if (e.x >= lastWidth + offset) {
                    caret.setLocation(width, 0);
                } else {
                    --ibeam;
                    caret.setLocation(lastWidth, 0);
                }
                ibeam = Math.min(Math.max(0, ibeam), length);
                gc.dispose();
            }
        });
        shell.pack();
        shell.open();
        while (!shell.isDisposed()) {
            if (!display.readAndDispatch()) display.sleep();
        }
        display.dispose();
    }
```

12.3 Summary

Canvas and Caret can be used to implement your own controls, the scope of which is beyond this book. However, the article entitled "Creating Your Own Widgets in SWT" on *eclipse.org* describes how to do this in detail.

CHAPTER 13

Draggable Controls

Draggable controls allow the user to customize the position and size of other controls within your program. Dragging a control should not be confused with drag and drop, which typically involves the transfer of data. When dragging a control, the user is configuring the user interface. This flexibility makes your application stand out from the competition.

13.1 Classes CoolBar and CoolItem

13.1.1 Example

13.1.2 CoolBar and CoolItem Hierarchies

13.1.3 CoolBar Styles (none)

Style	Description

13.1.4   CoolBar Events (none)

Event	Description

13.1.5   CoolItem Styles

Style	Description
SWT.DROP_DOWN	Indicates that the item can display a chevron

13.1.6   CoolItem Events

Event	Description
SWT.Selection	The drop-down chevron was selected

Cool bars, sometimes called *rebar controls*, provide an area where the user can dynamically reposition other controls. These are always children of the cool bar. Most of the time, cool bars are used to manipulate tool bars. This combination is so common that many people mistakenly believe that this capability is inherent in ToolBar.

Cool items, the "item children" of a cool bar, provide a "gripper" that allows the user to drag a control using the item. Sometimes when the user is dragging an item, part of the control might become clipped. A drop-down cool item is a special kind of item that is similar to a drop-down tool item. It allows the user to select a small drop-down chevron located within the cool item. When a cool item is used with a tool bar and the chevron is selected, a menu, list, or even another tool bar containing the strings and icons of the tool items that are no longer visible is often displayed.[1]

Cool bars have a reputation for being tricky and hard to program. This comes from the fact that they not only dynamically resize and reposition their items but also automatically resize themselves. This happens when the user drags a cool item to a new row, causing the cool bar to wrap and grow larger.

---

1. Sometimes programmers expect this behavior to be automatic. They are surprised when they need to write the code to make it happen. Because a cool item can reposition any kind of control, it's not always clear what should be displayed when the user presses the chevron. Other programs use the chevron to open a new shell instead of showing a menu.

Just as easily, the user can collapse a row by dragging an item onto another row. If a cool item is not properly configured, it may be given a zero size or behave strangely when rearranged. In addition, if your program is not prepared for the cool bar to change size dynamically, the other controls in the window will not be repositioned properly, relative to the new size of the cool bar. In this respect, CoolBar can be thought of as having "shell-like" behavior. For the same reason that you must be prepared to reposition controls when the user resizes a shell, you must also be ready to do this when the user resizes a cool bar.

13.1.7   Configuring CoolItem

The setControl() method is used to associate a control with a cool item.

> **setControl(Control control)**   Sets the control that will be positioned inside the cool item. When the cool bar positions the item, the control is moved and resized accordingly.

> **getControl()**   Returns the control that will be positioned inside the cool item.

Setting the control for a cool item merely associates the control with the item. It does not dictate or imply anything about the size of the item or how the cool bar will treat it when the other items are rearranged. Instead, each cool item has a preferred size, a minimum size, and a current size. The Cool-Bar layout algorithm uses these sizes to position and resize the items.[2]

> **setPreferredSize(int width, int height)**   Sets the preferred size of the item. If the *width* or *height* parameters are negative, zero is used instead. The *preferred size* of a cool item is the smallest size the item can have while showing all of its content. The preferred size is used by the cool bar to compute the initial size of the item and is also consulted during subsequent layouts, when the user is rearranging items.

> **setPreferredSize(Point size)**   Sets the preferred size of the item. Equivalent to setPreferredSize(size.x, size.y).

---

2. CoolBar layout should not to be confused with layout of controls, as described in the chapter Layout. CoolBar layout refers to the order, size, and wrap state of cool items.

Always Set the Preferred Size of a Cool Item

If you do not provide the preferred size for at least one item, the height of the CoolItem rows within the cool bar will be zero. The cool bar will draw strangely, and the user will be unable to interact with the items. For this reason, you *must* always set the preferred size of your items.

getPreferredSize()   Returns the preferred size of the item.

setMinimumSize(int width, int height)   Sets the minimum size of the item. The *minimum size* of a cool item is the smallest size that the user can resize the item. If you do not set this size, the user will be able to rearrange items so that none of the content of this item is showing. When a cool item is used to rearrange a tool bar, applications often set the minimum size of the cool item to the size of the first few tool items, then use the drop-down chevron to provide access to the rest of the items (see Using SWT.DROP_DOWN Cool Items in this section).

setMinimumSize(Point size)   Sets the minimum size of the item. Equivalent to setMinimumSize(size.x, size.y).

getMinimumSize()   Returns the minimum size of the item.

setSize(int width, int height)   Sets the size of the item. If the *width* or *height* parameters are negative, zero is used instead.

setSize(Point size)   Sets the size of the item. Equivalent to setSize(size.x, size.y).

Never Set the Size of a Cool Item

It is tempting to try to set the size of the item rather than configuring the preferred and minimum size. This should be avoided. Because cool bars rearrange their items, wrapping and shrinking them as necessary (based on the other items in the control and the current size of the cool bar), there is no guarantee that the size you set will be honored. Even when restoring the item as part of restoring the cool bar state from a previous program invocation, the CoolBar.setItem-Layout() method is more appropriate. Therefore, you should *never* set the size of a cool item. This method cannot be removed from SWT without breaking binary compatibility with previous releases.

getSize()   Returns a point that describes the size of the item. A new point is returned so that modifying the point will not affect the item.

getBounds()   Returns a rectangle that describes the size and location of the item, relative to the parent. A new rectangle is returned so that modifying the rectangle will not affect the item.

To determine the preferred size of an item, the computeSize() method for CoolItem is used. This method allows you to specify the client area of the cool item and compute the required size for the item, including the gripper.

computeSize(int wHint, int hHint)   Returns a point that is the preferred size of the item. The *wHint* and *hHint* arguments are normally the size of the content area but can be the special value SWT.DEFAULT (causing the cool item to return a small default size).

The following example program creates a cool bar that contains four separate tool bars. The computeSize() and setPreferredSize() methods are used to configure the cool bar so that each tool bar is completely visible when the shell is opened. The createItem() helper method creates a cool item and the tool bar that it contains. The static field *itemCount* is used to keep a running count of tool items that have been created so far so that each tool item has a unique label.

```
static int itemCount;
static CoolItem createItem(CoolBar coolBar, int count) {
    ToolBar toolBar = new ToolBar(coolBar, SWT.FLAT);
    for (int i = 0; i < count; i++) {
        ToolItem item = new ToolItem(toolBar, SWT.PUSH);
        item.setText(itemCount++ +"");
    }
    toolBar.pack();
    Point size = toolBar.getSize();
    CoolItem item = new CoolItem(coolBar, SWT.NONE);
    item.setControl(toolBar);
    Point preferred = item.computeSize(size.x, size.y);
    item.setPreferredSize(preferred);
    return item;
}

public static void main(String[] args) {
    Display display = new Display();
    Shell shell = new Shell(display);
    CoolBar coolBar = new CoolBar(shell, SWT.NONE);
    createItem(coolBar, 3);
    createItem(coolBar, 2);
    createItem(coolBar, 3);
    createItem(coolBar, 4);
```

```
    coolBar.pack();
    shell.open();
    while (!shell.isDisposed()) {
        if (!display.readAndDispatch()) display.sleep();
    }
    display.dispose();
}
```

Figure 13.1 shows the result of running this code.

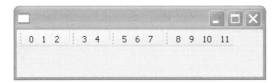

Figure 13.1

13.1.8   *Repositioning Other Controls When a CoolBar Is Resized*

Not only do the size and position of cool items change as the user repositions them, but the size of the cool bar can change, as well. To reposition the other controls in a window when this happens, you need to add an SWT.Resize listener to the cool bar.

The following main() method uses FormLayout (described in the chapter Layout) to place a cool bar at the top of a shell and a text control below it. When the user resizes the cool bar, an SWT.Resize listener calls Composite.layout(), causing the layout to reposition both the cool bar and the text control. If your program does not use Layout to position children, you can call setBounds() and setSize() to configure the controls instead.

Figure 13.2 shows the result after both the cool bar and shell have been resized.

```
public static void main(String[] args) {
    Display display = new Display();
    final Shell shell = new Shell(display);
    CoolBar coolBar = new CoolBar(shell, SWT.NONE);
    createItem(coolBar, 3);
    createItem(coolBar, 2);
    createItem(coolBar, 3);
    createItem(coolBar, 4);
    int style = SWT.BORDER | SWT.H_SCROLL | SWT.V_SCROLL;
    Text text = new Text(shell, style);
    FormLayout layout = new FormLayout();
    shell.setLayout(layout);
    FormData coolData = new FormData();
    coolData.left = new FormAttachment(0);
    coolData.right = new FormAttachment(100);
```

```
coolData.top = new FormAttachment(0);
coolBar.setLayoutData(coolData);
coolBar.addListener(SWT.Resize, new Listener() {
    public void handleEvent(Event event) {
        shell.layout();
    }
});
FormData textData = new FormData();
textData.left = new FormAttachment(0);
textData.right = new FormAttachment(100);
textData.top = new FormAttachment(coolBar);
textData.bottom = new FormAttachment(100);
text.setLayoutData(textData);
shell.open();
while (!shell.isDisposed()) {
    if (!display.readAndDispatch()) display.sleep();
}
display.dispose();
}
```

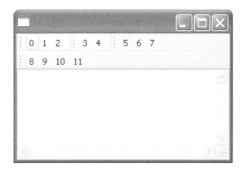

Figure 13.2

13.1.9   Using SWT.DROP_DOWN Cool Items

When the user rearranges a cool item to be smaller than its preferred size, this implies that some of the content within the item is clipped. A cool item that is created with the style SWT.DROP_DOWN shows a small drop-down chevron when this happens to indicate that clipped content is available. You can use the SWT.Selection event for CoolItem to provide alternate access to the clipped content when the user selects the chevron.

In the following example, the createItem() method creates a cool item with the SWT.DROP_DOWN style. It creates a tool bar and sets it into the item. An SWT.Selection listener is used to offer a menu of the tool items that are clipped when the user clicks on the chevron. If a tool item is obscured or partially displayed, it is included in the menu. Applications typically use the SWT.WRAP style when creating a tool bar to put into a cool item so that the tool items are either fully visible or hidden when the cool item becomes too small to show the entire tool bar.

Once the menu has been created, the x and y coordinates provided in the event are used to position it. Figure 13.3 shows the appearance after the chevron has been selected.

```
static int itemCount;
static CoolItem createItem(
    final CoolBar coolBar,
    int count) {
    final ToolBar toolBar =
        new ToolBar(coolBar, SWT.FLAT | SWT.WRAP);
    for (int i = 0; i < count; i++) {
        ToolItem item = new ToolItem(toolBar, SWT.PUSH);
        item.setText(itemCount++ +"");
    }
    toolBar.pack();
    Point size = toolBar.getSize();
    final CoolItem item =
        new CoolItem(coolBar, SWT.DROP_DOWN);
    item.addListener(SWT.Selection, new Listener() {
        Menu menu = null;
        public void handleEvent(Event e) {
            if (e.detail != SWT.ARROW) return;
            int i = 0;
            ToolItem[] items = toolBar.getItems();
            Rectangle client = toolBar.getClientArea();
            while (i < items.length) {
                Rectangle rect1=items[i].getBounds();
                Rectangle rect2=rect1.intersection(client);
                if (!rect1.equals(rect2)) break;
                i++;
            }
            if (i == items.length) return;
            Shell shell = toolBar.getShell();
            if (menu != null) menu.dispose();
            menu = new Menu(shell, SWT.POP_UP);
            for (int j = i; j < items.length; j++) {
                MenuItem item =new MenuItem(menu,SWT.PUSH);
                item.setText(items[j].getText());
            }
            Point pt = e.display.map(coolBar,null,e.x,e.y);
            menu.setLocation(pt);
            menu.setVisible(true);
        }
    });
    item.setControl(toolBar);
    Point preferred = item.computeSize(size.x, size.y);
    item.setPreferredSize(preferred);
    Rectangle minimum = toolBar.getItems()[0].getBounds();
    item.setMinimumSize(minimum.width, minimum.height);
    return item;
}
```

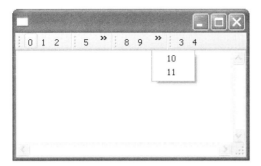

Figure 13.3

Note that the user can select items from the menu but the corresponding obscured tool item is not selected. You can easily fix this by adding an SWT.Selection listener to each instance of MenuItem and using notifyListeners() to forward the event to the tool item.

13.1.10   *Saving and Restoring the CoolBar Layout*

When users configure a cool bar, they are rearranging cool items and their associated controls to their liking. Cool items can wrap to a new line, become resized, and get reordered. When the program is restarted, the user expects the cool bar configuration from the previous invocation to be restored. Programs that do not restore the old cool bar state are frustrating, especially when the user has fussed to get the cool bar just right.

CoolBar provides the getItemOrder(), getItemSizes(), and getWrapIndices() methods to query the current state of the cool items. You can get this state before your program shuts down and save it in a configuration file.

>   **getItemOrder()**   Returns an array of the zero-based indices of the items. The array captures the visual order of the items and can be used to map the creation order to the order in which the items are currently displayed.

>   **getItemSizes()**   Returns an array of points that represent the current size of each of the items in the order that they are displayed.

>   **getWrapIndices()**   Returns an array of indices that represent the current wrap points of the items. When an index occurs in the array, this indicates that the item will appear on a new line.

The method that restores the layout of a cool bar is called setItemLayout().

setItemLayout(int[] itemOrder, int[] wrapIndices, Point[] sizes)   Sets the item order, the wrap indices, and sizes of each item in a cool bar. These three arrays are almost always the ones that were returned earlier by getItemOrder(), getItemSizes(), and getWrapIndices().

13.1.11   Locking the Cool Bar

Some users find cool bars annoying. They mistakenly reposition items, changing their order and the size of the controls that they contain. Other users reposition the items once and for all. The setLocked() method of CoolBar allows you to lock and unlock the position of every item in a cool bar.

setLocked(boolean locked)   Sets the locked state of the cool bar. When the cool bar is locked, the items cannot be repositioned.

getLocked()   Returns the locked state of the cool bar. By default, this value is false.

13.1.12   Searching Operations

CoolBar provides a number of searching operations that allow you to find items and indices.

getItem(int index)   Returns the item at the index, which is zero-based. If the index is out of range, an IllegalArgumentException ("Index out of bounds") is thrown.

getItemCount()   Returns the number of items in the cool bar.

getItems()   Returns an array of the items. This is a *copy* so that modifying it has no effect on the cool bar.

indexOf(CoolItem item)   Returns the zero-based index of the item. If the item is not found, −1 is returned.

13.1.13   CoolItem Events

SWT.Selection (SelectionEvent)

The SWT.Selection event (typed event SelectionEvent) is sent whenever the user selects the drop-down chevron on a cool item. The relevant event fields during a selection event for CoolItem are as follows.

Public Fields of Class Event That Are Valid during SWT.Selection

Field	Description
detail	This field contains SWT.ARROW if the drop-down chevron was selected.
x	The *x* coordinate to be used when positioning a widget for a drop-down cool item. Note that this value is in the coordinate system of the cool bar.
y	The *y* coordinate to be used when positioning a widget for a drop-down cool item. Note that this value is in the coordinate system of the cool bar.

Using SWT.Selection to Implement a Drop-Down Cool Item

A good example that uses the SWT.Selection event with a drop-down cool item can be found in the section Using SWT.DROP_DOWN Cool Items.

13.2   Class Sash

13.2.1   Example

13.2.2   Sash Hierarchy

13.2.3   Sash Styles

Style	Description
SWT.HORIZONTAL	Create a horizontal sash
SWT.VERTICAL	Create a vertical sash

13.2.4   Sash Events

Event	Description
SWT.Selection	The sash was dragged

A sash is a vertical or horizontal control that can be dragged by the user, just like a tracker, cool bar, or shell. Sometimes called *splitters*, they are almost always used to allow the user to resize controls within a shell.

Sash is a low-level mechanism to enable resizing. Sashes *do not* actually change their location or the location or size of other controls. Rather, a grayed image or another platform-specific graphic is moved. While the sash is being dragged, feedback is provided to your program using the SWT.Selection event.

Because using a sash to resize and position controls is the predominant use, a control that provides this functionality automatically, called *SashForm*, is implemented in the package *org.eclipse.swt.custom*.

13.2.5 Sash Events

SWT.Selection (SelectionEvent)

The SWT.Selection event (typed event SelectionEvent) is sent whenever the user drags a sash using the mouse or the keyboard. The relevant event fields during a selection event for Sash are as follows.

Public Fields of Class Event That Are Valid during SWT.Selection

Field	Description
detail	When the user is dragging the sash, this field contains SWT.DRAG
x	The proposed x coordinate of the sash
y	The proposed y coordinate of the sash
width	The proposed width of the sash
height	The proposed height of the sash
doit	When set to false, the sash will not move to the proposed coordinates

Using SWT.Selection to Resize Controls

Sashes are often used with FormLayout to allow the user to resize controls within a shell. An example of this can be found in the section Using FormLayout to Implement SashPane.

13.3   Class Tracker

13.3.1   Example

13.3.2   Tracker Hierarchy

13.3.3   Tracker Styles

Style	Description
SWT.RESIZE	Resize the rectangles instead of moving them
SWT.LEFT	Resize the left edge
SWT.RIGHT	Resize the right edge
SWT.UP	Resize the top edge
SWT.DOWN	Resize the bottom edge

13.3.4   Tracker Events

Event	Description
SWT.Move	The rectangles have been moved
SWT.Resize	The rectangles have been resized

Trackers allow the user to move or resize one or more rectangles on the screen. This action is sometimes called *rubber banding*. Because Tracker draws rectangles on top of other controls and the screen, special support is provided on some operating systems to avoid corrupting pixels on the desktop.

Tracker Should Have Been a Subclass of Dialog[3]

Tracker is a subclass of Widget but this is a mistake. A tracker behaves like a modal dialog, prompting the user and waiting for a result. Unfortunately, the class cannot be moved without breaking binary compatibility.

13.3.5 Creating a Tracker

Tracker provides two forms of the standard Widget constructor.

Tracker(Display display, int style)   Creates a new tracker on the display. The user is able to move or resize rectangles anywhere on the screen.

Tracker(Composite parent, int style)   Creates a new tracker with a Composite parent. The user is able to move or resize rectangles anywhere within the parent.

Trackers that allow the user to resize rectangles are created using the SWT.RESIZE style. When resizing, the user will drag either an edge or a corner, using the mouse or the keyboard. To indicate where the user should start, the SWT.LEFT, SWT.RIGHT, SWT.UP, and SWT.DOWN styles are used. Corners are specified using combinations of styles. For example, specifying SWT.DOWN | SWT.RIGHT indicates that resizing should happen in the bottom right corner.

13.3.6 Opening a Tracker

Trackers are opened in the same manner as Dialogs, using the open() method.

open()   Opens the tracker. This runs a modal loop that allows the user to move or resize the rectangles, using the mouse or the keyboard. If the mouse is down, the mouse is used to manipulate the rectangles. Otherwise, the keyboard is used. The modal loop ends when the close() method is called or when the user releases the mouse or presses the <Esc> or <Enter> key.

---

3. Dialogs are described in detail in the chapter Dialogs.

close()   Closes the tracker. If the user is interacting with the tracker, the interaction is cancelled.

13.3.7   Setting the Rectangles

Opening a tracker without setting any rectangles is not very useful. Normally, only one rectangle is provided.

setRectangles(Rectangle[] rectangles)   Sets the rectangles that the tracker draws. The rectangles are in the coordinate system of the parent. If the parent is the display, the rectangles are in screen coordinates.

getRectangles()   Returns the rectangles. This is a copy of the array so that modifying it has no effect.

13.3.8   Using Stippling and Cursors

Application programs use trackers for many different purposes. For example, a tracker could be used to move controls in a "GUI builder." To indicate where a control will be placed or whether dropping a control is valid, the GUI builder might need to change the cursor while tracking. This is done using setCursor().

setCursor(Cursor cursor)   Sets the cursor that is used by the tracker. Setting this value to null restores the default tracking cursor.

Some programs use trackers to implement tear-off controls. *Tearing off* a control happens when the user drags it with the mouse, causing it to be removed from its current shell and appear in a new shell. Tear-off controls can often be put back in their original shell, causing the new shell to be removed. To indicate that a control can be put back, programs sometimes use a tracker with a stippled effect. A stippled effect grays out the rectangles that the tracker draws.

setStippled(boolean stippled)   Sets the stippled effect. When true, the tracker draws with a stippled look.

getStippled()   Returns true if the tracker is drawing stippled, otherwise returns false.

13.3.9   Tracker Events

SWT.Move (ControlEvent)

The SWT.Move event (typed event ControlEvent) is sent whenever the user moves the rectangles within the tracker, using the mouse or keyboard. The relevant event fields during a move event for Tracker are as follows.

Public Fields of Class Event That Are Valid during SWT.Move

Field	Description
x	The x coordinate of the tracker
y	The y coordinate of the tracker

Using SWT.Move with Tear-Off Controls

Tracker actually plays a very small part in tearing off a control. However, Tracker is the class that is used to position the control, either within the parent or on the desktop. It is easy to see how Tracker can be used to move a control inside a shell but not so obvious why it is needed once the control is torn off. To understand why, recall that the window manager owns the shell trimming. When a shell is moved or resized, some window managers move an outline. Others move the shell. We need to know when the shell is finished moving in order to decide whether the control should be put back. This means that the SWT.Move event for shells cannot be used.

To decide when a control should be moved, a mouse tolerance factor is required. Otherwise, the user will move the control too easily. The main() method in this example creates the shell and the tear-off composite, and adds mouse listeners. The mouse down listener remembers the original mouse location. When the mouse moves outside of the rectangle defined by this point and the tolerance, a move() operation is started.

```
static final int TOLERANCE = 8;

public static void main(String[] args) {
    Display display = new Display();
    Color blue = display.getSystemColor(SWT.COLOR_BLUE);
    final Shell shell = new Shell(display);
    Composite composite = new Composite(shell, SWT.BORDER);
    composite.setBounds(10, 10, 100, 100);
    composite.setBackground(blue);
    Listener listener = new Listener() {
        Point point = null;
```

```
public void handleEvent(Event event) {
    switch (event.type) {
        case SWT.MouseDown :
            if (event.button == 1) {
                point = new Point(event.x,event.y);
            }
            break;
        case SWT.MouseMove :
            if (point == null) break;
            int x = point.x - event.x;
            int y = point.y - event.y;
            if (Math.abs(x) < TOLERANCE
                && Math.abs(y) < TOLERANCE) break;
            Control control =(Control)event.widget;
            move(shell, control, x, y);
            point = null;
            break;
    }
}
};
composite.addListener(SWT.MouseDown, listener);
composite.addListener(SWT.MouseMove, listener);
shell.setSize(200, 200);
shell.open();
while (!shell.isDisposed()) {
    if (!display.readAndDispatch()) display.sleep();
}
}
```

The move() operation takes the original shell, the control, and the mouse offset. If the control is reparentable, the bounds of the control and the original shell are queried and mapped to screen coordinates.

Next, a tracker is created using the control bounds and opened on the display. The tracker uses an SWT.Move listener to set the stippled look whenever the control rectangle is outside of the original shell rectangle. If the tracker is not cancelled, the rectangles are tested to see whether the user moved the rectangle inside the original shell.

If the rectangle is inside the original shell, the already torn-off control is being either put back or moved inside the shell. Putting back the control involves using setParent() to restore the original shell as the parent and disposing the torn-off shell. Whether the control is being put back or positioned, it must be placed inside the shell at the location determined by the tracker. The calls to setVisible() hide the control while it is being reparented and repositioned.

If the rectangle is outside the original shell, the control is being either torn off or moved on the desktop. Tearing off the control involves creating a new dialog shell for the control and using setParent() to reparent the control under it. Whether the control has just been torn off or not, the dialog shell is positioned on the desktop. Figure 13.4 shows the control being torn off.

```
static void move(Shell shell1, Control c2, int x, int y) {
    if (!c2.isReparentable()) return;
    Display display = c2.getDisplay();
    Rectangle rect = shell1.getClientArea();
    final Rectangle r1 = display.map(shell1, null, rect);
    rect = c2.getBounds();
    Shell shell2 = c2.getShell();
    Rectangle r2 = display.map(shell2, null, rect);
    r2.x -= x;
    r2.y -= y;
    final Tracker tracker = new Tracker(display, SWT.NONE);
    tracker.setRectangles(new Rectangle[] {r2});
    tracker.addListener(SWT.Move, new Listener() {
        public void handleEvent(Event event) {
            Rectangle r3 = tracker.getRectangles()[0];
            boolean inside = r1.intersection(r3).equals(r3);
            tracker.setStippled(!inside);
        }
    });
    if (!tracker.open()) return;
    r2 = tracker.getRectangles()[0];
    if (r1.intersection(r2).equals(r2)) {
        if (shell1 != shell2) {
            c2.setVisible(false);
            c2.setParent(shell1);
            shell2.dispose();
        }
        c2.setBounds(display.map(null, shell1, r2));
        if (!c2.getVisible()) c2.setVisible(true);
    } else {
        if (shell1 == shell2) {
            shell2 = new Shell(shell1, SWT.NONE);
            c2.setParent(shell2);
            c2.setLocation(0, 0);
        }
        int width = r2.width, height = r2.height;
        rect = shell2.computeTrim(r2.x, r2.y,width,height);
        shell2.setBounds(rect);
        if (!shell2.getVisible()) shell2.open();
    }
}
```

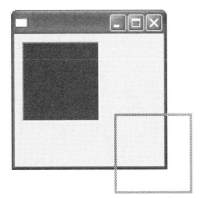

Figure 13.4

13.4   Summary

In this chapter, you learned how to use the draggable controls in SWT. Some controls, such as CoolBar, reposition themselves and their children. Others, such as Sash and Tracker, provide the mechanism to move or resize a control but require you to write the code to perform the operation. In either case, draggable controls provide user interface flexibility that is worth investigating for use in your program.

CHAPTER 14

Dialogs

The class Dialog is the abstract superclass of a hierarchy of dialogs that represent built-in platform dialog windows. A *dialog window* is a top-level shell that is used by the operating system to prompt for a value or inform the user that some condition has occurred. For example, a file dialog prompts the user for a file name, which can then be used by the programmer to open or create a file.

Dialogs vary wildly between platforms in terms of their look and feel. On some platforms, it is possible for native code to access the individual widgets that make up the dialog, whereas other platforms do not provide this capability. For this reason, dialogs are treated as black boxes in SWT. They may contain any number of native controls but these are not accessible to the programmer and not surfaced by any SWT API. More importantly, a dialog is not a widget; Dialog is not a subclass of Widget and does not have API or behavior in common with widgets.

14.1 Creation

Subclasses of class Dialog are created with the standard constructors.

Dialog(Shell parent)   Constructs a new instance, given a shell to use as its parent. The parent cannot be null.

Dialog(Shell parent, int style)   Constructs a new instance, given a shell to use as its parent, and a style value. The parent cannot be null.

Like Shell, Dialog supports modality, using the same modality bits as Shell (see Controls, Composites, Groups, and Shells). Three modality style constants are supported: SWT.PRIMARY_MODAL, SWT.APPLICATION_MODAL, and SWT.SYSTEM_MODAL.

As is evident in both constructors, a dialog is always created with a parent. When a dialog is created without style bits, the default behavior and modality is defined by the particular Dialog subclass.

Both the parent and the style can be queried after the dialog is created using getParent() and getStyle(). These methods are important when implementing your own dialog in order to create and configure the dialog shell.

14.2   Opening a Dialog

By convention, all dialogs implement the open() method. This method creates a shell and some controls, makes the shell visible, runs an event loop, and waits for the user to close the shell before proceeding. When the dialog is native, these operations are performed by the operating system. Custom dialogs implement this behavior using SWT API. The important factor that is common to both is that the open() method does not return until the dialog closes.

The type of result returned by the open() method depends on the particular dialog. For example, open() for ColorDialog returns an instance of class RGB, whereas open() for DirectoryDialog returns a directory path. Because the return value of this method is different between dialogs, open() cannot be implemented in Dialog.

Opening the Same Dialog Multiple Times

One feature of dialogs that is often overlooked is the ability to open the same dialog multiple times. For example, when the same instance of a file dialog is opened, the user will automatically be placed in the same directory as the last time the dialog was opened.

14.3   Setting the Title

All dialogs support the getting and setting of the title string. If a title is not specified, the dialog has an empty title, just like a shell. To set the title of a dialog, the setText() method is used.

setText(String title)   Sets the title of the dialog. The string must not be null.

The following code fragment sets the text for a dialog and opens it.

```
dialog.setText("Confirm Delete");
dialog.open();
```

In addition, the title of a dialog can be queried at any time using getText(). Once again, this method is important when implementing your own dialog in order to configure the dialog shell.

14.4   MessageBox

MessageBox is used to inform or alert the user that something important has occurred. By design, message boxes have a standard operating system appearance, usually taking the form of a window containing an icon, a message, and a row of buttons. On some platforms, they may also have different window trimming.

It is important to note that users are familiar with message boxes from other programs on the desktop. For this reason, applications that build their own message boxes instead of using class MessageBox risk looking out of place.

14.4.1   Creation

The MessageBox class supports a variety of standard operating system icons and buttons. The number of buttons, the icon, and the look of the message box are all configured using style bits. When style bits are not provided, a default message box is created.

The following code fragment creates a default message box.

```
//USELESS — MessageBox with no message text
MessageBox dialog = new MessageBox(shell);
dialog.setText("Information");
dialog.open();
```

Running this code fragment produces a message box with the title "Information," an information icon, and a single OK button.

14.4.2 MessageBox Icons

The following style bits are used to specify the type of message box.

Constant	Meaning
SWT.ICON_ERROR	Indicate that an error occurred
SWT.ICON_INFORMATION	Inform the user
SWT.ICON_QUESTION	Ask the user a question
SWT.ICON_WARNING	Warn the user
SWT.ICON_WORKING	Indicate work in progress

To create a message box that does not display an icon, create it without an icon style constant. As you would expect, only a single icon style constant can be used at a time. For example, the same message box cannot both warn the user and indicate an error.

The prefix ICON_ is a bit of a misnomer. Icon constants are used to create message boxes that have the correct operating system appearance for the situation. They may or may not contain any number of icons or controls.

14.4.3 MessageBox Buttons

The following style bit combinations are used to specify the buttons that will be displayed in a message box.

Style Bit Combination	Buttons Displayed
SWT.OK	A single OK button
SWT.OK | SWT.CANCEL	An OK and a Cancel button
SWT.YES | SWT.NO	A Yes and a No button
SWT.YES | SWT.NO | SWT.CANCEL	A Yes, a No, and a Cancel button
SWT.ABORT | SWT.RETRY	An Abort and a Retry button
SWT.ABORT | SWT.RETRY | SWT.IGNORE	An Abort, a Retry, and an Ignore button

Note that the result of using button style bits in combinations other than those specified above is undefined. Although it may be possible on some platforms to create a message box with the style SWT.YES | SWT.CANCEL, this is not guaranteed. For example, SWT.YES | SWT.CANCEL is not supported on Windows.

The following line of code creates a message box to notify the user of an error condition. The user can respond with *yes* or *no*.

```
MessageBox dialog = new MessageBox(shell,
    SWT.ICON_ERROR | SWT.YES | SWT.NO);
```

14.4.4 Setting the Message

A message box without a message is not useful. It informs the user that something has happened but gives none of the details. This sometimes happens by accident when a program is crashing and fails to load the message string. For this reason, it is recommended that all error message strings be preloaded. If you are using a message bundle to externalize strings, getting the string when your program starts and storing it in a static variable ensures that the string will be available when needed.

The message string can be accessed using the methods setMessage() and getMessage().

setMessage(String message)   Sets the message that describes the reason why the dialog was opened.

getMessage()   Returns the message that describes the reason why the dialog was opened.

The following code fragment creates a message box, sets the title, and uses setMessage() to set the message string before opening it.

```
MessageBox dialog = new MessageBox(shell);
dialog.setText("Information");
dialog.setMessage("Project was deleted.");
dialog.open();
```

14.4.5 Opening a Message Box

Message boxes are displayed using the open() method, which runs a modal message loop before returning a result. In the case of MessageBox, the result that is returned is one of the message box button constants (see the section MessageBox Buttons), indicating the button that was selected.

The following code fragment asks the user a question, allowing the user to respond with *yes* or *no* before proceeding.

```
int style = SWT.ICON_QUESTION | SWT.YES | SWT.NO;
MessageBox dialog = new MessageBox(shell, style);
dialog.setText("Question");
dialog.setMessage("Delete the Project ?");
if (dialog.open() == SWT.YES) {
    // code to delete the project goes here
}
```

Running this code produces the dialog shown in Figure 14.1 on Microsoft Windows XP.

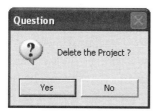

Figure 14.1   A question message box on Windows XP.

14.5 FileDialog

FileDialog allows the user to navigate the file system and enter a file name. Note that a file dialog simply prompts for a file name. It does not attempt to verify that the file name is valid for the platform or that the file exists.

The FileDialog class provides API to set the initial directory path and filter the file names that are displayed in the dialog. The programmer configures this behavior after the dialog has been created and before the dialog is displayed.

14.5.1 Creation

There are generally two scenarios where a file dialog is required: opening an existing file and saving to a file. The dialog that is displayed for each scenario often has a different appearance, even on the same platform. For that reason, the style bits SWT.OPEN and SWT.SAVE are used to identify the scenario for which the dialog is intended.

The following code fragment creates a file dialog to be used to save data and opens the dialog.

```
FileDialog dialog = new FileDialog(shell, SWT.SAVE);
dialog.open();
```

A file dialog can be multi- or single-select, allowing the user to enter more than one file name. The style bits SWT.SINGLE and SWT.MULTI are used to specify this behavior.

14.5.2   *Setting the Filter Path*

When a file dialog is opened, it offers the user a list of file names from which to choose. The list may be shortened so that only files that have a particular extension are displayed. This process is called *filtering*. For historical reasons, the absolute path to the directory that contains the files is also known as the *filter path*. The filter path is accessed using the following methods.

setFilterPath(String path)   Sets the directory whose contents will initially be displayed by the file dialog to the one described by the path, which can be null.

getFilterPath()   Returns the path to the directory that was selected at the time the file dialog was closed.

Setting the filter path to null causes the dialog to use the operating system default.

Note that the string that is used to specify the path follows the conventions for directory naming on the platform. For convenience, the dialog will accept either of the common path separators '\' or '/', but specifying a Windows-specific path that includes a volume name, such as *c:\temp*, will not work on Linux.

The following code fragment uses setFilterPath() to set the filter path to the home directory before the dialog is opened.

```
FileDialog dialog = new FileDialog(shell, SWT.SAVE);
dialog.setText("Browse for a File");
dialog.setFilterPath(System.getProperty("user.home"));
dialog.open();
```

14.5.3   *Setting the Filter Extensions*

The setFilterExtensions() method is used to filter the files that are displayed in a file dialog.

setFilterExtensions(String[] extensions)   Sets the list of filters that will be matched when deciding whether a file should be shown in the dialog. Each extension string is of the form **.extension*, where the special string "*.*" is used to match all files.

getFilterExtensions()   Returns the list of filters that will be matched when deciding whether a file should be shown in the dialog.

Some platforms do not support more than one filter extension. In this case, specifying more than one extension causes the file dialog to disable filtering. In this way, the user is able to select any file that was intended to be in the filter list.

Specifying a filter extension does not guarantee that the file name that is returned will end in that extension. Depending on the platform, the user may be able to type an arbitrary string into the dialog.

The following code fragment sets the title, filter path, and filter extensions to **.txt* and **.** before opening the dialog.

```
FileDialog dialog = new FileDialog(shell, SWT.SAVE);
dialog.setText("Browse for a File");
dialog.setFilterPath(System.getProperty("java.home"));
dialog.setFilterExtensions(new String[] {"*.txt", "*.*"});
dialog.open();
```

To provide a descriptive name for each extension on platforms that support multiple extensions, the setFilterNames() method can be used.

setFilterNames(String[] filterNames)   Sets the descriptive name for each of the filters set by the setFilterExtensions() method. The parameter should be the same length as the one passed to setFilterExtensions().

getFilterNames()   Returns the descriptive names for the filters if they were set.

The strings passed to this method are intended to describe the type of file represented by the filters. The following is the same code fragment that was used to set filter extensions, this time edited to provide a descriptive name for each extension.

```
FileDialog dialog = new FileDialog(shell, SWT.SAVE);
dialog.setText("Browse for a File");
dialog.setFilterPath(System.getProperty("java.home"));
dialog.setFilterExtensions(new String[] {"*.txt", "*.*"});
dialog.setFilterNames(
    new String[]{"Text Files (*.txt)", "All Files (*.*)"});
dialog.open();
```

Figure 14.2 shows a file dialog on Windows XP with the filter extension choices visible.

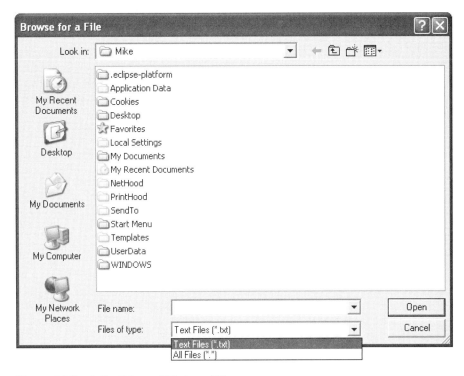

Figure 14.2 A file dialog on Windows XP.

14.5.4 Setting and Getting the File Name

These methods allow you to access the name of the selected file in the dialog.

setFileName(String name) Sets the name of the file that is initially shown when the file dialog is opened.

getFileName() Returns a string that is the name of the file chosen by the user. Note that this is the file name, not the full path to the file.

The getFileName() method is most useful after the dialog has been closed but can be called at any time. The file name that is returned is platform-specific but does not contain path separator characters.

To get multiple file names in a multiselect file dialog, the getFileNames() method is used.

getFileNames() This method returns an array of strings, each one in the same format as the string returned by getFileName().

By concatenating each string with the result of getFilterPath() after the dialog has closed, a complete path name can be constructed for each file. The following code fragment prompts for multiple file names and prints the complete path of each file name.

```
FileDialog dialog = new FileDialog(shell, SWT.MULTI);
dialog.setText("Browse for Files");
dialog.setFilterPath(System.getProperty("user.home"));
if (dialog.open() != null) {
    String path = dialog.getFilterPath();
    String[] names = dialog.getFileNames();
    for (int i = 0; i < names.length; i++) {
        System.out.println(path + names[i]);
    }
}
```

Multiselection and the FileDialog API

It is pretty easy to tell that multiselection capability was added to FileDialog after the first release of SWT. One clue is the fact that the methods setFileName() and getFileName() should be renamed and changed to take an array instead of a single string. Another indication is that the return value from opening the dialog should have been an array of strings. This would have been more consistent with other multiselect API in SWT, particularly the protocol of List, Tree, and Table. Unfortunately, these types of changes break binary compatibility with previous versions of SWT, so rather than modifying the existing API, the new getFileNames() method was added.

14.5.5   Opening a File Dialog

In addition to running a modal loop, the open() method for FileDialog returns the complete path name, including the file that the user selected. If the dialog was cancelled, null is returned. The result that is returned from open() is equivalent to the concatenation of getFilterPath() and getFileName().

The following complete program prompts the user for an image file using well-known image file extensions. If the user chooses a file, it is loaded into an image and displayed.

```
public static void main(String[] args) {
    Display display = new Display();
    Shell shell = new Shell(display);
    shell.setLayout(new FillLayout());
    Label label = new Label(shell, SWT.NONE);
```

```
FileDialog dialog = new FileDialog(shell, SWT.OPEN);
dialog.setText("Browse for a File");
dialog.setFilterPath(System.getProperty("user.home"));
dialog.setFilterExtensions(
    new String[] {
        "*.*",
        "*.bmp",
        "*.gif",
        "*.ico",
        "*.jpg",
        "*.png"});
dialog.setFilterNames(
    new String[] {
        "All Files",
        "BMP (*.bmp)",
        "GIF (*.gif)",
        "ICO (*.ico)",
        "JPEG (*.jpg)",
        "PNG (*.png)" });
Image image = null;
String path = dialog.open();
if (path != null) {
    image = new Image(display, path);
    label.setImage(image);
}
shell.pack();
shell.open();
while (!shell.isDisposed()) {
    if (!display.readAndDispatch()) display.sleep();
}
if (image != null) image.dispose();
display.dispose();
}
```

Figure 14.3 shows what this program looks like while prompting for the image file name on GTK.

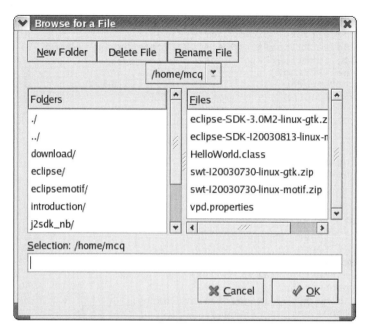

Figure 14.3   A file dialog on GTK.

14.6   DirectoryDialog

DirectoryDialog allows the user to navigate the file system and enter directory paths. On some platforms, directory dialogs closely resemble file dialogs.

14.6.1   Creation

DirectoryDialog is one of the simplest dialogs in SWT, supporting only modality styles bits. The following code fragment creates and opens a directory dialog.

```
DirectoryDialog dialog = new DirectoryDialog(shell);
dialog.open();
```

14.6.2   Setting the Message

Like a message box, a directory dialog without a message string can be confusing. When a message is not specified, the user is prompted for a directory but must remember why the directory was needed. In the same manner as MessageBox, the message string can be manipulated using the methods set-Message() and getMessage().

setMessage(String message)   Sets the message that describes the reason why the dialog was opened.

getMessage()   Returns the message that describes the reason why the dialog was opened.

The following code fragment creates a directory dialog, sets the title, and sets the message string before opening the dialog.

```
DirectoryDialog dialog = new DirectoryDialog(shell);
dialog.setText("Browse for a Directory");
dialog.setMessage("Choose a directory for the install.");
dialog.open();
```

14.6.3   Setting the Directory Path

As was true for FileDialog, setFilterPath() is used to set the initial directory path for a directory dialog.

setFilterPath(String path)   Sets the directory that will initially be displayed by the directory dialog to the one described by the path, which can be null.

getFilterPath()   Returns the path to the directory that was selected at the time the directory dialog was closed.

Calling setFilterPath(null) will restore the path to the operating system default.

The setFilterPath() Method Is Badly Named

By any measure, setFilterPath() is a poor name and does not reflect the functionality of the method. Unfortunately, setFilterPath() and the corresponding getter method cannot be removed without breaking the many clients of SWT. The best that could be done is to add an alias with a better name, such as set-DirectoryPath() or simply setPath(), and deprecate the old methods. However, adding an alias increases the size of SWT without adding new functionality.

The string that is used to represent the directory path is platform-specific. It should never be parsed directly but is suitable as a path name for file operations.

14.6.4 Opening a Directory Dialog

Directory dialogs are opened using the open() method. The directory path that was selected is returned. If the dialog was cancelled, null is returned. The following program prompts the user for a directory and fills a list with every file and directory name that it finds.

```
public static void main(String[] args) {
    Display display = new Display();
    Shell shell = new Shell(display);
    shell.setLayout (new FillLayout());
    int style = SWT.BORDER | SWT.H_SCROLL | SWT.V_SCROLL;
    List list = new List (shell, style);
    DirectoryDialog dialog = new DirectoryDialog(shell);
    dialog.setText("Browse for a Directory");
    dialog.setMessage("Choose a directory to list:");
    if (dialog.open() != null) {
        File file = new File(dialog.getFilterPath());
        list.setItems(file.list());
    }
    shell.pack();
    shell.open();
    while (!shell.isDisposed()) {
        if (!display.readAndDispatch()) display.sleep();
    }
    display.dispose();
}
```

Running this program on X/Motif will produce a directory dialog as shown in Figure 14.4.

Figure 14.4 A directory dialog on X/Motif.

14.7   ColorDialog

ColorDialog allows the user to select a color from a predefined color palette. Like the other built-in platform dialogs, color dialogs vary wildly in appearance across platforms. Some dialogs allow the user to choose a color from a color wheel or grid. Others offer an area for the user to enter integers to be used as color values. Some offer both.

Instances of class RGB are used to model device-independent red-green-blue color values. Instances of class Color are the result of allocating these red-green-blue values on a particular device.[1] Although it may seem counter-intuitive, ColorDialog uses RGB objects instead of Color objects. This makes the ColorDialog API consistent with the rules for allocating and freeing resource-based SWT objects. Instead of returning an allocated color that the programmer would need to free, a ColorDialog returns an RGB object.

14.7.1   Creation

Like DirectoryDialog, ColorDialog is simple, supporting only modality creation bits. The following code fragment creates and opens a color dialog.

```
ColorDialog dialog = new ColorDialog(shell);
dialog.open();
```

14.7.2   Setting the RGB

The methods setRGB() and getRGB() are used to access the color value that is selected in the dialog.

> **setRGB(RGB rgb)**   Sets the RGB value of the color that is initially shown when the dialog is opened. The parameter can be null, indicating that the color dialog will not select a particular color by default.

> **getRGB()**   Returns the RGB value of the color that the user selected.

14.7.3   Opening a Color Dialog

Like every other dialog, a color dialog is displayed using open(). As was described above, the value that is returned is the RGB value of the color that the user selected. If the dialog was cancelled, null is returned.

---

1. For more on the classes RGB and Color, see the Colors chapter.

The following code fragment creates a color dialog and sets the initial RGB value. The dialog is opened, and the color that the user selected is allocated.

```
ColorDialog dialog = new ColorDialog(shell);
dialog.setRGB(color != null ? color.getRGB() : null);
if (dialog.open() != null) {
    if (color != null) color.dispose();
    color = new Color(display, dialog.getRGB());
}
```

At the time this book was written, the Macintosh color dialog had the most powerful tools for specifying a color of any of the native dialogs on the supported platforms. Figure 14.5 shows what ColorDialog looks like on OS X.

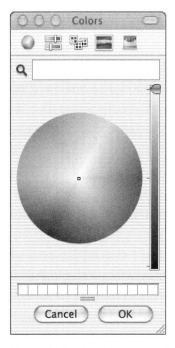

Figure 14.5   A color dialog on Macintosh OS X.

14.8   FontDialog

FontDialog allows the user to select a font from the available fonts on the system. Some fonts are highly platform-specific. For example, the Windows Wingdings font does not exist on other platforms. Windows also supports superscript, underline, and strikethrough fonts.

Like ColorDialog and for the same reason, FontDialog works with unallocated FontData objects instead of Font objects. For more on the classes FontData and Font, see the Fonts chapter.

14.8.1 Creation

FontDialog, like DirectoryDialog and ColorDialog, is simple. It supports only the modality creation bits. The following code fragment creates and opens a font dialog.

```
FontDialog dialog = new FontDialog(shell);
dialog.open();
```

14.8.2 Setting the FontData List

Unallocated fonts in SWT are represented by an array of FontData objects.[2] The methods setFontList() and getFontList() are used to access the font that is selected in the dialog.

setFontList(FontData[] fontData)   Sets the font that the dialog will initially select based on the given array of FontData objects.

getFontList()   Returns an array of FontData objects that describe the font that was selected by the user.

These methods are described further in the Fonts chapter, which includes several FontDialog-based examples.

14.8.3 Setting the RGB

Some platforms offer the capability to select a color at the same time as choosing the font. To support this feature, the methods setRGB(RGB) and getRGB() are provided. These methods behave in the same manner as the equivalent methods in class ColorDialog (see the ColorDialog section).

---

2. The reason an array of FontData instances (rather than a single instance of FontData) is used is described in detail in the Fonts chapter. Essentially, this was required to model the way fonts are dealt with on X/Motif.

14.8.4 Opening a Font Dialog

The following complete program allows the user to set the font and color of
the contents of a text widget.

```
public static void main(String[] args) {
    final Font[] font = new Font[1];
    final Color[] color = new Color[1];
    final Display display = new Display();
    Shell shell = new Shell(display);
    shell.setLayout(new RowLayout());
    int style = SWT.BORDER | SWT.H_SCROLL | SWT.V_SCROLL;
    final Text text = new Text(shell, style);
    text.setLayoutData(new RowData(100, 200));
    text.setText("Sample Text");
    Button button = new Button(shell, SWT.PUSH);
    button.setText("Set Font");
    final FontDialog dialog = new FontDialog(shell);
    dialog.setText("Choose a Font");
    button.addListener(SWT.Selection, new Listener() {
        public void handleEvent(Event event) {
            if (dialog.open() == null) return;
            if (font[0] != null) font[0].dispose();
            FontData[] list = dialog.getFontList();
            font[0] = new Font(display, list);
            text.setFont(font[0]);
            RGB rgb = dialog.getRGB();
            if (rgb != null) {
                if (color[0] != null) color[0].dispose();
                color[0] = new Color(display, rgb);
                text.setForeground(color[0]);
            }
        }
    });
    shell.pack();
    shell.open();
    while (!shell.isDisposed()) {
        if (!display.readAndDispatch()) display.sleep();
    }
    if (font[0] != null) font[0].dispose();
    if (color[0] != null) color[0].dispose();
    display.dispose();
}
```

Figure 14.6 shows the font dialog you would see if you ran this example
on Microsoft Windows XP.

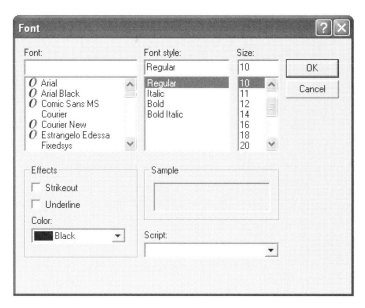

Figure 14.6   The font dialog on Microsoft Windows XP.

14.9   Summary

This chapter described the abstract class Dialog and the subclasses Message-Box, FileDialog, DirectoryDialog, ColorDialog, and FontDialog. Using these classes in your program rather than "rolling your own" gives your application polish and slick platform integration. Between operating system releases, native dialogs traditionally change. Dialogs, like the rest of SWT, are implemented using operation system facilities, ensuring that your application remains consistent with other programs on the desktop.

CHAPTER 15

Layout

A *layout* is an instance of a class that implements a positioning and sizing algorithm. Layouts are used to arrange controls within a composite automatically. Class Layout is not a subclass of class Widget, so it shares none of the Widget behavior. There is no operating system storage associated with a layout; thus, instances do not need to be sent the dispose() message when you are finished with them.

Layout offers several distinct advantages over explicitly positioning and sizing controls. Some of these are:

○ The ability to compute a good initial size of a composite

○ Automatic repositioning of child controls when a composite is resized

○ Operating system and locale (language)-independent positioning and sizing

○ Maintenance of layout code is often easier than the equivalent positioning and sizing code

Nevertheless, use of layouts is not mandatory. For example, on a platform such as a personal digital assistant where the screen and font size might not change, the size and position of controls may be known in advance. In this case, it is potentially simpler to position controls explicitly at pixel positions using setBounds(), setSize(), or setLocation().

Many operating systems provide rudimentary layout capabilities.[1] Unfortunately, most operating system layout algorithms are implemented as widgets and cannot be separated from the widget that they affect. In addition, native

---

1. Interestingly, Windows and the Macintosh are about the only modern operating systems that do not.

layout algorithms are quite diverse and make use of many platform-specific features in their implementation. Because native layouts have few common features and emulating their particular quirks on the other platforms would be difficult, layouts in SWT are not implemented using the platform mechanisms. Instead, a package of standard layouts has been created that provide a wide range of capabilities from simple space filling to very powerful and general forms. These layouts do not have platform-specific implementations. They can be found in the package *org.eclipse.swt.layout*.

15.1   When Are Layouts Invoked?

There are two situations in SWT when layout functionality is invoked. Both are the result of some action on a composite.

❍ The composite is resized (either programmatically or by the user)

❍ The layout() method of class Composite is called

When the composite is resized, the layout places the children of the composite at their new positions, using its layout algorithm. When a child control is resized, it may also contain a layout, causing the process to continue downward in the control hierarchy. The layout is invoked after the SWT.Resize event. This means that you can configure the layout just before it is invoked. Generally speaking, this is something that you will not need to do but there are cases when this feature can be useful (see Forcing Controls to Wrap).

Programmers new to SWT sometimes find it confusing that layout does not happen in more situations. For example, they expect layout to be invoked when a control is hidden, shown, or disposed of, or when a string is assigned into a label.[2] The problem with this approach is that only the programmer really knows when layout should occur. Because layout operations are expensive, layout should be invoked only when necessary. For example, if layout were to happen when each control is disposed of, multiple layouts and redraws would occur in the composite, causing a potential performance problem.[3] The section Forcing a Layout describes how you can make a layout happen.

---

2. One implication of this is that hidden controls are included in layout.

3. One possible way to perform automatic layout would be to implement something similar to the deferred update strategy used for painting. Every method that could change the preferred size of a control would need to queue a layout event. When the system is idle, the layout events would get merged into one. Although this kind of implementation was a possibility, we decided against it for complexity, portability, and performance reasons.

15.1.1   Layout and Z-Order

Most layouts position and resize their controls in the order that they appear in the children list of their composite. This means that when the z-order of a control is changed, using moveAbove() or moveBelow(), the order of the controls in the layout will change.[4] Some programs make use of this feature to move controls within a layout. If you do not change the z-order of a control, the layout order will not change.

15.2   Class Layout

Class Layout is the abstract superclass of all layout classes. Because layout algorithms are so diverse, class Layout does not have any public API or fields. This may seem odd at first. One might at least expect to find public methods to invoke the algorithm. Instead, each individual Layout class provides public API that is appropriate for its particular algorithm. The class Layout provides protected API that layouts must implement in order to interact with controls.

15.2.1   Setting a Layout

Layouts are pluggable. That is, any layout algorithm can be associated with any composite. As we previously stated, in many native widget toolkits, this is not the case.[5] To associate a layout with a composite, the setLayout() method is used.

> **setLayout(Layout layout)** Sets the layout for the composite. Although it is possible to invoke this method multiple times for a particular composite, in practice, application programs rarely do this. Layouts often require layout data that is stored with the child controls. This data is *layout-specific*, so when a new kind of layout is assigned, new layout data (or null) must also be assigned to every control in the composite.

---

4. FillLayout, RowLayout, and GridLayout are sensitive to z-order changes. FormLayout is not.
5. For example, Motif provides a widget, XmRowColumn, which positions children in rows or columns. To create a group box with radio buttons on Motif, it is necessary to create two native controls, the XmFrame that implements the group box and an XmRowColumn to position the children within it. SWT does not have this limitation.

getLayout()   Returns the layout. If the layout has never been set, null is returned.

SWT assumes that there is a one-to-one mapping between layout and its composite. The effect of using the same instance of Layout with more than one composite is undefined, and doing so should be avoided.

15.3   Layout Data

There are two ways to control how an instance of a particular Layout class behaves.

1. Each Layout class provides API that is specific to the algorithm that it implements.

2. Algorithm-specific layout data can be associated with each child control in the composite.

Layout data is any object that a particular layout can use to configure a control. The layout data typically holds some form of constraint description that provides additional information about how the control should be arranged, but the form of this description is completely up to the layout. It is important to remember that layouts are associated with composites, whereas layout data is associated with each of the children of the composite. The following methods on class Control are used to access the layout data.

setLayoutData(Object data)   Sets the layout data for the control. This layout data is consulted by the layout to configure the control when the position and size of the control are being computed.

getLayoutData()   Returns the layout data for the control or null if there is no layout data associated with it.

For each of the standard SWT Layout classes (that require layout data), there is a specific layout data class. For example, the class org.eclipse.swt.layout .RowLayout requires the layout data to be an instance of class org.eclipse .swt.layout.RowData. Attempting to use another class of layout data is an error and will result in a class cast exception. If you are implementing your own Layout classes, it is generally a good idea to create a new layout data class for each layout, but this is not a requirement.[6]

---

6. For example, a trivial layout that arranged each control at a fixed position and size might use a simple rectangle for layout data.

Layout data cannot be shared between controls because layouts almost always cache control-specific information inside the data object.

Not all layouts make use of layout data. For example, FillLayout does not.

15.4   Class FillLayout

FillLayout is the simplest layout. It *fills* the available space in a composite with the children of the composite in a single row or column. The available space is divided evenly among the children.

To create an instance of FillLayout, use one of the following constructors.

FillLayout()   Constructs a new instance. This is the same as new FillLayout(SWT.HORIZONTAL).

FillLayout(int type)   Constructs a new instance of the specified type. This type is used to specify the orientation of the layout, either SWT.HORIZONTAL or SWT.VERTICAL.

FillLayout provides the public fields *type*, *marginWidth*, *marginHeight*, and *spacing* that are described in Table 15.1.

Table 15.1   Public Fields of Class FillLayout

Field	Meaning
type	The orientation of the layout, one of SWT.HORIZONTAL or SWT.VERTICAL. The default value is SWT.HORIZONTAL.
marginWidth	The amount of space in pixels to be used as a margin to the left and right of the controls. The default value is zero.
marginHeight	The amount of space in pixels to be used as a margin at the top and bottom of the controls. The default value is zero.
spacing	The amount of space in pixels between controls. The default value is zero.

The following example program uses FillLayout to create a shell that contains a single push button.

```
public static void main(String[] args) {
    Display display = new Display();
    Shell shell = new Shell(display);
```

```
    shell.setLayout(new FillLayout());
    Button button = new Button(shell, SWT.PUSH);
    button.setText("Button");
    shell.pack();
    shell.open();
    while (!shell.isDisposed()) {
        if (!display.readAndDispatch()) display.sleep();
    }
    display.dispose();
}
```

When the shell is resized, the button is resized to fill the available space in the shell, as shown in Figure 15.1.[7]

Figure 15.1

Normally, FillLayout is used to position a single child within a composite that is typically a shell. It is rare that an application program needs to fill a space evenly with multiple children. Nevertheless, there are circumstances when this behavior might be desired. The following example shows a fill layout with multiple children.

```
public static void main(String[] args) {
    Display display = new Display();
    Shell shell = new Shell(display);
    shell.setLayout(new FillLayout());
    for (int i=0; i<12; i++) {
        Button button = new Button(shell, SWT.PUSH);
        button.setText("B" + i);
    }
    shell.pack();
    shell.open();
    while (!shell.isDisposed()) {
        if (!display.readAndDispatch()) display.sleep();
    }
    display.dispose();
}
```

---

7. The screenshots of the examples in this section were all made on Windows XP. This was done purely to allow easy comparison between them, because subsequent shots are frequently related. All of the layouts described in this chapter work equally well on all SWT platforms.

Figure 15.2 shows the window that results from running this code at two different sizes.

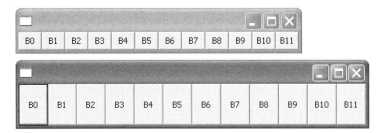

Figure 15.2

Here is an example of a fill layout that makes use of every field, with the resulting behavior shown in Figure 15.3.

```
public static void main(String[] args) {
    Display display = new Display();
    Shell shell = new Shell(display);
    FillLayout layout = new FillLayout();
    layout.type = SWT.VERTICAL;
    layout.marginWidth = 5;
    layout.marginHeight = 10;
    layout.spacing = 3;
    shell.setLayout(layout);
    for (int i=0; i<12; i++) {
        Button button = new Button(shell, SWT.PUSH);
        button.setText("B" + i);
    }
    shell.pack();
    shell.open();
    while (!shell.isDisposed()) {
        if (!display.readAndDispatch()) display.sleep();
    }
    display.dispose();
}
```

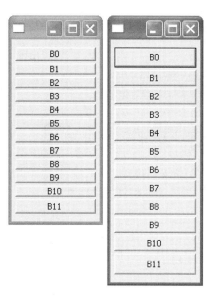

Figure 15.3

FillLayout is a very simple layout algorithm that is suitable for positioning only one control. RowLayout is a more flexible layout that is intended to position more than one control in a single row or column.

15.5 Classes RowLayout and RowData

RowLayout positions controls in either *rows* or columns but, unlike FillLayout, does not fill all the available space in the composite. RowLayout also differs from FillLayout because it is rarely used with a single control. Instead, RowLayout is most often used to position a row of buttons. Although more flexible than FillLayout, RowLayout implements a very specific positioning algorithm that is often unsuitable for general use without resorting to nesting.[8] For example, a single instance of RowLayout could not be used satisfactorily to position every control in a typical "Find/Replace" dialog. However, the dialog probably could be implemented using multiple row layouts and composites.

To create an instance of RowLayout, use one of the following constructors.

---

8. That is, it would require storing composites within composites purely to build a more complex layout.

RowLayout()   Constructs a new instance. This is the same as new RowLayout(SWT.HORIZONTAL).

RowLayout(int type)   Constructs a new instance of the specified type. This type is used to specify the orientation of the layout, either SWT.HORIZONTAL or SWT.VERTICAL.

RowLayout provides a number of fields (shown in Table 15.2) that provide flexibility over the positioning and sizing of controls within a row or column.

Table 15.2   Public Fields of Class RowLayout

Field	Meaning
type	The orientation of the layout, one of SWT.HORIZONTAL or SWT.VERTICAL. The default value is SWT.HORIZONTAL.
marginWidth	The amount of space in pixels to be used as a margin to the left and right of the controls. The default value is zero.
marginHeight	The amount of space in pixels to be used as a margin at the top and bottom of the controls. The default value is zero.
spacing	The amount of space in pixels between controls. The default value is 3.
wrap	Indicates that controls will be wrapped to the next row if there is insufficient space in the current row. The default value is true. See Row Layouts That Wrap.
pack	Indicates whether the size of each control will be configured using its RowData. If false, all controls are resized to the size of the largest control. The default value is true. See Row Layouts That Pack and Justify.
fill	Indicates whether all controls in a row (or column) will have the same height (or width). This field controls the opposite dimension of the layout. For example, when fill is true and type is SWT.HORIZONTAL, the height of each control in the row will be adjusted to be the tallest control in the row. When type is SWT.VERTICAL, the width of each control is adjusted to be the widest control in the column. The default is false. See Row Layouts That Fill.
justify	Indicates that any space remaining after the controls have been positioned should be allocated between the controls, increasing the spacing. The default is false. See Row Layouts That Pack and Justify.
marginTop	The amount of space in addition to the marginHeight to be added to the margin at the top of the controls. The default value is 3.

Table 15.2   Public Fields of Class RowLayout (continued)

Field	Meaning
marginRight	The amount of space in addition to the marginWidth to be added to the margin to the right of the controls. The default value is 3.
marginBottom	The amount of space in addition to the marginHeight to be added to the margin at the bottom of the controls. The default value is 3.
marginLeft	The amount of space in addition to the marginWidth to be added to the margin to the left of the controls. The default value is 3.

Default Margin and Spacing Values Should be Zero but They Are Not

In some of the Layout classes that define various margin and spacing values, the defaults are not zero. This seemed reasonable when they were first implemented but turns out not to be very useful. Programmers often expect controls to be packed tightly together by default and are surprised when they are not. As well, the default values often look wrong because there is no way to choose good values in advance, meaning that they will need to be reassigned. Unfortunately, this cannot be changed without breaking existing SWT applications. The moral of this story is: "Think before you choose a default."

To see the difference between FillLayout and RowLayout, here is the FillLayout program that positions multiple children recoded to use RowLayout, with the results shown in two different sizes in Figure 15.4.

```
public static void main(String[] args) {
    Display display = new Display();
    Shell shell = new Shell(display);
    shell.setLayout(new RowLayout());
    for (int i=0; i<12; i++) {
        Button button = new Button(shell, SWT.PUSH);
        button.setText("B" + i);
    }
    shell.pack();
    shell.open();
    while (!shell.isDisposed()) {
        if (!display.readAndDispatch()) display.sleep();
    }
    display.dispose();
}
```

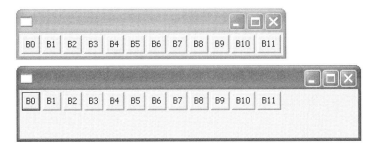

Figure 15.4

There are two important differences to note between the FillLayout and RowLayout versions of the code.

1. Each control in the row layout is a different size, whereas every control in the fill layout is the same size.

2. When the shell is resized, the controls in the row layout are not resized, as they would be using FillLayout. This makes RowLayout suitable when controls need to retain their size.

15.5.1   *RowLayout Does Rows and Columns*

Despite the name, RowLayout can be configured to position controls in columns instead of rows. Setting the type field to SWT.VERTICAL causes the orientation of the layout to be vertical. All of the concepts and fields that can be applied horizontally are applied vertically instead. Setting the type field to SWT.VERTICAL in the program that created the horizontal row of buttons in Figure 15.4 produces a vertical column of buttons.

Figure 15.5 shows the window that would result at two different sizes.

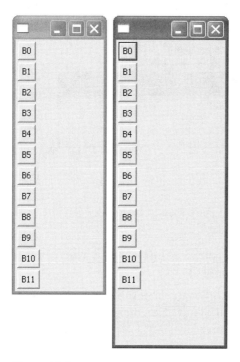

Figure 15.5

15.5.2   Row Layouts That Wrap

The *wrap* field of RowLayout governs the wrapping of controls. To cause a row layout to wrap, there must be insufficient space in the composite for a single row or column. The following example ensures that this will be true by first computing the width necessary to position one row of buttons, then resizing the shell to half that width. The result is shown in Figure 15.6.

```
public static void main(String[] args) {
    Display display = new Display();
    Shell shell = new Shell(display);
    RowLayout layout = new RowLayout();
    shell.setLayout(layout);
    for (int i=0; i<12; i++) {
        Button button = new Button(shell, SWT.PUSH);
        button.setText("B" + i);
    }
    Point size =
        shell.computeSize (SWT.DEFAULT, SWT.DEFAULT);
    shell.setSize (
        shell.computeSize (size.x / 2, SWT.DEFAULT));
    shell.open();
    while (!shell.isDisposed()) {
        if (!display.readAndDispatch()) display.sleep();
```

```
    }
    display.dispose();
}
```

Note that Figure 15.6 shows the *initial* result of the above code because resizing the shell horizontally will cause the wrapping to occur at different places.

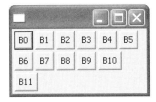

Figure 15.6

15.5.3   Row Layouts That Fill

Imagine a row of controls positioned by a row layout. The position of the next control in the row is dependent on the position of the previous one. If the controls all have different heights, the row of controls will be even on top but ragged on the bottom. To make the row of controls even on both the top and the bottom, the *fill* field is used. The *fill* field works in the opposite direction of the layout so that when the controls are being positioned in a row, the *fill* field affects the height.

The following example shows the *fill* field used with a vertical row layout. This example simulates a splash screen that contains an image and a progress bar. The result is shown in Figure 15.7.

```
public static void main(String[] args) {
    final Display display = new Display();
    Monitor primary = display.getPrimaryMonitor();
    Rectangle rect = primary.getClientArea();
    Class clazz = CH5_RowLayout5.class;
    Image image = new Image(display,
        clazz.getResourceAsStream("pyramid.jpg"));
    final Shell shell = new Shell(display, SWT.NONE);
    RowLayout layout = new RowLayout();
    layout.type = SWT.VERTICAL;
    layout.fill = true;
    shell.setLayout(layout);
    Label label = new Label(shell, SWT.NONE);
    label.setImage(image);
    final ProgressBar progress =
            new ProgressBar(shell, SWT.NONE);
    shell.pack();
    Rectangle bounds = shell.getBounds();
```

```
int x = rect.x
        + Math.max(0, (rect.width - bounds.width) / 2);
int y = rect.y
        + Math.max(0, (rect.height - bounds.height) / 2);
shell.setBounds(x, y, bounds.width, bounds.height);
shell.open();
display.timerExec(1000, new Runnable() {
        public void run() {
                int value = progress.getSelection();
                if (value < 100) {
                        progress.setSelection(value + 10);
                        display.timerExec(1000, this);
                } else {
                        shell.dispose();
                }
        }
});
while (!shell.isDisposed()) {
        if (!display.readAndDispatch()) display.sleep();
}
image.dispose();
display.dispose();
}
```

Figure 15.7

15.5.4   Row Layouts That Pack and Justify

When positioning its controls, a row layout needs to determine the desired width and height of each control. RowLayout can pack its controls to be as small as possible or resize each control to be the same size. The *pack* field controls this behavior.

When the *pack* field is true, controls are resized as small as possible. Setting this field to false disables packing and makes controls in the same row or column become the same size. This is the largest preferred size of every control in the composite.

If the composite is larger than the space necessary to position the controls, the *justify* field determines how to allocate the extra space. When true, the extra space is allocated between each child, increasing the space between children.

The following example uses both the *pack* field and the *justify* field to create a very simple custom message box, which is shown in Figure 15.8. RowLayout is used to position the OK and Cancel buttons, using the *pack* field to make them the same size and the *justify* field to center each button.

```java
public static void main(String[] args) {
    final Display display = new Display();
    Shell shell = new Shell(display, SWT.DIALOG_TRIM);
    RowLayout layout1 = new RowLayout();
    layout1.type = SWT.VERTICAL;
    layout1.fill = true;
    layout1.spacing = 10;
    layout1.marginWidth = layout1.marginHeight = 10;
    shell.setLayout(layout1);
    Label label = new Label (shell, SWT.NONE);
    label.setText ("This is a very simple MessageBox.");
    Composite composite = new Composite (shell, SWT.NONE);
    RowLayout layout2 = new RowLayout();
    layout2.pack = false;
    layout2.justify = true;
    layout2.marginWidth = layout2.marginHeight = 0;
    composite.setLayout(layout2);
    Button okButton = new Button(composite, SWT.PUSH);
    okButton.setText("OK");
    Button cancelButton = new Button(composite, SWT.PUSH);
    cancelButton.setText("Cancel");
    composite.pack();
    shell.pack();
    shell.open();
    while (!shell.isDisposed()) {
        if (!display.readAndDispatch()) display.sleep();
    }
    display.dispose();
}
```

Figure 15.8

15.5.5   *Using RowData to Configure Controls*

During the layout process, in order to determine the size of each control, most layouts call Control.computeSize(int, int, boolean) for each control (see Computing the Preferred Size in the Control Fundamentals chapter). RowLayout does this as well.

When RowData is *not* specified for a control, RowLayout uses SWT.DEFAULT for the width and height arguments to computeSize(). This causes each control to be the preferred size for the control, based on the contents of the control. When you want to set the size of a control explicitly, you can use RowData to override this behavior.

Can I Use setSize() to Configure the Control?

At first, one might expect that Control.setSize() could be used to set the size of the control to be used during layout. In fact, setSize() will *initially* resize the control. However, positioning and resizing controls is the job of the layout. When the layout algorithm is invoked, it ignores the current size of the controls and concentrates on providing new sizes that are based on the layout algorithm. Any previous positioning and sizing information, including the size you provided using setSize(), is overridden and lost.

Instances of RowData are created using one of the following constructors.

RowData()   Constructs a new instance. This is the same as new RowData(SWT.DEFAULT, SWT.DEFAULT).

RowData(int width, int height)   Constructs a new instance using the width and height values. These can be any positive integer or the special value SWT.DEFAULT.

RowData defines the *width* and *height* public fields (shown in Table 15.3) that provide flexibility over the size of a control within the layout.

Table 15.3   Public Fields of Class RowData

Field	Meaning
width	The amount of space in pixels to be used as the width hint for the control. The default value is SWT.DEFAULT.
height	The amount of space in pixels to be used as the height hint for the control. The default value is SWT.DEFAULT.

The following example uses RowData to reserve space in a list for about eight items. The width of the shell is about one quarter of the width of the primary monitor. The result is shown in Figure 15.9.

```
public static void main(String[] args) {
    Display display = new Display();
    Shell shell = new Shell(display, SWT.DIALOG_TRIM);
    RowLayout layout1 = new RowLayout();
    layout1.type = SWT.VERTICAL;
    layout1.fill = true;
    layout1.spacing = 10;
    layout1.marginWidth = layout1.marginHeight = 10;
    shell.setLayout(layout1);
    List list = new List(shell, SWT.BORDER | SWT.V_SCROLL);
    list.setItems(new String [] {"A", "B", "C", "D"});
    Monitor primary = display.getPrimaryMonitor();
    Rectangle rect = primary.getClientArea();
    int width = rect.width / 4;
    int height = list.getItemHeight() * 8;
    list.setLayoutData(new RowData (width, height));
    Composite composite = new Composite (shell, SWT.NONE);
    RowLayout layout2 = new RowLayout();
    layout2.pack = false;
    layout2.justify = true;
    layout2.marginWidth = layout2.marginHeight = 0;
    composite.setLayout(layout2);
    Button okButton = new Button(composite, SWT.PUSH);
    okButton.setText("OK");
    Button cancelButton = new Button(composite, SWT.PUSH);
    cancelButton.setText("Cancel");
    composite.pack();
    shell.pack();
    shell.open();
    while (!shell.isDisposed()) {
        if (!display.readAndDispatch()) display.sleep();
    }
    display.dispose();
}
```

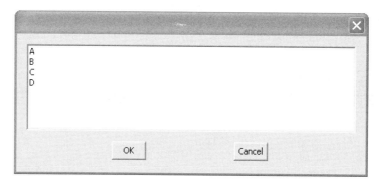

Figure 15.9

Despite the fact that RowLayout can be used to create multiple rows or columns, when *wrap* is set to true, the intent is for RowLayout to position controls in a single row or column. To position controls in multiple rows, GridLayout can be used.

15.6   Class GridLayout

GridLayout uses a powerful and complex algorithm to position controls within a *grid* of rectangular cells. Many user interfaces can be described as grids. This makes GridLayout appropriate for a wider range of applications than either FillLayout or RowLayout. In particular, GridLayout provides a good way to position every control within a window without resorting to nested composites. The average "Find/Replace" dialog can be defined using a single GridLayout. For an example of this sort of dialog, see Using GridLayout to Implement a Find Dialog.

GridLayout works by allowing you to configure explicitly the number of columns in the grid. Controls are assigned to columns in the order they are created, wrapping when the number of columns is exceeded. In this manner, the number of columns and the number of controls implicitly define the number of rows and the total number of cells. Within each cell, a control can be aligned to any side of the cell. For even more flexibility, controls can span cells horizontally or vertically.

Instances of GridLayout are created using one of the following constructors.

GridLayout()   Constructs a new instance. This is the same as new GridLayout(1, false).

GridLayout(int numColumns, boolean makeColumnsEqualWidth)
Constructs a new instance with the given number of columns. If
makeColumnsEqualWidth is true, the columns are all constrained to
be the width of the widest column.

Table 15.4 shows the public fields of class GridLayout.

Table 15.4 Public Fields of Class GridLayout

Field	Meaning
marginWidth	The amount of space in pixels to be used as a margin to the left and right of the controls. The default value is 5.
marginHeight	The amount of space in pixels to be used as a margin at the top and bottom of the controls. The default value is 5.
horizontalSpacing	The amount of space in pixels between controls in the horizontal direction. The default value is 5.
verticalSpacing	The amount of space in pixels between controls in the vertical direction. The default value is 5.
numColumns	The number of columns in the layout. Specifying the number of columns determines where the controls will wrap to the next row. The default value is 1.
makeColumnsEqualWidth	Indicates that all columns within the layout will have the same width. The default value is false.

The *numColumns* Field Is Inconsistently Named

To be consistent with naming conventions used by the rest of SWT, the *numColumns* field should have been named *columnCount*.

The following example creates a grid layout with a single column (which is
the default). Ignoring differences in margins and spacing, the end result, shown
in Figure 15.10, is equivalent to a vertical row layout that does not wrap.

```
public static void main(String[] args) {
    Display display = new Display();
    Shell shell = new Shell(display);
    shell.setLayout(new GridLayout());
    for (int i=0; i<12; i++) {
```

```
        Button button = new Button(shell, SWT.PUSH);
        button.setText("B" + i);
    }
    shell.pack();
    shell.open();
    while (!shell.isDisposed()) {
        if (!display.readAndDispatch()) display.sleep();
    }
    display.dispose();
}
```

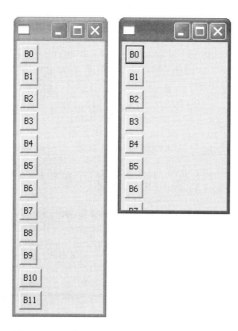

Figure 15.10

In the next example, in order to position controls in exactly one row, the *numColumns* field is used. As expected, assigning this field to the number of controls in the composite forces a single row, causing controls to be positioned like a horizontal RowLayout. Again, as in the example above, the result does not wrap. Figure 15.11 shows the result.

```
public static void main(String[] args) {
    Display display = new Display();
    Shell shell = new Shell(display);
    GridLayout layout = new GridLayout();
    layout.numColumns = 12;
    shell.setLayout(layout);
    for (int i=0; i<12; i++) {
        Button button = new Button(shell, SWT.PUSH);
```

```
        button.setText("B" + i);
    }
    shell.pack();
    shell.open();
    while (!shell.isDisposed()) {
        if (!display.readAndDispatch()) display.sleep();
    }
    display.dispose();
}
```

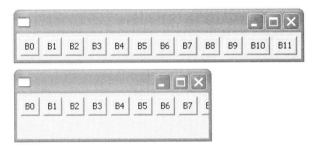

Figure 15.11

15.7   Defining the Grid

Generally speaking, a grid layout that contains a single column or row is uncommon. Normally, the *numColumns* field is used to force the row of controls to wrap, thereby defining both the number of columns and rows in the layout. For example, setting *numColumns* to 6 in the following example causes six columns and two rows.

```
public static void main(String[] args) {
    Display display = new Display();
    Shell shell = new Shell(display);
    GridLayout layout = new GridLayout();
    layout.numColumns = 6;
    shell.setLayout(layout);
    for (int i=0; i<12; i++) {
        Button button = new Button(shell, SWT.PUSH);
        button.setText("B" + i);
    }
    shell.pack();
    shell.open();
    while (!shell.isDisposed()) {
        if (!display.readAndDispatch()) display.sleep();
    }
    display.dispose();
}
```

Comparing the widths of the first column and the last column reveals that the last column is wider, as shown in Figure 15.12. Notice also that the number of columns does not change when the window is resized.

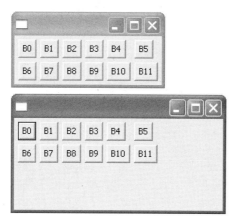

Figure 15.12

By default, in a GridLayout, the width of each column is determined by the width of the widest item in the column. To force the width of every column to be the same, the *makeColumnsEqualWidth* field is used. When set to true, the width of the widest column is used for every column. Adding the line

```
layout.makeColumnsEqualWidth = true;
```

to the above example will produce the result shown in Figure 15.13.

Figure 15.13

15.7.1 *Using GridData to Configure Controls*

In a similar manner to RowData, GridData can be used to configure many different properties of the control within a cell. Instances of GridData are created using one of the following constructors.

GridData()   Constructs a new instance. This is the same as new Grid-Data(SWT.DEFAULT, SWT.DEFAULT).

GridData(int width, int height)   Constructs a new instance using the width and height values. These can be any positive integer or the special value SWT.DEFAULT. The width and height values are assigned into the corresponding *widthHint* and *heightHint* fields. For a description of these fields, see Table 15.5.

The *widthHint* and *heightHint* Fields Are Inconsistently Named

To be consistent with naming conventions used by the rest of the layouts in SWT, the *widthHint* and *heightHint* fields should have been named *width* and *height*. Future versions of SWT may correct this problem by providing both sets of fields.

GridData(int horizontalAlignment, int verticalAlignment, boolean grabExcessHorizontalSpace, boolean grabExcessVerticalSpace)   Constructs a new instance. This is the same as calling new GridData(horizontalAlignment, verticalAlignment, grabExcessHorizontalSpace, grabExcessVerticalSpace, 1, 1).

GridData(int horizontalAlignment, int verticalAlignment, boolean grabExcessHorizontalSpace, boolean grabExcessVerticalSpace, int horizontalSpan, int verticalSpan)   Constructs a new instance and configures the fields of the grid data. For a description of each field, see Table 15.5.

GridData(int style)   Constructs a new GridData instance based on the GridData style "convenience constant." This constructor is not recommended. For details, see GridData "Convenience Constants" at the end of this section.

GridData defines many public fields that provide flexibility over the size and position of a control within a cell. Table 15.5 shows the public fields of class GridData.

Table 15.5 Public Fields of Class GridData

Field	Meaning
verticalAlignment	Specifies the vertical alignment of the control within a cell. This can be one of SWT.BEGINNING (or SWT.TOP), SWT.END (or SWT.BOTTOM), SWT.CENTER, or SWT.FILL.
horizontalAlignment	Specifies the horizontal alignment of the control within a cell. This can be one of SWT.BEGINNING (or SWT.LEFT), SWT.END (or SWT.RIGHT), SWT.CENTER, or SWT.FILL.
widthHint	The amount of space in pixels to be used as the width hint for the control. The default value is SWT.DEFAULT.
heightHint	The amount of space in pixels to be used as the height hint for the control. The default value is SWT.DEFAULT.
horizontalIndent	Specifies the number of pixels of indentation to be placed on the left side of the cell. The default value is 1.
horizontalSpan	Specifies the number of columns that the cell will fill.
verticalSpan	Specifies the number of rows that the cell will fill. The default value is 1.
grabExcessHorizontalSpace	Indicates that this cell will accept any excess horizontal space that remains after each cell has been placed. If more than one instance of GridData wants excess space, it is divided evenly among them. The default value is false.
grabExcessVerticalSpace	Indicates that this cell will accept any excess vertical space that remains after each cell has been placed. If more than one instance of GridData wants excess space, it is divided evenly among them. The default value is false.

Prior to R3.0, GridData Constants Were Not Defined in the Class SWT

Due to an oversight, the constants SWT.BEGINNING, SWT.CENTER, SWT.END, and SWT.FILL were defined inside of class GridData instead of class SWT. As of R3.0, these constants are defined in both classes. Because GridLayout is a very common layout, don't be surprised to see lots of code that still references the constants in class GridData. However, any new code you write should use the constants from the class SWT.

The following example sets the size of the first control out of every five controls in the composite.

```
public static void main(String[] args) {
    Display display = new Display();
    Shell shell = new Shell(display);
    GridLayout layout = new GridLayout();
    layout.numColumns = 6;
    shell.setLayout(layout);
    for (int i=0; i<12; i++) {
        Button button = new Button(shell, SWT.PUSH);
        button.setText("B" + i);
        if (i % 5 == 0) {
            button.setLayoutData (new GridData (64, 32));
        }
    }
    shell.pack();
    shell.open();
    while (!shell.isDisposed()) {
        if (!display.readAndDispatch()) display.sleep();
    }
    display.dispose();
}
```

The result of running this code is shown in Figure 15.14.

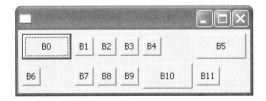

Figure 15.14

15.7.2   *Using GridData to Align Controls*

GridData is also used to align controls within cells. The GridData fields *verticalAlignment* and *horizontalAlignment* govern the alignment of the control. There are 16 possible combinations, as demonstrated by the following example.

```
public static void main(String[] args) {
    Display display = new Display();
    Shell shell = new Shell(display);
    GridLayout layout = new GridLayout();
    layout.numColumns = 5;
    shell.setLayout(layout);
    int[] alignment = new int[] {
        SWT.BEGINNING,
        SWT.CENTER,
        SWT.END,
        SWT.FILL,
    };
    String[] name = new String[] {"B", "C", "E", "F"};
    for (int i = 0; i < alignment.length; i++) {
        for (int j= 0; j < alignment.length; j++) {
            Button button = new Button(shell, SWT.PUSH);
            button.setText(name[i] + "," + name [j]);
            GridData data = new GridData();
            data.horizontalAlignment = alignment[i];
            data.verticalAlignment = alignment[j];
            button.setLayoutData(data);
        }
        Label label = new Label(shell, SWT.BORDER);
        GridData data = new GridData(128, 64);
        label.setLayoutData(data);
    }
    for (int i = 0; i < alignment.length; i++) {
        Label label = new Label(shell, SWT.BORDER);
        GridData data = new GridData(128, 64);
        label.setLayoutData(data);
    }
    shell.pack();
    shell.open();
    while (!shell.isDisposed()) {
        if (!display.readAndDispatch()) display.sleep();
    }
    display.dispose();
}
```

Given that "B" stands for SWT.BEGINNING, "C" for SWT.CENTER, "E" for SWT.END, and "F" for SWT.FILL, the buttons in Figure 15.15 show every possible cell alignment combination.[9] The first letter in each button rep-

---

9. The reason we couldn't use the full name for each constant was that the resulting window was just too big.

resents the value of the field *horizontalAlignment*, and the second letter describes the value of the field *verticalAlignment*.

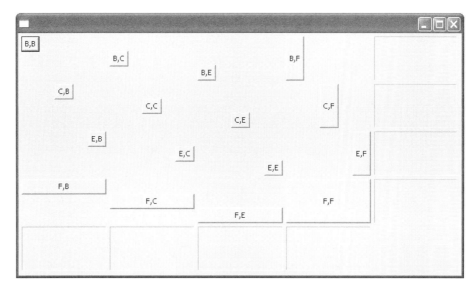

Figure 15.15

15.7.3 *Using GridData to Grab Excess Space*

When a composite is resized, extra space can be allocated among the cells using the GridData fields *grabExcessHorizontalSpace* and *grabExcessVerticalSpace*. These fields allow the space to be allocated in either the horizontal or the vertical direction. It is easy to imagine how this might be used to grow controls on the right and bottom edges of the grid as the composite resizes. However, the fact that any control in the grid can grab the extra space is often overlooked. For example, the following example defines three cells and allocates extra space in the middle cell when the shell is resized.

```
public static void main(String[] args) {
    Display display = new Display();
    Shell shell = new Shell(display);
    GridLayout layout = new GridLayout();
    layout.numColumns = 3;
    shell.setLayout(layout);
    for (int i=0; i<3; i++) {
        Button button = new Button(shell, SWT.PUSH);
        button.setText("Button" + i);
        GridData data = new GridData();
        data.horizontalAlignment = SWT.FILL;
        data.verticalAlignment = SWT.FILL;
```

```
        if (i == 1) {
            data.grabExcessHorizontalSpace = true;
            data.grabExcessVerticalSpace = true;
        }
        button.setLayoutData(data);
    }
    shell.pack();
    shell.open();
    while (!shell.isDisposed()) {
        if (!display.readAndDispatch()) display.sleep();
    }
    display.dispose();
}
```

As you can see in Figure 15.16, the middle cell grows when the shell is resized.

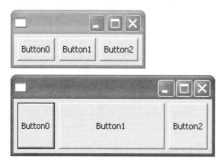

Figure 15.16

If more than one control grabs the extra space, it is distributed evenly among the cells that grab. The following example defines a grid with two rows and four columns. When the shell is resized, the extra space is allocated to every control, causing them to grow proportionally. Figure 15.17 shows the result.

```
public static void main(String[] args) {
    Display display = new Display();
    Shell shell = new Shell(display);
    GridLayout layout = new GridLayout();
    layout.numColumns = 2;
    shell.setLayout(layout);
    for (int i = 0; i < 8; i++) {
        Button button = new Button(shell, SWT.PUSH);
        button.setText("B" + i);
        GridData data =
            new GridData(SWT.FILL, SWT.FILL, true, true);
        button.setLayoutData(data);
    }
```

```
    shell.pack();
    shell.open();
    while (!shell.isDisposed()) {
        if (!display.readAndDispatch()) display.sleep();
    }
    display.dispose();
}
```

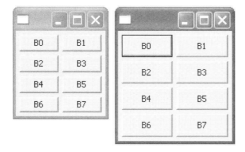

Figure 15.17

15.7.4   Using GridData to Span Rows and Columns

The real power and flexibility of GridLayout come from the ability to make controls span cells, either horizontally or vertically. The GridData fields *horizontalSpan* and *verticalSpan* contain the number of columns and rows that the control will cover. Alignment and size fields refer to the cells that are spanned, allowing many different combinations.

The following example uses *horizontalSpan* to create a very simple custom message box similar to the one created using RowLayout. The result is shown in Figure 15.18. Note that the grid layout has two columns. The label is spanning two horizontal cells in the first row, and the buttons are centered in the two remaining cells on the second row.

```
public static void main(String[] args) {
    Display display = new Display();
    Shell shell = new Shell(display);
    GridLayout layout = new GridLayout();
    layout.numColumns = 2;
    shell.setLayout(layout);
    Label label = new Label(shell, SWT.NONE);
    label.setText("This is a very simple MessageBox.");
    GridData labelData = new GridData();
    labelData.horizontalSpan = 2;
    label.setLayoutData(labelData);
    Button okButton = new Button(shell, SWT.PUSH);
    okButton.setText("OK");
    GridData okData =
        new GridData(SWT.CENTER, SWT.CENTER, true, true);
```

```
okButton.setLayoutData(okData);
Button cancelButton = new Button(shell, SWT.PUSH);
cancelButton.setText("Cancel");
GridData cancelData =
    new GridData(SWT.CENTER, SWT.CENTER, true, true);
cancelButton.setLayoutData(cancelData);
shell.pack();
shell.open();
while (!shell.isDisposed()) {
    if (!display.readAndDispatch()) display.sleep();
}
display.dispose();
}
```

Figure 15.18

15.7.5   Using Hidden Controls to Fill Space

One technique that is often associated with GridLayout is the use of hidden
controls that "take up space" during the layout. For example, the following
uses a hidden control to take the space in the first column, allowing the other
columns to become right-aligned as the shell is resized. The result is shown in
Figure 15.19.

```
public static void main(String[] args) {
    Display display = new Display();
    Shell shell = new Shell(display);
    GridLayout layout = new GridLayout();
    layout.numColumns = 3;
    shell.setLayout(layout);
    Label label = new Label (shell, SWT.NONE);
    label.setVisible(false);
    GridData labelData = new GridData();
    labelData.grabExcessHorizontalSpace = true;
    label.setLayoutData(labelData);
    Button okButton = new Button(shell, SWT.PUSH);
    okButton.setText("OK");
    Button cancelButton = new Button(shell, SWT.PUSH);
    cancelButton.setText("Cancel");
    shell.pack();
    shell.open();
    while (!shell.isDisposed()) {
        if (!display.readAndDispatch()) display.sleep();
    }
    display.dispose();
}
```

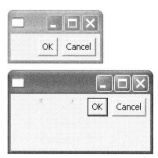

Figure 15.19

15.7.6 GridData "Convenience Constants"

When working with early versions of GridLayout, some programmers found creating and configuring GridData to be overly verbose. In an attempt to cut down on the number of lines of code necessary to create GridData objects, the GridData(int style) constructor was defined. In addition, convenience style constants (applicable only to this constructor) were *mistakenly defined* in class GridData instead of class SWT. Table 15.6 describes each constant and shows the equivalent field and setting.

Table 15.6 "Convenience Constants" of Class GridData

Constant	Meaning
HORIZONTAL_ALIGN_BEGINNING	horizontalAlignment = SWT.BEGINNING
HORIZONTAL_ALIGN_CENTER	horizontalAlignment = SWT.CENTER
HORIZONTAL_ALIGN_END	horizontalAlignment = SWT.END
HORIZONTAL_ALIGN_FILL	horizontalAlignment = SWT.FILL
VERTICAL_ALIGN_BEGINNING	verticalAlignment = SWT.BEGINNING
VERTICAL_ALIGN_CENTER	verticalAlignment = SWT.CENTER
VERTICAL_ALIGN_END	verticalAlignment = SWT.END
VERTICAL_ALIGN_FILL	verticalAlignment = SWT.FILL
GRAB_HORIZONTAL	grabExcessHorizontalSpace = true
GRAB_VERTICAL	grabExcessVerticalSpace = true
FILL_HORIZONTAL	horizontalAlignment = SWT.FILL grabExcessHorizontalSpace = true

Table 15.6 "Convenience Constants" of Class GridData (continued)

Constant	Meaning
FILL_VERTICAL	verticalAlignment = SWT.FILL grabExcessHorizontalSpace = true
FILL_BOTH	horizontalAlignment = SWT.FILL verticalAlignment = SWT.FILL grabExcessHorizontalSpace = true grabExcessVerticalSpace = true

In the final analysis, the "convenience constants" proved to be inconvenient[10] for at least the following reasons.

○ To begin with, they are in the wrong class, forcing programmers to remember them as a special case.

○ Due to their long and cryptic names, using these constants can be as verbose and hard to read as the original fields.

○ Because the constants are *create-only*, programmers had to learn two different ways to configure GridData objects to be able to change them after creation.

○ The "convenience constant" names do not map well to the field names, causing much confusion and consultation of the Javadoc.

To summarize, just *do not* use them.

To fix this problem for R3.0, two new constructors were added that allow you to set the corresponding fields directly when a grid data is created. Because these constructors are so new, we felt it was necessary to describe the "convenience constants," even though we do not recommend that you use them. There is (unfortunately) a significant amount of existing code that still uses them.

In the following code fragment, data1, data2, and data3 are equivalent.

```
GridData data1 = new GridData(GridData.FILL_BOTH);
GridData data2 =
    new GridData(SWT.FILL, SWT.FILL, true, true);
GridData data3 = new GridData();
data3.horizontalAlignment = SWT.FILL;
data3.verticalAlignment = SWT.FILL;
```

---

10. It's okay if you are laughing. The deeper issue here is that failing to make something convenient compounds the original problem by causing two inconvenient, confusing, and competing solutions.

```
data3.grabExcessHorizontalSpace = true;
data3.grabExcessVerticalSpace = true;
```

15.7.7 Using GridLayout to Implement a Find Dialog

The example in this section uses GridLayout to lay out controls in a typical find dialog. Before describing the code, we will first sketch the dialog and draw the grid, as shown in Figure 15.20.

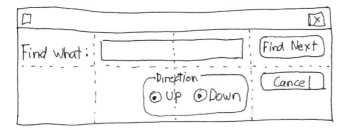

Figure 15.20 A sketch of a find dialog implemented using GridLayout.

The grid is defined to have four columns, and enough controls are created to fill two rows. The dialog contains a label with the string "Find what:", a text control, a "Direction" group with two radio buttons, and "Find Next" and "Cancel" buttons.

All of the controls are at their preferred size with the exception of the text control. To give the user enough room to type characters and to give the shell a sensible initial size, regardless of the resolution of the screen, a width hint is assigned to this control. A good width hint for the text control is the width of the monitor for the shell, divided by 7. Setting the width hint for the text control indirectly determines the preferred size of the shell.

In the first row, the label is placed in the first cell. It is horizontally aligned using SWT.FILL and centered vertically using SWT.CENTER.

Next, the single-line text control that spans two cells is placed in the cell beside the label. It is configured to grab the excess horizontal space so that when the shell is resized, it will grow horizontally. To ensure that the text control fills the horizontal space, it is horizontally aligned using SWT.FILL. To line up with the label, it is also centered vertically. The text control is also assigned the width hint.

Completing the first row, a button with the string "Find Next" is placed in the final cell and aligned in the same manner as the label.

The next row begins with the group of radio buttons. It spans three cells and is horizontally right-aligned using SWT.RIGHT. It is vertically aligned to the top of the cell using SWT.TOP. When the shell is resized, it will stay below the text control.

The last cell on the second row contains the Cancel button. It is horizontally aligned using SWT.FILL and vertically aligned using SWT.TOP. Like the group of radio buttons, it will stay below the Find Next button. Because both buttons use the SWT.FILL style, the third column in the grid will automatically be resized to be the width of the widest button.

Here is the code that creates the find dialog using GridLayout. Figure 15.21 shows the result.

```
public static void main(String[] args) {
    Display display = new Display();
    Shell shell = new Shell(display);
    shell.setText("Find (GridLayout)");
    Label label = new Label(shell, SWT.NONE);
    label.setText("Find what:");
    Text text = new Text(shell, SWT.BORDER);
    Button findButton = new Button(shell, SWT.PUSH);
    findButton.setText("Find Next");
    Group group = new Group(shell, SWT.NONE);
    group.setLayout(new RowLayout());
    Button upButton = new Button(group, SWT.RADIO);
    upButton.setText("Up");
    Button downButton = new Button(group, SWT.RADIO);
    downButton.setText("Down");
    downButton.setSelection(true);
    group.setText("Direction");
    Button cancelButton = new Button(shell, SWT.PUSH);
    cancelButton.setText("Cancel");

    /* Use a GridLayout to position the controls */
    Monitor monitor = shell.getMonitor();
    int width = monitor.getClientArea().width / 7;
    GridLayout layout = new GridLayout(4, false);
    layout.marginWidth = layout.marginHeight = 9;
    shell.setLayout(layout);
    GridData labelData =
        new GridData(SWT.FILL, SWT.CENTER, false, false);
    label.setLayoutData(labelData);
    GridData textData =
        new GridData(SWT.FILL,SWT.CENTER,true,false,2,1);
    textData.widthHint = width;
    text.setLayoutData(textData);
    GridData findData =
        new GridData(SWT.FILL, SWT.CENTER, false, false);
    findButton.setLayoutData(findData);
    GridData groupData =
        new GridData(SWT.RIGHT,SWT.TOP,false,false,3,1);
    group.setLayoutData(groupData);
    GridData cancelData =
        new GridData(SWT.FILL, SWT.TOP, false, false);
    cancelButton.setLayoutData(cancelData);

    shell.pack();
    shell.open();
```

```
    while (!shell.isDisposed()) {
        if (!display.readAndDispatch()) display.sleep();
    }
    display.dispose();
}
```

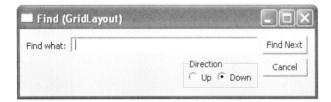

Figure 15.21

15.8 Class FormLayout

FormLayout is perhaps the most general and flexible layout in SWT. The layout algorithm is based on the concept of attachments. An *attachment* attaches the edge of one control either to the edge of another control or to a position within a composite. This very simple principle allows complex user interfaces to be created one element at a time. FormLayout has a further advantage over other layouts because it does not depend on the child order of the composite. This means that it is less sensitive to code changes and behaves better when controls are added and removed, either dynamically or when the code that creates the controls is updated.

It has one major disadvantage when compared with GridLayout. Because FormLayout has no concept of rows or columns, when attachments are used to create rows or columns of controls, FormLayout cannot automatically determine the largest control in the row or column and resize the other controls to match.

Table 15.7 shows the public fields of class FormLayout.

Table 15.7 Public Fields of Class FormLayout

Field	Meaning
marginWidth	The amount of space in pixels to be used as a margin to the left and right of the controls. The default value is zero.
marginHeight	The amount of space in pixels to be used as a margin at the top and bottom of the controls. The default value is zero.
spacing	The amount of space in pixels between controls. The default value is zero.

Unlike the other layouts, FormLayout needs FormData. A FormLayout example that does not have any corresponding FormData instances does not produce useful results.

15.8.1 Classes FormData and FormAttachment

FormLayout uses the class FormData to configure and position controls. Within each FormData, instances of class FormAttachment are used to describe the edges of the control.

Instances of FormData are created using one of the following constructors.

FormData() Constructs a new instance. This is the same as new FormData(SWT.DEFAULT, SWT.DEFAULT).

FormData(int width, int height) Constructs a new instance using the specified width and height values. These can be any positive integer or the special value SWT.DEFAULT.

FormData has the public fields shown in Table 15.8.

Table 15.8 Public Fields of Class FormData

Field	Meaning
width	The amount of space in pixels to be used as the width hint for the control. The default value is SWT.DEFAULT.
height	The amount of space in pixels to be used as the height hint of the control. The default value is SWT.DEFAULT.
left	The form attachment that describes the left edge of the control. The default value is null.
right	The form attachment that describes the right edge of the control. The default value is null.
top	The form attachment that describes the top edge of the control. The default value is null.
bottom	The form attachment that describes the bottom edge of the control. The default value is null.

FormData relies heavily on FormAttachment instances to describe the layout. Instances of FormAttachment are created using one of the following constructors.

FormAttachment(int numerator)   Constructs a new instance. This is the same as new FormAttachment(numerator, 100).

FormAttachment(int numerator, int denominator)   Constructs a new instance. This is the same as new FormAttachment(numerator, denominator, 0).

FormAttachment(int numerator, int denominator, int offset)   Constructs a new instance with the given numerator, denominator, and offset. The numerator and denominator together define a fraction of the width or height of the composite where the edge of the control will be placed. Once the edge has been determined, the control is placed at an offset from this position.

FormAttachment(Control control)   Constructs a new instance. This is the same as new FormAttachment(control, 0).

FormAttachment(Control control, int offset)   Constructs a new instance. This is the same as new FormAttachment(control, offset, SWT.DEFAULT).

FormAttachment(Control control, int offset, int alignment)   Constructs a new instance with the given control, offset, and alignment. The alignment field specifies where to attach within the other control. If this value is SWT.DEFAULT, the opposite edge is attached. For example, the right edge of the control will be attached to the left edge of the other control. The alignment parameter can also be one of SWT.LEFT, SWT.RIGHT, SWT.CENTER, SWT.TOP, or SWT.BOTTOM. Once the alignment has been determined, the control is placed at an offset from this position.

FormAttachment has the public fields shown in Table 15.9.

Table 15.9   Public Fields of Class FormAttachment

Field	Meaning
numerator	The numerator of the fraction that describes where the edge will be placed. The default value is zero.
denominator	The denominator of the fraction that describes where the edge will be placed. The default value is 100.
offset	The offset in pixels that is added to the edge once it has been placed. The default value is zero.

Table 15.9 Public Fields of Class FormAttachment (continued)

Field	Meaning
control	The control to which this edge is attached. The default value is null.
alignment	The alignment within the control to which this edge is attached. The default value is SWT.DEFAULT.

15.8.2 Overconstraining a Form

One thing that you might not have guessed right away when first learning about FormLayout is that leaving an edge of a control unattached is a fundamental and powerful technique. It allows the control to remain at a specific size instead of becoming fully constrained. When a control is *fully constrained*, both sides of a control are attached, causing the control to stretch and shrink when the edges are moved (also called *rubber banding*).

A common mistake when creating attachments is to overconstrain a control, which can cause cycles to occur. A *cycle* occurs when some edge of a control cannot be positioned without knowing the position of some edge of another control that in turn cannot be positioned without knowing the position of the first control. Although FormLayout detects cycles, it simply stops trying to position the edge it was working on when the cycle is detected and moves on to the next. One consequence of this is that if the z-order of one of the controls changes, overconstraining can lead to different layouts, because the algorithm might take a different path when computing the edges and stop in a different place when it detects the cycle.

Layout by Equation

Warning: You don't need to understand any of the following discussion in order to use FormLayout. Read on if you are curious about the implementation of FormLayout or skip this section if you hate math.

A form attachment can be thought of as defining the edge of a control in terms of the equation $y = ax + b$. The a term, represented by the numerator and denominator fields, defines a fraction of the width or height of the composite where the edge is placed. The b term represents an offset from the edge. When an edge is attached to another control, an implicit equation is defined in terms of the equations that define the edges of the other control. Layout is a simple matter of computing the complete set of equations for every edge and plugging in the current width or height of the composite. Computing the pre-ferred size of the composite is a bit more complicated. It involves solving another equation for each control that can impact the width or height of the composite. The equation is expressed in terms of the preferred size of the con-trol, and the solution to the set of equations is the smallest width and height value that satisfies each equation. It is not quite as straightforward as this because the equations contain degenerate cases.

15.8.3   Attaching an Edge as a Percentage

The following example defines the left edge of a button to be at a position that is 30% of the width of the composite. When the shell is resized, the left edge remains at 30%, and the size of the button does not change. Figure 15.22 shows the result.

```
public static void main(String[] args) {
    Display display = new Display();
    Shell shell = new Shell(display);
    FormLayout layout = new FormLayout();
    shell.setLayout(layout);
    Button button = new Button(shell, SWT.PUSH);
    button.setText("Button");
    FormData data = new FormData();
    data.left = new FormAttachment(30);
    button.setLayoutData(data);
    shell.pack();
    shell.open();
    while (!shell.isDisposed()) {
        if (!display.readAndDispatch()) display.sleep();
    }
    display.dispose();
}
```

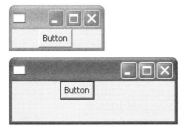

Figure 15.22

When both sides of a control are attached, the control is resized proportionally when the parent is resized. The following example centers a button horizontally by defining the left and right edges of the button to be 30% and 70% of the composite. As a result, the button fills 40% of the available area, leaving 30% of the space on either side. Figure 15.23 shows the result. Note the difference from the previous example.

```java
public static void main(String[] args) {
    Display display = new Display();
    Shell shell = new Shell(display);
    FormLayout layout = new FormLayout();
    shell.setLayout(layout);
    Button button = new Button(shell, SWT.PUSH);
    button.setText("Button");
    FormData data = new FormData();
    data.left = new FormAttachment(30);
    data.right = new FormAttachment(70);
    button.setLayoutData(data);
    shell.pack();
    shell.open();
    while (!shell.isDisposed()) {
        if (!display.readAndDispatch()) display.sleep();
    }
    display.dispose();
}
```

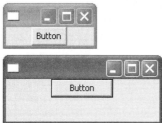

Figure 15.23

15.8.4 *Attaching an Edge at an Offset*

Very rarely, it is necessary to place a control at an absolute pixel position. Generally, this is not advisable because screen resolutions, font sizes, and internationalization issues all affect the final size of most user interfaces (see Using FormLayout to Implement SashPane for an example of when this is appropriate). FormLayout allows you to specify an absolute pixel position using offsets in the same way you might have used setLocation().

The following example positions two buttons within a form at (14, 35) and (73, 5).

```
public static void main(String[] args) {
    Display display = new Display();
    Shell shell = new Shell(display);
    FormLayout layout = new FormLayout();
    shell.setLayout(layout);
    Button button1 = new Button(shell, SWT.PUSH);
    button1.setText("Button 1");
    FormData data1 = new FormData();
    data1.left = new FormAttachment(0, 14);
    data1.top = new FormAttachment(0, 35);
    button1.setLayoutData(data1);
    Button button2 = new Button(shell, SWT.PUSH);
    button2.setText("Button 2");
    FormData data2 = new FormData();
    data2.left = new FormAttachment(0, 73);
    data2.top = new FormAttachment(0, 5);
    button2.setLayoutData(data2);
    shell.pack();
    shell.open();
    while (!shell.isDisposed()) {
        if (!display.readAndDispatch()) display.sleep();
    }
    display.dispose();
}
```

This example places the left and top edges of each button at a position that is "zero percent" of the width of the composite, leaving the offset to define the pixel position. Figure 15.24 shows the result.

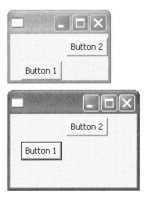

Figure 15.24

Offsets are more commonly used when attaching an edge to another control, which has the effect of leaving space between the controls.

15.8.5 Attaching an Edge to Another Control

The ability to attach the edge of one control to the edge of another is a particularly useful characteristic of FormLayout. It allows you to position one control, using any of the features of FormLayout, then to group other controls around it. Because the original control can be positioned relative to another control, this process is recursive and flexible.

The following example uses FormLayout to create a row of controls, just like RowLayout or GridLayout. This is achieved by attaching the left side of each control to the right side of the previous one. Figure 15.25 shows the result.

```
public static void main(String[] args) {
    Display display = new Display();
    Shell shell = new Shell(display);
    FormLayout layout = new FormLayout();
    shell.setLayout(layout);
    Button lastButton = null;
    for (int i=0; i<12; i++) {
        Button button = new Button(shell, SWT.PUSH);
        button.setText("B" + i);
        FormData data = new FormData();
        data.left = new FormAttachment(lastButton);
        button.setLayoutData(data);
        lastButton = button;
    }
    shell.pack();
    shell.open();
    while (!shell.isDisposed()) {
        if (!display.readAndDispatch()) display.sleep();
    }
    display.dispose();
}
```

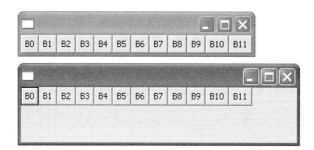

Figure 15.25

15.8.6 Attaching an Edge to an Opposite Edge of a Control

It is easy to imagine attaching the right edge of one control to the left edge of another. You can also attach an edge of one control to the opposite edge of another. For example, you can attach the right edge of a control to right edge of another control. When controls are attached in this manner, it seems that they would overlap. In fact, unless other attachments are defined to stop this from happening, they will. To stop this from occurring, attachments are defined in the opposite direction to move the control out of the way.

The following example aligns one button with another by attaching the left edge of the second button to the left edge of the first. The top of the second button is attached to the bottom of the first, moving it out of the way. The result is shown in Figure 15.26.

```
public static void main(String[] args) {
    Display display = new Display();
    Shell shell = new Shell(display);
    FormLayout layout = new FormLayout();
    shell.setLayout(layout);
    Button button1 = new Button(shell, SWT.PUSH);
    button1.setText("Button 1");
    FormData data1 = new FormData();
    data1.top = new FormAttachment(10);
    data1.left = new FormAttachment(30);
    data1.right = new FormAttachment(50);
    button1.setLayoutData(data1);
    Button button2 = new Button(shell, SWT.PUSH);
    button2.setText("B2");
    FormData data2 = new FormData();
    data2.left = new FormAttachment(button1, 0, SWT.LEFT);
    data2.top = new FormAttachment(button1);
    button2.setLayoutData(data2);
    shell.pack();
    shell.open();
    while (!shell.isDisposed()) {
        if (!display.readAndDispatch()) display.sleep();
    }
    display.dispose();
}
```

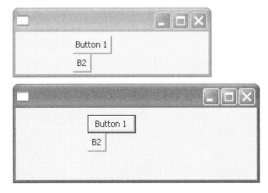

Figure 15.26

As you would expect, the same effect can be achieved in this example by giving both buttons the same left attachment. Specifically, the second button could be attached at 30% of the composite, just as the first one was. The main disadvantage of this approach is the copying of the logic that positions the controls. Code that uses FormLayout is generally easier to maintain and modify when the controls are positioned relative to one another, rather than duplicating the patterns of attachments.

15.8.7 Using FormLayout to Implement a Find Dialog

The following example uses FormLayout to implement the same find dialog from the section Using GridLayout to Implement a Find Dialog. Figure 15.27 shows a sketch of the dialog. The same controls are included, this time positioned with form attachments.

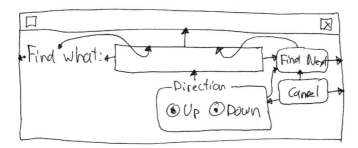

Figure 15.27   A sketch of a find dialog implemented using FormLayout.

First of all, the "Find what" label is attached on the left at zero percent, effectively anchoring it to the left edge of the shell. The top of the label is attached to the text control using SWT.CENTER. This causes the top of the label to be centered vertically with the text control. By leaving the right and bottom edges unattached, the label will be its preferred size and will not resize when the shell is resized.

Next, the text control is attached on the left to the label and on the right to the "Find Next" button. Because the text control is attached on both the left and the right, it will stretch when the shell is resized. The top is attached at zero percent, anchoring it to the top of the shell. The unattached bottom edge allows the text control to be at its preferred height.

The top of the Find Next button is attached in the same manner as the top of the "Find what" label to achieve a similar vertical alignment. Leaving the bottom edge of the button unattached causes it to be at its preferred height. By attaching the right edge to 100% (effectively the right edge of the shell),

the button will move when the shell is resized. It will follow the right edge of
the shell as the right edge moves but does not change size.

The "Direction" group is attached on the top to the text control and on
the right to the left edge of the Find Next button. Because the left and bottom
edges are not attached, the group will be at its preferred size.

Finally, the "Cancel" button is attached on the left to the Direction group,
on the top to the Find Next button, and on the right at 100% (effectively
attaching it to the right edge of the shell).

Here is the code fragment that positions the controls using FormLayout
instead of GridLayout. Figure 15.28 shows the result.

```
/* Use a FormLayout to position the controls */
Monitor monitor = shell.getMonitor();
int width = monitor.getClientArea().width / 7;
FormLayout layout = new FormLayout();
layout.spacing = 5;
layout.marginWidth = layout.marginHeight = 9;
shell.setLayout(layout);
FormData labelData = new FormData();
labelData.left = new FormAttachment(0);
labelData.top = new FormAttachment(text, 0,SWT.CENTER);
label.setLayoutData(labelData);
FormData textData = new FormData(width, SWT.DEFAULT);
textData.top = new FormAttachment(0);
textData.left = new FormAttachment(label);
textData.right = new FormAttachment(findButton);
text.setLayoutData(textData);
FormData findData = new FormData();
findData.right = new FormAttachment(100);
findData.top = new FormAttachment(text, 0, SWT.CENTER);
findButton.setLayoutData(findData);
FormData groupData = new FormData();
groupData.right = new FormAttachment(findButton);
groupData.top = new FormAttachment(text);
group.setLayoutData(groupData);
FormData cancelData = new FormData();
cancelData.left = new FormAttachment(group);
cancelData.right = new FormAttachment(100);
cancelData.top = new FormAttachment(findButton);
cancelButton.setLayoutData(cancelData);
```

Figure 15.28

15.8.8   Using FormLayout to Implement a SashPane

The following example uses FormLayout to implement a SashPane. FormLayout works well when combined with sash controls to allow the user dynamically to resize controls. Figure 15.29 shows a sketch of a shell that contains a list (with the contents *One, Two, Three*), a sash, and a text control. These controls are positioned using form attachments to allow the sash to resize the list and the text control, in conjunction with the FormLayout.

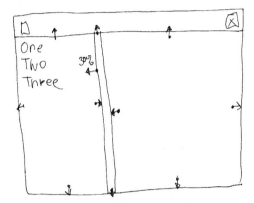

Figure 15.29   A sketch of a sash pane implemented using FormLayout.

The left, top, and bottom edges of the list are attached to the sides of the shell using zero and 100%, effectively attaching them to these edges of the shell. The right edge of the list is attached to the sash.

The top and bottom edges of the sash are attached to the top and bottom of the shell, and the left edge is attached at 30%. An SWT.Selection listener is added to the sash that creates a new left attachment for the sash and calls layout() to move the list and text control (see Forcing a Layout in this chapter). Once the user moves the sash, it is no longer positioned at a percentage. Instead, it is placed at the offset where the user moved it.[11] This means that the next time the shell is resized, the sash will not move, which is what the user expects.

Finally, the left edge of the text control is attached to the right edge of the sash, and the other edges are attached to the top, bottom, and right of the shell. Figure 15.30 shows how the appearance changes as the sash is moved.

---

11. This is an example of placing a control at an absolute pixel location.

```
public static void main(String[] args) {
    Display display = new Display();
    final Shell shell = new Shell(display);
    int style = SWT.BORDER | SWT.H_SCROLL | SWT.V_SCROLL;
    List list = new List(shell, style);
    list.setItems(new String[] { "One", "Two", "Three" });
    Sash sash = new Sash(shell, SWT.VERTICAL);
    Text text = new Text(shell, style);

    /* Create a FormLayout to configure the Sash */
    FormLayout layout = new FormLayout();
    shell.setLayout(layout);
    FormData listData = new FormData();
    listData.left = new FormAttachment(0);
    listData.right = new FormAttachment(sash);
    listData.top = new FormAttachment(0);
    listData.bottom = new FormAttachment(100);
    list.setLayoutData(listData);
    final FormData sashData = new FormData();
    sashData.left = new FormAttachment(30);
    sashData.top = new FormAttachment(0);
    sashData.bottom = new FormAttachment(100);
    sash.setLayoutData(sashData);
    sash.addListener(SWT.Selection, new Listener() {
        public void handleEvent(Event event) {
            if (event.detail != SWT.DRAG) {
                sashData.left =
                    new FormAttachment(0, event.x);
                shell.layout();
            }
        }
    });
    FormData data2 = new FormData();
    data2.left = new FormAttachment(sash);
    data2.right = new FormAttachment(100);
    data2.top = new FormAttachment(0);
    data2.bottom = new FormAttachment(100);
    text.setLayoutData(data2);
    shell.pack();
    shell.open();
    while (!shell.isDisposed()) {
        if (!display.readAndDispatch()) display.sleep();
    }
    display.dispose();
}
```

Figure 15.30

Layout Data Can Be Changed at Any Time

One technique that is often overlooked that applies to all layouts that have layout data is the ability to change layout data dynamically. For example, in the previous example, the left attachment of a control was changed to attach to an offset instead of a percentage. Another place where layout data can be changed is inside SWT.Resize listeners. This allows you to configure the data just before it is used.

15.9   Assigning Width and Height Hints

Recall from Control Fundamentals that the preferred size of a control is the smallest possible size that best displays its content. For controls such as buttons, labels, sliders, and scales, this is almost always the size that you want these controls to have in a layout. For other controls that can contain a great amount of content, the preferred size can be undesirable because it is too large. For example, the preferred height of a table that contains 1,000 items is almost certainly too tall and not useful in a layout.[12] Any control that uses scroll bars to make more content available is suspect. This means that you will probably need to assign width and height hints for these controls. In SWT, tables, trees, lists, and text controls almost always require width and height hints.

---

12. If the table is contained with a scrolling window, a table that is this tall might be appropriate.

Because SWT sizes are always measured in pixels, computing a good size for a control typically entails converting from some natural units (such as the number of characters) to pixel units.

15.9.1   Computing the Width Hint for a Table, Tree, List, or Text

Computing the preferred width of a table, tree, list, or multiline text control is quite tricky. There are a number of different approaches.

Some programs use the average character width of a font (using the getAverageCharacterWidth() method of FontMetrics)[13] and multiply this by some number of characters in order to compute a reasonable width. This approach suffers from the problem that the average character width can be very large on some locales. Specifically, Japanese and Chinese characters tend to be much wider than English characters. This means that shells can become too large, causing content to be clipped or unavailable. Instead of using the average character width for a font, other programs use the width of a wide English character, such as the letter W. This has the disadvantage that widths can be too small on locales that have wide characters, especially when most of the content consists of characters that are not English.

Perhaps the best approach is to choose a width that is a percentage of the monitor width where the shell is being opened. This has the advantage that the width of the control will always be proportional, regardless of locale.

15.9.2   Computing the Height Hint for a Table, Tree, List, or Text

You can compute the preferred height of a table, tree, list, or multiline text control using getItemHeight() and getLineHeight(). These methods return the height, in pixels, of a single item or line of text, so computing the preferred height is simply a matter of multiplying the return value times the number of items (or lines of text) that you want to display.[14] Note that you cannot simply use the height of the font for the control because, depending on both its type and the platform, there may be extra white space between the items.

Another approach is to use a percentage of the monitor height in the same fashion as the width was computed above. Hybrid strategies are also possible where the height of a control is set to the minimum of its preferred height, a percentage of the monitor height, or the height of a small number of items.

---

13. See the Width Measurements section of the Fonts chapter.

14. Obviously, this technique would not work when the height of an item is variable. In that case, the value returned would have to be an approximation. As of R3.0, SWT does not support variable item heights in any of these controls.

The following code fragment computes width and height hints for a table in a row layout. A RowData object is created for the table, indicating that the table should be tall enough to show about five table items and wide enough to display about 20 characters.

```
int height =
    5 * table.getItemHeight() + table.getHeaderHeight();
int width = 20 * fm.getAverageCharWidth();
table.setLayoutData(new RowData(width, height));
```

15.10   Which Layout Should I Use?

There is no simple answer to this question because some layouts are more effective than others, depending on the requirements. Here are some simple guidelines.

FillLayout is a good choice when you want to position a single control. FillLayout is very common in shells. Essentially, it allows you easily to put trim around a control. For example, FillLayout could be used when creating a shell that is a "floating palette" that contains only a tool bar. FillLayout could also be used to make a group in a dialog shell contain a single list control.

RowLayout is useful when you want a row or column of radio or check buttons. RowLayout is also useful when you want the layout to wrap. For example, it can be used to position thumbnails in a composite. Avoid using multiple row layouts and nested composites. Doing so creates unnecessary composites and increases code complexity.

GridLayout is the best choice for most user interfaces, especially data entry applications with many labels and text controls. In addition to the fact that these kinds of user interfaces are inherently grid-based, GridLayout automatically computes the maximum width and height of the cells, making it easy to create, for example, pairs of label and text controls that line up.

FormLayout is useful for user interfaces that are not inherently grid-based. If you want to position a control based on a percentage of the width or height or at an absolute position, FormLayout is a good choice. FormLayout has the added advantage that it does not depend on the order of the children in the composite. This makes it easy to remove controls by hiding them and changing attachments so that the hidden control is not referenced.

15.11   Forcing a Layout

When you set an attribute of a control that affects the preferred size of the control, the control has changed in a way that can affect layout. For example,

setting the text of a button can make the preferred size of the button smaller
or larger. In this case, the layout needs to be informed of the change. This is
called *forcing a layout*. If you do not force a layout, depending on the Layout
class, the change may not take effect until the next time the composite is
resized.[15]

There are other situations where you might want to force a layout. These
include the following.

❍ The contents of a control have changed.

❍ The layout data of a control has changed.

❍ The children list of the composite has changed.

❍ The layout has changed.

The layout() method of Composite is used to force a layout. There are two
versions of this method.

> **layout()**   Positions the children of the composite according to the
> algorithm encoded by the layout. Children are positioned within the
> client area of the composite. This method is equivalent to calling lay-
> out(true).

> **layout(boolean changed)**   Positions the children of the composite
> according to the algorithm encoded by the layout. Children are posi-
> tioned within the client area of the composite. The changed flag is an
> indication that the preferred size of a child has changed. When this
> parameter is true, any cached data that the layout might maintain
> concerning the children of the composite is thrown away and recom-
> puted. Some layouts cache the preferred size of children because it can
> be expensive to compute. When the composite is resized, the preferred
> sizes of the children are unchanged. In this case, the composite auto-
> matically calls layout(false) to indicate that the cache is still valid.

The following example forces a grid layout to reposition the children
when the text of a button is changed, as shown in Figure 15.31.

```
public static void main(String[] args) {
    Display display = new Display();
    Shell shell = new Shell(display);
    GridLayout layout = new GridLayout();
    layout.numColumns = 3;
    shell.setLayout(layout);
```

---

15. Some layouts cache the preferred size of a control and need to be told to clear the cache.

```
for (int i = 0; i < 12; i++) {
    Button button = new Button(shell, SWT.PUSH);
    button.setText("B" + i);
}
shell.pack();
shell.open();
Button button = (Button)(shell.getChildren()[0]);
button.setText("B1 is bigger");
//Force the layout to see the bigger button
shell.layout();
while (!shell.isDisposed()) {
    if (!display.readAndDispatch()) display.sleep();
}
display.dispose();
}
```

Figure 15.31

15.12   Forcing Controls to Wrap

Consider the following example that uses GridLayout to create a very simple dialog with a label, a list, and two buttons.

```
public static void main(String[] args) {
    Display display = new Display();
    final Shell shell = new Shell(display);
    GridLayout layout = new GridLayout();
    layout.numColumns = 2;
    shell.setLayout(layout);
    Label label = new Label(shell, SWT.WRAP);
    GridData labelData = new GridData();
    labelData.horizontalSpan = 2;
    labelData.horizontalAlignment = SWT.FILL;
    label.setLayoutData(labelData);
    label.setText(
        "This is lots of really nice text that " +
        "should wrap but does not. Is this a bug?");
    int style = SWT.BORDER | SWT.V_SCROLL | SWT.H_SCROLL;
    List list = new List(shell, style);
    list.setItems(new String[] {"A", "B", "C", "D"});
    GridData listData =
```

```
        new GridData(SWT.FILL, SWT.FILL, true, true, 2, 1);
    list.setLayoutData(listData);
    Button okButton = new Button(shell, SWT.PUSH);
    okButton.setText("Ok");
    Button cancelButton = new Button(shell, SWT.PUSH);
    cancelButton.setText("Cancel");
    shell.pack();
    shell.open();
    while (!shell.isDisposed()) {
        if (!display.readAndDispatch()) display.sleep();
    }
    display.dispose();
}
```

When the shell is resized to be smaller, the string in the label is clipped, despite the fact that the label was created with SWT.WRAP, as shown in Figure 15.32.

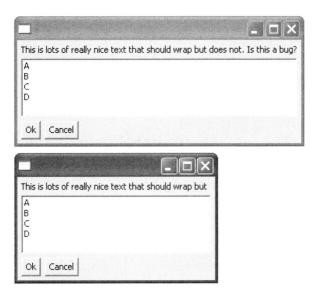

Figure 15.32

Actually, if you look closely, you will see that the string is actually being wrapped.[16] The problem is that the height of the label is not growing to show the wrapped string. This certainly looks like a bug. To understand why it is not, consider what happens when the string is even longer.

---

16. Notice how whole words appear and disappear when you resize.

```
label.setText(
    "This is lots of really nice text that " +
    "should wrap but does not. Is this a bug? " +
    "Well, not strictly speaking but adding too " +
    "much text looks bad as well. The problem is " +
    "that the label width needs to be specified " +
    "somehow instead of relying on the default.");
```

When the dialog opens, it is extremely wide—too wide, in fact, to show you a screen shot. This also seems like a bug. The problem is that in order for a control to wrap, a width other than SWT.DEFAULT must be specified. This comes from the fact that a control that can wrap does so only when there is insufficient space available. A further problem is that in general, a layout has no idea which controls can wrap and when it is appropriate to substitute a width value for SWT.DEFAULT.

Using Width Hints and SWT.Resize to Wrap a Label

The fix for both these problems is to provide a reasonable width hint when the layout data is created and to keep the width hint up to date when the shell is resized. Providing a reasonable width hint ensures that the dialog will start out at a sensible width. Keeping the hint up to date will make sure that Label wraps properly when the shell is resized. The following example code does this.

```
public static void main(String[] args) {
    Display display = new Display();
    final Shell shell = new Shell(display);
    GridLayout layout = new GridLayout();
    layout.numColumns = 2;
    shell.setLayout(layout);
    Label label = new Label(shell, SWT.WRAP);
    final GridData labelData = new GridData();
    labelData.horizontalSpan = 2;
    labelData.horizontalAlignment = SWT.FILL;
    Rectangle rect = shell.getMonitor().getClientArea();
    labelData.widthHint = rect.width / 4;
    label.setLayoutData(labelData);
    label.setText(
        "This is lots of nice text that really " +
        "should wrap but does not. Is this a bug?");
    int style = SWT.BORDER | SWT.V_SCROLL | SWT.H_SCROLL;
    final List list = new List(shell, style);
    list.setItems(new String[] {"A", "B", "C", "D"});
    GridData listData =
        new GridData(SWT.FILL, SWT.FILL, true, true, 2, 1);
    list.setLayoutData(listData);
    Button okButton = new Button(shell, SWT.PUSH);
    okButton.setText("Ok");
    Button cancelButton = new Button(shell, SWT.PUSH);
    cancelButton.setText("Cancel");
    shell.pack();
```

```
        shell.open();
        /* Adjust the width hint when the list resizes */
        list.addListener(SWT.Resize, new Listener () {
            public void handleEvent(Event event) {
                Rectangle bounds = list.getBounds();
                labelData.widthHint = bounds.width;
                shell.layout();
            }
        });
        while (!shell.isDisposed()) {
            if (!display.readAndDispatch()) display.sleep();
        }
        display.dispose();
    }
```

Notice that the resize listener is added to the list, not the shell. The technique used here is to allow a grid layout to position and resize the list, then use the width that was computed for the list as the width hint for the label. A layout is forced in the shell. If the text fits within the label, nothing happens. Otherwise, the grid layout repositions the controls, wrapping the label as shown in Figure 15.33.

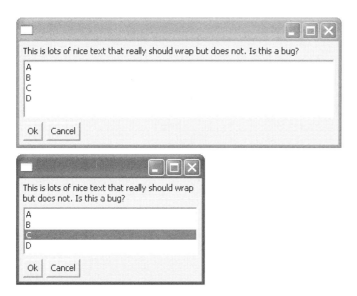

Figure 15.33

Also notice that this code has exactly the same bug in the height direction as it did when the label had too much text; if there are too many items in the list, the shell can get too tall.

Using Width Hints and SWT.Resize to Wrap a Tool Bar

The following example uses the same technique, this time with FormLayout.
A shell is created that contains a tool bar and a text control. The tool bar is
forced to wrap when the shell is resized to be too small to show all of the tool
items on one row. Listening for the SWT.Resize event on the shell and adjust-
ing the form data of the tool bar forces wrapping. The result is shown in Figure 15.34.

```
public static void main(String[] args) {
    Display display = new Display();
    final Shell shell = new Shell(display);
    int barStyle = SWT.FLAT | SWT.WRAP;
    final ToolBar toolBar = new ToolBar(shell, barStyle);
    for (int i=0; i<12; i++) {
        ToolItem item = new ToolItem(toolBar, SWT.PUSH);
        item.setText("Item " + i);
    }
    int style = SWT.BORDER | SWT.V_SCROLL | SWT.H_SCROLL;
    Text text = new Text(shell, style);
    FormLayout layout = new FormLayout();
    shell.setLayout(layout);
    final FormData toolData = new FormData();
    toolData.top = new FormAttachment(0);
    toolData.left = new FormAttachment(0);
    toolData.right = new FormAttachment(100);
    toolBar.setLayoutData(toolData);
    FormData textData = new FormData();
    textData.top = new FormAttachment(toolBar);
    textData.bottom = new FormAttachment(100);
    textData.left = new FormAttachment(0);
    textData.right = new FormAttachment(100);
    text.setLayoutData(textData);
    shell.addListener(SWT.Resize, new Listener() {
        public void handleEvent(Event e) {
            Rectangle rect = shell.getClientArea();
            toolData.width = rect.width;
        }
    });
    text.setFocus();
    shell.pack();
    shell.open();
    while (!shell.isDisposed()) {
        if (!display.readAndDispatch()) display.sleep();
    }
    display.dispose();
}
```

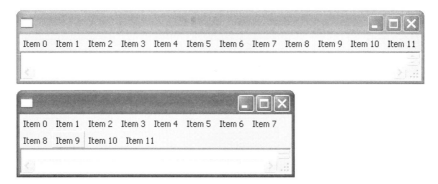

Figure 15.34

15.13   Summary

In this chapter, you have learned how and when to use FillLayout, RowLayout, GridLayout, and FormLayout. General Layout concepts and techniques for wrapping controls were described.

Layout is an expensive operation. When it is inefficient, the entire program suffers. Experience with programming native Motif applications, particularly fighting with native layout, convinced us that "less is more." Often, setting a string in a Motif program turned out to have a huge cost. Sometimes this was hidden (causing a hidden performance problem), but more often than not, the widgets were positioned either unnecessarily or incorrectly. This turned us off of automated layout. As a result, SWT layout is perhaps more manual than some programmers would like, but it is efficient.

Layout is an interesting area in SWT because it is not subject to the kind of operating system limitations and forced design decisions that constrain many of the other packages in the toolkit. It is an area of freedom, but with freedom comes responsibility.

PART II

Graphics

The SWT graphics routines model the kinds of constructs that are found in most graphical user interfaces: points, rectangles, regions, fonts, colors, images, and primitive graphics operations, such as line and circle drawing. These routines were created to allow applications to do the following tasks.

1. Control the appearance of SWT widgets by setting various aspects of their presentation, for example, by changing foreground and background colors, and setting the font used to display text.

2. Draw simple application-specific graphics, such as charts, flow diagrams, and images.

3. Create entirely new widgets whose presentations are drawn using graphics primitives (in other words, creating "custom" widgets).

We have already dealt in detail with the task of controlling a widget's appearance by setting its font, foreground and background colors, and so forth, so we will not cover that again here. In this part of the book, we will look at the details of the graphics routines that SWT provides, but before we get to that, it is important to note what the SWT graphics support does *not* provide.

3D   Three-dimensional modeling and rendering support is not directly part of the API because it is not required by most applications. However, the SWT implementers have created an experimental Java binding to OpenGL[1] called *org.eclipse.swt.opengl.* OpenGL is the most widely used standard for 2D and 3D graphics programming and is available on all the supported platforms, making it an excellent choice as the basis for an SWT 3D library. Unfortunately, the work on this is ongoing, and as of the writing of this book, there is recent evidence that the larger Java community is also becoming interested in creating a standard Java OpenGL binding. Because updating a book is quite a bit harder than updating a Web page, we will avoid talking further about org.eclipse.swt.opengl here. If you are interested in learning more about this, you should check out the developer resources on the SWT home page at Eclipse.org (http://www.eclipse.org/swt).

Advanced 2D   The SWT graphics routines do not cover all possible 2D drawing requirements. Compositing, complex image transformations, multicolored text, and other such advanced features are not provided by the base library. However, OpenGL does provide advanced 2D as well as 3D drawing capabilities, making the possibilities of interfacing SWT and OpenGL very exciting.

Video and animation   SWT does not have specific support for dealing with video streams or animation. Applications that need to display video can usually make use of the strong platform integration SWT provides to embed the system video player within the application (for example, via OLE on Microsoft Windows). Simple animation is possible using threading and the image drawing support described in the Images chapter. This is sufficient to create rollover images, spinning balls, and other similar capabilities you might require to create custom user interface elements, but it is clearly not an animation package.

---

1. More information about OpenGL can be found at http://www.opengl.org/.

Although all of the above topics are interesting and represent areas where the SWT implementers may focus their attention in the future, they are really beyond the scope of the problem that SWT graphics is trying to solve. The graphics routines were designed to provide access to the basic graphical capabilities of the platform, allowing applications to control the appearance of native widgets, to create new user-drawn custom widgets, and to do the kinds of simple graphics that applications frequently require. As is always true in SWT, they were built to map directly onto native platform capabilities, with a focus on good performance and a simple API.

There are excellent examples of the use of the graphics routines throughout the SWT library. In the custom widgets package, StyledText and its related support classes make extensive use of them; CTabFolder and CLabel are also good examples. The emulated widgets that are used when a platform widget is unavailable or incomplete on a particular platform are also typically written in terms of the graphics routines. The emulated CoolBar class is one such.

As a measure of how much *can* be done with SWT graphics, it is worth looking at the Graphical Editing Framework (GEF) created at Eclipse.org. GEF is a powerful tool for mapping application models onto graphical editors. It includes an advanced 2D graphics library, called *Draw2d*, which was built entirely on top of SWT. For more information, see http://www.eclipse.org/gef.

The remainder of this part of the book contains five chapters describing various aspects of the SWT graphics library.

❍ Graphics Fundamentals

❍ Color

❍ Fonts

❍ Images

❍ Cursors

All of these chapters contain information that is important for every SWT application. If you are new to SWT, reading through them in order is a good idea. Later chapters assume that you are familiar with the material from the earlier ones.

CHAPTER 16

Graphics Fundamentals

In this chapter, we introduce the SWT graphics model, including its coordinate system and basic data types, the graphics context (GC), simple line and figure drawing operations, and clipping support. The SWT color model, and text and image drawing operations are discussed in later chapters.

16.1 Points and Rectangles

The 2D coordinate system used by SWT is the one used by most graphics libraries, with the zero-point (0,0) at the top left corner of the drawing area and increasing values to the right[1] and downward, as shown in Figure 16.1.

All measurements are in pixels so, for example, the point at (20, 10) is 20 pixels from the left edge of the drawing area and 10 pixels down from the top edge.

---

1. When SWT applications are run in right-to-left language locales, they can be implemented so that the coordinate system is *mirrored* with the origin in the top right corner and *x* coordinates increasing from right to left.

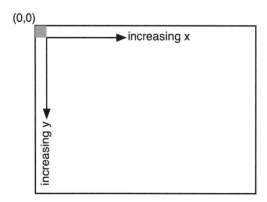

Figure 16.1 SWT coordinate system.

16.2 Class Point

Points in SWT are simple data structures. There is only one constructor.

Point(int x, int y)   Sets the public fields, x and y, to the provided values.

The x and y fields of Point are directly accessed to read or modify their values. Unlike many SWT objects, Point does not allocate any operating system resources, so there is no need for it to implement a dispose() method.

The primary purpose of an instance of class Point is to represent a structure for passing to or receiving from the operating system a pair of values. Every platform has at least one structure of this form that is used to represent values such as positions in the x-y coordinate plane and *width-height* pairs. In the SWT platform interface, Point instances are converted to and from these underlying structures. It is important to note that the range of values that are allowed in the operating system structures may be less than the range that can be stored in an *int* field, so the conversion from Point to operating system equivalent may cause values to be clipped. No error is generated in this case. Most applications do not hit this limit, because the smallest range of values across all supported platforms is –32768 to 32767 (i.e., a short). However, if you are using values outside that range, you will need to watch out for portability issues.

Because class Point is intended to be simply a data structure, it does not have any of the interesting API that would be associated with the abstract mathematical notion of points, such as translation, distance computation, or magnitude comparison. Effectively, all you can do with points is create them, modify their public fields, compare them for equality, and pass them to other routines.

> **Putting Points in Hashed Collections**
>
> Of course, all expert Java programmers know this one already, but one of the most common mistakes that people make with mutable data structures is to modify their fields after they have been stored, based on their hash values. The hashCode() method in class Point uses the values of *x* and *y*, so if you are storing points in hashed collections, you must not modify their fields after inserting them. We have seen variants of the code shown below on more than one occasion. Watch out; this kind of bug can be very subtle to find.
>
> ```
> Hashtable h = new Hashtable();
> Point p = new Point(100,100);
> h.put(p, "get the point?");
> p.x = 200;  // BAD BAD BAD: changes hashCode of p.
> ```

16.3   Class Rectangle

Like class Point, class Rectangle is used to model an operating system data structure. In this case, it is the normal (*x*, *y*, *width*, *height*) structure used to mark out a rectangular area of the *x-y* coordinate plane. Class Rectangle also has a single constructor.

> **Rectangle(int x, int y, int width, int height)**   Sets the public fields *x*, *y*, *width*, and *height* to the provided values.

In SWT terminology, the *location* of a rectangle is the point (*x*, *y*), and the *size* of a rectangle is the point (*width*, *height*). These terms are used throughout the API whenever a rectangular area is being described, for example, see getLocation() and getSize() defined in class Control.

Again, as is true for class Point, the range of values that are allowed in the operating system structure may be less than can be stored in an *int* field, so you need to be careful if you are using values that would not fit in a short.

Why Allow Values Larger Than a Short at All?

Point and Rectangle use *int* fields both because some operating systems do allow these values and because it gives you enough "head room" to do computations on the fields in your code, using values that would not fit in a short. For example, given two rectangles whose *x* and *y* values fit in a short, the following code will compute a new point halfway between their locations.

```
Point p = new Point (
        (rectangle1.x + rectangle2.x) / 2,
        (rectangle1.y + rectangle2.y) / 2);
```

Because the largest the sum of either the two *x* or *y* fields could be is

$$32767 + 32767 = 65534$$

which definitely fits in an *int*, this code does not need to deal with overflow.[2]

Rectangles are frequently used in operating system code when performing *hit testing* to detect whether a particular point (for example, the mouse cursor) is within the bounds of a rectangular area. Class Rectangle provides the method contains() for this purpose.

contains(Point p)   Returns true if *p* is within the bounds of the rectangle.

Another common use of rectangles is in *clipping* computations where it is important to detect whether two rectangular areas overlap and if so, to compute the area common to both and/or the smallest rectangle that covers both. In SWT, this can be done using the methods intersects(), intersection() or intersect(), and union().

intersects(Rectangle r)   Returns true if the area covered by the receiver overlaps the area covered by the parameter.

intersection(Rectangle r)   Returns a rectangle that describes the area where the receiver and the parameter overlap. If the rectangles do not overlap, a new empty rectangle (i.e., new Rectangle(0,0,0,0)) is returned.

---

2. Shorts are also cumbersome to work with in your code, because casting is often required when doing interesting calculations.

intersect(Rectangle r) Replaces *x*, *y*, *width*, and *height* in the receiver with new values that describe the area where the receiver and the parameter overlap. This can be used to reduce the amount of garbage objects that are created when computing the intersection of several rectangles.

union(Rectangle r) Returns the smallest rectangle that could contain both the parameter and the receiver.

Here is a code fragment that shows the use of these methods.

```
if (rectangle1.intersects(rectangle2)) {
    Rectangle intersection =
        rectangle1.intersection(rectangle2);
            // overlapping area
    Rectangle union =
        rectangle1.union(rectangle2);
            // smallest area covering both
}
```

16.4 The Graphics Context

In the SWT graphics world, class GC represents the principal interface to the graphics capabilities of the platform. It contains all of the routines that produce graphical output (such as line, rectangle, text, and image drawing) and all routines that query or set the graphical state of the platform (such as background and foreground colors, fonts, line styles, etc.). Because class GC covers such a wide range of functionality, we will talk about only the simple drawing operations and a few of the graphical state operations here. The remainder of the API methods will be described as they arise in the chapters that follow.

The standard constructor for GC takes an object that implements the Drawable interface.

GC(Drawable drawable) Constructs a new instance of class GC that is capable of painting on the given drawable.

GC(Drawable drawable, int style) Constructs a new instance of class GC that is capable of painting on the given drawable. The style flag is either SWT.RIGHT_TO_LEFT or SWT.LEFT_TO_RIGHT (more styles may be added in the future). If the style is SWT.RIGHT _TO_LEFT, the origin is mirrored to be in the top right corner.

Three classes in SWT implement the Drawable interface.[3]

Control   Drawing is typically done on particular controls in your application. Class Canvas, a subclass of Control, was created specifically to provide a surface on which an application may draw. Note that locations are specified relative to the control. Controls provide the method getClientArea() that returns a rectangular area on which your application may draw. See the Widgets part of the book for more on this.

Device   This allows drawing operations to be performed directly on the subclasses of class Device, currently, Display and Printer. Drawing on the display causes the graphics to be drawn directly "on the screen." Drawing on an instance of class Printer allows your application to generate printed output.

Image   Drawing on an image allows you to buffer your graphical operations or to create representations of them that can be written out to the file system. We will discuss this in the Images and Cursors chapter.

Once you have created a GC, you can use it to perform many kinds of drawing operations.

Points versus *int* Parameters

Graphical operations in SWT are often passed either a sequence of *int* parameters or a single parameter containing an array of *int* values. Consecutive pairs of these values are taken to represent the *x* and *y* coordinates of the endpoints for the figure being drawn. The methods were implemented this way, rather than passing in instances of class Point, to allow drawing to be performed without the creation of garbage. This pattern is common in the SWT API.

16.5   Graphics and Threads

Typically, application code invokes graphical operations from the user interface thread, as was described in the section Apartment Threading. However,

---

3. Note that you will never implement the Drawable interface in your classes. It is an implementation detail of SWT.

unlike the API provided by the widget classes, **this is not a requirement** for the drawing operations in class GC (although the GC must be created and disposed of in the user interface thread). Despite this, there are at least three good reasons to use the user interface thread for drawing.

1. **It is predictable.**   It is easier to implement code that does all drawing from the UI thread, because the relationship between when the graphics are drawn and when widget operations occur is predictable. For example, any code that performs a sequence of drawing operations in a background thread must be prepared to handle the fact that controls may be disposed of in the UI thread at any time. Contrast this to code that draws only from the user interface thread, which can be assured that once it begins running, no widget will be disposed of (unless the code itself does it) until after the code has completed.

2. **It is easier to manage.**   Because all user interface operations from non-user-interface threads would be wrapped with asyncExec() or syncExec(), graphical operations can be easily mixed with widget operations.

3. **It is bounded.**   On some operating systems, if many background drawing operations are performed without pauses between them, the platform cannot deal with them fast enough. In extreme cases, this can cause your application to freeze, crash, or even cause the operating system itself to behave unpredictably.

Why Are Graphics Calls Allowed from Non-User-Interface Threads?

The apartment-threading model used by SWT for the widget API was chosen because the platforms that SWT runs on require it. These same platforms either do not have constraints or have much relaxed versions of the same constraints when it comes to graphical operations. Because the platforms do not prevent graphics calls from other threads, it would be unproductive (and slower) for SWT to introduce artificial constraints on them.

Even though extra care is required when drawing from threads other than the user-interface thread, it is sometimes convenient to do so. An obvious example would occur when updating the graphical representation for a progress bar that is monitoring work done by a background thread. Because the drawing can be done without synchronizing with the user interface thread, the background thread will never have to wait for the user interface thread to be available. This both ensures that the background thread will run at maximum speed and eliminates the possibility of deadlock.

16.6   Line and Figure Drawing

There are several methods in class GC for drawing lines.

drawLine(int x1, int y1, int x2, int y2)   Draws a line between the point (x1, y1) and the point (x2, y2).

drawPolyline(int[] xyArray)   Draws lines between each of the points described by the pairs of (*x, y*) coordinates represented by consecutive values in the xyArray. In other words, it draws a line between the point (xyArray[0], xyArray[1]) and (xyArray[2], xyArray[3]), then draws a line between (xyArray[2], xyArray[3]) and (xyArray[4], xyArray[5]), and continues in this fashion until the end of the array is reached. If the variable *xyLen* held the length of the xyArray, the last line that is drawn is from (xyArray[xyLen-4], xyArray[xyLen-3]) to (xyArray[xyLen-2], xyArray[xyLen-1]). Because a single call to draw-Polyline() can draw a large number of lines, it is more efficient to call this if you are drawing a connected sequence of lines, rather than making multiple calls to drawLine() with each segment. The result of calling this method with an array containing an odd number of ints is undefined.

drawPolygon(int[] xyArray)   Behaves the same as drawPolyline(), except that after all the other lines are drawn, it draws a line between the last point in the xyArray and the first point in the xyArray. If, as above, the variable *xyLen* held the length of the array, the last line is drawn from (xyArray[xyLen-2], xyArray[xyLen-1]) to (xyArray[0], xyArray[1]).

Here is an example that uses drawLine() to draw radial lines outward from the center of a shell, then uses drawPolygon() to connect the endpoints together. You can change the value of the constant *sides* to control how many sides the resulting polygon has. For an interesting *Moiré pattern*,[4] try setting it to somewhere around 250.

---

4.   See, for example, Amidror, I. *The Theory of the Moiré Phenomenon.* Dordrecht, Netherlands: Kluwer, 1999.

```java
public class DrawLines {

static final int sides = 18;

public static void main(String[] args) {
    final Point center = new Point(0,0);
    final int[] radial = new int[sides*2];
    final Display display = new Display();
    final Shell shell = new Shell(display);
    shell.addListener(SWT.Resize, new Listener() {
        public void handleEvent(Event event) {
            Rectangle bounds = shell.getClientArea();
            center.x = bounds.x + bounds.width/2;
            center.y = bounds.y + bounds.height/2;
            for (int i = 0; i < sides; i++) {
                double r = Math.PI*2 * i/sides;
                radial[i*2] = (int)
                    ((1+Math.cos(r))*center.x);
                radial[i*2+1] = (int)
                    ((1+Math.sin(r))*center.y);
            }
        }});
    shell.addListener(SWT.Paint, new Listener() {
        public void handleEvent(Event event) {
            for (int i = 0; i < sides; i++) {
                event.gc.drawLine(
                    center.x, center.y,
                    radial[i*2], radial[i*2+1]);
            }
            event.gc.drawPolygon(radial);
        }});
    shell.setText("Draw Lines");
    shell.setSize(400, 400);
    shell.open();
    while (!shell.isDisposed()) {
        if (!display.readAndDispatch())
            display.sleep();
    }
    display.dispose();
}}
```

Notice that the resize listener[5] computes the center of the client area for the shell, then uses a for-loop and some basic trigonometry to find the endpoint of each radial line, which is saved in an array. In the paint listener, a line is drawn from the center to each endpoint, then the array of points is passed to a drawPolygon() call. Figure 16.2 shows the result.

---

5.   Remember to add the resize listener *before* you call setSize() on the shell. The code in the example does this, ensuring that the array of endpoints will be computed before the first attempt to paint the shell. Note that this example contains a potential bug: If the operating system picked a default size for the shell of 400 by 400, no resize event would be sent, and the example would fail to draw properly. This does not happen on any supported platform.

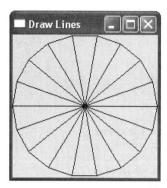

Figure 16.2   Results of running the DrawLines example on Windows XP.

SWT also provides API for controlling the appearance of the lines that are drawn. Setting the foreground color for the GC controls the color of the line. See the Colors chapter for more information on using colors. You can also set the width of the line, the line style, and whether it paints on top of the content that is there or inverts what is there, based on the line being drawn.

setLineWidth(int width)   Sets the width in pixels of the lines that are drawn. When the line width is greater than 1, drawing a line will cause approximately width/2 pixels to be drawn on each side of the mathematical line connecting the endpoints.

setXORMode(boolean xor)   If the boolean parameter is false, this will cause all drawing operations to replace the pixels of the destination Drawable with the source. This is the normal drawing mode. If the parameter is true, instead of replacing pixels in the destination, the new pixel values are calculated by computing the *exclusive or* of the color values of the foreground color and the old destination pixel color. The intent is to cause the drawing operation to be "erased" by invoking it a second time with the same parameters. Be careful when using setXORMode(true), however. In practice, the result tends to vary significantly from platform to platform. In particular, it is not implemented on the Macintosh because the platform does not support this operation.

setLineStyle(int style)   Sets the style of line that is drawn based on the parameter. Possible values are SWT.LINE_SOLID, SWT.LINE_DASH, SWT.LINE_DOT, SWT.LINE_DASHDOT, and SWT.LINE_DASH DOTDOT.

Here is an example, showing what it looks like when the line width is set to 10, and each of the line styles is used in turn.

```
public class LineStyles {
public static void main(String[] args) {
    final Display display = new Display();
    final Shell shell = new Shell(display);
    shell.addListener(SWT.Paint, new Listener() {
        public void handleEvent(Event event) {
            GC gc = event.gc;
            gc.setLineWidth(10);
            gc.setLineStyle(SWT.LINE_SOLID);
            gc.drawLine(10, 10, 200, 10);
            gc.setLineStyle(SWT.LINE_DASH);
            gc.drawLine(10, 30, 200, 30);
            gc.setLineStyle(SWT.LINE_DOT);
            gc.drawLine(10, 50, 200, 50);
            gc.setLineStyle(SWT.LINE_DASHDOT);
            gc.drawLine(10, 70, 200, 70);
            gc.setLineStyle(SWT.LINE_DASHDOTDOT);
            gc.drawLine(10, 90, 200, 90);
        }});
    shell.setText("Line Styles");
    shell.setSize(250, 150);
    shell.open();
    while (!shell.isDisposed()) {
        if (!display.readAndDispatch())
            display.sleep();
    }
    display.dispose();
}}
```

Note that, the actual *drawing* of the lines is done by the platform graphics routines. SWT maps the line style constants to one of the line styles supported by the platform, so the result will depend on whether the platform supports the specified style. On Microsoft Windows, for example, lines that are wider than one pixel are always drawn as though SWT.LINE_SOLID had been specified. Figure 16.3 shows the result of running the above program on Macintosh OS X.

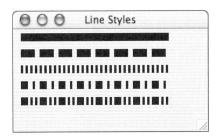

Figure 16.3   Result of running the LineStyles example on Macintosh OS X.

For each of the setter methods above, there is a matching getter method.

getLineWidth()   Returns the width in pixels that will be used to draw lines.

getXORMode()   Returns true if XOR mode will be used for drawing operations and false otherwise.

getLineStyle()   Returns the line style that will be used for drawing operations.

It is important to note that these methods query the values directly from the operating system. This means that regardless of how the values were set, either by your application or by the operating system itself, the values that are returned are always correct.

In addition to drawing lines and polygons, there are several other kinds of figures that can be drawn.

drawRectangle(int x, int y, int width, int height)   Draws a rectangle whose top left corner is at (x, y) and whose bottom right corner is at (x+width, y+height).

drawRectangle(Rectangle rect)   Equivalent to drawRectangle(rect.x, rect.y, rect.width, rect.height).

drawRoundedRectangle(int x, int y, int width, int height, int arc-Width, int arcHeight)   Draws a rectangle with corners rounded by drawing an arc that is one half arcWidth wide and one half arcHeight high at each corner, whose top left corner is at (x, y), and whose bottom right corner is at (x+width, y+height).

drawFocus(int x, int y, int width, int height)   Some platforms indicate the widget or item that has focus by drawing a rectangle in a particular style around it. On these platforms, drawFocus() draws a rectangle whose top left corner is at (x, y) and whose bottom right corner is at (x+width-1, y+height-1), that has the appearance of this *focus rectangle*. On other platforms, drawFocus() is similar to drawRectangle(). This method was intended to allow custom widget implementers to have a mechanism for matching the platform focus indicator. In practice, it is not very useful since many platforms use other mechanisms for indicating focus (such as the "border around the widget" that is used on X/Motif and Mac OS X).[6]

drawOval(int x, int y, int width, int height)   Draws an oval that is width+1 pixels wide and height+1 pixels high, centered at the point (x+(width/2), y+(height/2)). In other words, it draws the oval so that it would touch the edges of a rectangle drawn using the same parameters.

drawArc(int x, int y, int width, int height, int startAngle, int arcAngle) Draws a section of an oval that is width+1 pixels wide and height+1 pixels high, centered at the point (x+(width/2), y+(height/2)), starting at startAngle and extending around to startAngle+arcAngle. Angles are measured in degrees, with zero being horizontal, pointing toward the right, and increasing angles in the counterclockwise direction.

Here is an example showing the rectangle, oval, and arc drawing routines, and the use of XOR mode.

```
public class Figures {
public static void main(String[] args) {
    final Display display = new Display();
    final Color allOnes =
       new Color(display, 255, 255, 255);
    final Shell shell = new Shell(display);
    shell.addListener(SWT.Paint, new Listener() {
       public void handleEvent(Event event) {
          GC gc = event.gc;
          gc.drawRectangle(10, 10, 200, 100);
          gc.drawRectangle(
             new Rectangle (20, 20, 180, 80));
          gc.drawRoundRectangle(30, 30, 160, 60, 30, 20);
          gc.drawFocus(40, 40, 140, 40);
          gc.drawOval(50, 50, 120, 20);
          gc.setLineWidth(30);
          gc.setForeground(allOnes);
          gc.setXORMode(true);
          gc.drawArc(10, 80, 200, 180, 45, 90);
          gc.setXORMode(false);
       }});
    shell.setText("Figures");
    shell.setSize(250, 150);
    shell.open();
    while (!shell.isDisposed()) {
```

---

6.   The problem is exacerbated by the fact that most modern operating systems allow users to create *skins* that control the look of the widget, including the appearance when it has focus.

```
        if (!display.readAndDispatch())
            display.sleep();
    }
    allOnes.dispose();
    display.dispose();
}}
```

Running this example produces the result shown in Figure 16.4.

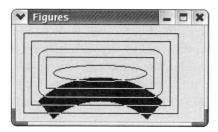

Figure 16.4   Result of running the Figures example on Linux GTK.

16.6.1 Filling

For each of the closed figure drawing routines including arcs (which are considered to be pie-shaped segments of a circle in this case) there is a fill method that matches the draw method. These methods fill the interior of the figure with the *background* color from the GC. Note that the interior of a figure does not include the right and bottom edges.[7]

fillRectangle(int x, int y, int width, int height)   Fills the interior of a rectangle whose top left corner is at (x, y) and whose bottom right corner is at (x+width, y+height) with the current background color.

fillRectangle(Rectangle rect)   Equivalent to fillRectangle(rect.x, rect.y, rect.width, rect.height).

fillRoundedRectangle(int x, int y, int width, int height, int arcWidth, int arcHeight)   Fills, with the current background color, the interior of a rectangle with corners rounded by drawing an arc that is one half arcWidth wide and one half arcHeight high at each corner, whose top left corner is at (x, y), and whose bottom right corner is at (x+width, y+height).

---

7. This behavior matches the X Windows system.

fillOval(int x, int y, int width, int height)   Fills the interior of an oval that is width+1 pixels wide and height+1 pixels high, centered at the point (x+(width/2), y+(height/2)) with the current background color.

fillArc(int x, int y, int width, int height, int startAngle, int arcAngle) Fills, with the current background color, a section of the interior of an oval that is width+1 pixels wide and height+1 pixels high, centered at the point (x+(width/2), y+(height/2)), starting at startAngle and extending around to startAngle+arcAngle. Angles are measured in degrees, with zero being horizontal, pointing toward the right, and increasing angles in the counterclockwise direction.

fillPolygon(int xyArray)   Fills the interior of the polygon that would be drawn by drawPolygon(xyArray) with the current background color. The *interior* of the polygon is computed using the *EvenOdd* rule.

The EvenOdd Rule

The EvenOdd rule states that to find out whether a given point is part of the interior of the polygon, draw a line from that point outward to another point some distance from the polygon, making sure that the line does not cross any of the polygon's vertices. If the line crossed an even number of edges, then the original point is outside the polygon. If the line crossed an odd number of edges, then the point is part of the interior of the polygon.

Here is another example similar to DrawLines above that uses fillPolygon and drawPolygon to draw an 11-pointed star. Notice that the EvenOdd rule causes some parts of the star to not be filled (see Figure 16.5). As with Draw-Lines, you can change the number of points in the star by modifying the variable *points*, although in this case, the value must be an odd number.[8]

```
public class FillPoly {

static final int points = 11;

public static void main(String[] args) {
    final Point center = new Point(0,0);
    final int[] radial = new int[points*2];
    final Display display = new Display();
```

---

8. Modifying the code to work with either an even or odd number of points is left as an exercise for the reader. The change is simple but makes the resulting code longer (because you must draw two polygons) without adding to the explanatory value.

```
final Color white =
    display.getSystemColor(SWT.COLOR_WHITE);
final Shell shell = new Shell(display);
shell.addListener(SWT.Resize, new Listener() {
    public void handleEvent(Event event) {
        Rectangle bounds = shell.getClientArea();
        center.x = bounds.x + bounds.width/2;
        center.y = bounds.y + bounds.height/2;
        int pos = 0;
        for (int i = 0; i < points; ++i) {
            double r = Math.PI*2 * pos/points;
            radial[i*2] = (int)
                ((1+Math.cos(r))*center.x);
            radial[i*2+1] = (int)
                ((1+Math.sin(r))*center.y);
            pos = (pos + points/2) % points;
        }
    }});
shell.addListener(SWT.Paint, new Listener() {
    public void handleEvent(Event event) {
        event.gc.setBackground(white);
        event.gc.fillPolygon(radial);
        event.gc.drawPolygon(radial);
    }});
shell.setText("Fill Polygon");
shell.setSize(400, 400);
shell.open();
while (!shell.isDisposed()) {
    if (!display.readAndDispatch())
        display.sleep();
}
display.dispose();
}}
```

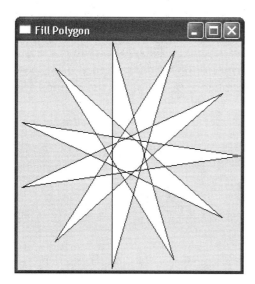

Figure 16.5   Result of running the FillPoly example on Windows XP.

16.7 Clipping and Regions

It is very common when implementing graphical user interfaces to need to control the parts of the drawing surface that are affected when a drawing operation is performed. This is called *clipping*. For example, you might want to constrain the area that you draw on in Figure 16.6 to be only the white rectangle.

Figure 16.6 A white rectangle on a gray rectangle.

SWT provides two calls on instances of class GC that set the area that can be drawn on to a given rectangle.

setClipping(int x, int y, int width, int height) Constrains drawing operations to affect only the rectangle whose top left corner is at (x, y) and whose bottom right corner is at (x+width, y+height).

setClipping(Rectangle rect) Given a rectangle passed as the parameter, this is equivalent to setClipping(rect.x, rect.y, rect.width, rect.height). If the parameter is null, this method removes any clipping that was previously set for the GC.

Unfortunately, being able to select a single rectangle to draw on is not very useful. In most cases, there are several areas where drawing must be allowed. The most obvious example of this occurs when repainting a widget because it is being resized larger. In this case, a minimum of two rectangles is required to delineate the area that has been uncovered. Figure 16.7 shows one example of how this could be represented.

All modern operating systems provide the ability to clip to multiple areas that are described by rectangles and polygons.[9] Typically, an operating system data structure is used to represent the collection of areas to draw on. SWT models this structure with class Region.

---

9. Some platforms allow more complex descriptions, but we will consider only rectangles and polygons here.

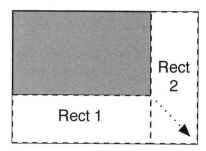

Figure 16.7 Two rectangles describing the new area.

16.7.1 Regions

Conceptually, Region represents the union of the areas covered by a collection of rectangles and polygons. Because the storage for a region is maintained by the operating system, you must follow the standard life cycle rules for SWT when working with them: If you create the region, you must call dispose() when you are done with it.

There are two constructors, both of which create an *empty region* (one that contains no rectangles or polygons).

Region()   Constructs a new empty instance of Region. This is equivalent to creating a region using the current device, normally the display that is associated with the current thread.

Region(Device device)   Constructs a new empty instance of Region that is associated with the given device.

Rectangles and polygons are added to the region using one of these methods.

add(Rectangle rect)   Adds the parameter to the collection of areas described by the region.

add (int[] pointArray)   Adds the interior of the polygon described by the pointArray (see fillPolygon() above) to the collection of areas described by the region.

add(Region rgn)   Adds all of the areas described by the parameter to the collection of areas described by the region.

If your application needs to decide whether a particular graphical element should be redrawn, it can do so by detecting whether the element intersects with the clipping region (see the More GC Clipping Methods section) using one of the following methods.

intersects(int x, int y, int width, int height)   Answers true if the rectangle whose top left corner is at (x, y) and whose bottom right corner is at (x+width, y+height) intersects with any of the areas contained in the region.

intersects(Rectangle rect)   Equivalent to intersects(rect.x, rect.y, rect.width, rect.height).

contains(int x, int y)   Answers true if the point (x, y) is contained by one of the areas in the region.

contains(Point p)   Equivalent to contains(p.x, p.y).

These methods invoke platform code to perform the tests and are typically quite efficient, even for regions containing a large number of areas. You can also compute the *bounding box* for the region using the method getBounds().

getBounds()   Returns the smallest rectangle that completely encloses all of the areas in the region.

Although you might assume that it would be useful to use this method to check quickly whether a point was even "in the same area" as some complex region, in practice, the platform code that is used to implement contains() does this optimization already.

As of R3.0 of SWT, class Region also provides API for subtracting areas (individual rectangles, polygons, or other regions) from the area described by a given instance of Region. This would be useful, for example, if you had a background area with areas "in front" that you did not want to draw on, something like the image shown in Figure 16.8. In this case, you could construct a region that would allow you to draw the gray area without damaging the white areas.

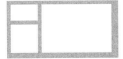

Figure 16.8   White rectangles "in front of" a gray rectangle.

To construct the region, you would first create a region representing the background area, then subtract from it each of the areas that should be "in front." Without the ability to subtract areas, you would have to manually compute a sequence of rectangles that represents only the gray parts.

The region subtraction API methods are as follows.

subtract(Rectangle rectangle)   Removes the rectangular area described by the parameter from the region.

subtract(int[] pointArray)   Subtracts the interior of the polygon described by the parameter (see fillPolygon() above) from the region.

subtract(Region region)   Removes all of the areas described by the parameter from the region.

16.7.2   More GC Clipping Methods

To force a GC to clip to a given region, you call this version of the setClipping method:

setClipping(Region r)   Constrains drawing operations to affect only the areas contained in the region. As was true with setClipping(Rectangle rect), if the parameter is null, this method will remove any clipping that is set for the GC.

You can also get the clipping area, either as a rectangle or a region, from the GC.

getClipping()   Returns the rectangle that is the bounding box for the current clipping region associated with the GC. If a clipping region was not set, this method returns the bounds of the drawing area.

getClipping(Region region)   Replaces the contents of the parameter with a copy of the areas from the clipping region associated with the GC. If a clipping region was not set, this method replaces the contents of the parameter with a single rectangle describing the bounds of the drawing area.

Why Not Return the Region?

The method getClipping(Region region) seems to have a somewhat "unnatural" shape. Rather than force the user to create a region that is then changed to

> represent the clipping area, would it not be better to simply have a "getClip-ping()" method that *returns* the region?
>
> The problem is that it violates one of the fundamental SWT patterns: Any object that you must send the dispose() message to when it is no longer needed is *always* created in your code via a constructor. Maintaining the consistency of the rule is very important for the programmer to be able to detect "leaked" resources. That is why in this case the API requires you to create the region, then pass it to the method.

Here is an example that attempts to fill the entire client area of a shell with a different random color each time the paint listener is invoked. The shell is created with the SWT.NO_REDRAW_RESIZE style so only the area that has been uncovered will be included in the clipping region (see the Painting and Resizing chapter for more on this). Resizing the window to be larger generates the distinctive "backward L" shape shown in Figure 16.9.

```
public class ClippingRegion {
public static void main(String[] args) {
    final Random rand =
        new Random(System.currentTimeMillis());
    final Display display = new Display();
    final Shell shell = new Shell(
        display,
        SWT.SHELL_TRIM | SWT.NO_REDRAW_RESIZE);
    shell.addListener(SWT.Paint, new Listener() {
        public void handleEvent(Event event) {
            GC gc = event.gc;
            // problem with color usage here (see text).
            Color color = new Color (display,
                rand.nextInt(256),
                rand.nextInt(256),
                rand.nextInt(256));
            gc.setBackground(color);
            gc.fillRectangle(shell.getClientArea());
            color.dispose();
        }});
    shell.setText("Clipping Region");
    shell.setSize(250, 150);
    shell.open();
    while (!shell.isDisposed()) {
        if (!display.readAndDispatch())
            display.sleep();
    }
    display.dispose();
}}
```

Figure 16.9 shows what this looks like when the window is incrementally resized to be larger; a new backward L is produced for each paint event, leading to the "banded" look in the image. You can also try dragging another window in front of the ClippingRegion shell to see what areas are painted as parts of the shell become visible.[10]

Figure 16.9

Note that the code for the ClippingRegion example is *not correct* as shown above. We will be looking at this further in the next chapter, but if you are interested in spotting the flaw yourself, you should consider the way colors are used.

---

10. On some platforms, such as Mac OS X, the SWT.NO_REDRAW_RESIZE flag is ignored. In this case, the example will always fill the entire window with a single color.

CHAPTER 17

Colors

SWT supports a straightforward but powerful model for dealing with color information. Simple uses of color are supported by providing a number of easily accessed, pre-built color values. For more complex applications, complete control over the colors that are displayed is possible.

17.1 Class RGB

The simplest color-related class in SWT is RGB. Instances of this class are descriptions of particular abstract colors, represented as three 8-bit quantities modeling the red, green, and blue components of the color.[1] This is less accuracy than would be required by some high-end photo applications, but it is fine for almost all other uses. There is no operating system storage associated with RGB; thus, instances do not have a dispose() method. They have no interesting API, only a constructor that sets the public fields, which are subsequently accessed directly.

> **RGB(int red, int green, int blue)** Constructs a new instance of RGB that has its *red*, *green*, and *blue* fields set to the given values.

---

1. This is typically called the *primary additive color model*. The color being represented is the color that would result if the light from three sources, one red, one green, and one blue, with intensities relative to the given values, were mixed together.

This code fragment creates an instance of RGB, then prints out the values of its fields.

```
RGB rgb = new RGB(19, 255, 100);
System.out.println(rgb.red+" "+rgb.green+" "+rgb.blue);
```

To convert an RGB into something that is useful for drawing, you need to allocate operating system storage for the color. This allows the platform to manage how the color value that you are requesting is converted to the color you get. To understand why this is necessary, we need to look briefly at *color depths* and *color models*.

The *depth* of a display or image is the number of bits that are used to represent a single pixel. The maximum number of colors that can be handled simultaneously is equal to one more than the largest value that can be stored in the given number of bits. Most operating systems support working at depths of 1, 8, 16, and 24 bits. Some operating systems support other values. There are two standard ways to encode color information, called *color models*,[2] with the choice between them typically being made based on depth. The two models are called *direct* color and *indexed* color.

17.1.1 Direct Color

Direct color is almost invariably used when the depth is 16 bits or greater. In this model, the color to be displayed is mapped by packing the red, green, and blue values of the color into a range of bits in the pixel value. So for example, in a 24-bit-depth direct color display, the system will usually map the 8-bit red value from the color to the high-order 8 bits of the pixel value, the 8-bit green value from the color to the middle 8 bits of the pixel value, and the 8-bit blue value from the color to the low-order 8 bits of the pixel. In other words:

$$\text{24-bit pixel value} = \text{red} << 16 + \text{green} << 8 + \text{blue}$$

For 16-bit-depth direct color displays, the rule is usually 5 bits of red, 6 bits of green, and 5 bits of blue. In this case, there is less precision possible in the result than there is in the original color value, so the RGB values will be clipped, something like this:

---

2. In this case, *color model* denotes the strategy used to describe the color **within operating systems and associated hardware**. This differs from the additive color model described in the previous footnote, which is an abstract notion of how colors can be represented.

16-bit pixel value = (red >> 3) << 11 + (green >> 2) << 5 + (blue >> 3)

Direct color could even be used if the depth were only 8 bits, in which case, only 2 or 3 bits of precision per color could be used. For example:

8-bit pixel value = (red >> 6) << 6 + (green >> 5) << 3 + (blue >> 5)

Here we see the real problem with the direct color model. If the depth is low, the number of bits available to represent the color is also low. Using the above formula to store colors directly in 8 bits means that only four possible red, eight possible green, and eight possible blue values can be represented. Because precision is lost in the representation, the color that is displayed will not match the color that was requested. The indexed color model was introduced to fix this problem.

17.1.2   Indexed Color

The indexed color model takes the range of possible pixel values as indices into a table containing color values. Because of this, although the maximum *number* of colors is still equal to one more than the largest value that can be stored in the bit depth, the **precision of the representation** is controlled by the size of the values in the color table. So for example, an 8-bit-depth display with a 24-bit color table could have at most 256 simultaneously displayed colors, but for each color, a full 24-bit representation could be maintained.

The problem with the indexed color model is *color management*. Because the number of entries in the color table is usually 256 or less, there are frequently fewer entries available than your application needs. This is particularly true if it must share the available colors with the other applications that are running on the platform. When no more colors are available and you attempt to perform a drawing operation that uses a color that had not previously been allocated, the platform may deal with the problem in one or more of the following ways.

❍ It may return an error indicating that the color could not be allocated or simply pick the entry representing the color black and use that.

❍ It may look through the table to find the color that is the closest match to the color you requested.

❍ It may attempt to use a *dithering* strategy where it performs the drawing operation using a pattern made from two or more of the colors that were previously allocated.

In addition to the above, some platforms give each application its own color table, swapping in the color table for the application as it becomes active. This allows the application to have the greatest chance of displaying the colors it requires but causes the display to "flash" as you switch between applications, because all applications must redraw themselves to handle the change in available colors.

The indexed color model is discussed further when we talk about images (see for example the section PaletteData).

17.2   Class Color

Instances of class Color are used to represent the actual color values that have been allocated in the operating system. Because these objects hold on to operating system memory, you must follow the standard life cycle rules for SWT when working with them: If you create the Color, you must call dispose() when you are done with it.

Colors can be created using one of two constructors.

Color(Device device, RGB rgb)   This constructs a new instance of Color, suitable for displaying on the specified Device (Display or Printer), that is the result of attempting to allocate the color specified by the RGB value.

Color(Device device, int red, int green, int blue)   This is equivalent to new Color(device, new RGB(red, green, blue)).

RGB or ColorData?

The convention in SWT is that for every class that models some platform data structure, for example, XXX, if there is a parallel class that provides a description of that platform data but does not use operating system resources, it will be called XXX*Data*. Thus, for Font objects there is FontData, for Image objects there is ImageData, etc. By this rule, class RGB should have been called *Color-Data* because that is its purpose. In any case, you can remember this to remind yourself of the association between RGB and Color.

Colors are always allocated on a particular device and are useful only on that device. It is a programming error to use a color that was allocated on one device on some other device, so for example, if you wanted to get a red color for use on a both a display and a color printer, you would need to allocate both, something like the following.

```
RGB red = new RGB(255, 0, 0);
displayRed = new Color (myDisplay, red);
printerRed = new Color (myPrinter, red);
```

Once you have created a color, you can find out how close you were to getting the color you requested by using the following methods.

getRed()   Answers the red component of the color that was allocated.

getGreen()   Answers the green component of the color that was allocated.

getBlue()   Answers the blue component of the color that was allocated.

getRGB()   Answers a new instance of RGB containing the color components that were allocated.

These methods query the actual color values that were allocated in the operating system. For direct color devices, the result will be either the exact red, green, and blue values you requested or an approximation of them based on the depth of the display (as was described in the Direct Color section). For indexed color devices, the result could be the exact values, some close match to the values, or simply all zeros (i.e., black) based on whether a new color index was available to be allocated and the color allocation policy of the platform.

If you believe your application will need to run on an indexed color display, you should be as frugal as possible when it comes to allocating colors. Allocate them only when needed and dispose of them as soon as they are no longer required. Remember though, that once you draw something with a particular color, you should hold onto the color as long as it is visible. If you do not, the appearance could change wildly when the color it was drawn in is reallocated with a different value.

On direct color displays, color management is less important, because at least an approximation of the colors you are looking for will always be available. However, it is still good practice to manage your colors.

This leads us to an interesting point. Take a look at the example that we wrote in the More GC Clipping Methods section.[3] Given what you now know about colors, can you see what is wrong with that code?

---

3. No really, take a look.

In the paint listener, the example creates a color, draws with it, then immediately disposes of it. On an indexed color display, this would have the effect of painting an area of the screen with the color, then immediately giving up ownership of the "slot" in the table of color values. If some other application running on that display attempted to allocate a color, it could get the same slot in the color table. If that application then changed the color stored in the slot, the area painted by the example would *change color* to match it.

Even worse is the fact that even if there are no other applications running, the next time the example paint listener is invoked, *it* allocates a color slot, probably the one it just released. This will cause the previously painted area to be changed to the new color. Thus, when the example paints the new area, it will be the same color as the previous area, preventing you from seeing the distinction between them and making the example useless.

Here is a new version of the example that allocates a selection of random colors first, then uses them to show the clipping region in action, and finally frees the colors when the application is about to exit. This is the correct way to write the example.

```
public class ClippingRegion2 {
public static void main(String[] args) {
    final Display display = new Display();
    final Shell shell = new Shell(
        display,
        SWT.SHELL_TRIM | SWT.NO_REDRAW_RESIZE);
    final Random rand =
        new Random(System.currentTimeMillis());
    final Color[] colors = new Color[16];
    for (int i=0;i<colors.length; ++i) {
        colors[i] = new Color (
            display,
            rand.nextInt(256),
            rand.nextInt(256),
            rand.nextInt(256));
    }
    shell.addListener(SWT.Paint, new Listener() {
        public void handleEvent(Event event) {
            GC gc = event.gc;
            gc.setBackground(
                colors[rand.nextInt(colors.length)]);
            gc.fillRectangle(shell.getClientArea());
        }});
    shell.setText("Clipping Region");
    shell.setSize(250, 150);
    shell.open();
    while (!shell.isDisposed()) {
        if (!display.readAndDispatch())
            display.sleep();
    }
    for (int i=0; i<colors.length; ++i) {
        colors[i].dispose();
```

```
    }
    display.dispose();
}}
```

Color management in SWT is one of those places where the need to support multiple platforms with different ways of dealing with a feature has led to an API that is not as simple as we would have liked. Because indexed color displays are becoming less and less common, it may be that we need to look at the SWT color model again. In any case, that is a topic for future research. In the meantime, to make applications that have only simple color requirements easier to write, a collection of standard color values, called *system colors*, was introduced.

17.3 System Colors

System colors are a collection of standard colors that are pre-allocated by the SWT library. Because you do not allocate these colors, you should not call their dispose() method. The constants that are used to choose the color are implemented in the class SWT (as you would expect), and the following method, defined on the class Device, is used to access them.

> **getSystemColor (int colorConstant)**   Returns an instance of class Color, the predefined system color represented by the given color constant.

Table 17.1 shows the color constants and the RGB values of the colors that are returned.

Table 17.1   System Color Constants

Constant	Red	Green	Blue
SWT.COLOR_BLACK	0	0	0
SWT. COLOR_DARK_RED	128	0	0
SWT. COLOR_DARK_GREEN	0	128	0
SWT. COLOR_DARK_YELLOW	128	128	0
SWT. COLOR_DARK_BLUE	0	0	128
SWT. COLOR_DARK_MAGENTA	128	0	128
SWT. COLOR_DARK_CYAN	0	128	128
SWT. COLOR_DARK_GRAY	128	128	128

Table 17.1   System Color Constants (continued)

Constant	Red	Green	Blue
SWT. COLOR_GRAY	192	192	192
SWT. COLOR_RED	255	0	0
SWT. COLOR_GREEN	0	255	0
SWT. COLOR_YELLOW	255	255	0
SWT. COLOR_BLUE	0	0	255
SWT. COLOR_MAGENTA	255	0	255
SWT. COLOR_CYAN	0	255	255
SWT. COLOR_WHITE	255	255	255

The getSystemColor() method is *redefined* in class Display to provide additional colors based on constants that represent the window system-specific values for things such as the "default background color for widgets." Table 17.2 shows the added color constant values that can be passed to the getSystemColor() method in class Display. Note that these colors do not work on printers.

System Colors Are a Failure

Using these system colors can improve your chances of matching the platform look when implementing new widgets, but as is true with the drawFocus() method, this works only to the extent that SWT can determine the correct values. If the operating system supports the notion of skins, particularly ones that call code in the skin to draw themselves, it may not be possible to determine what the correct values are. Even if it is possible, this does not necessarily mean that you can duplicate the appearance that the skin is providing.

The only long-term solution to the problem is to make the native skinning support available via SWT, something that the SWT team continues to investigate.

Table 17.2   Additional System Color Constants Defined in the Class Display

Constant	Meaning
SWT.COLOR_INFO_FOREGROUND	Tool tip foreground
SWT.COLOR_INFO_BACKGROUND	Tool tip background
SWT.COLOR_TITLE_FOREGROUND	Title bar foreground
SWT.COLOR_TITLE_BACKGROUND	Title bar background
SWT.COLOR_TITLE_BACKGROUND_GRADIENT	Second title bar background
SWT.COLOR_TITLE_INACTIVE_FOREGROUND	Inactive title bar foreground
SWT.COLOR_TITLE_INACTIVE_BACKGROUND	Inactive title bar background
SWT.COLOR_TITLE_INACTIVE_BACKGROUND _GRADIENT	Second inactive title bar background
SWT.COLOR_WIDGET_DARK_SHADOW	Dark shadow areas
SWT.COLOR_WIDGET_NORMAL_SHADOW	Normal shadow areas
SWT.COLOR_WIDGET_LIGHT_SHADOW	Light shadow areas
SWT.COLOR_WIDGET_HIGHLIGHT_SHADOW	Highlight shadow areas
SWT.COLOR_WIDGET_FOREGROUND	Default widget foreground
SWT.COLOR_WIDGET_BACKGROUND	Default widget background
SWT.COLOR_WIDGET_BORDER	Default widget border
SWT.COLOR_LIST_FOREGROUND	List widget foreground
SWT.COLOR_LIST_BACKGROUND	List widget background
SWT.COLOR_LIST_SELECTION	List selection background
SWT.COLOR_LIST_SELECTION_TEXT	List selection foreground

The GRADIENT versions of the title background color are intended to map onto the gradient fill style used for window titles in Microsoft Windows 98 and Windows 2000, as shown in Figure 17.1. Because this look is no longer being used in the standard Windows XP appearance and was never used on the other supported platforms, these GRADIENT constants may eventually be phased out.

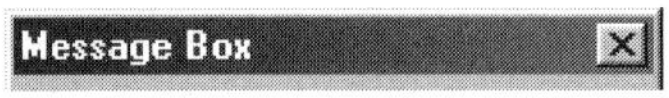

Figure 17.1 Gradient-filled titles as used in Windows 98.

Because many operating systems allow the default foreground and background colors of widgets to be specified for each type of widget (not just list widgets), the above set of system colors is clearly incomplete. This, combined with the fact that SWT may or may not be able to determine these colors on all platforms, makes it not a good idea to rely heavily on them.

In general, the best way to determine good default choices for foreground and background colors for a particular widget is to create one (or the closest analog among the native widgets) and query the colors from it. For example, if you were building a new kind of list widget, you could get good colors to use from an instance of the List class, as follows.

```
List list = new List(shell, SWT.SINGLE);
RGB foreground = list.getForeground().getRGB();
RGB background = list.getBackground().getRGB();
list.dispose();
```

Because SWT simply creates the widget in the operating system when you ask it to, the colors that the widget uses will always be the default colors. This is true for many of the standard widgets properties, including fonts.

CHAPTER 18

Fonts

All modern graphical user interfaces provide some mechanism for specifying the appearance of text that is displayed. The degree of control that platforms provide over this can vary significantly, and on several of the platforms that SWT supports, there is significant ongoing work in this area. We use the term *font* (note lowercase) to describe generally the platform objects that specify text appearance. SWT abstracts these objects using three classes: FontData, Font, and FontMetrics.

18.1 Class FontData

Instances of class FontData are descriptions of fonts. They can represent either an abstract, user-oriented specification of a font, or a precise, platform-specific description of a font, depending on how they are created. No operating system storage is allocated for FontData objects, and they do not have a dispose() method.

To request a font with a particular name, size, and style, create an instance of class FontData, using the following constructor.

FontData(String name, int height, int style)   The font name must be the name of a font that is available on the platform, the height is specified in points,[1] and the style must be one of SWT.NORMAL, SWT.ITALIC, SWT.BOLD, or (SWT.BOLD | SWT.ITALIC).

---

1. A *point* is a unit of measure common in the printing industry. It is equivalent to 1/72 of an inch.

This constructor creates an instance of FontData that matches the values you provided; however, it may not exactly match any font that is installed on the platform.

FontData instances can also be created by other SWT API methods in ways that cause them to match exactly a particular platform font. Two common ways to do this are as follows.

1. Using the FontDialog class (see the FontDialog section in Part 1 or Using More Than One Instance of FontData below for more on this).

2. Calling the getFontList() method of class Device.

The getFontList() method looks like the following.

getFontList(String faceName, boolean scalable)   Answers an array of FontData instances that match exactly fonts that are available on the device. If faceName is null, all fonts are returned; otherwise, only fonts with names that are equal (using case-insensitive comparison) to faceName are provided. The scalable flag indicates whether bitmapped or scalable fonts should be returned.

18.1.1   *Scalable versus Bitmapped Fonts*

Some platforms distinguish between fonts where each glyph[2] is represented as a fixed size bitmap and fonts that use an algorithmic description of each glyph that allows them to be scaled to arbitrary sizes. There are several types of scalable (or, as it is sometimes called, *outline*) font systems, including TrueType; OpenType; PostScript Types 1, 3, and 5; and MetaFont .mf format.

There are advantages and disadvantages to both bitmap and scalable fonts. Bitmap fonts, when they are well designed, can look better than scalable fonts, but they can typically be used only at the sizes they are created. Even if the platform will scale them to other sizes, the results are usually ugly. Scalable fonts, by definition, are available at a wide range of sizes but require very complex descriptions and rendering engines in order to look good.

Some platforms do a better job than others at rendering scalable fonts, so the implementation of getFontList() includes a flag that allows you to choose whether you want to return scalable fonts in the result. If the flag is true, only scalable fonts are returned; if it is false, only bitmap fonts are returned.

---

2. A *glyph* is the actual "image" that a particular character has in a specific font.

Here is a simple application that writes to System.out a list of the names of all fonts on the default display. It calls getFontList() twice, once to get the bitmap fonts and once to get the scalable fonts. It then builds a set of the font names to remove duplicates caused by FontData objects being returned that represent several different sizes and styles of the same named font. Finally, it sorts and prints the results.

```
public class ListFonts {
public static void main(String[] args) {
    final Display display = new Display();
    Set s = new HashSet();
    // Add names of all bitmap fonts.
    FontData[] fds = display.getFontList(null, false);
    for (int i=0; i<fds.length; ++i)
        s.add(fds[i].getName());
    // Add names of all scalable fonts.
    fds = display.getFontList(null, true);
    for (int i=0; i<fds.length; ++i)
        s.add(fds[i].getName());
    // Sort the result and print it.
    String[] answer = new String[s.size()];
    s.toArray(answer);
    Arrays.sort(answer);
    for (int i=0; i<answer.length; ++i) {
        System.out.println(answer[i]);
    }
    display.dispose();
}}
```

18.1.2   Character Encoding and Locale

A *character encoding* is a mapping between the symbols in an alphabet and numbers that represent those symbols. Java uses the 16-bit *Unicode* encoding to represent characters. On almost all platforms supported by SWT, the font rendering code in the operating system directly supports text-drawing operations using this encoding. In other words, on these platforms, **when a character to be drawn is passed to SWT, the character is already represented by a 16-bit integer that the operating system can use to find the appropriate glyph.** If the font that is being used to do the drawing contains that glyph, it will be properly displayed. If the font does not contain the glyph, either the platform substitutes a glyph from some other font that matches that Unicode value or some distinguished glyph (usually either a "box" or question mark) is displayed to indicate that the glyph is not available. See the section Using More Than One Instance of FontData for a description of how some platforms can control this substitution process.

The *locale* of a platform is a description of the language, country, and character encoding that have been selected by the user (using whatever support the platform provides for this). In Java, the locale is represented by an instance of class Locale containing a language code, country code, and variant. The language code is a lowercase two-letter string described by the ISO-639 specification. The country code is an uppercase two-letter string described by ISO-3166. The variant part of a locale is platform-specific.[3]

To specify a locale in SWT, a string having the same form as the string representation of a Locale instance is used.

<language code>_<country code>_<variant>

In this case, the variant part specifies the character encoding that should be used if there is more than one choice for the given language/country pair.

> **Why Not Just Use Locale?**
>
> As we indicated in the introduction, SWT runs on a wide range of platforms, including ones that use J2ME. The J2ME 1.0 spec does not include class Locale, so for compatibility reasons, we use a String representation instead.

For SWT implementations that do not support Unicode text drawing (currently only Windows 98 and Motif in "non UTF-8" mode), each font must be treated **as though it had its own character encoding**. When a character is passed to SWT to be drawn, the 16-bit integer Unicode value that represents the character must be converted by SWT to a new number that can be used to look up the glyph using the encoding for the specific font. Typically on these platforms, fonts are installed that match the encoding chosen for the current locale, so by default, SWT will convert from Unicode to that encoding before doing the drawing operation. If you need to use a specific font that uses some encoding other than the one in the current locale, you must identify the correct locale to SWT using the following FontData method.

setLocale(String locale)   Sets the locale that will be used to determine the character encoding for FontData. This value is *ignored* on Unicode platforms.

There is a matching getter method.

---

3. For more on this, see the Javadoc for class java.util.Locale.

getLocale()   Answers the locale that was previously set via setLo-
cale() or null if it has not been set.

Important: Do Not Use

It is important to remember that applications almost never need to invoke the
setLocale() API. It is required only by applications that are running on non-
Unicode platforms and need to display text using a font whose character encoding differs from the default for the platform.

18.1.3   Remembering Font Choices

When you call the toString() method of a FontData object, it will answer a
string that contains an exact description of the FontData. This string can then
be passed to the following FontData constructor.

FontData(String description)   Constructs a new instance based on
the description.

It is important to note that this description string is *platform-specific*. It will
not work on platforms other than the one on which it was created.[4] The only
real use for this is to allow an application to create an external description of
the fonts that it is using so that the same fonts can be used each time it is started.
This would be required, for example, if the application allowed the user to
change fonts via FontDialog and needed to remember the choice between invo-
cations. Here is a simplified example of what that would look like.

```
public static FontData chooseFont(Shell parent) {
    FontData fd;
    String fdString = null;
    FontDialog dialog = new FontDialog(parent);
    final String fileName = "the-font";

    // Get FontData string from file if it exists
    try {
        FileReader fr = new FileReader(fileName);
        StringBuffer buf = new StringBuffer();
        for (int ch = fr.read(); ch >= 0; ch = fr.read())
```

---

4. This actually does make some sense. Because the string exactly describes the particular platform
   font, attempting to use the font description on another platform would be equivalent to attempting to use the font from one platform on a different one.

```
        buf.append((char) ch);
    fr.close();
    fdString = buf.toString();
} catch (IOException e) { }
if (fdString != null)
    dialog.setFontData(new FontData(fdString));

fd = dialog.open();

// If a font was chosen, save the FontData string.
if (fd != null) {
    FileWriter ofw;
    try {
        ofw = new FileWriter(fileName);
        ofw.write(fd.toString());
        ofw.close();
    } catch (IOException e1) { }
}

return fd;
}
```

The example code begins by attempting to read the representation for a FontData from a file. If it finds one, it seeds the font dialog with this value so that the dialog will show a matching font when it is opened. If the user picks a font, its representation is written back out to the file for next time and the FontData is returned.[5] Obviously, in a real application, you would split this into two pieces, one that attempts to get the previous value and one that allows the user to choose a new value and save it (because you would not want to display a font dialog each time the application needed the FontData). You would also want to make the file input code more robust. There is a third limitation in this code, related to the way FontData objects are mapped to fonts, which we will discuss further in the next section.

18.2 Class Font

Fonts are device specific objects. Because they hold onto operating system memory, you must follow the standard life cycle rules for SWT when working with them: If you create the Font, you must call dispose() when you are done with it.

Font instances can be created using one of the following constructors.

---

5. In the source code that is provided with this book, this chooseFont() function is part of the RememberFont.java example in package *part2*. RememberFont simply displays a button that opens a font dialog and remembers the font that is selected between times it is opened (even if the example exits and is restarted).

Font(Device device, FontData fd)   Constructs an instance of Font for use on the given device, based on the description given by the Font-Data parameter. The font that is created will be the best match for the description but can be significantly different if, for example, there is no font on the system whose name matches the name given in the FontData.

Font(Device display, String name, int height, int style)   This is equivalent to Font(device, new FontData(name, height, style)).

Instances of class GC provide accessors for setting and getting the font. Note that you can pass in an instance of Font that was created only on the same device as the one that is associated with the GC.

setFont(Font font)   Causes the given font to be used for all text operations on the GC. If the parameter is null, the default font for the GC is used.

getFont()   Gets the font that is being used by the GC. If a font had not previously been explicitly set on the GC, the result will be the font associated with the Drawable on which the GC was created. For widgets, this will be Widget's current font; for devices, it will be the *system font* for the device.

The system font for a device can be queried using this method.

getSystemFont()   Returns the font that the device will use to draw text if some other font has not been explicitly set.

Here is an example that shows the correlation between the default font in GC on a device and the system font for the device.

```
public class GetSystemFont {
public static void main(String[] args) {
    Display display = new Display();
    System.out.println("System Font is:");
    printFontData(display.getSystemFont().getFontData());
    System.out.println("Font in GC on Display is:");
    GC gc = new GC(display);
    printFontData(gc.getFont().getFontData());
    gc.dispose();
    display.dispose();
}
private static void printFontData(FontData[] fds) {
    String style;
    for (int i=0; i<fds.length; ++i) {
```

```
                    FontData fd = fds[i];
                    switch (fd.getStyle()) {
                        case SWT.NORMAL: style = "NORMAL"; break;
                        case SWT.BOLD: style = "BOLD"; break;
                        case SWT.ITALIC: style = "ITALIC"; break;
                        case (SWT.BOLD|SWT.ITALIC):
                            style = "BOLD|ITALIC"; break;
                        default:
                            style = "STYLE("+fd.getStyle()+")";
                    }
                    System.out.println(
                        "    FontData[" + i + "] " + fd.getName() +
                        ", " + fd.getHeight() +
                        ", " + style);
            }
}}
```

Running this example produced the following output on a Macintosh OS X machine.

```
System Font is:
    FontData[0] Geneva, 13, NORMAL
Font in GC on Display is:
    FontData[0] Geneva, 13, NORMAL
```

Notice that in this example, printFontData() is coded to take an *array* of FontData instances. This is required because of the way the getFontData() method on class Font is specified:

getFontData()   Returns an array of FontData instances that provide an exact description of the font.

If you are wondering why an array of FontData instances could be required to represent the font, read on.

18.2.1   Using More Than One Instance of FontData

There is a third form of the Font constructor, which takes as a parameter an array of FontData objects.

Font(Device device, FontData[] fds)   Constructs a Font for use on the given device, based on the given array of FontData instances.

This constructor was created because some platforms allow text to be drawn using a collection of fonts, rather than a single font. The only current example of this is X/Motif, where the equivalent operating system structure is called a *FontSet*.

The value of supporting a collection of fonts in graphics operations is that it allows the system to take several fonts that separately only partially cover the range of required glyphs (as was noted in Character Encoding and Locale) and effectively merge them together to create one *union font*[6] that contains all needed glyphs.

Here is an example of how that could be used: Assume that a given system had several fonts, for example, *Times*, *Courier*, etc., that provide only the glyphs specified by the ISO-8859-1 "Latin-1" character encoding, which is an 8-bit encoding commonly used by many North American and European countries. If this system also had another font that had glyphs for all the Unicode characters and the user asked for the Times font, the system could return a union font that contained first the Times font, followed by the standard Unicode font. Given this, any characters with glyphs in the Times font could be drawn in Times; any other characters would be drawn by the Unicode font. By doing this kind of *font substitution*, it is possible to draw text in multiple fonts without requiring each one to contain all possible Unicode characters.

Current X/Motif implementations use this mechanism extensively, sometimes creating union fonts made from five or more other fonts. To allow applications built with SWT the greatest degree of control over the font substitution process, the SWT API was extended to allow arrays of FontData objects to be used in several places where previously only single FontData instances were allowed. Although adding this support was important for us to be able to provide real national language support on Motif, it has two significant drawbacks for the developer.

1. Picking the right fonts is difficult.

2. Applications need to use different API to deal with arrays of FontData instances.

The first problem arises from the fact that only the platform has enough information to decide which glyphs are present in a particular font and how these fonts should be composed to create the union font. It is *possible* for a smart developer to duplicate this process, given a deep knowledge of the fonts on a particular system, but there are no guarantees that the mapping will be constant across platforms or even across other occurrences of the same platform. The situation is not as bad as it sounds, however. Because the default font used by widgets and drawables is chosen by the platform, if you do not change the font, it will be a union font if that is the platform default. In addi-

---

6. This is not a term used in SWT but is useful for the purposes of this discussion. From the perspective of an SWT program, a union font is simply another font.

tion, because the FontDialog class uses the platform dialog for choosing fonts, it can return union fonts.

The *way* that FontDialog communicates the union font to the application leads us to the second problem. As we have already shown, SWT uses an array of FontData instances to represent a union font, but the FontDialog class is specified to return a single instance of FontData as its result. To get around this, after the dialog has exited, you can get the full list of FontData instances using the following FontDialog method.

> **getFontList()**   Answers the array of FontData instances that represents the last font chosen by the user or null if no font was chosen.

Similarly, to set the initial font to be displayed by FontDialog, you can use a setter method that takes an array.

> **setFontList(FontData[] fds)**   Sets the font that FontDialog will display based on an array of FontData instances.

The return value for the dialog is just the first instance of FontData that would have been returned by the getFontList() method. If you use this instance of FontData to create a new font, SWT will attempt to produce a reasonable union font for you, but it is not guaranteed to be the same as the one returned by the dialog.

Here is a new version of the chooseFont() method example from the Remembering Font Choices section that has been rewritten to use arrays of FontData instances.[7] Notice that an array of FontData instances is read from or written to the file by storing the descriptions one per line, and getFontList() and setFontList() are used to access the dialog.

```
public static FontData[] chooseFont(Shell parent) {
    FontData fd[];
    FontDialog dialog = new FontDialog(parent);
    final String fileName = "the-font";

    // Get FontData strings from file if it exists
    ArrayList inputFDs = new ArrayList(10);
    try {
        BufferedReader reader =
            new BufferedReader(
                new FileReader(fileName));
```

---

7. In the source code that is provided with this book, this chooseFont() function is part of the Show-Font.java example in package *part2*. ShowFont allows the user to choose a font and displays a line of text using it.

```
        String line = reader.readLine();
        while (line != null) {
            inputFDs.add(new FontData(line));
            line = reader.readLine();
        }
        reader.close();
    } catch (IOException e) { }
    if (inputFDs.size() > 0) {
        fd = new FontData[inputFDs.size()];
        inputFDs.toArray(fd);
        dialog.setFontList(fd);
    }

    dialog.open();
    fd = dialog.getFontList();

    // If a font was chosen, save the FontData strings.
    if (fd != null) {
        try {
            BufferedWriter writer =
                new BufferedWriter(
                    new FileWriter(fileName));
            for (int i=0; i < fd.length; ++i) {
                writer.write(fd[i].toString());
                writer.newLine();
            }
            writer.close();
        } catch (IOException e1) { }
    }

    return fd;
}
```

Note that the original version of this function *will work* on all platforms. The only interesting difference between them is that on X/Motif, this version of the function preserves the exact font choice made by the user, whereas the original version will manufacture a font based on a single instance of FontData.

18.2.2 Rules for Writing Platform-Independent Font Code

What then have we learned from this rather lengthy discussion of Font and FontData? To be maximally portable across all platforms, your application should always assume that more than one instance of FontData is required to represent a font. It should also avoid setting fonts in widgets to "hand constructed" fonts if possible, either by simply not setting the font in the widget and allowing the platform to provide a default value or by using FontDialog (and the getFontList() method) to choose the font.

If you are writing your own custom widget and you want to pick a font that is appropriate for the platform, a good way to do this is to create an instance of a similar existing widget, then query its font. For example, if you were building a new kind of text widget, you could get the default font from an instance of a text widget.

```
Text text = new Text(shell, SWT.MULTI);
Font textFont = text.getFont();
text.dispose();
```

This way, your widget would use the same font as the native text widgets by default, regardless of the platform.

18.3   Drawing Text

There are five different text-drawing routines provided by SWT. As with all other drawing operations, they are implemented in class GC. The result is always drawn inside a rectangular area whose top left corner is specified by the values passed as the x and y parameters. We will discuss further how the text is aligned in this area in the FontMetrics section.

The first two text-drawing routines do not interpret the string to be drawn in any way. For maximum performance, they simply pass the string along to the raw platform text-drawing routines.

> **drawString(String string, int x, int y, boolean isTransparent)**   Draws the string at position (x, y) relative to the origin of the Drawable associated with the GC. The text is drawn in the foreground color of the GC. If the isTransparent flag is false, the rectangular area around the text is filled with the background color of the GC.

> **drawString(String string, int x, int y)**   Equivalent to drawString(string, x, y, false).

These methods provide the fastest text-drawing performance in SWT. However, the result of calling these methods with a string containing special characters (such as tab ('\t') or newline ('\n')) or with characters that do not have matching glyphs in the font that is set into the GC is *indeterminate*. Some platforms may embed "missing character" glyphs in the result, and some platforms may simply ignore the characters.

The remaining three text-drawing operations provide varying degrees of special interpretation of the string to be drawn, at the cost of some performance:

drawText(String string, int x, int y, int flags)   This method is similar to drawString() but is considerably more flexible. As with draw-String(), this draws the string at position (x, y) relative to the origin of the Drawable associated with the GC. The flags parameter is constructed using bitwise-or with one or more of the constants from Table 18.1.

Table 18.1   drawText() Constants

Constant	Meaning
SWT.DRAW_DELIMITER	Embedded line break characters cause the text to display on multiple lines.
SWT.DRAW_TAB	Embedded tab characters cause text display to align with the next tab stop. The width of a tab stop is platform- and font-specific (usually equivalent to eight spaces).
SWT.DRAW_MNEMONIC	Embedded ampersand characters (&) cause the following character to be underlined in the style the platform uses to indicate mnemonics. Pairs of ampersands (&&) are displayed as a single ampersand.
SWT.DRAW_TRANSPARENT	Prevents the area around the text from being filled with the background color.

It is important to note that the interpretation of these flags is platform-specific. If the platform provides direct support for the drawing styles, that support will be used by the implementation.

drawText(String string, int x, int y, boolean isTransparent)   If the isTransparent flag is true, this is equivalent to drawText(string, x, y, SWT.DRAW_DELIMITER | SWT.DRAW_TAB | SWT.TRANSPAR-ENT). If the isTransparent flag is false, this is equivalent to draw-Text(string, x, y, SWT.DRAW_DELIMITER | SWT.DRAW_TAB).

drawText(String string, int x, int y)   Equivalent to drawText(string, x, y, false).

Here is an example that shows the result of drawing the text "&Hello,\tWorld\nfrom\tOttawa" using the various drawing methods.

```
public class DrawText {

static final String string =
    "&Hello,\tWorld\nfrom\tOttawa";

public static void main(String[] args) {
    final Display display = new Display();
    final Color white =
        display.getSystemColor(SWT.COLOR_WHITE);
    final Color gray =
        display.getSystemColor(SWT.COLOR_GRAY);
    final Color black =
        display.getSystemColor(SWT.COLOR_BLACK);
    final Shell shell = new Shell(display);
    shell.addListener(SWT.Paint, new Listener() {
        public void handleEvent(Event event) {
            Rectangle bounds = shell.getClientArea();
            int top = bounds.y;
            int left = bounds.x;
            GC gc = event.gc;
            int yAdvance = bounds.height / 10;
            gc.setBackground(gray);
            gc.fillRectangle(bounds);
            gc.setBackground(white);
            gc.setForeground(black);
            gc.drawString(
                string, left, top, false);
            gc.drawString(
                string, left, top + yAdvance, true);
            gc.drawText(
                string, left, top + (2 * yAdvance), false);
            gc.drawText(
                string, left, top + (4 * yAdvance), true);
            gc.drawText(
                string, left, top + (6 * yAdvance),
                SWT.DRAW_DELIMITER | SWT.DRAW_TAB |
                SWT.DRAW_MNEMONIC);
            gc.drawText(
                string, left, top + (8 * yAdvance),
                SWT.DRAW_MNEMONIC);
        }
    });
    shell.setText("Draw Text");
    shell.setSize(400, 400);
    shell.open();
    while (!shell.isDisposed()) {
        if (!display.readAndDispatch())
            display.sleep();
    }
    display.dispose();
}}
```

Running this example on Windows XP produces the output shown in Figure 18.1.

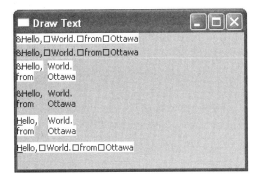

Figure 18.1

18.3.1   Rules for Writing Platform-Independent Text-Drawing Code

As of R3.0 of SWT, the SWT team has worked around most of the inconsistencies between the various platform text-drawing routines. Of course, there will always be minor differences in appearance but that is to be expected because matching the platform appearance is a feature of SWT.

In earlier versions, if you intended to run your application on several platforms, your only reasonable option was to use the *drawString (String string, int x, int y, boolean isTransparent)* method with isTransparent set to true. To be fully portable, you also needed to ensure that the strings that were drawn did not include any of the special characters tab (\t), newline (\n), carriage return (\r), or ampersand (&).

Using the drawString() methods is probably still the best answer unless you need the mnemonic drawing capability of drawText(). Often, this is more effective anyway, because it allows for exact control over the drawing behavior.

18.4   Class FontMetrics

If you look at the implementation of the DrawText example, you can see that it uses the rather primitive strategy of splitting the vertical space in the shell into 10 equal-sized chunks (see the variable *yAdvance*), then aligns each of the text-drawing calls with the start of a chunk. Obviously, this is less than ideal because if the example window is resized to be much smaller, the text lines will draw on top of each other. To fix this problem, the code would need to measure the height of the text being drawn and move down an appropriate amount for each line. This kind of operation, called a *measuring* operation, is extremely common when building user interfaces that do text drawing. Some other examples of where this might be important are as follows.

○ Displaying lines of text using multiple fonts or styles

○ Wrapping text to fit within a fixed size area

○ Drawing the I-beam between characters

○ Aligning text with other drawings[8]

Many different measurements are required to perform these operations, but we begin by looking again at the notion of the "height" of a font.

18.4.1 Height Measurements

You will remember that when FontData instances are constructed, one of the parameters passed in is the *height*. There is an accessor on class FontData (getHeight()) that returns the height of the font. This seems as though it would be exactly what we are looking for except for two fundamental problems.

It is measured in points. The SWT graphics model uses pixels to specify positions on the Drawable. Given the Device method getDPI(), which returns the number of *dots per inch*, or DPI (in both the horizontal and vertical directions) for the device, you could convert a value specified in points to a value specified in pixels using the formula

$$\text{device.getDPI}().y \times \text{heightInPoints} \div 72$$

Unfortunately, this equation is not guaranteed to generate an integer result. So for example, with a 90-DPI display and a 7-point font, the height would be 8.75 pixels. Because the way the system renders the font is platform-specific, the system could render the font 8 pixels high, 9 pixels high, or even 8.75 pixels high, using anti-aliasing techniques to render the fractional pixel value.

Some platforms lie. On some platforms, particularly those that do font substitution, even though the font is specified to be a particular size, for example, 7 points, some of the glyphs may be larger than 7 points in height. It may be, for example, that the font that contained the Japanese Kanji symbols could not be reasonably rendered at less than 10 pixels in height. In this case, when one of those symbols was included in text to be drawn, the text would require 10 pixels, rather than 8.75 (based on the numbers above).

Together, these problems mean that you cannot simply use the height of an instance of FontData to measure how many rows of pixels high the text will be on the screen.

---

8. This includes things such as centering captions under images in graphs and drawing the "red squiggle" underline used as an error indicator in the Eclipse Java editor.

SWT uses a separate class, called *FontMetrics*, to hold onto the API methods related to font measurement. An instance of FontMetrics is created by asking a GC for the metrics for the font that it is using.

getFontMetrics()   Returns an instance of FontMetrics that describes the font that is in use by the GC.

Why Is getFontMetrics() Not a Font Method?

By defining this method on class GC, it is clear that the result is specific to the font that will be used for drawing on that GC and keeps all the measurement-related API in the same place. It is also convenient because application code is typically handed an instance of GC (for example, in a paint listener) that already has a font set. If the application is simply going to use this font (and not change to a new one), defining the method on GC means that the application can ask for FontMetrics directly, rather than asking for the font first, then getting Font-Metrics from there.

Class FontMetrics has a number of methods that provide measurement information about the font. To compute the height of the font, as was required in the discussion above, you would use the following.

getHeight()   Answers the amount of vertical space that is required to hold any text displayed in this font.

If we build a new example (called, for example, DrawText2), changing the line in the DrawText example that computes the amount of space to leave from

```
int yAdvance = bounds.height ÷ 10;
```

to

```
int yAdvance = gc.getFontMetrics().getHeight();
```

the new example creates a window like the one shown in Figure 18.2. Notice that in this example, resizing the window does not change the positions of the lines of text, which are always drawn with "just enough" space between them.

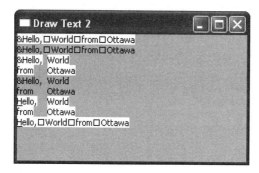

Figure 18.2

Applications may require several other kinds of height measurements. Consider for example the image shown in Figure 18.3. Notice that the text written in both the small font and the large font "sits on" the dotted line. This line is called the *baseline* for the font.

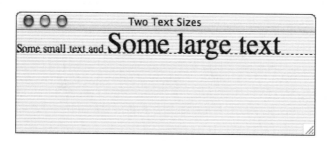

Figure 18.3

In addition to the height returned by getHeight(), instances of class FontMetrics provide three other vertical measurements for the font that they describe.

getAscent()   Returns the distance in pixels between the baseline of the font and the top of the "full-height" glyphs.

getDescent()   Returns the distance in pixels that glyphs can extend below the baseline.

getLeading()   Returns the amount of space in pixels that should be left above the ascent area to accommodate exceptionally tall glyphs, such as accented capitals (e.g., Á).

Figure 18.4 shows the relationship between these three measurements.

Figure 18.4   Font height measurements.

Given the above measurements, to compute the distance between the top of the area in which the text is drawn and the baseline, you add together the leading and ascent, thus:

$$\text{distance to baseline} = \text{leading} + \text{ascent}$$

Knowing this, to align the baselines of two fonts of different sizes, as we did in Figure 18.3, you add the difference between the distances to the baselines to the y coordinate of the starting location where the *smaller* text is drawn. Here is the code for the TwoTextSizes example that was used to create Figure 18.3. Notice that the variable *yAdvance* is set to the amount to add to the y coordinate of the smaller text.

```
public class TwoTextSizes {

static final String smallText = "Some small text and ";
static final FontData smallFD =
    new FontData("Times", 14, SWT.NORMAL);
static final String largeText = "Some large text";
static final FontData largeFD =
    new FontData("Times", 36, SWT.NORMAL);

public static void main(String[] args) {
    final Display display = new Display();
    final Font smallFont = new Font(display, smallFD);
    final Font largeFont = new Font(display, largeFD);
    final Shell shell = new Shell(display);
    shell.addListener(SWT.Paint, new Listener() {
        public void handleEvent(Event event) {
            Rectangle bounds = shell.getClientArea();
            int top = bounds.y;
            int left = bounds.x;
            GC gc = event.gc;
            gc.setFont(largeFont);
            FontMetrics fm = gc.getFontMetrics();
            int largeBaseline =
                fm.getAscent() + fm.getLeading();
            gc.setFont(smallFont);
            fm = gc.getFontMetrics();
            int smallBaseline =
```

```
                    fm.getAscent()+fm.getLeading();
                int yAdvance = largeBaseline - smallBaseline;
                int xAdvance = gc.stringExtent(smallText).x;
                gc.drawString(
                    smallText, left, top+yAdvance, true);
                gc.setFont(largeFont);
                gc.drawString(
                    largeText, left+xAdvance, top, true);
                gc.setLineStyle(SWT.LINE_DOT);
                gc.drawLine(
                    left, largeBaseline,
                    left+bounds.width, largeBaseline);
            }
        });
        shell.setText("Two Text Sizes");
        shell.setSize(400, 400);
        shell.open();
        while (!shell.isDisposed()) {
            if (!display.readAndDispatch())
                display.sleep();
        }
        display.dispose();
}}
```

18.4.2 Width Measurements

In the TwoTextSizes example code, in addition to aligning the baselines of the
two fonts, we needed to compute how much horizontal space is used to display "Some small text and " (including the trailing space) so that when "Some
large text" is displayed, it exactly abuts the small text. To do this, we used the
following GC method.

> **stringExtent(String string)**   Answers a point describing the width and
> height in pixels of the rectangle that would be covered if the given
> string were painted using the method drawString(String string, int x,
> int y) and the font that is set in the GC.

There are similar methods that return the equivalent width and height
measurements for strings that are drawn with drawText(). As was true of
drawString() versus drawText(), these methods are slower than stringExtent().

> **textExtent(String string)**   Answers a point describing the width and
> height in pixels of the rectangle that would be covered if the given
> string were painted using the method drawText(String string, int x, int
> y) and the font that is set in the GC.

> **textExtent(String string, int flags)**   Answers a point describing the
> width and height in pixels of the rectangle that would be covered if

the given string were painted using the method drawText(String string, int x, int y, int flags), the same flags, and the font that is set in the GC.

For the TwoTextSizes example, we computed the horizontal distance to move the start of the large text as follows.

```
int xAdvance = gc.stringExtent(smallText).x;
```

Using textExtent() in DrawText2

Given that the above methods return both the width *and height* of the rectangle that the text covers, we could have used them to set the vertical spacing in the DrawText2 example as well. In fact, this would have been a better implementation, because we could then guarantee that the "multiline" text (displayed using drawText()) was spaced correctly, rather than assuming as we did that it was exactly two times the height of a single line. Using getFontMetrics().getHeight() instead allowed us to introduce class FontMetrics simply, with only a single line change in the example.

There are a few other measuring operations worth noting. You can discover the average width of a character in the font using the following Font-Metrics method.

getAverageCharWidth()   Answers the average width of the characters in the font described by the font data.

Although this is sometimes used to compute preferred sizes for controls,[9] it is only an average and depending on the font, may not be what you would expect. For example, in a Unicode font, the average width, if it takes into account all of the characters, would typically be much wider than one that has only Latin-1 glyphs.

You can also compute the width of a particular character in the font that is in use in a GC using the GC methods getCharWidth() and getAdvance-Width().

---

9. Because preferred sizes are measured in pixels, you could use, for example, 40 times the average character width as the width of a text control that should be able to display *approximately* 40 characters per line.

getCharWidth(char c)   Answers the amount of horizontal space taken up by the character in the current font. This does not include any extra space left around the character if it were drawn as part of a multicharacter string.

getAdvanceWidth(char c)   Answers the amount of space that this character would take up if it were drawn as part of a multicharacter string. Effectively, this is the distance that a cursor or selection rectangle should be "advanced" horizontally to move past the character.

The getAdvanceWidth() method is most useful when building, for example, a text editor where the I-beam cursor or text selection is moved left and right when the arrow keys are pressed. Unfortunately, this does not work for language scripts that support contextual forms.

Ligatures and Contextual Forms

A *ligature* is an arrangement of one or more characters that is displayed as though it were a single glyph (see Figure 18.5). The use of ligatures in traditional printing systems came from the desire to emulate early calligraphic styles. SWT does not provide any special support for this kind of "stylistic" use of ligatures. If a font contains a glyph for a ligature, it can be displayed by specifying its appropriate Unicode value (e.g., the code for the lowercase "fi" ligature is "\uFB01"). However, SWT treats this as a single character, so for example, you could *not* use

```
getAdvanceWidth('f')
```

to place the I-beam cursor between the *f* and the *i* of the "fi" ligature.

Figure 18.5   The "fi" ligature.

Ligatures represent one example of a *contextual form* where the shape of a letter depends on where it appears in the text, both with respect to surrounding characters, and whether it is at the start or end of a line. Some language scripts cannot be properly represented without support for contextual forms.

As of the writing of this book, SWT supports contextual forms for BIDI (bidirectional languages, such as Arabic) on Microsoft Windows only. This support is provided via class BidiUtil in the package *org.eclipse.swt.internal*. The class is *internal* because the investigation to determine whether the functionality it provides is available and appropriate on all platforms is still pending. BidiUtil is used by the StyledText widget to implement functional BIDI editing support. There is also ongoing work on "TextLayout" classes that will be the replacement for this functionality in R3.0.

CHAPTER 19

Images

Images are 2D arrangements of pixels used to represent the kinds of displayable "pictures" found in computers, such as digital photos, desktop backgrounds, icons, and graphical Web page content. In this chapter, we investigate the support that SWT provides for reading, writing, manipulating, and displaying images.

As was true with the color and font support, two main classes are used to represent images within SWT: one to represent the image in a device-independent fashion (class ImageData) and one to represent it in a form suitable for display on a particular device (class Image).

Several methods are provided for loading images from and saving images to files and streams. These vary from easy-to-use API for simple tasks to powerful support that allows arbitrary control over color allocation, reading of multiple-frame images, and incremental loading with notification. The simple mechanisms are covered as they arise in the discussion of the classes Image and ImageData. The more powerful mechanisms are covered in the section Loading Images.

19.1 Class ImageData

Instances of class ImageData contain a device-independent representation of an image. The storage for this representation is allocated within the Java heap. No operating system storage is associated with ImageData instances, and they do not need to be disposed of.

461

The simplest way to create an instance of ImageData is to use one of the following constructors.

ImageData(String fileName)   Constructs a new instance by reading a representation of it from the file with the given name. The SWTException ("i/o error") is thrown if the file could not be read. The SWTException ("Invalid image") is thrown if the contents of the file could not be interpreted as an image.

ImageData(InputStream stream)   Constructs a new instance by reading a representation of it from the given stream. The SWTException ("i/o error") is thrown if an error occurs while reading the stream. The SWTException ("Invalid image") is thrown if the contents of the stream could not be interpreted as an image.

These methods parse the contents of the file or stream to detect which of the standard image file formats (shown in Table 19.1) was used to represent the image. If no errors occur while reading, an instance is returned that contains a representation of that image.[1]

Table 19.1   Supported Image File Formats

Abbreviation	Type Constant	Format Name
GIF	SWT.IMAGE_GIF	Graphics Interchange Format
JPEG	SWT.IMAGE_JPEG	Joint Photographic Experts Group
PNG	SWT.IMAGE_PNG	Portable Network Graphics
TIFF	SWT.IMAGE_TIFF	Tagged Image File Format
BMP	SWT.IMAGE_BMP	Microsoft Windows Bitmap
BMP	SWT.IMAGE_BMP_RLE	Microsoft Windows run-length-encoded Bitmap
ICO	SWT.IMAGE_ICO	Microsoft Windows Icon

---

1. If the file contains more than one image, only the first one is returned. For more on this, see the section Loading Images.

ImageData instances have a large number of public fields that can be directly accessed by application code. Most of these should be treated as read-only, particularly for images that are read from files or streams. Table 19.2 lists the public fields and their meanings.

Table 19.2   Public Fields of Class ImageData

Field	Brief Description (see below for more)
width	Width of the image in pixels
height	Height of the image in pixels
depth	Color depth of the image as described in the Colors chapter
scanlinePad	Each image scan line is a multiple of this many bytes
bytesPerLine	Number of bytes per image scan line
data	Array of bytes containing the pixel data
palette	PaletteData describing the color palette for the image
transparentPixel	Pixel value to make transparent, or –1 for none
maskData	Array of bytes containing a 1-bit mask (icons only)
maskPad	Each mask scan line is a multiple of this many bytes
alphaData	Array of bytes containing 1-byte-per-pixel alpha values
alpha	A single global alpha value for all pixels; overrides alphaData
type	Type of image; one of the type constants from Table 19.1
x	x coordinate of offset to use when painting the image
y	y coordinate of offset to use when painting the image
disposalMethod	Type of transition between images
delayTime	Delay before displaying next image (in hundredths of a second)

There are enough fields in class ImageData to be overwhelming. It helps to think of them as being broken up into three categories: image attributes, transparency, and multi-image animation support.

19.1.1 *ImageData Fields That Are Image Attributes*

Several of the fields in ImageData are used to describe the content and fundamental structure of the image. These are as follows.

type   The *type* field in an image is set to one of the type constants from Table 19.1 when the image is loaded. Note that this describes the external representation of the image, not the format of the ImageData itself.

width and height   The *width* and *height* fields describe the dimensions of the image that the ImageData represents. See the section The *data* Field below, which describes how these are used to control which pixels are drawn.

data, bytesPerLine, and scanLinePad   The *data* field contains the storage for the pixels of the image. The *bytesPerLine* and *scanLinePad* fields describe the alignment of that storage. See the section The *data* Field below, which describes this in full detail.

depth   The *depth* field represents the pixel depth of the image. As was discussed in the Colors chapter, this is the number of bits that will be used to represent a single pixel. Valid depths for ImageData are 1, 2, 4, 8, 16, 24, and 32.

palette   ImageData instances can use either a direct or an indexed color model, controlled by a PaletteData instance stored in the *palette* field. See also the Class PaletteData section for more on this.

For images with an indexed color model, it is possible to obtain directly an array containing the RGB values from the palette by calling the ImageData method.

getRGBs()   Answers an array containing the RGBs from an indexed palette or null if the palette stored in the ImageData uses a direct color model.

The data *Field*

The pixel values that make up the image are stored in the *data* field, which is an array of bytes. Depending on the depth, 1–4 bytes are used to represent the pixels. When the depth is less than 8, multiple pixels can be packed in a single byte.

For largely historical reasons, if the image uses 2 bytes per pixel, the pixels are stored with the least significant byte first. If the image uses 3 or 4 bytes per pixel, the pixels are stored with the most significant bytes first. If your application is going to access the *data* field directly, you just need to know the ordering.

Note that the number of bits used to represent a pixel is always rounded up to the next byte boundary. For example, if the *depth* is 15, two (whole) bytes will be used.

The image is always stored within the *data* field in the same order that is used by the SWT coordinate system. Thus, the first pixel in the data is in the top left corner of the image, followed immediately by the remaining pixels in the first row (increasing *x* coordinate). The *bytesPerLine* field describes how many bytes have been used to represent each row of pixels. This value can be larger than the number of bytes that would be strictly required to represent the image, in which case the *width* field ensures that only the intended pixels are displayed. Similarly, the *height* field controls how many rows of pixels, often called *scanlines*,[2] are drawn.

In some image formats, each row must be a multiple of a given number of bytes. In ImageData, this value is stored in the *scanlinePad* field, and *bytes-PerLine* will always be a multiple of the *scanlinePad*.

The following methods in class ImageData can be used to access the contents of the *data* field without needing to worry about the internal representation.

getPixel(int x, int y)   Returns the pixel value stored at (x,y).

getPixels(int x, int y, int getWidth, int[] pixels, int startIndex)   Copies *getWidth* pixel values starting from (x,y) into the int array starting at offset startIndex.

getPixels(int x, int y, int getWidth, byte[] pixels, int startIndex)   Same as getPixels(int x, int y, int getWidth, int[] pixels, int startIndex) except that it takes a byte array to copy values into. This version is faster but can be used only for images whose depth is 8 or less.

setPixel(int x, int y, int pixel)   Sets the pixel value stored at (x,y) to the given value.

setPixels(int x, int y, int putWidth, int[] pixels, int startIndex)   Copies *putWidth* pixel values from the int array starting at offset startIndex into ImageData starting at (x,y).

---

2. The word *scanline* comes from the way images are displayed on a CRT monitor, where each horizontal sweep of the electron gun "scans a line" of pixels across the tube.

setPixels(int x, int y, int putWidth, byte[] pixels, int startIndex)   Same as setPixels(int x, int y, int putWidth, int[] pixels, int startIndex) except that it takes a byte array to copy values from. This version is faster for images whose depth is 8 or less.

Class PaletteData

The *palette* field of ImageData contains an instance of class PaletteData. The fields in a PaletteData (shown in Table 19.3) describe the palette that is used by a particular instance of ImageData.

Table 19.3   Public Fields of Class PaletteData

Field	Meaning
isDirect	True if palette is direct, false if it is indexed
colors	For an indexed palette, array of RGB instances describing the colors
redMask	Bit mask used to pull the red component of a direct color out
greenMask	Bit mask used to pull the green component of a direct color out
blueMask	Bit mask used to pull the blue component of a direct color out
redShift	Amount to shift red component of a direct color after masking
greenShift	Amount to shift green component of a direct color after masking
blueShift	Amount to shift red component of a direct color after masking

The *isDirect* field controls whether the palette is using a direct or indexed color model and in turn which of the other fields are used.

If *isDirect* is true, then the palette is using a direct color model. In this case, the red, green, and blue components of the color represented by a particular pixel value are computed like this.[3]

```
int r = pixel & redMask;
r = (redShift < 0) ? r >>> -redShift : r << redShift;
int g = pixel & greenMask;
g = (greenShift < 0) ? g >>> -greenShift : g << greenShift;
int b = pixel & blueMask;
b = (blueShift < 0) ? b >>> -blueShift : b << blueShift;
```

---

3. Copied from the implementation of PaletteData.getRGB(int pixel).

As this code shows, the various ...*Shift* values can be negative, implying that the masked value should be rotated right, rather than shifted left. In this way, any direct encoding scheme that can be represented by an integer value can be used.

If *isDirect* is false, the palette is using an indexed color model. In this case, the field *colors* will contain an array of RGB values that describes the colors that are used by the image. Computing the red, green, and blue components of the color represented by a particular pixel is simply a matter of indexing into the *colors* array and returning the resulting RGB.

To simplify mapping between pixel values and colors, the following PaletteData method can be used.

getRGB(int pixel)   Returns an instance of class RGB that represents the color described by the given pixel value.

There is an equivalent method for converting from RGB to a pixel value.

getPixel(RGB color)   Returns the pixel value that is equivalent to the given instance of RGB. For a direct palette, this will construct the answer based on the mask and shift values for each of the colors. For an indexed palette, the colors array will be scanned for an exact match to the given RGB. If an exact match is not found, an SWTException (ERROR_INVALID_ARGUMENT) will be thrown.

Note that for an indexed palette, a simple equality test is used when converting from RGB to pixel value. It is possible to implement a more powerful mapping strategy by scanning the available colors using application code, either by accessing the *colors* field directly or by using getRGBs():

getRGBs()   If *isDirect* is false, this returns the array of RGB instances that is the indexed palette of the receiver. If isDirect is true, this method returns null.

Images on Indexed Color Displays

Applications that attempt to display color images on indexed color displays often end up with unsatisfactory results. This is not an SWT issue but is simply a side effect of the clash between the high color usage of images and, as we discussed in the Colors chapter, the limited number of simultaneous colors that are available on the device.

Each platform handles color allocation and image display differently, but colors in the image that are also in the color table of the display will usually be used directly. This leads to an optimization that is sometimes possible when displaying images that have indexed palettes: By "pre-allocating" the colors from the palette of the image, it is possible to greatly increase the likelihood that those colors will be used when the image is displayed. This can be as simple as creating an instance of class Color for each, something like the following.

```
RGB[] rgbs = theImageData.getRGBs();
Color[] colors = null
if (rgbs != null)
    colors = new Color[rgbs.length; ++i)
    for (int i=0; i<rgbs.length; ++i)
        colors[i] = new Color(display, rgbs[i]);
}
```

Unfortunately, there are several problems with this strategy.

○ Most significantly, modern GUIs have typically already used more colors than are available in the device color table, so attempting to allocate new ones will be ineffective.

○ For the greatest chance of success, the colors that should be pre-allocated first are the ones that are most prevalent or "important" in the image. This is costly to compute in the general case, requiring some kind of caching strategy or application-specific knowledge (e.g., "It's a danger sign, so we need the color red").

○ Direct color images, unless they are carefully constructed, typically use a very large number of colors, making this strategy infeasible for them. In addition, computing the list of colors that are used by the image would require application code to scan each pixel.

○ If more than one image is going to be used, color pre-allocation must take all of the images into account. This is particularly problematic if the set of images being displayed is dynamically varying, as it would be in a Web browser, for example.[4]

○ Colors that have been pre-allocated have to be managed by the application to ensure that they are not disposed of until the image is no longer being displayed but are disposed of as soon as possible to allow other colors to be allocated.

Because of these issues, most applications do not attempt to pre-allocate colors, simply relying on the platform to do the best job that it can.

---

4. Web browsers, if they do color pre-allocation at all, usually allocate a set of colors that are optimally distributed across the visual color range (called a *color cube*). Using these colors and dithering algorithms to transform the image before displaying it is usually good enough for a Web page.

19.1.2 ImageData Fields That Affect Transparency

Transparency is the quality that allows light to pass through something. When a computer image is displayed on a screen (or elsewhere), transparent areas allow the previous contents of the area to remain visible. Partial transparency is also possible, in which case the previous contents are blended with the contents of the image.

Because transparency is represented in different ways in the various image file formats, ImageData objects have several ways to describe transparency.

maskData The *maskData* field is used only in ImageData instances that represent icons (i.e., the type is SWT. IMAGE_ICO). These are usually created by reading them from .ICO format files. The field contains an array of bytes, describing a 1-bit-per-pixel mask, stored in the same order as the pixels in the *data* field. When the icon is displayed, any pixels for which the corresponding bit in the *maskData* is zero will not be painted.

maskPad Each scanline in the maskData should be a multiple of this number of bytes. Code that creates .ICO files by writing out Image-Data instances should use a maskPad of 4.

transparentPixel If a value other than –1 is stored in the *transparentPixel* field, anywhere the pixel value shows up in the image data, that pixel will not be displayed when the image is painted. This form of transparency is frequently found in GIF images with indexed palettes.

alpha Setting the *alpha* field to a value in the range 0 to 255 will cause the *entire* image to vary in transparency from completely invisible (alpha == 0) to completely opaque (alpha == 255). This form of transparency is frequently used to layer images on top of each other. Setting *alpha* to –1 will cause it to be ignored.

alphaData The alphaData is an array of bytes with a byte for each pixel in the *data*. It allows the transparency to be set **for each pixel separately** where, as above, a value of zero means the pixel will be invisible, and 255 means that it is fully visible.

Note that if *alpha* is set to a value from 0 to 255, any values in *alphaData* are ignored. Thus, if you want to override the *alphaData* of an image in your application, you can set *alpha* to 255. If you want the *alphaData* values to be applied, *alpha* should be set to –1.

Class ImageData provides several accessors for the *alphaData* field:

getAlpha(int x, int y)   Returns the *alpha* value for the pixel at (x,y).

getAlphas(int x, int y, int getWidth, byte[] alphas, int startIndex)
Copies *getWidth* alpha values from (x,y) in the alphaData into the byte array starting at offset startIndex.

setAlpha(int x, int y, int alpha)   Sets the *alpha* value for the pixel at (x,y) to the *alpha* parameter, which should be in the range −1 to 255.

setAlphas(int x, int y, int getWidth, byte[] alphas, int startIndex)
Copies *getWidth* alpha values from the byte array starting at offset startIndex into the *alphaData* starting at position (x, y).

Here is a simple example that displays a GIF image to show the effect of the last three kinds of transparency (because maskData is applicable only to icons). The example loads a file containing an image with a diamond-shaped figure in the center on a white background. The pixel value for the white background is pre-set in the file to be the *transparentPixel*. After an image is created from the ImageData, its *transparentPixel* is set to −1, and its *alpha* is set to 150. A second image is created from this. Finally, the *alpha* is set to −1, and the *alphaData* is used to vary the transparency from completely transparent at the top to opaque at the bottom. This is used to create a third image. When the example window is asked to paint, it fills the background with gray, then draws the three images on top.[5] The result is shown in Figure 19.1. Notice that the first image displays only the diamond pattern in the center, that the gray background can be seen through the second image, and that the third image "fades in" from top to bottom. The code looks like the following.

```
public class TransparentImages {

public static final String
    resourceName = "transparent1.gif";

public static void main(String[] args) {
    final ImageData data = new ImageData(
        TransparentImages.class.
            getResourceAsStream(resourceName));
    final Display display = new Display();
    final Image img = new Image(display, data);
    data.transparentPixel = -1;
    data.alpha = 150;
    final Image img2 = new Image(display, data);
    data.alpha = -1;
    byte[] alphas = new byte[data.width];
```

---

5. Image creation and drawing are covered in the Image section. We needed to use them here to show you the result of changing the transparency values.

```
for (int i = 0; i < data.height; ++i) {
    Arrays.fill(alphas, (byte)(255.0*i/data.height));
    data.setAlphas(
        data.x, data.y+i, data.width, alphas, 0);
}
final Image img3 = new Image(display, data);
final Shell shell = new Shell(display, SWT.SHELL_TRIM);
final Color gray =
    display.getSystemColor(SWT.COLOR_GRAY);
shell.addListener(SWT.Paint, new Listener() {
    public void handleEvent(Event event) {
        event.gc.setBackground(gray);
        event.gc.fillRectangle(shell.getClientArea());
        event.gc.drawImage(
            img,
            data.x,data.y,data.width,data.height,
            10,10,data.width,data.height);
        event.gc.drawImage(
            img2,
            data.x,data.y,data.width,data.height,
            20+data.width,10,data.width,data.height);
        event.gc.drawImage(
            img3,
            data.x,data.y,data.width,data.height,
            30+(2*data.width),10,
                data.width,data.height);
    }
});
shell.setText("Load Transparent Images");
shell.setSize(350, 180);
shell.open();
while (!shell.isDisposed()) {
    if (!display.readAndDispatch())
        display.sleep();
}
img.dispose();
img2.dispose();
img3.dispose();
display.dispose();
}}
```

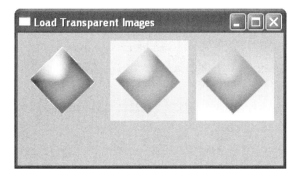

Figure 19.1   transparentPixel, alpha, and alphaData images.

The following two ImageData methods support working with images with transparency.

getTransparencyType()   Returns an *int* value, which will be one of the following constants: SWT.TRANSPARENCY_NONE, SWT.TRANS-PARENCY_MASK, SWT.TRANSPARENCY_PIXEL, or SWT.TRANS-PARENCY_ALPHA.

getTransparencyMask() Returns a new ImageData with a depth of one that represents the mask image for the ImageData. This method will do something reasonable only if the transparency type is SWT.TRANSPARENCY_MASK or SWT.TRANSPARENCY_PIXEL.

19.1.3   *ImageData Fields for Animation Support*

The GIF file format is flexible enough to model simple animations, represented as multiple images in the file, with extra information describing a location to display the image, the display time of each image and the transition to use as subsequent images are displayed. The remaining public fields in an Image-Data, *x, y, delayTime*, and *disposalMethod*, capture this information, allowing you to implement code that displays the animation.

x and y   These fields contain offsets that should be applied when *displaying* the image. For example, if an image was supposed to be drawn at location (100, 100) but the *x* field contained 10 and the *y* field contained 20, the image should be painted at (110, 120). These fields are typically set only for animated GIFs.

delayTime   This is the time to display the current image before transitioning to the next one, measured in hundredths of a second. Some early versions of the GIF spec incorrectly identified the delay time to be a number in seconds. Because displaying a GIF that used the erroneous definition would cause it to animate too quickly to see, applications that display animated GIFs frequently bound the minimum delay time to be 3 or more (i.e., 30 milliseconds per frame).

disposalMethod   This specifies a graphical operation to perform after the current image has been displayed for its full *delayTime* but before the next image is displayed. In other words, it is the graphical operation to perform to transition between images. Table 19.4 shows the possible values for disposalMethod.[6]

Table 19.4   disposalMethod Constants

Constant	Description
SWT.DM_UNSPECIFIED	No transition was specified
SWT.DM_FILL_NONE	Leave the existing image in place
SWT.DM_FILL_BACKGROUND	Fill the area with the background color
SWT.DM_FILL_PREVIOUS	Restore the previous image

Most applications treat the SWT.DM_UNSPECIFIED disposal method as being equivalent to SWT.DM_FILL_NONE. For compatibility with the greatest number of existing animated GIFs, your code should do this, as well.

SWT does not provide direct support for displaying animated GIFs. However, it is simple to implement this kind of animation using the image-drawing routines provided with SWT. We will provide example code that shows how to do this, but first we need to look at class Image in more detail.

19.2   Class Image

Instances of class Image represent images whose storage is organized in a format that is suitable for display on a particular device. Because of their device-specific representation, the operations that SWT provides for Images can be implemented using the native functionality of each platform. This includes making use of hardware graphics accelerators on platforms that support them. Images implement the interface Drawable, so all of the GC drawing methods can be applied to Images.

Image instances hold onto operating system memory, so you must follow the standard life cycle rules for SWT when working with them: If you create an Image, you must call dispose() when you are done with it.

---

6. The name "disposalMethod" and the names of the constants in Table 19.4 are based on the terminology used in the GIF89a specification. Since they were created to represent exactly the concepts from that spec, the same terms were used (modulo the variable case conventions used by SWT). Remember though, that disposalMethod has nothing to do with disposing of the ImageData.

As we saw in the TransparentImages example, an instance of Image can be created from an ImageData using the constructor.

Image(Device device, ImageData data)   Constructs a new instance from the given ImageData.

Two convenience constructors are provided that remove the interim step when creating an instance of Image from ImageData that was constructed from a file or stream:

Image(Device device, String fileName)   Equivalent to Image(device, new ImageData(fileName)).

Image(Device device, InputStream stream)   Equivalent to Image(device, new ImageData(stream)).

Currently, these are for convenience only and do not provide any performance benefit over using the equivalents. However, optimized versions may be provided in the future.

In addition, as is true for the ImageData constructors, if the file or stream contains more than one image, only the first one is used.

In all of the above constructors, the instance of Image that is created is initialized to contain the content from the ImageData. After the image has been created, it can be modified by drawing on it using methods from class GC. If the entire area of the image is going to be modified, for example by using fillRectangle() to set it to a solid color, it is simpler to create a "blank" instance of Image using one of the following constructors.

Image(Device device, int width, int height)   Constructs a new instance that is the given width and height. The entire area of the resulting image will be filled with a single color, typically white.

Image(Device device, Rectangle bounds)   Equivalent to Image(device, bounds.width, bounds.height). Note that the x and y fields of the bounds rectangle are ignored.

The remaining two Image constructors are used when creating special-purpose images to be displayed by user interface controls.

Image(Device device, ImageData source, ImageData mask)   Constructs a special instance, called an *icon image*, based on the source and mask. Icon images have their *type* slot set to SWT.ICON to distinguish them from normal images, which have the *type* set to

SWT.BITMAP. The ImageData parameters must have the same *width* and *height*, and the mask must have *depth* == 1. When the resulting image is displayed, any pixels that were black in both the source and mask will be transparent.

Image(Device device, Image sourceImage, int flag)   Constructs a new instance by copying and (optionally) transforming the sourceImage. The flag should be one of the SWT constants IMAGE_COPY, IMAGE_DISABLE, or IMAGE_GRAY.

Table 19.5 lists the valid flag values and their meanings. On platforms that do not have native support for these operations, something reasonable is done. In any case, the appearance of the resulting image will vary between platforms.

Table 19.5   Image Transformation Constants

Constant	Description
SWT.IMAGE_COPY	Make an identical copy of the original
SWT. IMAGE_DISABLE	Make a copy that looks like a "disabled" image
SWT.IMAGE_GRAY	Make a copy that looks "grayed out"

19.2.1   Image Drawing

Once an image has been constructed, it can be used with the various SWT drawing operations. An image can be either a source (when painting the image on a canvas, for example) or, as was previously mentioned, a target for drawing. Because class Image implements the Drawable interface, any of the GC drawing operations can be used to draw on an image. The line, figure, and text-drawing routines have already been covered, so we will concentrate here on the drawing operations that are specific to images.

To draw an image onto a Drawable, the following GC methods can be used.

drawImage(Image image, int x, int y)   Copies the image onto the Drawable on which the GC was created, starting at position (x, y). The operation replaces the rectangular area of the Drawable defined by (x, y, image.width, image.height) with the pixels from the image.

drawImage(Image image, int srcX, int srcY, int srcWidth, int srcHeight, int destX, int destY, int destWidth, int destHeight) Copies a rectangular area from the image onto a potentially different-sized area of the Drawable on which the GC was created. The operation replaces the rectangular area of the Drawable defined by (destX, destY, destWidth, destHeight) with the pixels in the image defined by the area (srxX, srcY, srcWidth, srcHeight). The rectangular area from the source image is **scaled to fit** the destination area.

Any transparency information that was present in the ImageData that the Image was created from is used when drawing, so it is possible to "blend" the Image with the contents of the Drawable by, for example, varying the alpha-Data of the original ImageData.

Here is an example that shows how to build a trivial "magnifying image viewer" by getting an image from a resource file, then displaying a scaled version of part of it in a shell. In this case, moving the shell selects a different area of the image to display by mapping the position of the shell to a screen position.[7]

```
public class Magnifier {

public static final String resourceName = "Camel.JPG";

public static void main(String[] args) {
    final ImageData imgData = new ImageData(
        Magnifier.class.getResourceAsStream(resourceName));
    final Display display = new Display();
    final Image img = new Image(display, imgData);
    final Color white =
        display.getSystemColor(SWT.COLOR_WHITE);
    final Shell shell = new Shell(display,
        SWT.SHELL_TRIM | SWT.NO_BACKGROUND);
    shell.addListener(SWT.Move, new Listener() {
        public void handleEvent(Event event) {
            shell.redraw();
            shell.update();
        }});
    shell.addListener(SWT.Paint, new Listener() {
        public void handleEvent(Event event) {
            Rectangle r = shell.getClientArea();
            Point p = display.map(shell, null, r.x, r.y);
            r = new Rectangle(
                -p.x + 50, -p.y + 50,
                imgData.width * 2, imgData.height * 2);
            event.gc.drawImage(
                img,
```

---

7. This simple trick works surprisingly well. It is worth trying the example to see it in action.

```
                    0, 0, imgData.width, imgData.height,
                    r.x, r.y, r.width, r.height);
                Region rgn = new Region();
                rgn.add(shell.getClientArea());
                rgn.subtract(r);
                event.gc.setClipping(rgn);
                event.gc.fillRectangle(shell.getClientArea());
                rgn.dispose();
            }});
        shell.setText("Magnifier");
        shell.setBounds(400, 300, 300, 200);
        shell.open();
        while (!shell.isDisposed()) {
            if (!display.readAndDispatch())
                display.sleep();
        }
        img.dispose();
        display.dispose();
    }}
```

The result of invoking this example is shown in Figure 19.2. The magnification factor is currently set to 2. You can change this by modifying the line in the example that is drawn in boldface above.

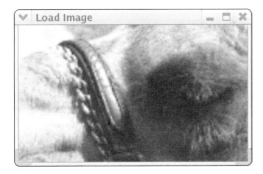

Figure 19.2 Result of running the Magnifier example on GTK.

In addition to drawing an image on a Drawable, it is also possible to perform the inverse operation, copying the existing contents of the Drawable onto an image, using copyArea():

copyArea(Image image, int x, int y) Replaces the contents of the image with the content from the rectangular area bounded by (x, y, image.width, image.height) in the Drawable on which GC was created. If the requested area extends outside the bounds of the Drawable, the corresponding areas in the target image are painted white.

This method can be used whenever a "snapshot" of the state of a Drawable is required. Because displays are Drawables, copyArea() can be used to create a "screen snapshot" if required.

Controls are also Drawables, but when using copyArea with a control, it is critical to remember one very important detail: **Controls use the contents of the display as their "drawing area."** This implies that it is possible to copy only the *visible* area of a control. Any areas of the control that are hidden by other widgets or that extend past the edges of the screen cannot be copied. Attempting to do so will cause the corresponding areas in the destination image to be replaced with white.[8]

Here is an example that shows that only the visible area of the control is copied.

```
public class CopyAreaTest {

Display display;
Color canvasBackground;
Shell shell;
Canvas canvas1, canvas2;

public static void main(String[] args) {
    new CopyAreaTest().run();
}
void run() {
    display = new Display();
    Color c1 = display.getSystemColor(SWT.COLOR_YELLOW);
    Color c2 = display.getSystemColor(SWT.COLOR_CYAN);
    shell = new Shell(display, SWT.SHELL_TRIM);
    canvas1 = new Canvas(shell, SWT.BORDER);
    canvas1.setBackground(c1);
    canvas1.setBounds(10, 10, 150, 100);
    canvas2 = new Canvas(shell, SWT.BORDER);
    canvas2.setBackground(c2);
    canvas2.addPaintListener(new PaintListener() {
        public void paintControl(PaintEvent e) {
            GC gc = new GC(canvas1);
            Rectangle r = canvas1.getClientArea();
            Image img = new Image(display,
                r.width, r.height);
            gc.copyArea(img, r.x, r.y);
            e.gc.drawImage(img, 20, 20);
            img.dispose();
            gc.dispose();
        }});
    canvas2.setBounds(40, 60, 190, 140);
```

---

8. If you decide to use copyArea() on a control, you need to test your application carefully to ensure that it will do what you expect. Depending on the code, the behavior can be inconsistent between platforms. For example, in some circumstances, on Microsoft Windows, copying outside the visible area of a control can copy the contents of the underlying widget instead of filling with white.

```
canvas2.moveAbove(null);
shell.setSize(300, 240);
shell.setText("Copy Area Test");
shell.open();
while (!shell.isDisposed()) {
    if (!display.readAndDispatch())
        display.sleep();
}
display.dispose();
}}
```

The example creates two overlapping instances of Canvas. When the paint listener for the front canvas is invoked, it attempts to use copyArea() to copy the contents of the back canvas, and then uses drawImage() to paint the snapshot onto the front canvas. Figure 19.3 shows that the overlapping area is undefined (in this case, it is white).

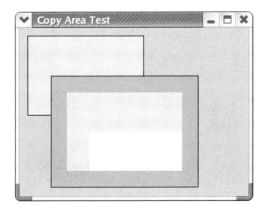

Figure 19.3   Result of running the CopyAreaTest example on Motif.

Removing Transparency from an Image

It is occasionally necessary to convert an image that has transparent areas into one that does not. One situation where this arises occurs when setImage() is used with button and label controls: On some platforms, images with transparency will not display properly when set as the image for a label or a button.[9]

You might think that the obvious way to remove the transparency from an image would be to fill a second image with the desired background (let's say, for simplicity, a solid color), then paint the original image onto the second

9.   In fact, "icon images" (images whose *type* field is SWT.ICON) were introduced to handle this case. See the constructor descriptions in the Class Image section for more information.

image, and copy the second image back onto the first. The code would look something like the following.

```
Rectangle r = imageWithTransparency.getBounds();
Image img = new Image(display, r.width, r.height);
GC gc = new GC(img);
gc.setBackground(backgroundColor);
gc.fillRectangle(r);
gc.drawImage(imageWithTransparency, 0, 0);
gc.copyArea(imageWithTransparency, 0, 0);
gc.dispose();
```

Unfortunately, this code will not work. The problem is that the transparency information in the original image is *not modified* by the call to copy-Area(). In other words, copying the nontransparent image back onto the original will have no effect on the original image.

It is important to remember this constraint when working with Image: In general, once an instance of Image has been created, it is not possible to modify the fields that describe its transparency. If your application needs to work with transparency, it must work with the ImageData instances that the images are created from. This is reasonable, if inconvenient, because the only way to create an Image that has transparent areas is to start from an ImageData that does also. In the Cursors chapter, there are several examples that manipulate ImageData instances, including their transparency, in order to create custom cursors.

Although there is no way to change the transparency of an image in general, there *is* actually one kind of Image that can have its transparency modified, using the following Image method.

setBackground(Color background)   For images that were created from ImageData that used the *transparentPixel* field to describe transparency, this method will replace any areas that were previously transparent with the given background color. It is an error to call this method more than once on the same Image instance or with null.

This method was specifically implemented to allow images with transparent backgrounds, which were created from simple GIF files, to be set into buttons and labels. The code to do this would look something like the following.

```
imageWithTransparency =
    new Image(display, "something.gif");
Button b = new Button(shell, SWT.PUSH);
imageWithTransparency.setBackground(b.getBackground());
b.setImage(imageWithTransparency);
```

The following method will return the color that would be replaced if set-Background() was going to do anything.

getBackground()   For images that were created from ImageData that used the *transparentPixel* field to describe transparency, this method will return the color that the transparentPixel maps to. For other images, this method returns null.

Note that the setBackground() method *modifies* the image to remove the transparency so that, unlike most accessors,

```
anImage.setBackground(anImage.getBackground());
```

does have an effect.

19.3 Animation

In the ImageData Fields for Animation Support section, we noted that we would provide an example of how to display animated images. Based on the information presented there and what we have learned above, we can now implement code that displays the animation.

To begin with, let us assume we are given an array of ImageData instances that represent the frames of the animation. In addition, each ImageData instance will have its *delayTime* field set to control how long the frame should be displayed and its *disposalMethod* field set to describe how to transition between that frame and the next. Our task is to display the resulting animation on a canvas.

One possible algorithm to display the animation would be as follows.

1. Get the first ImageData in the array.

2. Convert the ImageData to an image and display it on the canvas.

3. Delay for the time set in the *delayTime* field of the ImageData.

4. If the current image is the last one, we are done; otherwise, get the next ImageData from the array.

5. If the *disposalMethod* field is SWT.DM_UNSPECIFIED[10] or SWT.DM_FILL_NONE, go to step 2.

6. If the *disposalMethod* field is SWT.DM_FILL_BACKGROUND, fill the canvas with the background color, then go to step 2.

---

10. Refer back to the ImageData Fields for Animation Support section for the description of these constants.

Leaving aside the SWT.DM_FILL_PREVIOUS disposal method for a moment, let us consider this algorithm.

The intent of the SWT.DM_FILL_NONE disposal method is to leave the previous frame visible so that the next image can be painted on top of it. The algorithm implements this behavior but runs into a problem if the visible area of the canvas increases. Say, for example, that the canvas is contained within a shell that is hidden behind some other shell. If the shell containing the canvas is brought to the front of the desktop, the canvas will need to draw the entire "current frame" of the animation. If the current frame was created using SWT.DM_FILL_NONE, the algorithm would have to redraw the previous frame, then draw the current image on top of it. In fact, if the previous frame were also constructed with SWT.DM_FILL_NONE, the algorithm would have to display the frame before that, and so forth.

It seems as though it would be a good idea to remember the current frame of the animation as it is created, so that it could be used to repaint the canvas as its visibility changes. As we saw in the Image Drawing section, copyArea() could be used to make a snapshot of the *visible area* of the canvas but unfortunately, at the time it would need to be called, the canvas may not be visible—this is exactly the problem.

The normal solution to this is to use *double buffering*. Rather than drawing the current frame of animation directly on the canvas, it is created on a separate image. Any time that the Canvas needs to be painted, the "buffered" copy is drawn onto it with drawImage().

The SWT.DM_FILL_PREVIOUS disposal method adds another wrinkle to the problem. It indicates that the current frame should be replaced with the previous frame before drawing the new image on top of it. Applying the same logic as for SWT.DM_FILL_NONE, this could be implemented using the double-buffering strategy by keeping the last *two* frames of animation.

There is one further optimization that can be made to the algorithm. If we assume that the number of frames in the animation is relatively small and that it is going to be shown more than once (say, in a continuous loop, or each time a button is pressed), it would make sense to keep *all* of the buffered frames. Because any given frame will be the same each time the animation is shown, holding onto it will mean that the time to draw it is incurred only once. Of course, if the number of frames or the size of them individually is large, keeping all of them around may require too much space. In this case, it would be better to use the form of the algorithm that buffers only two frames.

For our example code, we will pre-render all of the frames. This is desirable—for demonstration purposes, at least—because it allows us to separate the code that renders the frames from the code that draws them.

The following method takes an array of ImageData instances and returns an array of Image instances that contain the animation frames.

```
Image[] convertImageDataToImages (
        ImageData[] ids,
        Color defaultBackground)
{
    if (ids == null) return null;
    Image[] answer = new Image[imageData.length];

    // Step 1: Determine the size of the resulting images.
    int width = 0, height = 0;
    for (int i = 0; i < imageData.length; ++i) {
        ImageData id = imageData[i];
        width = Math.max(width, id.x + id.width);
        height = Math.max(height, id.y + id.height);
    }

    // Step 2: Construct each image.
    int transition = SWT.DM_FILL_BACKGROUND;
    for (int i = 0; i < imageData.length; ++i) {
        ImageData id = imageData[i];
        answer[i] = new Image(display, width, height);
        GC gc = new GC(answer[i]);

        // Do the transition from the previous image.
        switch (transition) {
            case SWT.DM_FILL_NONE:
            case SWT.DM_UNSPECIFIED:
                // Start from last image.
                gc.drawImage(answer[i-1], 0, 0);
                break;
            case SWT.DM_FILL_PREVIOUS:
                // Start from second last image.
                gc.drawImage(answer[i-2], 0, 0);
                break;
            default:
                // DM_FILL_BACKGROUND or anything else,
                // just fill with default background.
                gc.setBackground(defaultBackground);
                gc.fillRectangle(0, 0, width, height);
                break;
        }

        // Draw the current image and clean up.
        Image img = new Image(display, id);
        gc.drawImage(
            img,
            0, 0, id.width, id.height,
            id.x, id.y, id.width, id.height);
        img.dispose();
        gc.dispose();

        // Compute the next transition.
        // Special case: Can't do DM_FILL_PREVIOUS on the
```

```
        // second image since there is no "second last"
        // image to use.
        transition = id.disposalMethod;
        if (i == 0 && transition == SWT.DM_FILL_PREVIOUS)
            transition = SWT.DM_FILL_NONE;
    }
    return answer;
}
```

Step one of the code computes the maximum size that the images would have to be in order to display all of the ImageData instances: The x and y offsets of each ImageData are added to their width and height, and the maximum values are remembered. The x and y fields indicate where each should be drawn, as was previously noted. For the animation, this allows us to overlay smaller images, positioned at arbitrary locations, on top of earlier ones.

Step two computes the array of frames. For each frame, it performs the following steps.

1. It creates a new instance of Image to represent the frame.

2. It fills in the new instance based on the disposalMethod of the *previous* frame (stored in the local variable *transition*). For SWT.DM_FILL _NONE or SWT.DM_UNSPECIFIED, it copies the contents of the last Image instance. For SWT.DM_FILL_PREVIOUS, it copies the contents of the second to last Image instance. For anything else, it fills the new image with the background color.[11]

3. It copies the contents of the current ImageData onto the new Image instance.

Given the array of images that describes each of the animation frames, drawing them is easy. The canvas that will show the animation is set up to draw the current frame whenever it is asked to paint, as in the following.

```
canvas.addPaintListener(new PaintListener() {
    public void paintControl(PaintEvent e) {
        Image img = getCurrentImage();
        if (img == null) {
            // Erase the whole canvas
            e.gc.setBackground(canvasBackground);
            e.gc.fillRectangle(canvas.getClientArea());
        } else {
            // Display the image, then erase the rest
            e.gc.drawImage(img, drawX, drawY);
            Region theRest = new Region(display);
```

---

11. For the first frame, the code presets the transition to be DM_FILL_BACKGROUND, forcing the frame to be initially filled with the background color.

```
                        e.gc.getClipping(theRest);
                        theRest.subtract(drawBounds);
                        e.gc.setClipping(theRest);
                        e.gc.setBackground(canvasBackground);
                        e.gc.fillRectangle(canvas.getClientArea());
                        theRest.dispose();
                    }
        }});
```

This will handle both switching between animation frames and redrawing the canvas as its visible area changes. The getCurrentImage() method uses the *int* stored in the field *currentImage* to get one of the images to display.

```
protected Image getCurrentImage() {
    if (images == null) return null;
    return images[currentImage];
}
```

The method getDelayTime() answers the value of the *delayTime* field of the current ImageData, converted to milliseconds. In order to handle GIF files that have abnormally short delay times set (as described in the ImageData Fields for Animation Support section), the method optionally adds in a 30-millisecond delay if the system property SLOW_ANIMATION is set.

```
int getDelayTime() {
    if (SLOW_ANIMATION)
        return imageData[currentImage].delayTime * 10 + 30;
    else
        return imageData[currentImage].delayTime * 10;
}
```

Finally, the example code uses timerExec[12] to schedule when each image should be displayed. Switching to the next animation frame is simply a matter of incrementing the *currentImage* field and asking Canvas to redraw itself:

```
void startAnimationTimer() {
    // If there is only one image, don't start a timer.
    if (images.length < 2) return;
    display.timerExec(
        getDelayTime(),
        new Runnable() {
            public void run() {
                if (canvas.isDisposed()) return;
                currentImage =
                    (currentImage+1) % images.length;
                drawCurrentImage();
```

---

12. See the section Timers in the Display chapter.

```
                    // If this is the last image in the
                    // animation, check if we are looping
                    // forever, or still have more loops to
                    // do. If not, don't restart the timer.
                    if (currentImage+1 == images.length &&
                            animationLoopCount != 0 &&
                                --animationLoopCount <= 0)
                            return;
                    display.timerExec(getDelayTime(), this);
            }});
    }
```

That is it. The code is relatively compact but contains enough ideas that were not covered to be worth studying further. In the source code that is provided with this book, all of the above comes from the ShowAnimation.java example in package *part2*. ShowAnimation prompts for an animated GIF to display, loads the images contained in it, then displays the animation. The next section looks at how to load images, including those that represent multiple frames of animation.

19.4   Loading Images

In the Class ImageData and Class Image sections, we described how to load images from files and input streams, using constructors. These constructors are sufficient for many applications, but they suffer from several limitations.

○ Some image file formats, such as GIF, are capable of representing several images in a single file. The constructors can access only the first image.

○ The constructors only load images. Many applications also need to *save* images, that is, to be able to create image files from images that they have produced internally.

○ Once the constructors have been invoked, they do not return until the image has been completely read from the file or stream. Because of this, they cannot be used in applications such as Web browsers, which incrementally display images as they are being loaded.

The ImageLoader class was implemented to provide these missing capabilities.

19.4.1   *Class ImageLoader*

Instances of class ImageLoader represent the process of loading or saving image files and streams. No operating system storage is associated with Image-

Loader instances, and they do not need to be disposed of. They are not associated with a display and can be created and used in any thread.

ImageLoader instances can be reused to load and/or save multiple images but support only one operation at a time. In other words, at any given moment, an instance of ImageLoader can be either loading from a single source or saving to a single destination. Once that operation has completed, it can perform another operation.

Class ImageLoader provides a single constructor.

ImageLoader() Constructs a new ImageLoader instance, which is ready to load and save images.

Instances have a number of public fields that can be directly accessed by application code. Table 19.6 lists the public fields and their meanings.

Table 19.6 Public Fields of Class ImageLoader

Field	*Brief Description (see below for more)*
data	Array of ImageData instances containing the images
backgroundPixel	GIF89a Background Color Index
logicalScreenHeight	GIF89a Logical Screen Height
logicalScreenWidth	GIF89a Logical Screen Width
repeatCount	Number of times to display an animation

After a load operation completes, the *data* field will contain an array of ImageData instances, one for each image that was stored in the file. To save one or more images, you would first set the *data* field to an array containing ImageData instances that represent them, then invoke the save operation.

The *backgroundPixel, logicalScreenHeight,* and *logicalScreenWidth* fields contain information that is available as part of the GIF89a standard. They are useful only when loading from a GIF source, in which case they are set to the corresponding values. The *backgroundPixel* is the index into the color table of the color that describes the transparent areas for each image.

The *logicalScreenHeight* and *logicalScreenWidth* fields describe the width and height of the area that should be used to display the images, which is not strictly related to the sizes of the images contained in the file. The fields may demarcate an area that is larger than would be required to display any of the images or a smaller area indicating that the result should be clipped.[13]

The *repeatCount* field holds the number of times to display an animation that was loaded. This field is also useful only when loading GIFs. It is set to the value stored in a particular GIF Application Extension Block defined by Netscape 2.0 (which has since become something of a standard) if it is present. A value of zero in this field implies that the animation should loop indefinitely.

19.4.2   Loading Multiple Images

The simplest use of an ImageLoader is just to load all of the images from a file or stream using one of the following methods.

> **load(InputStream stream)**   Returns an array of ImageData instances that were created by reading the contents of the stream, which must be in one of the standard image file formats (shown in the Class ImageData section in Table 19.1). It also sets the *data* field to the result before returning it.

> **load(String filename)**   Returns an array of ImageData instances that were created by reading the contents of the file named by the parameter, which must be in one of the standard image file formats (shown in the Class ImageData section in Table 19.1). It also sets the *data* field to the result before returning it.

In the Animation section, we carefully avoided describing the code that created the array of ImageData instances that were rendered by the convert-ImageDataToImages() method. As an example of how to use load(), here is the image loading code from the ShowAnimation example.

```
boolean loadImages(String fileName) {
    if (fileName == null) return false;
    try {
        loader = new ImageLoader();
        imageData = loader.load(fileName);
        if (imageData.length == 0) return false;
        images = convertImageDataToImages(
```

---

13. In the Animation section, we described code that computed the size of the area required to draw all of the images in their entirety based on the *x, y, width,* and *height* fields of each ImageData. Although it would have been more correct to use logicalScreenHeight and logicalScreenWidth for this, by computing the size in the code, we avoided talking about the ImageLoader class, which had not yet been described. The ShowAnimation2.java example in package *part2* is a minor variation of ShowAnimation.java that uses logicalScreenHeight and logicalScreenWidth.

```
            imageData,
            canvasBackground);
      animationLoopCount = loader.repeatCount;
      drawBounds = images[0].getBounds();
      drawBounds.x += drawX;
      drawBounds.y += drawY;
   } catch (SWTException t) {
      System.err.println("Got an exception:" + t);
      t.printStackTrace(System.err);
      return false;
   }
   return true;
}
```

Note that the actual image loading code is trivial. It simply creates an image loader, uses it to load the named file (as provided by FileDialog), then checks that some images were loaded.

19.4.3   Saving Images

Saving images with ImageLoader[14] is also easy. Class ImageLoader provides two methods for saving images.

> **save(OutputStream stream, int format)** Converts the array of ImageData instances, stored in the *data* field of the ImageLoader, into the external image file format specified by the parameter, then writes it to the specified output stream. The format parameter should be one of the file format constants shown in Table 19.1 in the Class Image-Data section.

> **save(String filename, int format)** Converts the array of ImageData instances, stored in the *data* field of the ImageLoader, into the external image file format specified by the parameter, then writes it to the named file. The format parameter should be one of the file format constants shown in Table 19.1 in the Class ImageData section.

For both methods, the ImageData instances must have a color depth and dimensions that are compatible with the file format that is specified, or an SWTException (various) will occur. However, if the *data* array contains multiple images but the file format can represent only one, ImageLoader will silently choose the first image to save.

---

14. Yes, it was an unfortunate name choice.

Only One to a Customer

As of the time this book was written, ImageLoader supports writing out only a single ImageData instance, regardless of the format that is specified. This means, for example, that it is not possible to construct animated GIF images using SWT.

The API *is* specified in terms of an array of ImageData instances, however, and it would make sense to allow saving of multiple images for the formats that support it. This is likely to happen eventually, but if you are keen to see it, the best thing to do is *get involved*. Talk to the committers on the SWT team, enter bug reports, and create patches to fix the problem. Help us to make the tool *you* want to use!

This code fragment shows how to save an image (stored in the variable *image*).[15]

```
ImageLoader loader = new ImageLoader();
loader.data = new ImageData[] {image.getImageData()};
loader.save(filename, SWT.IMAGE_JPEG);
```

The JPEG file format is a compressed representation, where the amount of compression that is performed is specified in terms of a quality factor. The JPEG encoder used by SWT has a fixed quality factor of 75, which provides a reasonable balance between image size and quality.

19.4.4   Using a Background Thread to Load Images

For applications that simply need to load a selection of small images from the file system (to represent icons in their user interfaces, for example), it is reasonable to load all of the images as part of the application initialization code. This would be an issue, however, if the time to load the images became large, because the application would be unresponsive until loading was complete. Several factors can affect the loading time, including the following.

○ The application requires many images.

○ The individual images are quite large.

○ The images are stored on a slow or unpredictable source, such as a network connection.

---

15. This code can be found in the SavePoly.java example in package *part2*. The example builds an image of a 5-pointed star, then saves it to the file Star.jpeg.

As was stated in the introduction to the Class ImageLoader section,
ImageLoader instances do not need to be run from the user interface thread;
one possible solution, if the loading time becomes problematic, is to use a second thread to load the images, something like the following.[16]

```
loading = true;
loader = new ImageLoader();
message("loading");
new Thread(new Runnable() {
    public void run() {
        try {
            ImageData[] answer = loader.load(str);
            if (answer == null) return;
            images = new Image[answer.length];
            lastImageIndex = answer.length - 1;
            for (int i = 0; i <= lastImageIndex; ++i)
                updateImage(i, answer[i]);
        } catch (Throwable t) {
            message(t.toString());
        } finally {
            loading = false;
            message(null);
        }
    }
}).start();
```

Because the images are being loaded by a second thread, the user interface
thread is free to run the event loop, keeping the user interface responsive. For
comparison to another version of this code in the next section, here are a few
of the more salient details of this example.

❍ The variable *loading* can be used by code in the user interface thread to
   decide whether the images are still being loaded.

❍ The *images* variable is a slot that holds the array of loaded Image
   instances.

❍ The updateImage() method creates the Image instance and stores it into
   images, then updates a canvas to show it, as shown below.

```
void updateImage(int index, ImageData imageData) {
    final int idx = index;
    final ImageData id = imageData;
    display.syncExec(new Runnable() {
        public void run() {
            images[idx] = new Image(display, id);
            int x = shiftAmount(idx);
```

---

16. This code comes from the BackgroundLoadImage.java example in package *part2*. Background-
    LoadImage provides a text field to enter a URL and a canvas to display the image(s) that are
    loaded from it.

```
                              canvas.redraw(x,0,id.width,id.height,false);
                              canvas.update();
                     }
           });
}
```

○ The code in updateImage() uses syncExec() to allow the user interface to be updated from the image loading thread.

○ Calling redraw() followed by update() has the effect of forcing the image to be displayed before the method returns.

○ Finally, for image sources that contain more than one image, the example displays the images in a horizontal row in the canvas. The shiftAmount() method returns the *x* coordinate of the position where the image should be displayed.

Incremental Display

One of the features of modern Web browsers is the ability to display incomplete representations of images incrementally as they are being loaded. If you have ever seen an image on a Web page that appeared quickly but was initially fuzzy, becoming clearer over time, you have seen this effect.

The code in the previous section keeps the user interface responsive, but it does not provide any kind of incremental display. In this section, we describe how to implement incremental feedback using class ImageLoader and modify the example code to provide it.

Incremental display in SWT is based on the fact that the image formats themselves support incremental loading by modeling each of the (increasingly accurate) partial images in their representation. For GIF images, this support is called *interlacing*, and the equivalent for JPEG images is called *progressive JPEG*. Each time one of the partial images has been completely read by Image-Loader, it notifies any listeners that have been added using the standard listener-and-event mechanism.

addImageLoaderListener(ImageLoaderListener listener)   Adds a listener to the list of listeners that will be notified when an image has been partially loaded.

removeImageLoaderListener(ImageLoaderListener listener) Removes the listener from the list of listeners that will be notified when an image has been partially loaded.

The ImageLoaderListener interface declares a single method that is called whenever the partially loaded image is available to be displayed.

imageDataLoaded(ImageLoaderEvent event)   Provides incremental feedback during image loading based on the information contained in the event.

ImageLoaderEvents contain three fields, as shown in Table 19.7.

Table 19.7   Public Fields of Class ImageLoaderEvent

Field	Description (also see below)
imageData	ImageData for the image being loaded
incrementCount	Number of times this image was updated
endOfImage	True if the image has been completely loaded

The *imageData* field contains a representation of the image that is being loaded. Successive events will contain increasingly accurate representations (and increasing *incrementCount* values) until the final form is provided. When the *imageData* field contains the final form of the image, the *endOfImage* flag is also set to true. At this point, it is the responsibility of the application to remember that if another event is received, it will be for the *next image* in a multiple image source.

It is important to note that the ImageLoader does not guarantee that an event will be generated for all possible partial representations, nor does it guarantee that an event will be sent when the last image is completely loaded. For this reason, application code should always rely on the return result of the load() method (or the value of the *data* slot in ImageLoader) as the definitive version of the images.

To see how this all fits together, here is an updated version of the background image loading code from the previous section.[17]

```
loading = true;
loader = new ImageLoader();
loader.addImageLoaderListener(
        new ImageLoaderListener() {
    public void imageDataLoaded(ImageLoaderEvent e) {
        updateCurrentImage(e.imageData);
        if (e.endOfImage)
```

---

17. This code comes from the IncrementalLoadImage.java example in package *part2*. Incremental-LoadImage behaves exactly like BackgroundLoadImage except that it provides incremental feedback while loading.

```
                        ++lastImageIndex;
        }
    });
    message("loading");
    new Thread(new Runnable() {
        public void run() {
            try {
                lastImageIndex = 0;
                ImageData[] answer = loader.load(str);
                for (int i = 0; i < answer.length; ++i)
                    if (images[i] == null)
                        updateImage(i, answer[i]);
                loading = false;
            } catch (Throwable t) {
                message(t.toString());
            } finally {
                loading = false;
                message(null);
            }
        }
    }).start();
```

The obvious difference between the two versions is that this one hooks the image loader listener. Notice that the listener calls updateCurrentImage(), which calls updateImage() with the index of the image that is currently being loaded.

In the new version, the index of the loading image is maintained in the slot *lastImageIndex*. Remember that in the previous version, *lastImageIndex* was set after all images were loaded to be the final size. In this version, it is set to zero initially and is incremented each time an event is received whose *endOfImage* flag is true.

Because the updateImage() method may now be called multiple times for each image, it needs to handle the case where the slot in the *images* array may already contain an image. If so, it simply disposes of the old version, because the ImageData it has just been given is a more accurate representation of it.

```
void updateImage(int index, ImageData imageData) {
    final int idx = index;
    final ImageData id = imageData;
    display.syncExec(new Runnable() {
        public void run() {
            ensureSpace(idx);
            if (images[idx] != null)
                images[idx].dispose();
            images[idx] = new Image(display, id);
            int x = shiftAmount(idx);
            canvas.redraw(x,0,id.width,id.height,false);
            canvas.update();
        }
    });
}
```

The ensureSpace() call handles the case where the *images* array is not large enough to hold the image. This could not happen in the previous version, because the *images* array was not constructed until all images had been read. In the new version, the array is initialized to be a reasonable size but must be prepared to grow if too many images are loaded.

The changes that are required in your code to provide incremental feedback are relatively simple. The two versions of the example code were carefully constructed to identify the nature of these changes, and we hope it has done so. One aspect of the problem that was not covered is the trade-off between incremental display and loading time. Obviously, the more work that is done *while* the image is being loaded, the longer the loading will take. This can be managed by bounding the number of times that updates are performed, based, for example, on the time since the last update occurred.

In the next chapter, we look at cursors, which are used to set the appearance of the hardware mouse cursor.

CHAPTER 20

Cursors

With the exception of Windows CE, all of the supported SWT platforms provide an on-screen pointer called a *cursor*. Typically, the cursor is positioned by moving a mouse, trackball, or other similar input device, but its position may also be set by application code. Cursors are described by two attributes, *shape* and *hotspot*.

shape   The *shape* of a cursor is its image on the screen. Platforms may restrict the number of colors that are available to draw the shape, the valid sizes for the shape, or both.

hotspot   The *hotspot* is the point within the bounds of the cursor shape that is aligned with the on-screen pointer. Thus, when mouse events occur, the point in the event is the point, relative to the screen, of the hotspot for the visible cursor.

In SWT, cursors are modeled by instances of class Cursor. Cursor instances hold onto operating system memory, so you must follow the standard life cycle rules for SWT when working with them: If you create the Cursor, you must call dispose() when you are done with it.

20.1   System Cursors

Operating systems that use cursors provide a selection of standard ones, called *system cursors*, which are intended to represent various states of the user interface. There are several good reasons for using system cursors.

○ Applications that display system cursors when they are in a corresponding state provide useful information to the user, allowing them to apply their knowledge of the operating system to the specific application.

○ If newer versions of the operating system provide cursors with a different shape, the application will display the new cursor, preventing it from looking dated. A similar problem arises when a new operating system "skin" that contains custom cursors is used.

○ The system cursors provided by some platforms are more interesting than the ones that applications can create. For example, they may be animated.

○ Applications that create their own cursors must either restrict the shapes they use to be ones that can be displayed on all platforms or write platform-specific code.

SWT provides access to the system cursor shapes using the following constructor.

Cursor(Device device, int style)   Constructs an instance that represents the platform equivalent of the cursor described by the style parameter, which must be one of the constants described in Table 20.1. If the platform does not provide the specified cursor, a reasonable alternative is returned.

Table 20.1   System Cursor Constants

Constant	Meaning	Typical Shape
SWT.CURSOR_ARROW	Default shape	Arrow pointing diagonally up left
SWT.CURSOR_WAIT	Application is busy	Hourglass or watch
SWT.CURSOR_APPSTARTING	Application is active but still available	Hourglass overlayed on an arrow
SWT. CURSOR_CROSS	For targeting x-y positions	Crosshairs, plus sign

Table 20.1   System Cursor Constants (continued)

Constant	Meaning	Typical Shape
SWT.CURSOR_HELP	Application will provide help on selected item	Question mark
SWT.CURSOR_UPARROW	Selection from below	Arrow pointing up
SWT.CURSOR_IBEAM	For selecting text	Vertical line with marks at each end
SWT.CURSOR_NO	Capability is not available	Circle with a line through it
SWT.CURSOR_HAND	For moving items on screen	Hand
SWT.CURSOR_SIZExx	Resizing cursors (see below)	Arrows indicating resizing direction

The *resizing cursors* are used when the user is changing the dimensions of an on-screen object, such as a control or an application-drawn shape, by dragging one of its edges. They are usually represented either as an image of the edge or corner being dragged, or as one or more arrows showing the directions in which size changes can be made. Table 20.2 shows the resizing cursor constants and their uses.

Table 20.2   Resizing Cursor Constants

Constant	Meaning
SWT.CURSOR_SIZEALL	All directions
SWT.CURSOR_SIZENESW	Two-directional top right to bottom left
SWT.CURSOR_SIZENS	Two-directional top to bottom
SWT.CURSOR_SIZENWSE	Two-directional top left to bottom right
SWT.CURSOR_SIZEWE	Two-directional left to right
SWT.CURSOR_SIZEN	Vertically starting from top edge
SWT.CURSOR_SIZES	Vertically starting from bottom edge
SWT.CURSOR_SIZEE	Horizontally starting from right edge
SWT.CURSOR_SIZEW	Horizontally starting from left edge
SWT.CURSOR_SIZENE	Diagonally starting from top right corner

Table 20.2   Resizing Cursor Constants (continued)

Constant	Meaning
SWT.CURSOR_SIZESE	Diagonally starting from bottom right corner
SWT.CURSOR_SIZESW	Diagonally starting from bottom left corner
SWT.CURSOR_SIZENW	Diagonally starting from top left corner

20.1.1   Seeing the System Cursors

In the code that is provided with the book, there is an example called *System-Cursors.java* in package *part2*. This example opens a shell containing a vertical stack of label controls. Each one has its text set to the name of one of the system cursor constants and its cursor set to the corresponding cursor. By passing the mouse pointer over the labels, you can see what the cursors look like on the platform you are running on.

The code to implement the SystemCursors example is not particularly interesting, so it is not reproduced in its entirety here. Essentially, after looking up each of the cursors by name, it runs this loop, which creates and configures the label widgets.

```
for (int i=0; i < cursorNames.length; ++i) {
    label = new Label(shell, SWT.BORDER);
    label.setText(cursorNames[i]);
    label.setCursor(cursors[i]);
}
```

Figure 20.1 shows what SystemCursors looks like when run on one of the authors' Linux machines. In this case, the mouse pointer is over the CURSOR_WAIT label, which is actually displaying an animated, full-color hourglass.

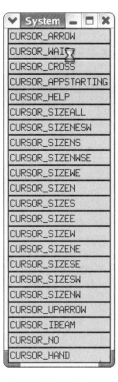

Figure 20.1   The result of running the SystemCursors example on X/Motif.

20.2   **Custom Cursors**

For situations where none of the system cursors is appropriate, SWT also provides a mechanism for creating cursors with arbitrary shapes. Class Cursor implements two constructors that take ImageData instances[1] for this purpose. The first one is as follows.

> **Cursor(Device device, ImageData source, ImageData mask, int hotspotX, int hotspotY)**   Constructs a cursor that has a shape based on the source and mask ImageData instances and whose hotspot is at the point (hotspotX, hotspotY). The source and mask must have the same dimensions and a depth of 1. The mask can also be null, in which case the source must be an icon, as defined in the Class Image

---

1. For consistency, the constructors should have taken instances of a "CursorData" class that would provide the device-independent representation of a cursor. They do not. Remember that Image-Data instances are used instead.

section of the Images chapter, or have a transparent pixel. Many platforms restrict the size of the cursor that can be created using this constructor.

This constructor hooks into low-level, operating system-specific cursor drawing routines that vary significantly from platform to platform. Because it uses the low-level routines, it can, on platforms that support them, produce a style of cursor that has four possible pixel values:

1. Black pixels

2. White pixels

3. Transparent pixels

4. "Inverting" pixels

The definition of *inverting* in this case also varies from platform to platform but typically either toggles black and white pixels under the cursor or inverts pixels under the cursor based on the color table (similar to setXOR-Mode()). In any case, this mode is largely a holdover from the earliest days of graphical user interfaces, where it was used because it was easy to implement, rather than a good user interface design.

It is effectively impossible to create a cursor that has the same appearance on all platforms using the above constructor, so **it should be avoided**.[2] It is much easier to use this second Cursor constructor to create portable applications.

Cursor(Device device, ImageData source, int hotspotX, int hotspotY)
Constructs an instance that has a shape based on the source Image-Data and whose hotspot is at the point (hotspotX, hotspotY).

Cursors built using this constructor are not displayed using the low-level cursor handling routines. Because of this, they cannot show the inverting pixels that were described above. However, the image that is used to create the cursor can be much larger when using this constructor, and on all platforms other than the Macintosh, the result will display at the full size. On Mac OS X, the cursor handling routines used by SWT do not handle images larger than 16 by 16 pixels. On this platform, the image is scaled down to that size before being displayed.

---

2. If you absolutely must see this API in action, you can look at the CustomCursorWithMask.java example in package *part2*. This example is a variant of the other *CustomCursor* examples, but running it produces significantly different effects on each platform.

The remainder of this chapter shows how to create custom cursors using the second constructor.

20.2.1   *Black and White Cursors*

For almost all uses, a custom cursor that is drawn using black, white, and transparent pixels is efficacious. All of the desktop platforms that SWT supports provide the ability to display this kind of cursor, so good application portability can be achieved. Remember though, that the best strategy is still to use the system cursors wherever possible.

In this section, we will discuss an example that starts with a color image, produces a black/white/transparent image from it, then uses that to create a cursor. We start from a color image, in this case, both to demonstrate some simple image manipulation using SWT and for comparison with another version of the code introduced later. The first step is to draw the image, a blue and yellow, 5-pointed star on a white background. This is quite similar to the code that was shown in the FillPoly example in the Graphics Fundamentals chapter, so we will not reproduce it here.[3]

Converting an ImageData to Black/White/Transparent

The next step is to convert the image to a black/white/transparent ImageData to be passed to the constructor. This can be encapsulated in a method that takes an ImageData representing the image and the pixel value (in that Image-Data) that should be transparent. It will return a new ImageData with the desired attributes, something like the following.

```
static ImageData
   makePixelTransparent(ImageData id, int pixel) {

   // Downsample to 3 color (black, white, transparent).
   int w = id.width, h = id.height;
   int pixelRow[] = new int[w];
   RGB[] colors = new RGB[3];
   RGB transparent = new RGB(128, 128, 128);
   colors[0] = black;
   colors[1] = white;
   colors[2] = transparent;
   int colorsIndex = 0;
   PaletteData p = id.palette;
   PaletteData p2 = new PaletteData(colors);
   int pixelRow2[] = new int[w];
   ImageData id2 = new ImageData(id.width,id.height,2,p2);
   id2.transparentPixel = 2;
```

---

3. The code can be found in the CustomCursorBlackAndWhite.java example in package *part2*.

```
        for (int j=0; j < h; ++j) {
            id.getPixels(0, j, w, pixelRow, 0);
            for (int i=0; i < w; ++i) {
                if (pixelRow[i] == pixel)
                    pixelRow2[i] = 2;
                else
                    pixelRow2[i] = mapPixel(p,pixelRow[i],p2);
            }
            id2.setPixels(0, j, w, pixelRow2, 0);
        }
        return id2;
}
```

The code begins by building a PaletteData with three colors in it: black, white and an arbitrary color (we chose gray) that will be marked as transparent in the answer. It then sets that PaletteData into a new ImageData of depth 2, which will be the result. It also sets the *transparentPixel* of the result to 2 (the transparent pixel we chose).

Notice that the code uses a for loop that copies pixels from the source to the destination a whole row at a time, using getPixels() and setPixels(). For each pixel in the source ImageData, the code checks whether it is the same as the transparent pixel and if so, it sets the corresponding pixel in the result to 2. If the source pixel is not the transparent pixel, we call mapPixel to convert from a pixel value in the PaletteData of the source to one in the new Palette-Data we created.

```
static int mapPixel(
        PaletteData source,
        int sourcePixel,
        PaletteData dest)
{
    RGB color = source.getRGB(sourcePixel);
    if (color.red+color.green+color.blue > (128*3))
        return dest.getPixel(white);
    else
        return dest.getPixel(black);
}
```

This code performs a very simple translation, mapping all pixels in the source that represent colors whose red, green, and blue components sum to more than those of 50% gray (i.e., 128 + 128 + 128) to white in the destination. The rest are mapped to black.

Once we have created the black/white/transparent ImageData, we can construct a cursor from it. Here is the code from the example that makes the image and builds the cursor.

```
    Image starImage =
        new Image(display, cursorWidth, cursorHeight);
```

```
drawStar(display, starImage);
ImageData starImageData = starImage.getImageData();
starImage.dispose();
starImageData = makePixelTransparent(
        starImageData,
        starImageData.getPixel(0, 0));
Cursor cursor = new Cursor (
        display,
        starImageData,
        cursorWidth / 2, cursorHeight / 2);
```

Notice that we chose the pixel in the top left corner of the image as the transparent pixel, because we knew that would be drawn in the white background color by the drawStar() method. The hotspot is set to the center of the cursor shape. Figure 20.2 shows the appearance of the resulting cursor on GTK. Although a 100- by 100-pixel cursor is too large for most applications, it may be appropriate for those that target children or the vision-impaired.

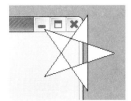

Figure 20.2   The result of running the CustomCursorBlackAndWhite example on GTK.

Cursor Size Limits

Some platforms do not allow cursors to be larger than a given size or have a "preferred" size for cursors. For example, on Mac OS X, cursors are 16 by 16 pixels. To ensure that you are creating a cursor at a reasonable size for the platform, you can use the following method, which is defined in class Display.

getCursorSizes()   Returns an array of points that represents the preferred cursor sizes on the current platform.

Cursors should normally be created at one of the sizes returned by this method. Cursors that are created with one of these sizes are guaranteed to be displayed at that size. Creating a cursor with some other size may cause it to be scaled to one of the preferred sizes. This method is new in R3.0 of Eclipse.

20.2.2 Color Cursors

When the portability that black/white/transparent cursors provide is not an overriding concern, it is also possible to create a color cursor by passing ImageData that describes a color image to the second Cursor constructor. If we had the image of a star in blue and yellow on a white background from the last example, creating a cursor with a blue and yellow star on a transparent background is simple.[4]

```
Image starImage =
    new Image(display, cursorWidth, cursorHeight);
drawStar(display, starImage, points);
ImageData starImageData = starImage.getImageData();
starImage.dispose();
starImageData.transparentPixel =
    starImageData.getPixel(0, 0);
Cursor cursor = new Cursor (
    display,
    starImageData,
    cursorWidth / 2,
    cursorHeight / 2);
```

This code gets the pixel in the top left corner of the ImageData, sets the transparentPixel for the ImageData to that pixel, and constructs the cursor from it. In versions of SWT prior to 3.0, this code worked on Microsoft Windows but produced variable results on the other platforms. If the ImageData had a direct palette, it was displayed as a black rectangle everywhere but on Windows. However, if the image had an indexed palette, the shape of the star was displayed. As of R3.0, the shape is always displayed on platforms that do not support color cursors.

Converting an ImageData to Indexed Color

In our example, the code that draws the star will produce an ImageData with an indexed palette only if the display was using an indexed color model at the time the image was created. To create an indexed palette version of the Image-Data, the first step is to construct the indexed PaletteData for it. Here is a routine that creates such a PaletteData using an extremely simplistic algorithm; the first *maxColors* different colors from the image are used.[5]

---

4. The code is part of the CustomCursorInColor1.java example in package *part2*.
5. The code is part of the CustomCursorInColor2.java example in package *part2*.

```
private static PaletteData
    getIndexedPalette(ImageData id, int maxColors)
{
    int w = id.width, h = id.height;
    RGB[] colors = new RGB[maxColors];
    Arrays.fill(colors, new RGB(0, 0, 0));
    HashSet colorSet = new HashSet(maxColors);
    int color = 0;
    PaletteData p = id.palette;
    int pixelRow[] = new int[w];
    for (int j=0; j<h && color<colors.length; ++j) {
        id.getPixels(0, j, w, pixelRow, 0);
        for (int i=0; i<w && color<colors.length; ++i) {
            RGB rgb = p.getRGB(pixelRow[i]);
            if (!colorSet.contains(rgb)) {
                colorSet.add(rgb);
                colors[color++] = rgb;
            }
        }
    }
    return new PaletteData(colors);
}
```

For a real application, the algorithm would need to be more complex, taking into account the area of the image covered by each of the colors, the contrast between them, and so forth. Given the star image we are working with, the simple version will be acceptable. Note that, we cannot simply assume that the three original colors we chose (blue, yellow, white) are the only colors that will appear in the image. On Macintosh OS X, for example, the line drawing routines use anti-aliasing to improve the appearance of the result. This can generate many "interim" colors that are not specified by the application code.

Given the code to create the indexed palette, here is a method that will convert an ImageData to one that uses an indexed palette if it does not already use one:

```
static ImageData makeIndexed(ImageData id) {
    if (!id.palette.isDirect) return id;
    int w = id.width, h = id.height;
    PaletteData p = id.palette;
    PaletteData p2 = getIndexedPalette(id, 256);
    int pixelRow[] = new int[w];
    int pixelRow2[] = new int[w];
    ImageData id2 =
        new ImageData(id.width, id.height, 8, p2);
    for (int j=0; j < h; ++j) {
        id.getPixels(0, j, w, pixelRow, 0);
        for (int i=0; i < w; ++i) {
            pixelRow2[i] = mapPixel(p, pixelRow[i], p2);
        }
        id2.setPixels(0, j, w,pixelRow2, 0);
    }
    return id2;
}
```

Notice the similarity between this and the makePixelTransparent()
method in the CustomCursorBlackAndWhite example. In fact, the new version of makePixelTransparent() would be simply as follows.

```
static ImageData
    makePixelTransparent(ImageData id, int pixel)
{
    ImageData id2 = makeIndexed(id);
    id2.transparentPixel =
        mapPixel(id.palette, pixel, id2.palette);
    return id2;
}
```

The new version of the mapPixel() routine must map to one of the colors
in the palette, rather than to just black or white, as does the one in Custom-
CursorBlackAndWhite. Because the PaletteData method getPixel() will throw
an exception if the RGB value that is passed in is not an exact match for one
of the colors in it, the code must get the colors first, using getRGBs(), then scan
them for the closest match.

```
static int mapPixel (
        PaletteData source,
        int sourcePixel,
        PaletteData dest)
{
    RGB[] RGBs = dest.getRGBs();
    RGB matchColor = source.getRGB(sourcePixel);
    int closestMatch = -1;
    int closestDiff = 256*3;
    for (int i=0; i < RGBs.length; ++i) {
        RGB c = RGBs[i];
        int diff =
            Math.abs(c.red - matchColor.red) +
            Math.abs(c.green - matchColor.green) +
            Math.abs(c.blue - matchColor.blue);
        if (diff == 0) return i;
        if (diff < closestDiff) {
            closestDiff = diff;
            closestMatch = i;
        }
    }
    return closestMatch;
}
```

Once the indexed palette ImageData has been created, the code to build a
cursor from it looks exactly like that shown in the CustomCursorBlackAnd-
White example. Because the pictures in the book are black and white, including an illustration of the result of running this example would not be

particularly elucidating. If you have access to a Microsoft Windows machine, you can try running it there to see the effect.

Finally, we realize that the code in this section is not specifically related to cursor construction. It is our hope that by providing a context for the discussion, this has made both the custom cursor and the image manipulation topics more interesting.

PART III

Applications

If you have read the book to this point, you should have a good understanding of how SWT works. The many examples and code fragments have given you a toolkit of useful patterns for writing SWT programs. What has been missed, however, was the end-to-end story showing how the pieces all fit together in real-world applications.

In this part of the book, we will provide two examples that show how SWT can be used to build interesting, first-class, native platform applications using portable Java code—the ideal of SWT.

The first application is *Minesweeper*. This is a simple game that most people have seen before. Our version uses a custom widget to display the board, simple image handling to display the action, and timers to track progress. It runs well on all the supported platforms and shows that you can build something good without adding a lot of baggage.

The second application is a powerful file explorer called (naturally enough) *FileExplorer*. This example is significantly larger but includes everything that would be required in a commercial application, including a modern GUI, drag-and-drop support, and internationalization. It also supports the launching of other applications by double-clicking. Finally, it is a multithreaded application that demonstrates how you can use threads to keep the user interface responsive while long operations are executing.

Our goal here is not to "pad the book" with the code for these applications, however. As we said in the Introduction, we believe that "a program is worth a thousand words." To really understand what these applications do, you are going to have to read the code for them. The two chapters in this part of the book are intended to be the "study guides" to direct you through that code. They describe what the applications are intended to do and the basic program structure, and they identify the "points of interest"—those patterns that will almost certainly show up in the applications that you build.

CHAPTER 21

Minesweeper

Minesweeper is one of those addictive little games that have appeared on every platform, in a multitude of variations. Ours is a simple implementation, but it plays well and is small enough to leave on your machine.[1]

21.1 How to Play

For those who have not seen it before, here is a brief explanation of how to play Minesweeper.

The basic premise of the game is that it is your job to mark the locations of all the explosives (mines) in an area. The playing field is made up of a rectangular grid of initially hidden squares. Above the playing field, there are two numeric displays; one indicates the number of mines left to be found, and the other shows how much time you have spent on this puzzle. The timer does not start until you have clicked on the playing field.

The area above the playing field also includes a button to start a new game. The Start button doubles as a status indicator. It normally shows a smiling face but shows a happy face (with a bigger smile) when you have solved the puzzle or a sad face if you set off a mine. Figure 21.1 shows what the board looks like just before a new game is started.

---

1. It even runs on Windows CE. That platform does not support buttons with images, however, so if you were planning to deliver on Window CE, you would probably end up tweaking the code to match the platform user interface guidelines better.

Each time you *left-click* on a hidden square in the playfield, one of three things can happen.

1. If the square contains a mine, it explodes, ending the game.

2. If there is a mine in one of the squares that is immediately beside the one you clicked on (either horizontally, vertically, or diagonally), a number from 1 to 8 is displayed in the square, indicating the total number of mines that surround it.

3. If there are no mines in squares that neighbor the square you clicked, the square is displayed as a blank space, and all squares around it are tested as though you clicked on them.

The last point has the effect of recursively revealing all the empty squares around the square you selected, stopping at the squares that contain numbers.

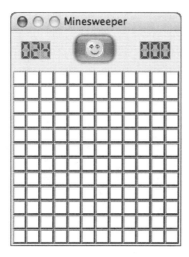

Figure 21.1   Minesweeper on Macintosh OS X.

As you continue to left-click on squares on the board, you will eventually be able to identify places where there are mines. In Figure 21.2, for example, there must be a mine in the square on the diagonal down and to the right from the square being pointed at, because the square indicates that there is one mine surrounding it, and there is only one hidden square left.

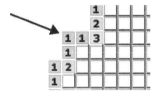

Figure 21.2   Square that shows the location of a mine.

Once you have identified a square with a mine in it, you can *right-click* on the square to put a flag there, indicating that you believe it is a mine location. Each time you do this, the counter showing the remaining mines is decremented. To win the game, you must correctly identify the locations of all mines.

As an added feature, if you right-click on a square that has already been identified as a mine location, the marker changes to a question mark (and the counter is incremented). This can be used to identify places that you think *might* be mine locations. Right-clicking on a square containing a question mark simply removes it, returning the square to the hidden state.

21.2   Implementation Notes

The structure of the Minesweeper application is simple enough that it does not require much explanation. It has basically the same shape as the other examples in the book and is built from just four classes.

> **Minesweeper:** the class containing the main() method
>
> **Counter:** a custom widget to display a three-digit counter
>
> **Timer:** a subclass of Counter that increments once a second
>
> **Board:** a custom widget to display the playing field

21.2.1   Class Minesweeper

The main() method in this class creates the shell and the controls that make up its contents and adds various listeners, then runs the event loop until the shell is disposed of. Notice that SWT.MouseDown and SWT.MouseUp listeners are added to the board to control the image that is displayed on the "new game" button.

The SWT.MouseUp listener also checks whether the game is over, updating the display accordingly. This is a common pattern in SWT: Widgets (in this case, the Board custom widget) know how to display themselves and hold onto the state required to do so, but the application logic resides in the application classes. Our bias toward this kind of implementation is based on the behavior of the platform widgets: They typically deal with very simple objects (strings or images) and any higher-level interpretation of those objects is the responsibility of the application.

Note that Minesweeper is "NLS[2]-ready," even though it uses only a single string, the title. The method getMessage(String key) looks for a "mine-sweeper" resource bundle and if it is found, uses it to look up the key that is passed in. If the bundle is not found, the key itself is returned (which is what happens in the code as it is distributed). Simply adding the bundle will allow you to change the title to match your locale.

The interesting behavior in the application comes from the three other classes, which are all custom widgets.

21.2.2   *Class Counter*

The Counter class is quite generic and could be used in other applications that require a three-digit counter control. It is a good example of how easy it is to create new, custom, nonnative widgets with SWT.

The constructor for the class adds SWT.Paint and SWT.Dispose listeners, then reads in GIF images that contain the digits to display (into the slot *images*[3]). The SWT.Dispose listener takes care of disposing of the images. The SWT.Paint listener draws the current value of the counter (stored in the slot *value*), which can be accessed using setValue() and getValue().

For the counter control to participate in the layout process, we must define the computeSize(int wHint, int hHint, boolean changed) method. See The Preferred Size of a Control section in the Controls chapter for a description of how this works. In this case, we ensure that the control has enough space to hold the three digits and any associated trim.

Surprisingly, that is all that is required to make this widget. Because it is built as a subclass of Canvas, all listeners that Canvas supports can also be added to the widget. This would allow you, for example, to add a mouse listener to reset Counter if your application required it.

21.2.3   *Class Timer*

Timer is a subclass of Counter and presents itself in exactly the same way. It differs from Counter in that as long as it is "started," it increments the value

---

2. National Language Support.

3. For an application that uses many instances of Counter, it would presumably be better to maintain the images in a static slot, but this implementation keeps things simple.

that it displays once per second. It adds the new API start(), stop(), and reset() to control the timing aspects.

The code that increments the timer is stored in a runnable (created in the constructor), which is scheduled using timerExec(). See the Timers section of the Display chapter for more on this.

21.2.4 Class Board

Class Board is the most interesting class in the application. The class itself implements the Listener interface, and the constructor adds the instance as the listener for all events that it requires. For simple applications, this is a convenient way to avoid the creation of numerous anonymous inner classes. The handleEvent() method for the class uses a switch statement to forward the work to an appropriate helper method.

For each square, several pieces of information need to be maintained.

❍ Has the square been clicked on?

❍ Is there a mine in the square?

❍ Has the user flagged the square as a mine?

❍ Has the user flagged the square with a question mark?

❍ How many mines surround the square?

One possible way to represent this would have been to create a "Square" class and store a two dimensional array of Square instances in Board. However, because the Square instances would essentially be pure data structures, we instead chose to use a very simple form of the Flyweight Pattern[4] to represent the information: Rather than keep a separate instance for each square in the board, we use three arrays, which are stored in slots in Board.

> **selected** A 2D array of booleans that contains true if the square has been clicked on and false otherwise.

> **images** A 2D array of images that contains an image that represents the true state of the square: a count of the number of neighboring mines, a mine, an explosion, a "wrong" indicator (marked as a mine but was not), or null.

> **guesses** A 2D array of Images that contains the image of what the user believes the square represents: a flag, a question mark, or null.

---

4. See *Design Patterns* by Gamma, Helm, Johnson, and Vlissides.

To keep the code as small as possible, at the cost of making the result somewhat less readable, the contents of these arrays are accessed directly to implement the game logic. For example, the select(GC gc, int i, int j, int width, int height) method checks "images [i][j] == null" to decide whether it should recur to check surrounding squares, because when the image is null, there are no mines around the square. Given that the actual game logic is not as interesting as the SWT code, this kind of simplification is acceptable.

As was true of class Counter, Board overrides the computeSize(int wHint, int hHint, boolean changed) method from class Composite so that it can return a reasonable size to hold the entire grid of squares. It does not, however, override any other methods, relying instead on the simple solution of adding listeners for all relevant events to itself. The board is drawn from within the SWT.Paint event; selection is handled by the mouse events; and SWT.Dispose is used to clean up the extra graphical resources that were acquired. Neat and simple.

CHAPTER 22

FileExplorer

Every platform has some kind of graphical utility for browsing the contents of its file systems. Macintosh OS has Finder. Microsoft Windows has Explorer. Linux has a host of options, including Nautilus, KFM, Kruiser, TkDesk, DFM, Xplore—the list is endless. We have implemented a new file system browser comparable in power to the native platform utilities that we call *File-Explorer*.

22.1 Features

Figures 22.1 and 22.2 show what FileExplorer looks like running on Microsoft Windows and Macintosh OS X, respectively. The client area of the application shell contains four main sections.

1. A tool bar containing a combo for selecting the file system root to browse (really useful only on Windows) and several tool items that invoke common operations.

2. A tree for walking the directory hierarchy.

3. A table showing the contents of the selected directory.

4. A status line that shows information about the selection.

Typically, you would use the tree to walk down the file hierarchy to the directory you are interested in, then use the information in the table to find a particular file. Double-clicking on the file will cause it to open in an editor. You can also use menus (either from the menu bar or the context menu) to act on selected files and directories. This includes deleting or renaming existing files and directories, and creating new files and directories.

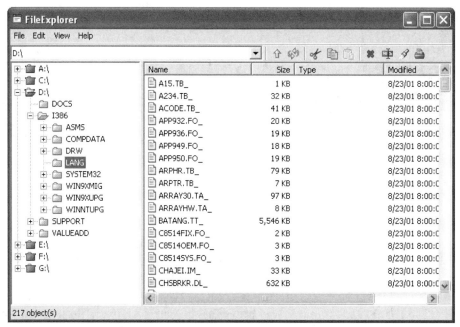

Figure 22.1   FileExplorer running on Windows XP.

Some of the more interesting features of FileExplorer include the following.

Flexible Layout   Notice that the four sections of FileExplorer fill the available space in the shell. The tool bar, the status area, or both may be hidden via menu items, and the relative space taken up by the tree and table can be varied by dragging the sash that appears between them.

Drag-and-Drop Support   You can move files and directories from place to place in the directory hierarchy using the appropriate mouse gesture for the platform.

Application Launching   Double-clicking on a file in the table will launch the native tool available for editing files of that type, if it can be determined.

Multithreading   Many of the operations implemented by FileExplorer provide incremental feedback as they operate.

In-Place Editing   Selecting the Rename menu item allows a file or directory to be renamed by typing a new name into an in-place editing window that appears over the item.

We will look at how each of these features is implemented in the next section.

Figure 22.2   FileExplorer running on Macintosh OS X.

22.2   Implementation Notes

22.2.1   *Flexible Layout*

The FileExplorer shell uses FormLayout to arrange its children. Initially, the table, the tree, and the sash between them are attached to the tool bar at the top and the status label at the bottom. The View menu allows you to hide the tool bar or status label. This is accomplished by changing the attachment of the table, tree, and sash to be relative to the edge of the shell, then hiding the tool bar or label. For example, here is the code that toggles the visibility of the tool bar.

```
if (toolItem.getSelection ()) {
    FormData treeData = (FormData) tree.getLayoutData ();
    treeData.top = new FormAttachment (toolBar);
    FormData sashData = (FormData) sash.getLayoutData ();
```

```
        sashData.top = new FormAttachment (toolBar);
        FormData tableData = (FormData) table.getLayoutData ();
        tableData.top = new FormAttachment (toolBar);
} else {
        FormData treeData = (FormData) tree.getLayoutData ();
        treeData.top = new FormAttachment (0);
        FormData sashData = (FormData) sash.getLayoutData ();
        sashData.top = new FormAttachment (0);
        FormData tableData = (FormData) table.getLayoutData ();
        tableData.top = new FormAttachment (0);
}
toolBar.setVisible (toolItem.getSelection ());
shell.layout ();
```

Notice that the selected state of the item is queried to decide whether the tool bar should be shown or hidden. Notice also the explicit call to layout() to cause the appearance to change.

22.2.2 Drag-and-Drop

In SWT, drag-and-drop (we say "D&D") support is implemented using native drag-and-drop facilities. The package that implements this support is *org.eclipse.swt.dnd*. D&D support is implemented in an application by creating a DragSource for the control that items will be dragged from and a Drag-Target for the control they will be dragged to. The example creates a DragSource and a DragTarget for both the table and the tree, allowing items to be moved by dragging them to either control.

Where things start to get interesting, however, is that because the D&D support uses the native facilities, you can also drag files between FileExplorer and the native file browsers on platforms that support this.

Taking the Transfer

To be able to drag files between FileExplorer and native applications, FileExplorer needs to warn the platform that the thing that is being dragged represents a file. In SWT, setting the *transfer* of the DragSource (using setTransfer()) to an instance of org.eclipse.swt.dnd.FileTransfer does this.[1] Similarly, setting the *transfer* of a DropTarget to a FileTransfer indicates that the target can accept files from other platform applications.

---

1. Actually, the transfer is set to an *array* of transfers. This allows multiple versions of the same objects to be dragged from a DragSource or received at a DropTarget. For example, an application might include both text and RTF versions of a text selection.

> Subclasses of class org.eclipse.swt.dnd.Transfer describe the format of the item that is being dragged. The predefined transfer types, which map to native types on most platforms, are TextTransfer (plain text), RTFTransfer (rich text), Image-Transfer (images), and FileTransfer (files). You can also define new types of transfers.

In the FileExplorer source, the DragSource and DragTarget instances are created by the following methods.

createDragSource(Control control)   Associates a DragSource for a FileTransfer with the given control. DragSourceListener is added to the DragSource.

createDropTarget(Control control)   Associates a DropTarget for a FileTransfer with the given control. DropTargetListener is added to the DropTarget.

Looking at these methods should provide a good start toward working with the drag-and-drop support.

22.2.3 Application Launching

Most modern operating systems provide support for mapping between iden-tifiers for content types (such as MIME types or file extensions) and the native applications that are capable of manipulating content of those types. In SWT, this application launching support is implemented by the Program class in the package *org.eclipse.swt.program*. An instance of class Program represents a specific external program that is capable of handling one or more content types. Static methods in class Program are provided that return the available programs and the content types for which there are mappings. The simplest way to use this support is to *launch* the content file.

> **launch(String fileName)**   This static Program method attempts to find an external program that is capable of handling the file named by the argument and, if one is found, causes it to be started by the oper-ating system, with the file name passed to it as an argument. If a com-patible program can be successfully started, this method returns true. If a program cannot be found or if one is found but fails to start, false is returned. As a special case, if the file name describes a file that can

itself be executed by the operating system (for example, an .EXE file on Microsoft Windows), the file is launched directly.

The FileExplorer example launches the selected file when the table receives a DefaultSelection event. The handler for this is implemented in the following method.

tableDefaultSelected(TableItem[] items)   For each item that represents a directory, the matching entry in the tree is expanded (or collapsed if it was already expanded). For items that represent files, the file is launched.

The code to launch the file is trivial and looks like this.

```
String name = file.getAbsolutePath ();
if (!Program.launch (name)) {
    MessageBox dialog =
        new MessageBox (shell, SWT.ICON_ERROR | SWT.OK);
    dialog.setText (shell.getText ());
    dialog.setMessage (
        getMessage (
            "Could not launch \"{0}\".",
            new Object [] {name}));
    dialog.open ();
}
```

This is the simplest way to use the Program class. Class Program provides other capabilities that we have not included here, and it is worth looking at its API if you get a chance. For example, you can use the findProgram() method to return an instance of Program, then ask this program for an image to display. This would allow you, for example, to show a specific image for each type of file that is shown in the table.

22.2.4 Multithreading

The FileExplorer application uses multithreading to allow different file operations to run in parallel. These operations include deleting a file or hierarchy, copying a file or hierarchy, and filling the table in the background. These operations are described by a hierarchy of classes under the abstract class FileOperation.[2]

2. FileOperation is not intended to be a general-purpose "operation" class, but you could implement a more general version if this were required.

FileOperation always runs in a separate thread. The user interface will wait until either the operation completes or the *expectedTime* (in FileOperation) has passed. The user interface then calls the isDone method to see whether the operation has completed. This allows us to support both operations that complete quickly (without notification in the user interface) and longer running operations that display a progress dialog.

Progress is reported to the user interface by calling the following method.

check(File file, boolean increment)   Called by the FileOperation as it does work. The method should be called once with *increment* set to true each time a file is about to be processed, but it can be called an arbitrary number of times with *increment* set to false. The user interface uses this information and the aforementioned *expectedTime* value to display and update a progress dialog.

Look at the code for DeleteOperation to see a simple operation.

22.2.5   *In-Place Editing*

Native tables and trees sometimes provide built-in support for directly editing the contents of an item that they are displaying. This support is typically quite limited. Because this support was either not available or not sufficiently powerful across all platforms, the SWT implementers chose to provide a separate, platform-neutral, in-place editing mechanism, rather than attempt to manifest the native capabilities.[3] The classes that provide this capability are found in the *org.eclipse.swt.custom* package. The class ControlEditor has subclasses TreeEditor and TableEditor[4] that allow an arbitrary control to be laid out "on top of" a field in a tree or table. Application code can use this to build an in-place editor by doing the following.

1. Creating an editor for the field to be edited.

2. Setting the editor control to be one that is appropriate for the editing task. This could be a text, a combo, a button to launch a separate editing window, or even a custom, application-specific control (such as a "color picker").

3. Setting the value that is displayed by the control to the value in the field.

---

3. This decision may be revisited in the future. Some platforms dictate a certain look for in-place editing.

4. And class TableTreeEditor, which provides these capabilities for org.eclipse.swt.custom.TableTree instances.

4. Running an event loop until a new value has been entered.

5. Setting the new value back into the field.

Depending on the application, you may also have to disable accelerators for the application menu and tool bar to prevent unexpected behavior.

In the FileExplorer example, renaming of files and directories is implemented using in-place editing. The code that does this is found in the following.

rename(ControlEditor editor, Composite composite, Item item, Rectangle bounds)   Given an editor for the item, a composite (either Table or Tree), the item to be edited, and the initial bounds for the editor, use the editor to rename the item.

This method is called from either rename(TreeItem item) or rename(TableItem item). These methods simply construct an instance of the appropriate editor class, then call the above method to do the work.

22.2.6   Other Design Notes

Here are some other areas of the code that are worth looking at.

Enabling the ToolBar Icons   The paste icon in the tool bar needs to be enabled whenever there is something in the platform clipboard that can be pasted into the current directory in FileExplorer. Because the contents of the clipboard can be changed by other applications, the simplest way to do this is to poll the clipboard at regular intervals. In FileExplorer, the createToolBarTimer() method does this by setting up a timerExec to check the clipboard contents every 250 milliseconds. This pattern is quite common (it is used by the Microsoft Office applications, for example) and does not cause significant overhead as long as the polling frequency is not too high.

Updating Tree and Table   Each time the above polling loop runs, if an operation is in progress, Table and Tree are checked to see whether they need to be updated. This has the effect of incrementally filling in the table and tree as the operation is running.

Retargeting the Menus   Several actions, such as Rename in the Edit menu, always apply to the selected file or directory. To implement this behavior, the slot *toolBarTarget* is set to either Tree or Table whenever they are given focus. See the method FileExplorer.getSelectedItems().

PART IV

Next Time

As we said in the Preface, there is more to SWT than we could fit in one book. What we have tried to do on these pages is give you a deep understanding of the fundamentals and a valuable reference for the native widgets. We hope that you find this valuable, and we look forward to hearing from you on the SWT newsgroup.

Thanks,
Mike and Steve

Index

A

Accelerators, 48–50, 198
add() method, 11, 167–168
add() (to region), 422
addDisposeListener(), 21
addFilter(), 93–94
addImageLoaderListener(), 492
addListener(), 18, 91
Advanced controls, 209, 257
    classes TabFolder/TabItem *see* Tab-
        Folder/TabItem
    classes Tree/TreeItem *see* Tree/TreeItem
alpha (ImageData field), 469
alphaData (ImageData field), 469–470
append(), 157
Application data, 122–123
    named/unnamed, 25
    see also Display
Applications, xx, 511–512
    see also FileExplorer; Minesweeper
asyncExec(), 101–102
    from user interface thread, 106, 107c, 108
    queue code for user interface thread exam-
        ple, 103–104
    TableItems creation in an "idle handler"
        code example, 245c–246c
AWT/Swing, xxvii–xxix

B

Basic controls, 135, 179
    class button *see* Button

class combo *see* Combo
class label *see* Label
class list *see* List
class text *see* Text
beep(), 127
BIDI *see* Bidirectional languages
Bidirectional languages (BIDI), support,
    458–459
Bounds, 65–66, 65f, 112–113
Button, 132
    class button
        alignment, 142
        arrow buttons, 145–146
        button events, 140–141, 146–147
        button styles, 140
        check buttons, 142–143
        example, 140
        hierarchy, 140
        push buttons, 142
        radio buttons, 144–145, 146–147
        text and images, 141
        toggle buttons, 145
    default button, 290
bytesPerLine field (image), 464

C

Canvas, 132, 302
    tab group traversal implementation exam-
        ple, 45–46
    see also Class Canvas

Caret, 132, 148, 296–297, 302
  see also Class Caret
Character, 33
  Convenience Constants, 33t
  generated control characters, 34
Character encoding, 439
check(), 525
checkItems() method, 219
checkPath() method, 219
checkSubclass(), 15–16
Class Canvas
  events, 296
  example, 295
  hierarchy, 295
  painting in a Canvas, 296
  scrolling, 297–298
  styles, 296
  see also Caret
Class Caret
  bounds/size/location, 298–299
  events, 298
  example, 298
  hierarchy, 298
  Input Method Editor font, 300
  styles, 298
  visibility, 299–300
  writing single-line text editor code example,
    300c–302c
Class Composite
  events, 278
  example, 277
  getting children, 278
  hierarchy, 277
  and Layout, 279
  styles, 277
  see also Tab traversal
Class Control
  context menus, 275
  cursors, 276–277
  events, 274
  example, 273
  foreground/background/font, 275–276
  hierarchy, 273
  parent/shell/monitor, 275

styles, 274
tool tips, 276
Class Group
  events, 279–280
  example, 279
  hierarchy, 279
  styles, 279
  text setting, 280
Class Shell
  closing a Shell, 285
  creation/no trim coding example, 287,
    287c–288c
  creation/nonstandard trim, 286–287
  creation/standard trim, 286
  default button, 290
  events, 282, 292–294
  example, 280
  hierarchy, 281
  menu bar setting, 285
  minimizing/maximizing/restoring, 289–290
  modality, 289
  nonrectangular, 290–291
    coding example, 291c–292c
  opening a Shell, 283–284
  styles, 281
  text and image methods, 282–283
Class SWT, 10
Classes ScrollBar and Slider
  configuring options, 268–269
  events, 265–266, 269–272
  example, 265
  hierarchy, 265
  historical background, 266
  increment/page increment, 268
  range operations, 267
  selection and thumb, 267–268
  styles, 265
clearSelection(), 155
Client area, 66–67, 67f, 113
close(), 93, 285
Color(), 430
Colors, 427
  Class Color, 430–433
  coding example allocating random colors in
    clipping region, 432c–433

preallocation issues, 468
System Colors, 433–434
    constants, 433t–434t, 435t, 436
    GRADIENT versions, 435
see also RGB/Class RGB
Combo, 132
    box, 174
    class combo, 175
        drop-down combo resizing, 177
        events, 174–175, 177–178
        example, 173
        hierarchy, 174
        list methods, 176–177
        styles, 174
        text methods, 175–176
Common Widgets, xxvi–xxvii
computeSize(), 77, 307
Constructors
    convenience constructors, 11
    use of operating system resources, 8
Consuming a key, 28
    coding example, 38–39
Containment, 273
Containment hierarchy, 14
contains(), 408, 423
Context menu request, 59–60
Contextual forms, 458–459
Control, 16, 130, 294
    see also Advanced controls; Basic controls;
        Class Composite; Class Control; Class
        Group; Class Shell; Draggable con-
        trols; Menu/MenuItem; Range-based
        controls; ToolBar/ToolItem
Control (Drawable interface), 410, 478
Control fundamentals, 65, 88
    enabling/disabling, 74–75
    preferred size, 76
        computing, 77
        packing, 76–77
    visibility, 72–73
    z-order, 74
    see also Bounds; Client area; Moving/Resiz-
        ing; Painting
Control.setMenu(), 14

CoolBar/CoolItem, 132
    Class CoolBar/CoolItem
        and clipped content code example,
            309c–311c
        CoolBar events, 304
        CoolBar style, 303
        CoolItem configuring, 305–307
        CoolItem events, 304, 312–313
        CoolItem styles, 304
        example, 303
        hierarchies, 303
        locking CoolBar, 312
        saving/restoring CoolBar layout, 311–312
        searching operations, 312
    CoolBar resize and control repositioning
        coding example, 308c–309c
    create cool bar with four tool bars coding
        example, 307c–308c
    "item children" (cool items) and "gripper,"
        304
    rebar controls (cool bars), 304
    "shell-like" behavior, 305
copy(), 157
copyArea(), 477
createDragSource(), 523
createDropTarget(), 523
Cursor(), 498, 501, 502
Cursor, 497
    color, 506
    converting an ImageData to indexed color
        coding example, 506, 507c–508c
    custom cursors, 501–503
        black and white, 503
        coding example converting ImageData to
            black/white/transparent, 503c–505c
        size limits, 505
    hotspot, 497
    inherited, 277
    multiple, 277
    resizing cursors, 499
        constants, 499t–500t
    setting, 276
    shape, 497
    system cursors, 498, 500
        constants, 498t–499t
cut(), 157

D

Data *see* Application data
data field (image), 464–465
Decorations, class, 131
delayTime (ImageData fields), 472
depth field (image), 464
deselect(), 171, 240–241
deselectAll(), 171, 221, 241
detail field issues, and traversal codes, 43–44,
    45t
Device (Drawable interface), 410
Dialog(), 323
Dialogs, 323, 341
    ColorDialog, 337, 338f
        creation, 337
        opening, 337–338
        setting RGB, 337
    creation, 323–324
    dialog window, 323
    DirectoryDialog, 334, 336f
        creation, 334
        directory path setting, 335
        message setting, 334–335
        opening, 336
    FileDialog, 328, 331f, 334f
        coding example for image file using file
            extensions, 334c–333c
        creation, 328–329
        filter extensions setting, 329–330
        filter path setting, 329
        multiselection capability, 332
        opening, 332
        set/get file name, 331–332
    FontDialog, 338–339, 341f
        creation, 339
        FontData List setting, 339
        opening (coding example), 340c
        RGB setting, 339
    MessageBox, 325
        buttons, 326–327
        creation, 325
        icons, 326
        opening, 327–328
        setting message, 327
    opening, 324
    title setting, 324–325

Display(), 91
Display, 16–17, 89, 128
    application data, 122–123
        dismissal alignment, 123–124
    application naming, 90
    beep, 127
    cursor control/location, 116
        getting cursor control, 116–118
        setting/getting cursor location, 118
    depth and DPI, 118–119
        system colors, 120
        system font, 120
        system information, 119
    double-click time, 127
    events/listeners, 91–93
    life cycle, 90–91
    querying, 26
    updating, 121–122
    see also Event filters; Event loop; Monitors;
        Runnables; Shells; Threading; Timers
disposalMethod (ImageData fields), 472–473
dispose(), 12
    vs. close, 285
    (display destruction), 91
    and system objects, 119
disposeExec(), 95
DisposeListener interface, 22
    see also Widget events
doit field issues
    input validation, 39
    and traversal implementation/stop, 44, 45t
Drag-and-drop request, 60–61
    in application example, 522–523
Draggable controls, 303, 321
    Class CoolBar/CoolItem *see* CoolBar/
        CoolItem
    Class Sash *see* Sash
    Class Tracker *see* Tracker
Drawable interface, 410
    and controls, 478
drawArc(), 417
drawFocus(), 416–417
drawImage(), 475–476
drawLine(), 412
drawOval(), 417
drawPolygon(), 412

drawPolyline(), 412
drawRectangle(), 416
drawRoundedRectangle(), 416
drawString(), 448, 451
drawText(), 449

E

Eclipse Project, xix
EvenOdd rule, 419
Event filters, 93–94
Event loop, 96, 111
    event queue flushing, 97
    inactivity detection using timer, 109–110
    reading/dispatching, 96–96
    sleeping/waking, 97–100
Events, 17–18
    Class event (Public Fields), 19t
    filters, 18
    Focus events, 30, 30t, 31f
    Key events, 32–33, 32t
    Move, 68–69, 68t
    Resize, 69–70, 70t
    Selection events, 61–62, 62t
    Text events, 159–164
    Typed, 22t–23t
    Untyped, 20t–21t
    see also Keyboard support; Listeners;
        Mouse events; Traversal events;
        Widget events

F

FileExplorer (sample application), 519
    application launching, 523–524
    drag-and-drop, 522–523
    features, 519–521, 526
    in-place editing, 525–526
    layout flexibility, 521–522
    multithreading, 524–525
fillArc(), 419
FillLayout(), 347
fillOval(), 419
fillPolygon(), 419
fillRectangle(), 418
fillRoundedRectangle(), 418

fillTable() method, 243
    coding example, 244c
Filtering process, 329
    filter path, 329
Filters *see* Event filters
Flicker reduction, 84–85, 86–87
Flooding, 104
Focus control (keyboard events), 28, 116
    forcing, 29–30
    setting, 29
Focus events, 30–31
Font(), 443, 444
FontData(), 437, 441
Fonts, 437
    Class Font, 442–443
        coding rules for platform independent
            fonts, 447–448
        using more than one font, 444–447
    Class FontData, 437–438
        character encoding, 439
        locale, 439–441
        scalable vs. bitmapped fonts, 438–439
        tracking font choices, 441–442
    Class FontMetrics, 451–452, 453
        height measurements, 452
        invalid data issues, 452
        methods, 453–454
        TwoTextSizes coding example,
            455c–456c
        width measurements, 456–458
    drawing text, 448–449
        coding example, 450c, 451f
        drawText() constants, 449t
        rules for platform-independent code,
            451
forceActive(), 284
forceFocus(), 29–30
FormAttachment(), 379
FormData(), 378
FormLayout code example (cool bar and shell
    resize), 308c–309c
Fragile superclass problem, 14–15

G

GC *see* Graphics/class Graphics Context (GC)
GC(), 409

getAccelerator(), 49
getActiveShell(), 115
getAdvanceWidth(), 458
getAlignment(), 139, 235
getAlpha/s(), 470
getAscent(), 454
getAverageCharWidth(), 457
getBackground(), 220, 238, 276, 481
getBlue(), 431
getBounds(), 66, 112–113, 189, 242, 299, 307, 423
getCharWidth(), 458
getChecked(), 217, 237
getChildren(), 278
getClientArea(), 67, 113
    centering Shell on primary monitor example, 113c–114c
getClipping(), 424–425
getControl(), 187, 255, 305
getCursorControl(), 117–118
getCursorLocation(), 118
getCursorSizes(), 505
getData(), 25
getDefaultButton(), 290
getDescent(), 454
getDisabledImage(), 190
getDismissalAlignment(), 123–124
getDisplay(), 26
getDoubleClickTime(), 127
getEchoChar(), 151
getEnabled(), 75, 190, 197
getExpanded(), 214
getFileName(), 331–332
getFilterExtensions(), 329
getFilterNames(), 330
getFilterPath(), 329, 335
getFocusControl(), 116
getFont(), 220, 238, 276, 300, 443
getFontList(), 339, 438, 446
getFontMetrics(), 453
getForeground(), 220, 237, 276
getGrayed(), 217, 237
getGreen(), 431
getHeaderHeight(), 231
getHeaderVisible(), 231
getHeight(), 453
getHorizonBar(), 267

getHotImage(), 190–191
getIconDepth(), 119
getImage(), 137, 141, 185, 197, 234, 236, 254, 283
getImageBounds(), 242
getIncrement(), 264, 268
getItemCount(), 215, 256, 312
getItemHeight(), 167, 231–232
getItemOrder(), 311
getItems()/getItem()/getItemCount(), 166–167, 193, 200, 215, 230, 242, 256, 312
getItemSizes(), 311
getLayout(), 346
getLeading(), 454
getLineCount(), 151
getLineDelimiter(), 153
getLineHeight(), 151
getLineStyle(), 416
getLinesVisible(), 231
getLineWidth(), 416
getLocale(), 441
getLocation(), 66, 299
getMaximum(), 261, 263, 267
getMenu(), 198, 275
getMenuBar(), 285
getMessage(), 327, 335
getMinimum(), 261, 263, 267
getMinimumSize(), 306
getMonitors(), 112, 275
getPageIncrement(), 264, 268
getParent(), 9–10, 275
getParentItem(), 215
getPixel/s(), 465, 467
getPreferredSize(), 305–306
getPrimaryMonitor(), 112
getRectangles(), 317
getRed(), 431
getRGB(), 337, 431, 464, 467
getRowCount(), 191
getSelection(), 143, 155, 170, 185, 221, 240, 255, 261, 264, 268
getSelectionCount(), 221
getSelectionIndices(), 170, 255
getShells(), 115–116, 275
getSize(), 66, 299, 307
getStippled(), 317

getStyle(), 10–11
getSystemColor(), 433
getSystemFont(), 443
getTabList(), 42
getText(), 137, 141, 150, 184, 197, 234, 236,
    254, 280, 283
getTextLimit(), 159
getThread(), 100
getThumb(), 268
getToolTipText(), 189, 254, 276
getTopIndex(), 158, 241
getTopItem(), 221
getTransparencyMask(), 472
getTransparencyType(), 472
getVericalBar(), 267
getVisible(), 73, 300
getWidth(), 186, 234
getWrap Indices(), 311
getXORMode(), 416
Grab control, 54
Graphical Editing Framework (GEF), 403
Graphics, xviii, 401–403
    3D, 402
    advanced, 2D, 402
    class Graphics Context (GC), 409–410
    Class Point, 406–407
        points in hashed collections, 407
    Class Rectangle, 407–409
    clipping, 421, 424–426
    line and figure drawing, 412–413, 414f
        coding example (rectangle/oval/arc and
            XOR model), 417c–418c, 418f
        controlling line appearance, 414–415
        filling, 418–419, 419c–420c, 420f
        Moira pattern, 412
        and platform graphics routines,
            415–417
    points and rectangles, 405
    regions, 422–424
    and threads, 410–412
    video and animation, 402
Grid *see* Layout
Graduate(), 365
Griddled(), 360–361
Group, 132
GK. widget toolkit, 27
GUI (graphical user interface), xix

H
height field (image), 464
"Hit test" operations, 193, 242
HTML, and user interfaces, 1

I
I-beam *see* Caret
Idle handlers, 106–108
    coding example creating TableItems,
        245–246
Image(), 474–475
Image (Drawable interface), 410
ImageData(), 462
imageDataLoad(), 493
ImageLoader(), 487 T
Images, 461
    animation, 481
        algorithm, 481–482, 483c–486c
        double buffering, 482
    Class Image, 473–475
        image copying, 477–478
            ∫coding example, 478c–479c
        image drawing, 475–476
            ∫coding "magnifying image viewer,"
                476c–477c
        removing transparency, 479–481
    Class ImageData, 461–462
        data field, 464–466
        fields affecting transparency, 469–470
        fields for animation support, 472–473
        image attributes fields, 464
        indexed color display images, 467–468
        isDirect field, 466 467
        palette field, 466
        public fields, 463f
        transparency coding example,
            470c–471c, 471f
    Class ImageLoader, 486–487
        coding example, 493c–494
        multiple images, 488–489
        saving images, 489–490
    Class PaletteData, 466–467
    disabled, 190
    hot, 190–191

loading, 486
   background thread, 490–492
   incremental display, 492–495
   normal, 190
indexOf(), 193, 200, 242, 256, 312
Inheritance hierarchy, 14
Input Method Editor (IM/IME), 27, 300
Input validation, *doit* field issues, 39
insert(), 156
Interlacing, 492
intersection(), 408
intersects(), 408, 409, 423
isEnabled(), 75, 190, 197
isFocusControl(), 29
isSelected(), 170, 240
isVisible(), 73, 300
Item, 130, 166
   see also List/class list

K

Keyboard shortcut (menu accelerator), 48–50,
   198
Keyboard support, 28, 51
   accelerators, 48
      specification, 49–50
      text, 50
   characters/key codes/state masks, 33–39
   "consuming" a key, 28
   focus control (keyboard events), 28, 116
      forcing, 29–30
      setting, 29
   focus events, 30–31
   inactivity detection using timer, 110–111
   key events, 32–33
   traversal events, 42–48
   traversal keys, 39
      mnemonic, 39–40
      tab, 41–42
   window system keys, 50–51
keyCode field, 34–35

L

Label, 132
   class label, 135f
      alignment, 138–139
      label events, 136–137
      label hierarchy, 136
      label styles, 136
      separators, 139
      text/images, 137–138
      wrapping, 138
launch(), 523
layout(), 393
Layout, 343–344, 399
   advantages, 343
   assigning width/height hints, 390–391
      computing height hint
         (Table/Tree/List/Text), 391–392
      computing width hint
         (Table/Tree/List/Text), 391
   Class FillLayout, 347
      fill layout with multiple children coding
         example, 348c–349c
      fill layout using all fields coding exam-
         ple, 349c–350c
      shell creation with single push button
         coding example, 347c–348c
   Class FormLayout, 377–378
      class FormAttachment, 378–380
      class FormData, 378
      edge attached at offset, 382–383
      edge attached as percentage, 381–382
      edge attached to another control, 384
      edge attached to opposite edge of con-
         trol, 384–386
      implementing a find dialog, 386–387
      implementing a SashPane, 388, 389c, 390f
      overconstraining a form, 380–381
   Class Griddled, 360–361
      coding example *numColumns* field used,
         362c–363c
   Class Layout, 345
      setting, 345–346
   Classes RowLayout/RowData, 350–352
      RowData to configure controls, 358–360

RowLayout and column controls, 353–354

RowLayout and filling, 355–356

RowLayout and packing/justifying, 357

RowLayout and wrapping, 354–344

defining grid, 363–364

"convenience constants" (Graduate), 373–375

Graduate for aligning Controls, 368c–369c

Graduate for Controls configuration, 364–367

Graduate to grab excess space coding example, 369c–371c

Graduate to span rows/columns coding example, 371c–372c

Griddled to implement a Find Dialog coding example, 375–376, 376c–377c

hidden controls usage coding example, 372c

sizing controls coding example, 367c

FillLayout/RowLayout coding examples, 352c–353

forcing, 392–394

forcing controls to wrap code example, 394c–395c, 395f, 396

margin/spacing issues, 352

selection criteria, 392

usage, 344

composite resized, 344

layout() method of class Composite called, 344

width hints and SWT.Resize to wrap label coding example, 396c–398c

width hints and SWT.Resize to wrap tool bar coding example, 398c–399c

and z-order, 345

Leaf items, 214

Ligature, 458

List, 133

class list

adding items, 167–168

deselecting/selecting items, 170–171

example, 164

item height, 167

list events, 165–166, 172–173

list hierarchy, 165

list styles, 165

removing items, 168

scrolling, 171–172

searching, 172

selection setting methods, 169–170

setting items, 166–167

single-/multiselect lists, 166

Listeners, 17, 23–24

typed, 21–23

untyped, 18–21

see also Events

load(), 488

Locale, 439–441

M

map() method forms, 124

Mapping coordinates, 124

maskData (ImageData field), 469

maskPad (ImageData field), 469

Measuring operation *see* Fonts/Class Font-Metrics

Menu accelerator (keyboard shortcut), 48–50

Menu bar setting, 285

Menu/MenuItem, 133

cascade/submenus, 196

class Menu/MenuItem, 206–207

buttonlike MenuItems, 196–197

example, 194

hierarchy, 194

indcx-based operations, 200

main menus, 198, 198c–199c

Menu events, 195, 201–203

Menu styles, 194

MenuItem events, 195–196, 203–207

MenuItem styles, 195

MenuItems with accelerators, 198

MenuItems that show others, 198

pop-up menu creation, 199, 200c

separator-like MenuItems, 197

drop-down menus, 196
pop-up/context menus, 196
MenuItem.setMenu(), 13
MessageBox *see* Dialogs
Minesweeper (sample application), 513
    Class Board, 517–518
    Class Counter, 516
    Class Minesweeper, 515–516
    Class Timer, 516–517
    implementation notes, 515
    overview, 513–515
Mirroring, 124–125
    coding example of Shell alignment,
        125c–126c, 127f
Mnemonic traversal, 39–40
    mnemonic strings, 40t
Modality, 282, 289
Monitors, 112, 112f
    Shell positioning coding example, 114c
    see also Bounds; Client area
Mouse, 53–54
    intercept (coding example), 75c–76c
    wiggly mouse problem, 98–100
Mouse events, 54, 56t–57t, 63
    buttons/coordinates, 54–56
    context menu request, 59
    displaying example, 58c–60c
    double-click events, 57–58, 127
    drag-and-drop request, 60–61
    selection operation on widget, 61–62
    state masks, 55–56, 55t
moveAbove(), 74
moveBelow(), 74
Moving/Resizing, 68

N

Native widgets, xvii, 129–130
    class hierarchy, 130, 131f
Nesting *see* Containment
Notebooks *see* TabFolder
notifyListener(), 19
numColumns, 361, 363
    coding example, 362c–363c

O

open(), 284, 316
org.eclipse.swt.events, typed listeners and
    event classes, 21

P

pack(), 76–77, 234
Painting, 77–78
    background color control, 86
        and flicker reduction, 86–87
    in a canvas, 296
    deferred update strategy, 78
    events, 78–79, 78t, 80f
    forcing an update, 81
    redraw, 80–81
        turning off, 82
    repainting/resizing, 82–85
palette field (image), 464
Parent parameter, 9–10
paste(), 158
Platform, xxi
Point(), 406
Point class, 66
Pointing device *see* Mouse
Points vs. *int* parameters, 410
Position parameter, 11
ProgressBar, 132
    Class ProgressBar
        example, 259
        hierarchy, 259
        indeterminate ProgressBar, 262
        ProgressBar events, 260
        ProgressBar styles, 260
        range operations, 261
        selection of "fill rectangle" extent, 261
    creating shell with progress bar coding
        example, 260c–261c
Progressive JPEG, 492

R

R3.0, Table performance improvements, 244
Range-based controls, 259, 272
    Class ProgressBar *see* ProgressBar
    Class Scale *see* Scale
    see also Classes ScrollBar and Slider

readAndDispatch(), 96
Rebar controls, 304
Rectangle(), 407
redraw(), 80
Region(), 422
remove(), 168, 239
removeAll(), 168–169, 222, 238–239
removeDisposeListener(), 22
removeFilter(), 94
removeImageLoaderListener(), 492
removeListener(), 18, 19, 91
Resizing *see* Moving/Resizing
RGB(), 427
RGB
    Class RGB, 427–428
        direct color, 428–429
        indexed color, 429–430
    see also Dialogs/ColorDialog
RowData(), 358
RowLayout(), 351
Rubber banding, 380
    see also Tracker
Runnables (runnable execs), 95

S

Sash, 132
    Class Sash; example, 313
    events, 313–314
    hierarchy, 313
    styles, 313
save(), 489
Scale, 132
    Class Scale
        events, 262–263, 264
        example, 262
        hierarchy, 262
        increment/page increment, 264
        range operations, 263
        selection, 264
        styles, 262
    thumb, 263
        and selection, 264
    ticks, 263
    trough, 263
scanLinePad field (image), 464

scroll(), 297–298
Scrollable, 130
ScrollBar, 133
    creation, 266–267
    and tables, 228
    and trees, 212
    see also Classes ScrollBar and Slider
select(), 171, 241
selectAll(), 154, 171, 221, 241
Separators, 139
setAccelerator(), 49
setActive(), 284
setAlignment(), 139, 235
setAlpha/s(), 470
setAppName(), 90
setBackground(), 220, 238, 276, 480
setBounds(), 68, 299
setCaret(), 296–297
setChecked(), 217, 237
setClipping(), 421
setControl(), 187, 255, 305
setCursor(), 276, 317
setCursorLocation(), 118
setData(), 25
setDefaultButton(), 290
setDisabledImage(), 190
setEchoChar(), 151
setEnabled(), 75, 190, 197
    intercept mouse events example, 75c–76c
setExpanded(), 214
    and SWT.Selection, 215
setFileName(), 331
setFilterExtensions(), 329
setFilterNames(), 330
setFilterPath(), 329, 335
setFocus(), 18, 29
setFont(), 220, 238, 276, 300, 443
setFontList(), 339, 446
setForeground(), 220, 237, 275
setGrayed(), 217, 237
setHeaderVisible(), 231
setHotImage(), 190
setImage(), 137, 141, 184, 197, 234, 236, 237, 254, 283
setIncrement(), 264, 268
setItemLayout(), 312

setItems()/setItem(), 166
    and Table, 231
setLayout(), 345
setLineStyle(), 414
setLinesVisible(), 231
setLineWidth(), 414
setLocale(), 440
setLocation(), 68, 199, 299
setMaximum(), 261, 263, 267
setMenu(), 198, 198c–199c, 275
setMenuBar(), 285
setMessage(), 327, 335
setMinimum(), 261, 263, 267
setMinimumSize(), 306
setPageIncrement(), 264, 268
setPixel/s(), 465–466
setPreferredSize(), 305–306
setRectangles(), 317
setRedraw(), 82
    creating Table items coding example,
        244–245
setRegion(), 290–291
setRGB(), 337
setSelection(), 143, 154, 169–170, 185, 221,
        239–240, 255–256
    with ScrollBar and Slider, 267–268
    ScrollBar and Slider applications, 267–268
    and string selection, 155c–156c
    and SWT.Selection event, 143
    within ProgressBar, 261
    within Scale, 264
setSize(), 68, 299, 306
    and Control configuration, 358
setStippled(), 317
setTabList(), 42
setText(), 137, 141, 149, 184, 196, 234, 236,
        254, 280, 283
setTextLimit(), 159
setThumb(), 268
setToolTipText(), 189, 254, 276
setTopIndex(), 158, 171, 241
setTopItem(), 221
setValues(), 269
setVisible(), 73, 199, 299
setWidth(), 186, 234
setXORMode(), 414

Shell(), 286
Shells, 16–17, 132
    active state, 283–284
    dialog, 282
    and Display, 115
        getting the Active Shell, 115
        getting Focus Control, 116
        getting list of Shells, 115–116
    top-level, 282
    see also Class Shell
showItem(), 222, 242
showSelection(), 158, 172, 221–222, 241
sleep(), 96
Slider, 133
    see also Classes ScrollBar and Slider
Smalltalk, xxv
    influence on SWT, xxv–xxvii
Splitters, 314
stateMask field, 35–37, 35t, 36t
Stippled effect, 317
stringExtent(), 456
Style parameter, 10–11
StyledText, 149
subtract() (from region), 424
SWT (Standard Widget Toolkit), xix, 1
    acquisition of, xxxv–xxxvi
        available drops/platforms, xxxvi–xxxvii
        full source via Eclipse, xxxl–xlii
    command line arguments, xxxix
    Eclipse plug-ins development, xliii
    exception/error checking, 9, 12
    "HelloWorld" (sample program),
        xxviii–xxix, 3–4
    indexing and range operations, 150
    installation as an extension, xxxviii–xxxix
    overview, xx–xxi
        efficiencies, xxii–xxiii
        history, xxv–xxviii
        implementations, xxi
        "look and feel," xxiii–xxiv
    packages, xxx–xxxii
        and memory constraints, xxxii–xxxiv
    run components, xxxiv–xxxv
    stand-alone and Mac OS X, xxxix–xl
    see also Class SWT; Events; Keyboard sup-
        port; Listeners; Native widgets;

Widget hierarchy; Widget life cycle
SWT.Activate event, 294
SWT.Arm (ArmEvent), 204
    updating status line example, 204, 205c,
        206f
SWT.ARROW, 146
SWT.BAR, 198
SWT.BUTTON_MASK, 55–56
SWT.CASCADE, 198
SWT.CHECK, 142–143, 185, 196
SWT.Close event, 92, 92c–93c
    for Shell, 292–293
        preventing a Shell from closing code
            example, 293c–294c
SWT.Collapse (TreeEvent), 225–226
SWT.Deactivate event, 294
SWT.DefaultSelection (SelectionEvent), 159,
        172, 177, 178, 222–223
    "recently typed" list coding example,
        177c–178c
    and Table events, 247
    and TableColumn events, 250
SWT.Deiconify event, 294
SWT.Dispose event, 92, 92c–93c
SWT.DragDetect event, 60–61
SWT.DROP_DOWN(), 187–189, 196
    code example with CoolItems, 309c–311c
SWT.Expand (TreeEvent), 223
    coding example (fill tree lazily), 223–225
SWT.FLAT, 191–192
SWT.FocusIn/SWT.FocusOut case examples,
        30–31
SWT.FULL_SELECTION, 229
SWT.Help (HelpEvent), 203, 206
SWT.Hide (MenuEvent), 202, 204
SWT.HIDE_SELECTION, 229
SWT.HORIZONTAL/VERTICAL, 183
SWT.H_SCROLL, 266–267
SWT.Iconify event, 294
SWT.INDETERMINATE, 262
SWT.KeyDown()/SWT.KeyUp(), 32–33
    coding examples, 37–39
    doit field issues, 39
SWT.LEFT/CENTER/RIGHT styles
    and buttons, 142
    and labels, 138–139

SWT.MenuDetect event, 59–60
SWT.Modify (ModifyEvent), 159, 179
    invalid input warning to user, 161c–162c
    track modified state of text control exam-
        ple, 160c–161c
SWT.Move (ControlEvent)
    Shell "follows the parent" example, 69c
    TableColumn usage, 251
    track a parent Shell example, 70c–71c
    for Tracker, 318
        coding example with tear-off controls,
            318c–320c
SWT.NO_BACKGROUND, and flicker reduc-
        tion, 86–87
SWT.NO_REDRAW_RESIZE, 83–84
    and flicker reduction, 84–85
SWT.Paint event, 78, 78t
    draw in a canvas coding example, 79, 79c,
        80f
SWT.PASSWORD style, 150–151
SWT.POP_UP style, 196, 199
SWT.PUSH, 142, 185
SWT.RADIO style, 144–145, 185, 196
SWT.Resize
    coding example with width hints to wrap
        label, 396c–397c
    coding example with width hints to wrap
        tool bar, 398c–399c
    move/resize children example, 71c–72c
    TableColumn usage, 251
SWT.Selection event, 143, 146, 172, 177, 178,
        193–194, 203
    CoolItem events, 312–313
    implementing a drop-down ToolItem, 194
    print current selection example, 172c–173c
    with radio buttons, 146–147
    for Sash events, 314
    Scale changes, 264
    for ScrollBar and Slider events, 269
        scroll a list of strings case example,
            269–270, 270c–272c
    and **setExpanded**(), 215
    TabFolder event, 256
        manual paging coding example,
            256c–257c

and Table events, 247
   check box table coding example, 248c
and TableColumn events, 248
   sort items in a Table coding example,
      248c–250c
and TreeItem, 211, 222
SWT.SEPARATOR, 186, 192, 197
SWT.SHADOW_OUT, 192
SWT.Show (MenuEvent), 201–202
SWT.SINGLE/MULTI, 149
SWT.Size, track a parent Shell example,
   70c–71c
SWT.TOGGLE, 145
SWT.Traverse() event *see* Traversal events
SWT.Verify (VerifyEvent), 162c–164c
SWT.V_SCROLL, 266–267
SWT.WRAP style, 138, 157, 191
   and TableItem, 235
syncExec(), 101–102
   in **fillTable**() implementation coding exam-
      ple, 246c–247c
   running code in user interface thread exam-
      ple, 102, 102c–103c
System font, 120
System objects, 119

T

Tab traversal, 41, 278
   tab group, 41
   tab item, 41
   tab ordering specification, 42
TabFolder/TabItem, 132
   classes TabFolder/TabItem
      example, 251
      hierarchies, 251
      searching operations, 256
      TabFolder events, 251, 256–257
      TabFolder styles, 251
      TabFolders paging modes, 252–253
      TabFolders selection methods, 255–256
      TabItem events, 252
      TabItem page controls, 254–255
      TabItem styles, 252
      TabItem text and images support,
         253–254
      TabItem tool tips, 254

Table/TableItem/TableColumn, 132–133
   classes Table/TableItem/TableColumn
      checked/grayed table items, 237
      deselecting/selecting items, 240–241
      example, 226
      full row selection, 229
      get items, 230
      headers/grid lines, 231
      hiding selection, 229
      hierarchies, 226
      hit testing operations, 242–243
      item height, 231–232
      "list mode," 230
      multiple-column tables, 231–234
      program examples large tables,
         244c–247c
      removing table items, 238–239
      scrolling, 241–242
      selection setting methods, 239–240
      table column alignment, 235
      table column width, 234–235
      Table events, 227, 247
      Table styles, 227
      TableColumn events, 228–229,
         248–251
      TableColumn styles, 227
      TableItem events, 227
      TableItem foreground/background/font,
         237–238
      TableItem styles, 227
      text and images in table column, 234
      text and images in table item, 235–237
   performance improvements, 244
   program example multiple table columns,
      233c, 234f
   program example one table column, 232c
   setItems() method issue, 231
   virtual tables, 243
   see also **asyncExec**(); **setRedraw**()
tableDefaultSelected(), 524
Tearing off control, 317
   coding example, 318c–320c
Text, 133
   button support, 141
   class text
      clipboard operations, 157–158
      echo character, 151

example, 147
hierarchy, 148
inserting/appending, 156–157
line delimiters, 152–153
lines/line height, 151–152
passwords, 150–151
scrolling, 158
single-line/multiline controls, 149
string operations, 149–150
substring selection, 153–156
text events, 148–149, 159–164
text limits, 158–159
text styles, 148
wrapping, 157
label support, 137
textExtent(), 456–457
Threading
apartment threading, 100–101
and creating table items coding example,
246c–247c
and *flooding*, 104
free threading, 101
multithreading in application example,
524–525
user interface thread, 100
syncExec() vs. asyncExec() issues,
104–106
see also **asyncExec**(); Graphics/and threads;
syncExec()
Thumb, 263, 264
Ticks, 263
timerExec(), 108
Timers, 108–109
detecting event loop inactivity, 109–110
detecting keyboard inactivity, 110–111
ToolBar/ToolItem, 129, 133
classes ToolBar/ToolItem, 106–207
bounds (tool item), 189
button-like ToolItems, 184–186
drop-down feature, 187–189
enabling/disabling tool items, 189–190
example, 181
flat tool bar, 191–192
hierarchies, 181
image supports, 190
searching/"hit test" operations, 193
separator above tool bar, 192

separator-like ToolItems, 187
tips (tool item), 189
ToolBar events, 182
ToolBar style, 182
ToolItem events, 182–183, 193–194
ToolItem styles, 182
wrapping tool bar, 191
Tool Tips, 184
ToolItems creation coding example,
185c–186
Tracker, 133
Tracker(), 316
Tracker
Class Tracker
creation, 316
events, 315, 318–320
example, 315
hierarchy, 315
opening, 316–317
setting rectangles, 317
stippling/cursor use, 317
styles, 315
and Dialog, 316
rubber banding, 316
transparentPixel (ImageData field), 469
Traversal events, 42–43, 43t
SWT.Traverse() event, 43
implementing tab group traversal,
45–46
implementing text traversal, 46–47
intercept traversal, 47–48
keyboard traversal codes, 44t
managing traversals, 44, 45t
public fields, 43t
Tree/TreeItem, 133
classes Tree/TreeItem
checked/grayed tree items, 217–218,
218c–219c, 220f
example, 210
expanding/collapsing, 214–215
hierarchical operations, 215–217
hierarchies, 210
hierarchy creation, 212, 213c
removing items, 222
scrolling, 221–222
selection, 220–221
and SWT.Selection, 211–211

texts/images, 213–214
Tree events, 210, 222–226
Tree styles, 210
TreeItem events, 211
TreeItem foreground/background/font,
    220
TreeItem styles, 211
Trimmings, 282
Trough, 263
type field (image), 464

U

union(), 409
update() method, 121–122
    forcing a paint event, 81

V

Visibility, 72–73

W

wake(), 98
    coding example, 99c–100c
Widget, xvii–xviii, 1, 7, 26, 130
    and application data, 25–26
    constructor use of operating system
        resources, 8
    custom, xxiv–xxv
    heavyweight, 130
    lightweight, 130

selection, 61–62
    see also Common Widgets; Native widgets
Widget events, **SWT.Dispose**(), 24–25
Widget hierarchy
    containment hierarchy, 14
    controls/composites/Shells/Display, 16–17
    importance of, 9
    inheritance hierarchy, 14
    non-control widgets, 17
    subclassing, 14–16
        "final" tag issue, 15–16
Widget life cycle, 7
    creation overview, 8
    disposal of, 12
        rules, 13–14
    parameters, 9
        parent parameter, 9–10
        position parameter, 11
        style parameter, 10–11
    standard constructors, 8–9
width field (image), 464

X

X/Motif implementations, 444–445
x/y (ImageData fields), 472
XML, and user interfaces, 1

Z

Z-order, 74
    and layout, 345